After the Second Flood

Other books by Michael Hamburger

Criticism

Art as Second Nature

A Proliferation of Prophets: essays on German literature
    from Nietzsche to Brecht

The Truth of Poetry: tensions in modern poetry from
    Baudelaire to the 1960s

Translations (all German/English texts)

German Poetry 1910–1975: an anthology

East German Poetry: an anthology

Paul Celan: Poems

Peter Huchel: The Garden of Theophrastus and Other
    Poems

Poetry

Variations

Collected Poems

Modern German Literature: II

Essays on post-war German literature

After the Second Flood

MICHAEL HAMBURGER

St. Martin's Press
New York

First published in the United States of America in 1986

Printed in Great Britain

ISBN 0-312-00087-1
       0-312-00088-X (pbk)

**Library of Congress Cataloging-in-Publication
Data**

Hamburger, Michael.
   After the second flood.

   Includes index.
   1. German literature—20th century—History
and criticism. I. Title.
PT403.H22 1986   830'.9'00914   86-22008
ISBN 0-312-00087-1
ISBN 0-312-00088-X (pbk)

The publishers acknowledge the financial assistance
of the Arts Council of Great Britain

Typesetting by Paragon Photoset, Aylesbury
Printed in England by SRP Ltd, Exeter

Contents

Preface

This book had its inception as part of a projected series of volumes that were to constitute my 'collected critical writings'. When that project was modified, by a new emphasis on the subjects and periods most of those writings were about, it also became a sequel to the second volume in the series, *A Proliferation of Prophets*, which dealt with German authors from Nietzsche to the Second World War. That volume, though, was largely a collection of existing essays, rewritten only where disturbing anachronisms had arisen. The present work posed much greater difficulties. Post-war German literature is not only still in progress, but was so thoroughly conditioned by historical and political peculiarities that a purely critical approach would have been unhelpful to all but specialists; and the pieces I had written on specific authors or works proved too miscellaneous to make anything like a coherent study. I therefore decided that all such material called for a re-working so drastic as to amount to the writing of a new book.

A special difficulty was that I do not believe in histories of literature. A purely critical approach, for me, is one confined to single works, or single authors at the most; and one that concentrates on their singularity, their quiddity, not on the general trends that are the historian's concern. In the case of this book, however, criticism of that kind had to be balanced against the need to give unspecialized readers some intimation of the diversity of writing in German in the forty years that have passed since the end of the war. The last thing I wished to produce was the 'survey' to which histories degenerate when their matter is too recent to have been sifted by the mere passage of time. Yet, to intimate the diversity, I had to mention more names than I had the space or capacity to flesh with criticism proper.

Needless to say, this study does not cover, or attempt to cover, all the imaginative writing published in the two Germanys, Austria and German-speaking Switzerland since 1945. For one thing, writing for the theatre had to be virtually left out, only because I am not a theatre-goer and do not consider myself competent to write about plays as theatre, rather than as literary texts. Ignorance, forgetfulness and blind spots further limited my choice. What is more, some of the authors who have meant most to me, as a reader and translator, could be mentioned only in passing here, because their work demands a kind of minute attention which the nature and perspective of this study forbade.

Paul Celan is one of those authors. Criticism of his work has reached a stage where only new discoveries or insights can decently be offered. The excellence of his work is recognized by those who respond to it, and cannot be conveyed by generalization to those who do not. Other writers were omitted or skimped because their work did not fit into my various themes and contexts: Günter Bruno Fuchs, Christoph Meckel and Rainer Brambach are a few of these who occur to me. Many good novelists, especially those of the GDR, are missing because I cannot read everything, far less do justice to everything I have read. My own preoccupation with poetry and with prose that has some of the density and concentration of poetry will be apparent.

I have no regrets about the almost total exclusion of secondary literature, when the primary literature alone was much more than one study can comprise. Even critics and theorists of literature distinguished enough as writers to have qualified for inclusion on those grounds had to make way for imaginative writers here. For the same reasons, no scholarly apparatus in the form of notes, bibliography or biographical summaries could be appended. A bibliography alone of so many writers and their works, as well as English translations of them, where they exist, would have taken up more space than was practicable or in character. The text incorporates publication dates and such biographical facts as were relevant and indispensable.

This book is addressed to the 'common', 'general' but literate reader, to whom an interest in literature is, or used to be, as natural as his or her other concerns, curiosities and pursuits. If this kind of reader is obsolete or obsolescent, in a world tending more and more to technical specializations and indifference to anything beyond them, so are this book and its assumptions. In that case the book is dedicated to the memory of that same reader, who will have to be reborn if anything like a civilization is to survive.

M. H.
Suffolk, January 1986

I   After the Second Flood

1

If isolation, division and confusion were conspicuous in German literature between the wars, and even before the First World War, the collapse of the Third Reich—and of its cultural *Gleichschaltung* or homogenization, a uniformity upheld by the violent suppression or destruction of all that was different and separate—could not possibly offer an immediate remedy. Many of the 'liberated' Germans of 1945 were like those discharged prisoners who have lost any capacity to cope with the complexities of freedom, and whose response to them is bewilderment and fear. The breakdown of so many material amenities of civilization exacerbated a sense of doom in those who had accommodated themselves to the new order. The ideological void left by its collapse was experienced as a 'spiritual zero point'. The protecting prison walls had been demolished. There was nowhere to turn for shelter or security.

True, some sort of continuity was provided by the survival and re-emergence of established writers who had belonged either to the 'inner emigration' or to the Christian and conservative opposition that had not been totally destroyed, even after the purges of 1944. It is one of the 'inner emigrants', Wilhelm Lehmann, from whose poem 'Nach der Zweiten Sintflut' I have taken my title. In many cases, though, it was as hard for the inner emigrants to re-establish themselves as it was for the emigrants proper, since many of them had been silenced by the Third Reich and were remembered by only a tiny minority of older readers.

As for the so-called 'resistance' or opposition in literature, it was more remarkable for courage and stubbornness than for any literary qualities that could serve as a model or starting-point for new writing. In diction and form the Christian exhortations of poets like Rudolf Alexander Schröder, Werner Bergengruen, Albrecht Goes and Reinhold Schneider, written during or after the Third Reich, were so antiquated that they could only allegorize, never sensuously grasp and enact, the realities they condemned. Their poems could not resist the National Socialist order because, as poems, they did not penetrate it, merely upheld a moral or religious alternative to it which some of their readers had accepted in any case, while conforming outwardly. R. A. Schröder's poems have their place in a tradition of Protestant devotional poetry going back to the seventeenth century, a tradition to which they constantly allude even in their diction. Their very nature made them a 'second reality' at best, parallel to, but not contiguous with, the secular order they opposed.

Reinhold Schneider, a Roman Catholic, was one of those writers who paid the price for opposition, and it seems almost indecent to apply aesthetic criteria to the work of such men. His sonnet 'Der Antichrist' of 1938, with a sub-title suggesting that it was based on a painting by Luca Signorelli—when in fact his model was Hitler—shows that he would have had to pay the ultimate price to make his poem as direct as it needed to be if it was to be an effective act of resistance. In translating the sonnet, I had to modify one line, the seventh, because its rhetoric was so inappropriate to what we know to have been Schneider's true subject, a vegetarian and teetotaller.

Er wird sich kleiden in des Herrn Gestalt,
Und seine heilige Sprach wird er sprechen
Und seines Richteramtes sich erfrechen
Und übers Volk erlangen die Gewalt.

Und Priester werden, wenn sein Ruf erschallt,
Zu seinen Füssen ihr Gerät zerbrechen,
Die Künstler und die Weisen mit ihm zechen,
Um den sein Lob aus Künstlermunde hallt.

Und niemand ahnt, dass Satan aus ihm spricht
Und seines Tempels Wunderbau zum Preis
Die Seelen fordert, die er eingefangen;

Erst wenn er aufwärts fahren will ins Licht,
Wird ihn der Blitzstrahl aus dem höchsten Kreis
Ins Dunkel schleudern, wo er ausgegangen.

He will put on the person of the Lord
And mouth the holy language that was His,
Usurp the seat of judgement, brashly seize
Authority and win the crowd's accord.

And when his voice commands them, at his feet
Grovelling priests will break their implements,
Wise men and artists, privy to his intents,
In flattering celebration will compete.

That through him Satan speaks, not one has guessed,
Nor how he builds his temple at the cost
Of captive souls, his tribute gathered in;

Not till the highest circle is his quest
Will lightning hurl him from that glory, tossed
Into the dark that was his origin.

Although Schneider's vocabulary in other poems is no less impervious to immediate experience and usage, here the Last Judgement
paintings of Signorelli do seem to have served him as an alibi. Daring as
it was, this poem could do no harm to Hitler or his régime, if only
because they had broken out of the Christian order, establishing a new
one that combined a primitive, atavistic ideology with the ability to
enforce it with all the resources of bureaucracy and technology. (This
was clear to one Roman Catholic resistance writer, if to no one else to
the same degree—to the philosopher, cultural historian and polemicist
Theodor Haecker, who had seen through the mendacious propaganda
that sustained the First World War, and lived to record his brave and
radical opposition to the Third Reich, for which he was arrested in 1933
and 1940. An English version of the notebooks he wrote during the
Second World War, published in West Germany after Haecker's death
in 1944, appeared in 1950 as *Journal in the Night*.) To demonize or
diabolize Hitler—who had also been prudent enough to enter into a
concordat with Schneider's Church—was to make sure from the start
that this sonnet could never hit its target. Schneider's prediction of
doom was to be fulfilled, it is true; and after the event questions of
responsibility, guilt and commitment became the dominant preoccupation of many German writers.

Reinhold Schneider was a contributor to the widely read and discussed anthology *De Profundis* published in 1946. In a speech delivered
at the Humboldt University, East Berlin, in May of the following year,
Peter Huchel commented:

Why is it that in an anthology like *De Profundis* that contains only poems by
authors who lived in Germany during the twelve Nazi years, we find more
good landscape poems than work that confronts the age? . . . How did it
come about that, with few exceptions, we have no resistance literature like
the French? The reason is that our best poets— and again I mean those who
in no way compromised with the Nazis— even then ascended into the
mountain ranges of poetic vision and, detached from every reality, on the
highest glaciers engaged in a dialogue with the infinite in metaphysical
solitude, when at the foot of the mountains, cities and villages had long been
ravaged by fire and human beings killed. It was a flight from responsibility.
And even where they did touch on contemporary issues, they struggled
alone and in the dark against destiny, instead of fighting political and social
powers. The reason is that in their increasing isolation they could see only
the questionableness of all life and action, and had lost all sense of kinship
with a community. A decade of fascist dictatorship and total isolation had
been enough to stifle German literature.

Like Wilhelm Lehmann, Peter Huchel became one of the survivors of the 'inner emigration' who succeeded in bridging this gap between an archetypal and an historical vision. Of the veritable explosion of exhortatory and protesting literature set off in the early post-war years, very little has survived. Rudolf Hagelstange's morally searching sonnet sequence *Venezianisches Credo*. written in 1944, when Hagelstange was a soldier, suffered from the same incapacity to find images and diction that interlocked with his themes, the same elevated nineteeth century rhetoric at odds with twentieth century realities, as Schneider's earlier sonnet; and his sequence, published in 1946, was among the outstanding books of poems of that period. The more ambitious works of prose fiction published in those years, like Hermann Kasack's *Die Stadt hinter dem Strom* (1947), tended towards allegory and abstraction. The realities mentioned by Huchel seemed to elude the grasp of both poets and prose writers—with exceptions that did not emerge until later years.

British and American realism in fiction, French existentialism, and all the innovations in poetry from which German-language writers inside the Third Reich had been cut off, now had to be assimilated, as Huchel also implied. If, generally speaking, commitment in the immediate post-war years and in West Germany was religious rather than humanist, at least among the older writers, Sartre's *littérature engagée*, which he himself regarded as a last philosophical vindication of humanism, exercised a wide appeal in Germany. Commitment there had rarely taken the same form as in France. Nor had a common concern with existential thought led to similar decisions. Sartre's humanism—if it was a humanism, as he claimed—rested on the traditional involvement of French intellectuals in political and social issues, a tradition not firmly established in Germany. Whatever hold this kind of humanism may have maintained over German intellectuals in the Wilhelminian era was threatened by the impact of vitalistic, anti-rational creeds on the one hand, the outbreak of the First World War on the other. Yet a new humanism, often existentially based, did emerge during and after that war; and if we look for a counterpart of 'engagement' in Sartre's sense, it is to be found in inter-war writers of the Expressionist generation like the early Werfel, Hasenclever and Toller, all of whom looked to the extreme Left for the realization of their humanist ideals.

It is no accident, therefore, that the work of Wolfgang Borchert, which has survived those immediate post-war years, now seems so close in mood and spirit to that of the inter-war Expressionists. Borchert's early death, in his twenties in 1947, was seen as a direct consequence of his brave defiance of authority as a civilian and soldier in the Third Reich. Yet the anger he voiced in his stories and in his play *Draussen vor der Tür* spoke to and for a whole generation of bewildered and self-pitying ex-soldiers who had not defied the régime.

The *Gruppe 47*, a loose association of younger writers that became prominent, powerful and controversial in the course of the next decades, was founded mainly in response to a general awareness that German writers and intellectuals had failed to offer any effectual opposition of the kind associated with the French *Résistance*. At that time the immediate problems of German writers seemed so acute and pressing as to cut across all differences in outlook, personality and creed. The determination to avoid a repetition of that failure was enough to cement the association; and strictly political differences had not yet become pronounced, when responsibility for government, in any case, had not yet been assumed by Germans. Those differences, and clashes of personality, did arise in later decades and eventually led to the dissolution of the Group.

Even before the rehabilitation of Gottfried Benn—whose *Statische Gedichte* appeared in Switzerland in 1948, but did not receive a German licence until the following year—a Nietzschean stance at once anti-Christian and anti-humanist continued to appeal to German readers, mainly of the older generation. Differences between the existentialist schools of Heidegger and Sartre became explicit in Heidegger's *Über den Humanismus*, a letter addressed to Jean Beaufret in Paris. In this letter—appended to his *Platons Lehre von der Wahrheit*—Heidegger dissociated himself from all those systems which he regarded as humanistic, including Christianity, Marxism and Sartre's existentialism, because all of them were 'metaphysical'. Of his own thinking he wrote that 'it has no result. It has no effect. It is sufficient to its own nature (*Wesen*) merely by virtue of being (*indem es ist*).'

This definition of autonomous thinking is strikingly similar to Gottfried Benn's definition of autonomous art. Much of Heidegger's postwar thinking, in any case, took poetry as its starting-point; and Nietzsche's demolition of metaphysics was the premiss of Benn's poetry as it was of Heidegger's thought. 'Works of art', according to Benn, 'are phenomena, historically ineffective, without practical consequences. That is their greatness.' If the link seems tenuous or accidental, another is provided in Benn's definition of his creed of *Artistik* as 'the attempt of Art to experience itself as a meaning within the general decay of all meaning', a re-formulation of Nietzsche's attempt to salvage art from the moral and metaphysical wreckage his own thinking had exposed or brought about. For another decade or so, autonomous, self-sufficient thinking, like autonomous, self-sufficient art, conflicted with the trend towards commitment and a new realism. In literature, it was the names of Benn and Brecht that polarized the conflict.

2

The work of Ernst Jünger, a writer who is neither a pure philosopher nor a poet, is also relevant in this context, since Jünger's work has run the whole gamut of those conflicting attitudes, from political and social activism to extreme detachment. After the First World War Ernst Jünger, who had won the highest award for gallantry as a young officer, glorified the dangers and hardships of modern war, disparaged pain, and welcomed the technical revolution that so disturbed fellow writers with humanist or pacifist commitments. His book *Der Arbeiter* of 1932 could be understood as a glorification of the technology that the National Socialists were to harness to their ideology, in so far as the book could be understood at all on the level of political and social realities, when it was distinguished by a prose style so abstract and opaque that it can also be read as an exercise in self-sufficient thinking. Like Stefan George, Ernst Jünger was one of the few eminent writers of the time whom the Nazis fervently wished to claim as a forerunner and supporter; and Jünger's political activism had been dedicated to causes upheld by the nationalistic, anti-democratic fringe groups that abounded in the Weimar Republic. By 1934, however, Jünger had not only re-assessed his political allegiances in the light of new events, but had begun to have second thoughts about war and peace, militarism and technology, corporatism and individualism.

The transition from extreme activism and vitalism to extreme aesthetic detachment can be followed in Jünger's diaries of the war years, published in 1949 as *Strahlungen*. Like Gottfried Benn, Jünger had returned to the Army, 'the aristocratic form of emigration', as Benn called it, though as a Staff Officer Jünger could not become quite as unpolitical as the medical officer Benn. As an officer attached to the German G.H.Q. in Paris, Jünger had unusual opportunities to keep in touch with current developments both in politics and literature. He was the intimate friend of General Speidel and other generals. He mixed socially with such French writers as Cocteau, Jouhandeau, Giraudoux, Léautaud and Henri Thomas. No writer was better placed to convey the weird atmosphere of Paris under the Occupation from a point of view which, though independent, was closer to that of the occupying army than to that of the *Résistance*. Jünger seems to have regarded himself as a member of a cosmopolitan élite, rather than as an executive of German policy. Needless to say, his detachment could not always be maintained. He was troubled by scruples, contradictions, and rumours of atrocities perpetrated by the military and civilian executives of Party politics. His visits to Germany and to the Eastern Front, also recorded in the diaries, left him in no doubt as to the true nature of the war, or the physical destruction and demoralization it would entail. The failure of the military plot against Hitler—with which Jünger sympathized and in which he was remotely implicated—endangered many of his friends and former political allies. Jünger's son was arrested for making 'unpatriotic' remarks, then killed in the Italian campaign. Though Jünger's diaries continued to record his purchase of rare books, his collecting of insects, plants and minerals, his study of the Bible and works on anthropology, biology and history, there is a growing sense of doom, a suggestion that he was fiddling while Rome burned. In fact Jünger's minute analyses of dreams, his constant theorizing and aestheticizing in the diaries, and his account of wholly private pursuits and curiosities, come to read very strangely in this historical context. Here is a characteristic reflection:

> About illnesses: There are differences here in their effect on the imagination, and these do not correspond to the different degrees of danger. For instance I feel more inclined to put up with disorders of the lungs or of the heart than disorders of the stomach, the liver, or the abdomen generally. It seems that, even merely in regard to the flesh, there are higher and lower ways of dying.

What is extraordinary about such a reflection—recorded at the time of mass carnage, by a man wearing the uniform of a German officer—is its imperviousness. One may sympathize with the diarist's resolve not to be overwhelmed by developments which, in any case, he had predicted in earlier works, but rather to build up inner reserves against a seemingly disastrous future; but to generalize about 'high' and 'low' ways of dying in 1941 amounts to a tactlessness (that is, a lack of contact) quite staggering in a writer who claimed a special insight into the meaning of age. The same unreality pervades the whole diary, as it pervades much of Jünger's later work; and in this Jünger is truly representative of those cultured Germans who dissociated themselves from Nazism out of an aesthetic or 'aristocratic' fastidiousness.

In the diaries Stulpnagel, the German Commander-in-Chief, studies Spinoza between despatches. Speidel, in the course of an important interview with Jünger, quotes the opening lines of Platen's poem 'Tristan', which equates the attraction of beauty with the attraction of death. While on the Russian front, Jünger himself goes out to collect specimens of local insects, without showing much awareness of whether the men around him are privileged to die a superior sort of death. His comment on the excursion is characteristic: 'This kind of thing also helps me to preserve my dignity, as a symbol of my world of free will.'

Like his brother, the poet Friedrich Georg Jünger, Ernst Jünger has become an implacable enemy of technologies and technicians out to destroy that dignity and the residual freedom of individual wills; and even in the diaries there are pointers to a metanoia in the direction of Christian spirituality. 'Doctrines based purely on economics', Jünger noted there, 'inevitably lead to cannibalism'. Yet one wonders whether that observation rests on an aesthetic, rather than a moral or spiritual, foundation, and may recall that Kierkegaard's exasperation with the 'priests and professors' of Christendom led him to be quite explicit about his preference even for cannibals. The difference is one between existential passion and a cold, theorizing self-absorption.

As a novelist, therefore, Jünger has found utopian or political allegory a more congenial medium than any form of realistic fiction. Compared to Ernst Jünger's, even some of the characters of Thomas Mann or Herman Hesse 'reek of the human'; and since his allegories show the same reluctance to be specific and unambiguous as his expository prose in *Der Arbeiter*, it is hard to know what to make of them. His *Auf den Marmorklippen*, (1939), for instance, was interpreted as a veiled condemnation of the Nazi regime—and was presented as such to readers outside Germany, with a Swiss edition in 1943 and an English translation (*On the Marble Cliffs*) in 1947. The same book, however, was published in a 'Wehrmachtsausgabe'—an army edition—in Paris in 1942, for distribution among those fighting Hitler's war. Jünger's friends in the High Command may have had something to do with that; but they could not have got away with it if Jünger's allegory had been unambiguous, its dominant concerns more ethical than aesthetic and utopian.

Even his post-war allegory *Heliopolis* (1949) has more in common with his diaries and expository writings than with any novel by any writer other than Jünger, because of Jünger's incapacity—ascribed by Baudelaire to the dandy (or aesthete)—'to get outside himself', *sortir de soi-même*. His characters are personified ideas; and the action is always symbolic, partly of recent history, as Jünger saw it, partly of a hypothetical order that might be established in the future, if an 'aristocracy of the spirit or mind' (*Geist*) were to prevail. In some regards this allegory suggests a reversal of Jünger's early beliefs; and Jünger has had the rare courage never to disown any part of his work, but to declare that it is to be judged as a whole. In *Heliopolis* the élite envisaged by Jünger has become an élite not of power, but an 'élite formed by suffering'. It shows a new concern with the victims and the oppressed— the Parsees and Melitta of the book—even if the sympathy, too, remains somewhat abstract and general. The true substance of both the novel and the diaries is to be found in reflections and *obiter dicta*, and in exquisite passages of descriptive or evocative prose. Even the nearest thing to true fiction in *Heliopolis*, a complete short story told by one of the characters, Ortner, recalls the Romantic fairy tales of E. T. A. Hoffmann. For all the stylistic felicities and reflective profundities of Jünger's mature works, they leave one with a sense of acute disparity between the general and the particular, between Jünger's readiness to theorize about the age and his inability to present credible individual characters or to convey what it feels like to be alive in our time. In all his researches into symbolic lore, anthropology and world history he seems to have overlooked the traditional location of the deepest feelings not in the lungs or heart, but in the bowels. It is as though human life as it is were altogether too low a thing to be compatible with Jünger's dignity and fastidiousness.

There is a striking parallel between Jünger's development and that of André Malraux after the Second World War. Much as Malraux turned from a cult of action and activism to the contemplation of a *musée imaginaire*, Ernst Jünger turned to meditations on such subjects as hour-glasses and the measurement of time in different civilizations. Jünger's advocacy of 'Waldgang' (literally 'forest-going') also shows an affinity with Heidegger's withdrawal from moral, social or political '*engagement*'. The significant title of a collection of Heidegger's later essays in 1950 was *Holzwege* (woodland paths). Both titles have assumed a somewhat ironic overtone since the dying off of those German forests that have so engaged the imaginations of Germans for centuries.

True, Jünger's later books include meditations on seemingly topical themes. In *Der Gordische Knoten* (1953) he dealt with relations between East and West, but in terms so general once more as to be 'historically ineffective', in the manner of Benn's self-sufficient art and Heidegger's self-sufficient thinking. Jünger saw the conflict between East and West as one between two ancient, almost archetypal, rather than historical, and radically opposed traditions, not only of government—Eastern despotism against Western freedom—but of religion and philosophy. Here Jünger was much concerned with different methods and codes of warfare, a subject he had written about since his youth, drawing on first-hand experience, but considered in this book as manifestations of those basic principles to which he attributes the opposition between East and West. This opposition, though, emerges as not strictly geographical, ethnic, or even historical. So one is left with little more than two basic principles, which are also treated psychologically, as conflicting urges at work in all human beings, and mythically, as the conflict between Cain and Abel. In that context Hitler is treated as an Eastern despot, rather than as the ruler of a Western nation—a characteristic side-stepping of concrete realities. Needless to say, Jünger is now on the side of the West, as defined in his book: 'That men should be powerful in their lives and acts, but that in this power they should restrict themselves by the observance of divine and earthly laws: this we account great.' Such, according to Jünger, is the Western view; yet by no means every European would agree with him that the exercise of power is one of the requisites of greatness, and the majority of younger German post-war writers were to disagree with that most radically. As for the 'divine and earthly laws', difficulties about them ever since the Middle Ages have hinged on questions of what 'divine and earthly laws', precisely and specifically, are recognized at any one place or time, whether in the East or in the West. Jünger's conclusion, therefore, was inevitably vague. He states that 'essentially, it is the European who has lost the last two world wars', and goes on to ask whether it will be the same European's fate to become an inverted Saturn, 'devoured by his children', or else to survive because 'the armed men growing up from the dragon's teeth he has sown will proceed to annihilate one another'. These 'dragon's teeth' are the science and technology Jünger had once glorified. There is an intimation that world government could resolve the conflict. To translate these large concepts into political realities, however, remains almost as difficult as with earlier works like *Der Arbeiter*.

World government is the subject of Jünger's later treatise, *Der Weltstaat* (1960), but again his argument moves vertically, from plane to plane, where a horizontal movement is needed. Instead of careful distinctions and definitions on a single plane of reality, we get generalizations that leap from fact to symbol, from history to myth or archetype, and back again. The same had been true of his earlier *Das Sanduhrbuch* (1954), which sets up another polar antinomy between the 'abstract, mechanical time' that prevails where mechanical clocks are in use, and the 'natural elemental time' of the hourglass and other primitive chronometers. This antinomy, too, turns out to be partly obvious, partly specious. 'Timeless' works of art have been produced by persons wearing wrist-watches, and 'natural' time experienced between one chime of the clock, if not one tick of the clock, and the next. It is the humourless ponderousness of Jünger's generalizations that has exasperated many of his readers to the point of having no patience with his later works, for all their distinction of manner and their integrity. As a solitary and almost anachronistic survivor from an era that the foreshortening of German history has made remote, Jünger has remained active and unbowed throughout four post-war decades, and a figure still capable of arousing controversy.

3

Each in his way, Heidegger, Benn and Jünger perpetuated the Nietzschean ideal of lone intellectual heroism, of an 'aristocracy' that is not the head of an organic body, but is distinguished by complete separateness, independence and daring—a head without a body, one is tempted to call it, in view of some of the extravagance to which the ideal has given rise; and in view of the paradox, that such heads without bodies have shown an astonishing readiness to abandon themselves uncritically to corporative movements and ideologies that were anything but aristocratic. Ernst Jünger's attempts to make his peace with traditional values were defeated by his tendency to 'leave out too much'—Hofmannsthal's criticism of Stefan George. Neither his fastidious style nor his often complex themes have healed that rift between body and head, between ideas and their embodiment in ways of life and specific institutions, let alone in individual men and women. His literary gifts have failed to coalesce with the realities of the post-war world, as they once did coalesce with the experience of total war.

In this Jünger was not alone in the immediate post-war years, when the social realities of post-diluvial Germany seemed to offer little or nothing that could be assimilated by the imagination, if only because even those continuous normalities which had persisted both under Nazism and after its collapse were so overshadowed by the magnitude of the catastrophe as to seem unfit for literary treatment. This was a problem for prose writers more than for poets; and it affected even writers of fiction with a clear-cut religious or ethical commitment that exempted them from the prevalent bewilderment. If they tried to deal with recent history, as Albrecht Goes, a Lutheran minister who had served as an army chaplain, did in his long story *Das Brandopfer* (1954), the inescapable questions of good and evil drove them towards a moral tendentiousness not conducive to good realistic fiction. That is one reason why ambitious novels of this period, like Hermann Kasack's already mentioned, or Stefan Andres' *Die Sintflut* (1949 ff.)—the Second Flood once more!—tended towards utopian or apocalyptic allegory. Another was the German addiction to comprehensive, all-embracing novels of ideas or whole societies, like Thomas Mann's *The Magic Mountain* among those most familiar to English readers, though many writers less familiar to them could be named. Such ambitious novels were to render nothing less than a whole world, with its dominant tensions and issues, and these might well appear not as primarily social or political, let alone economic, but as primarily philosophical or mythical. It was left to a later group of post-war writers, from Hans Erich Nossack to Hans Werner Richter, Ernst Kreuder, Heinrich Böll and the Austrian Hans Lebert (with a single powerful novel of 1960, *Die Wolfshaut*) to evolve new forms of realism, whether in the superficial sense of topicality or in the deeper sense of imaginative penetration of given realities.

Hans Henny Jahnn, a controversial, but never widely read dramatist and novelist in the inter-war years, produced the most idiosyncratic and distinguished of those large-scale, visionary novels, his trilogy *Fluss ohne Ufer*, whose fourth and last volume, *Epilog*, did not appear until 1961. Best known in his lifetime as an organist, designer of organs, musicologist (with the very great distinction of having devoted himself to the rediscovery of the works of Gesualdo), but also as a breeder of horses and a scientist who specialized in the study of hormones, Jahnn might have been a Goethean synthesist if he had been less hectic and obsessed, or if the age had permitted the kind of serenity and balance that he lacked. As it was, he remained a prophet figure largely without honour in his own country or any other, though with a small number of devoted admirers. One of these, the Swiss critic Walter Muschg— author of a 'Tragic History of (German) Literature'—found it necessary in Jahnn's lifetime to compile a large anthology of extracts from this remarkable author's works, not only because most of them had long been out of print, but also because Jahnn's excellence as a prose writer was more apparent in such extracts than in long works so bizarre that very few readers could make sense of any of them as a whole. Amongst other things, Jahnn was prophetic in his concern with ecology, his unsentimental understanding of animals, and his conviction in later years that an anthropocentric civilization must inevitably destroy itself. His cult of eroticism, though more Platonic than Freudian, offended the squeamish by embracing both heterosexual and homosexual love. In the immediate post-war period, Jahnn's warnings against nuclear technology, his opposition to the partition of Germany (and therefore to the Cold War), and the visionary intensity of his imaginative writing made him even more of a pariah than he had been in the Weimar Republic and before his retirement to the Danish island of Bornholm. Nor was it the enormous length and scale of *Fluss ohne Ufer* alone that alienated the general novel-reading public. Even his very short novel *Die Nacht aus Blei* (1956), salvaged by Jahnn from his drafts for a longer work not finished when he died in 1959, is an apocalyptic fantasy so dream-like and mysterious as to defy interpretation as an allegory, except perhaps in terms of Jahnn's own cults and obsessions in earlier works. Though Jahnn could be minutely realistic in passages of his longer works and some of his descriptive writing was more vivid than any other German novelist's of his time, few younger post-war writers could learn from him, as Günter Grass professed to have learnt from Alfred Döblin—a novelist with whom Jahnn had some affinities. (Among English writers, only John Cowper Powys could provide material for interesting comparisons and contrasts.) Jahnn's topicality is not to be found on the surface, or in the plots, of his imaginative prose.

It was an Austrian writer of Jünger's and Jahnn's generation, Heimito von Doderer, who did succeed in reconciling the demands of social realism with the grand design of what he called 'the total novel'. In that, as an Austrian, he had the advantage of such pre-war models as Musil's *The Man Without Qualities*, Hermann Broch's *The Sleepwalkers* and Elias Canetti's *Die Blendung* (translated as *Auto da Fé*). As long ago as 1778, Goethe's friend J. H. Merck had written a treatise on 'The lack of the Epic Spirit in Germany'. If so many outstanding German novelists strike their non-German readers as provincial, that was not because they lived in the provinces—so did Jane Austen and Flaubert—nor even because the German-speaking countries had no capital comparable to London or Paris. There was always Vienna; but not a single great novel dedicated to its *genius loci* throughout the eighteenth and nineteenth centuries. What was lacking was a writer with the capacity to turn his particular city, or province, into the centre of the world. To do so for Vienna must have been part of Doderer's incentive when he planned his two long novels *Die Strudlhofstiege* (1951) and *Die Dämonen* (1956). Those novels celebrate Vienna as it was never celebrated in the days of its imperial glory; and they do so not so much by showing Vienna to have been the geographical, cultural or political centre of Europe at a particular period, the 1920s, as by making it the setting of a 'world theatre', a stage on which universal passions and obsessions are acted out. The *teatro del mundo* may suggest moral allegories and social types, rather than characters. Although Doderer regarded himself as a traditionalist and conservative, both in politics and in literature, the tradition in which he was rooted was that of nineteenth-century realism. Since his psychology, too, was almost exclusively concerned with the way in which individuals perceive, or refuse to perceive, reality, his very objection to Freudian depth psychology was that its researches are directed towards what is typical in human nature. An individual, to Doderer, is inseparable from the outer realities to which that individual responds or fails to respond.

For Doderer, as for Jünger and Brecht, the First World War was a decisive and formative experience. In an autobiographical sketch he wrote:

> 'At the age of 19 he wore what has long been a historical costume, with its gay colours, red and blue: the uniform of an Imperial Austrian officer of the Dragoons. At 23 he was a lumberjack deep in the virgin forest of Siberia; at 24 a printer; at 25 he hiked through the Kirghiz Steppes on foot; still in the same year he became a student of history in Vienna. At 29 he had put this, too, behind him, as well as the publication of his first books.'

These first books were a collection of poems and a short novel, *Die Bresche*. Two other books followed in 1930, but it was not till 1938, with the publication of his novel *Ein Mord den Jeder Begeht*, that Doderer became at all widely known. His next novel, *Ein Umweg* (1940), is set in seventeenth-century Austria, but it was as much a psychological novel as the other.

In the Second World War Doderer served in the German Air Force, on the Russian Front once more and in several other countries. Of his return to Austria after the war he wrote:

> Already he had made what has remained his most important discovery, bearing both on the mechanics of the mind and on outward events: that of the indirect way; that of making thought conform to life, as opposed to the attempts, made all around him incessantly, to make life conform to

thought—attempts that inevitably lead to dogmatism, to reformism, and finally to the totalitarian State.

Doderer's *magnum opus*—large in every sense of the word—was published on his sixtieth birthday. (The American translation, *The Demons*, appeared five years later, in 1961, and was not welcomed as a major work.) Its less ambitious prelude, or ramp, *Die Strudlhofstiege*—a mere 909 pages, compared with the 1345 of *Die Dämonen*—had been in print since 1951. Though each work is complete in itself, the two works are complementary in that some of the principal characters appear in both; and chronologically, too, the action of *Die Dämonen* is a sequel to that of *Die Strudlhofstiege*. Since Doderer worked on the longer novel for twenty-five years, in one sense the shorter one is the later of the two; it therefore alludes to themes and events that were treated more fully in *Die Dämonen*. A shorter and much slighter novel of Doderer's, *Die Erleuchteten Fenster* (1950), was entirely devoted to one of the minor characters in *Die Strudlhofstiege*, the civil servant Zihal, who 'grows human' after his retirement by developing, and finally overcoming, a mania for peeping at female neighbours from the window of his flat—with a meticulous and compulsive thoroughness taken over from his former profession.

This comic and seemingly trivial episode in the life of one of his minor characters points to Doderer's most constant and serious pre-occupation, and to one of his major distinctions as a novelist. His peculiar psychology—or demonology, to give its correct name—is so fascinating as to deserve study in its own right; and Doderer did, in fact, enlarge on it theoretically in his published journals and notebooks, *Tangenten* (1964). The merit of Doderer's psychology, as opposed to the various orthodoxies which he described as 'disinfected demon-ology', is that it embraces the whole individual in relation to his or her environment, instead of positing one dominant and universal urge called *libido* or self-assertion or what have you. It is a humanistic psychology, not a clinical one. Doderer's choice of the title *The Demons*, in defiance of the rule that titles must not be duplicated, was intended as a tribute to Dostoevsky; but it is also a pointer to his application of his own demonology, quite different from Dostoevsky's, to a great variety of characters. None of these becomes a 'case' or even a type. The demons that possess them may be quite pleasant to live with—for a time; but they create a 'second reality', a cage in which some, at least, of their faculties become atrophied.

Doderer's realism, therefore, was more than a literary mode. His characters develop by breaking out of this second, or secondary, reality and liberating themselves. Yet they need no therapy other than the moment of self-discovery that may come when they least expect it, a shock treatment offered by life itself; most often by a word, an image or a smell that unravels a whole complex of past experience. Here Proust's *madeleine* suggests a precedent; but to Doderer this kind of recall is more than a trigger for the evocation of one man's life.

The protagonist of *Die Strudlhofstiege*, for instance, is a soldier; a soldier uncommonly dumb—without being an ox—not very literate, conventionally decent, awkward, inhibited. Doderer shows the gradual awakening of Melzer's 'civilian sense', which not only unties his tongue but releases him from a vicious pattern of frustrated love. Far from recoiling from such a character, Doderer's sensibility is at its finest where he retraces the pattern to an incident in Melzer's early life, his visit to Vienna on leave and his meeting, on the train that will take him back to Bosnia, with the superior officer whose friendship becomes a compensation for Melzer's failures as a civilian and a lover. Melzer's love-sickness and the promise of a bear-hunt in Bosnia fuse and conflict during the journey itself; the bear-hunt, with all its associations, wins.

This becomes Melzer's 'second reality', symbolized by the bear-skin rug, his trophy, that he takes back with him into civilian life after the war. *Die Dämonen* presents some thirty characters more or less securely trapped in their various 'second realities'. These may be sexual, political, ethical, or even linguistic, relatively harmless or utterly destructive of others or themselves. The novel is more ambitious, too, in giving an account of the whole of Austrian society at a critical period and, by implication, of the dangers that threaten this society. If the book can be said to have a hero at all, he is none of the three main characters–Geyrenhoff, Stangeler and Schlaggenberg—who embody certain phases or aspects of the author's own life. Geyrenhoff, a retired civil servant with a private income, is the principal narrator. René von Stangeler, the young historian who spent several years as a prisoner of war in Siberia, had already been prominent in *Die Strudlhofstiege* and in Doderer's early novel *Das Geheimnis des Reichs* (1930). Though even the name seems to indicate an *alter ego* of the author's, Doderer can no more be identified with Stangeler, in the long novel, than with Kajetan von Schlaggenberg, who resembles him in being a novelist with a brilliant and original mind. The most exemplary characters in the book—and Doderer was old-fashioned enough to admit exemplary characters, to maintain a scale of values—may be far removed from their author's person and circumstances: Prince Croix, for instance, and Leonhard Kakabsa, the young working man who studies Latin and becomes librarian to the Prince.

Schlaggenberg's 'second reality' takes the form of an obsession with corpulent ladies or fat women; he 'collects' them, follows them in the street, advertises for them, compiles statistics of their weight, measurements and other particulars—in search of the perfect fat woman. But every ideal, like every ideology, is suspect to Doderer—not excluding Plato's *Republic*. Schlaggenberg, of course, does his best to pass off this mania as a joke, as a merely cerebral protest against the current fashion in women's figures. Yet he is half aware of its connection with his broken marriage and his unhappiness. Another character, the rich businessman Herzka, is obsessed with the trial and punishment of witches. Doderer interpolates a complete 'document', in sixteenth-century German, recording the capture, trial and punishment of two would-be witches by one of Herzka's distant forebears.

In other instances the 'second reality' is overtly political or ideological. Imre von Gyurkicz, a talented artist and caricaturist, is driven to political action and to his death by his inability to come to terms with his middle-class, perhaps partly Jewish, descent which he tries to conceal by assuming an implausible Hungarian title. Gyurkicz, too, keeps trophies of his past, but he tells lies about their provenance, even to himself. The action of *Die Dämonen* culminates in a political event, the burning down of the Vienna *Justizpalast* on 15 July 1927. Gyurkicz is shot while inciting the crowd to violence. On the extreme Right there is the retired German cavalry officer Baron von Eulenberg, who slides from conservatism into reaction. Geyrenhoff's nephew, Körger, has the cynicism and the ruthlessness of a younger generation that will take up the Nazi cause. On a different plane, the thief and murderer Meisgeier, who also dies horribly on 15 July, shares their hatred of the old order.

There is no neat division between the different forms of possession. A sexual fixation may crystallize into an ideology, and vice versa. The 'second reality' of Charlotte von Schlaggenberg, Gyurkic's mistress for a time, consists in her compulsion to become a professional violinist, though she suffers agonies in forcing herself to practise. Her conversion to reality is a sudden one. Others, like Stangeler, have to experience many little changes of direction—*tropoi*, Doderer calls them—detours and setbacks to arrive at their true selves.

For all his originality, Doderer did not see himself as an avant-garde writer, let alone an experimental one. 'No intellectual act is wholly practicable except on an absolutely conservative basis', Stangeler remarks in *Die Strudlhofstiege*. Since Doderer did not keep up the naturalist convention of non-intervention—summed up in Flaubert's definition of the novelist as being 'like God in His universe, present everywhere, visible nowhere'—it is permissible to guess that Doderer agreed with Stangeler's remark, though his conservatism was of that generous, catholic and liberal kind to be found in other Austrian writers, from Grillparzer to Hofmannsthal, and perhaps only in Austria. It is a principle, a way of life and a cast of mind that has nothing to do with class or party, far less with material interests, nor with the insistence on an ideal *status ante* or *status quo*. That would be ideology. Since it aims not at exclusiveness, but at integration, it is also the opposite of snobbery. The only crushing snub that occurs in *Die*

Dämonen is administered by Prince Croix to a middle-class youth who has sneered at Leonhard's working-class origin; but the young man is the son of Mary K., whom Croix treats as his equal. What he snubs is Hubert K.'s snobbery, not his class.

That Austrian conservatism, of course, is a thing of the past, and one that may have become quite unintelligible to later generations both in Austria and the two Germanys. *Die Dämonen* was never a topical novel or a political one, though it did clarify some of the crucial issues of the century, including political ones. Without that distance of thirty years between the action of the novel and its completion, it would not have become what it is. That distance is one of its dimensions, as important as its spatial structure or its range. Because Doderer set out to impose order on a pandemonium, and because he was sure of his centre, he could explore every periphery and lunatic fringe of human life, every linguistic tangent, without waywardness or eccentricity. Diplomats, doctors, factory workers, financiers crooked or straight, policemen, prostitutes, lawyers, soldiers commissioned or otherwise, musicians, house porters, the proprietor and manageress of a shady café, an American lepidopterist, historians, landladies and a whole crowd of adolescents—all these and their worlds Doderer weighed up, co-ordinated and illuminated; and never by the merely conventional lights to which Balzac, for instance, resorted when his experience or imagination gave out. Above all, his book was a vindication of reality, and the possibility of fully inhabiting it. To live fully in the present, he suggested, one must be at peace with the past. Hence his need for those thirty years between the concept and its execution.

Its scale and intricacy alone make *The Demons* a wholly untypical novel of the 1950s, by which time younger German and Austrian writers had learned from British and American models to be wary of 'total', encyclopedic, novels; and Doderer's next novel, *Roman No. 7: Die Wasserfälle von Slunj* (1963), was kept at a farther remove from superficial topicality by its setting in late nineteenth-century England and Austria. Except in his comic *jeu d'esprit Die Merowinger* of 1962, and a few of the short pieces collected in *Die Peinigung der Leder-beutelchen* (1959), Doderer deliberately restrained his exuberant fancy, his proclivity to elaborate, baroque inventions and erudite, polyglot word-play. (A streak of peculiarly Austrian grotesquerie in all his works connects it with that of the painter and writer Albert P. Gütersloh, whom Doderer called his master.) Yet, whatever their subjects, his novels are no more historical than they are topical; and though he made use of realistic conventions, his novels were exploratory in a way that relates them to those of Proust or Musil rather than those of Thomas Mann. This has less to do with formal structure than with the novelist's attitude to his characters, their behaviour and development; and, ultimately, with an attitude to reality itself. In his diaries Doderer wrote:

But the story-teller must never acknowledge any theme at all, of which his characters then become a vehicle, because merely in doing so he makes the theme absolute and raises it above its true level—that is, its existence in the psychology of the characters alone. A 'theme' can exist only as something *imagined by individual persons* in the novel; no other kind of existence is justified here, and most certainly not an existence as a guiding concept in the author, whose business is only to imagine persons, not ideas.

Doderer, then, explored reality through his characters, and it was the process of exploration itself that mattered. Of one of his recurrent characters he remarked that 'Stangeler is converted to the complexity of life', and those words convey the essence not only of Doderer's psychology, but of his seemingly conventional realism.

Because the simplification or suppression of life's complexity has a great deal to do with the evils of our time, from bureaucracy, blinkered specialization and personal obsession to ideological fanaticism, mass hysteria and the totalitarian state, Doderer's novels were more topical than they seemed—and may still seem to those who have dismissed them from their awareness—besides being more convincing and therapeutic than novels in which ideas and trends of our time are merely allegorized. The last war and its issues, as such, were not touched upon in Doderer's fiction. As he mentioned in his war-time diaries, with specific reference to the difference between his response and that of Ernst Jünger, he experienced that war as a 'second reality', with no other wish than to survive it and return to a 'real world'. Yet Doderer's demonology anticipated and included the issues of that war, as the psychology of Musil, Broch and Canetti anticipated and included them in novels written before the war, not least because of Doderer's identification of stupidity with a failure to grasp the 'complexity of life'. Unlike Thomas Mann in *Dr Faustus*, Doderer's *The Demons* is a work that does not demonize evil, but de-demonizes it by making it understandable. It is there, above all, that the work of this Austrian traditionalist links up with the endeavours of a younger generation of German writers to understand and face up to the past.

II De-demonization

1

Doderer himself commented on a German peculiarity to which he attributed much that happened in this century, as well as the antipathy to things German among other nations. In the late nineteenth and early twentieth centuries, he noted in his *Tangenten*, Germans tended to lose the faculty of 'unconscious thinking', and, consequently, to 'act incessantly out of an extension of conscious thinking', a narrow track which is 'that of inhumanity'. Doderer connected this trend with the philistinism that treats 'so-called cultural possessions' (*Kulturgüter*, an untranslatable word) as commodities, cut and dried, useful in their way and eminently respectable, but unrelated to other pursuits and therefore forbidding, 'like a large house with open doors and windows, clean and polished—but quite empty inside.' He went on to observe: 'That kind of person who habitually regards all things of the mind as opposed to 'life' (what could they possibly mean by this life?!) is the embodied result of the split between form and content which the nineteenth century bequeathed to us.'

A de-humanized and schematic intellectuality precipitates a violent reaction in favour of 'life', conceived as pure impulse and pure unconsciousness. Many instances of this reaction were touched upon in my book *A Proliferation of Prophets*, in writers as diverse as Nietzsche, Gottfried Benn and Thomas Mann. To treat this reaction as 'demonic', though, perpetuates the split, instead of healing it, since demons are made responsible for an entirely human failure to achieve a modicum of integration.

Doderer was not alone in seeing that this split between 'form and content', or between abstract knowledge and vital experience, is intimately bound up with the split between fantasy and reality in modern literature, and German literature especially. Hermann Broch was preoccupied with this dilemma, often to the point of doubting that imaginative literature could be anything but morally pernicious in his time. Elias Canetti, too, presented an extreme and gruelling instance of the alienation in his novel *Die Blendung* (1935, first reissued in Germany in 1948), whose three parts are called 'A Head without a World', 'Headless World', and 'World in the Head'. Like Broch and Doderer, Canetti was led to psychological, sociological and historical studies by his need to grapple with the dilemma; and Canetti's plays too, investigate various obsessions that amount to a loss of reality.

The temptation to demonize violent eruptions of destructive unreason was hard to resist. Even Broch did so in his unfinished novel *Der Versucher* (1935-51), in which he tried to show how an alpine village community is threatened by the outbreak of a creed clearly meant to be identified with National Socialism. Traditional notions of good and evil alone proved unable to account for such a phenomenon; and one reason may be that the fascination of unreason was not connected dialectically to the ossification of reason in educational institutions that turned literature, art and knowledge into commodities. Under National Socialism, too, Germans were taught to take pride in their 'cultural possessions', but these now served only as weapons to be used against any glimmering of true perception in the 'bearers' of German culture (*Kulturträger*, another untranslatable word.)

2

Only lyrical poetry proved capable of bridging the pre-war and post-war eras without too immediate or drastic a confrontation with the breakdown of values that called all literature in doubt after 1945. In the cases of Benn and Brecht, one reason is that neither had accepted those values in any case. Another is that lyrical poets had found it easier to go underground in the Third Reich, merely by keeping silent, or publishing their work in tiny editions that escaped notice; and poetry had its own way of counterpointing immediate perceptions with timeless and universal concerns, of placing 'real toads' in 'imaginary gardens', as Marianne Moore put it. After the belated rediscovery of Brecht's poetry in both German Republics, demands for overt political 'commitment' even in verse became so peremptory for a time as to virtually banish the work of those poets who made no concession to the trend; but a measure of continuity had been maintained even by those poets, whether they were read or ignored. Later, it was to become apparent that Brecht, too, had built on a tradition, though not on the Romantic-Symbolist tradition that had dominated European poetry for nearly two centuries.

Wilhelm Lehmann was one of those who bridged the eras. Born in 1882—almost a generation earlier than either Jünger or Doderer—he was overshadowed in his youth by the poet Oskar Loerke, whom he revered. His first book of poems had not appeared until 1935, from a small press dedicated to resistance. Like Edwin Muir, with whom he had affinities—though Robert Graves was the English poet to whom he felt closest—he wrote some of his best poems at an age at which the energies of most lyrical poets have begun to flag. In 1946 Lehmann was one of the first of the survivors to re-emerge, with his collection *Entzückter Staub*; and the title of his 1935 collection, significantly, had been *Antwort des Schweigens*—'Answer by Silence'.

Like Loerke, Lehmann had kept clear of fashions and movements, including the Expressionist movement so powerful in their youth; but Loerke and Lehmann themselves became the founders of what was to be regarded as a school—the one which a post-war poet and critic, Hans Egon Holthusen, was to label 'the marsh-and-bog poets'. Their influence was traced not only to Elisabeth Langgässer, Oda Schäfer and Horst Lange, fellow survivors in the Third Reich, but to Günter Eich, Karl Krolow, Heinz Piontek and other poets who became prominent in later decades, up to the 1980s. In some cases the label has been affixed only because such poets wrote 'nature poems', amongst other things; and Lehmann, together with Loerke, had originated a kind of 'nature poetry' at once more precise and less sentimental than the Romantic prototype that had persisted throughout the previous century (with rare and distinguished exceptions like Mörike and Annette von Droste-Hülshoff).

Wilhelm Lehmann observed the phenomena of nature in the light of myth and history. His poems could be botanically and zoologically specific without being naturalistic, since every particular he evoked was at once itself and more than itself, through its association with historical and mythical archetypes. 'Nature poetry', let alone 'marsh-and-bog poetry', tells us nothing about this peculiarity, when both Loerke and Lehmann could, and did, write poems just as good about cities and civilization—seen from the same perspective as their 'nature poems'. To Lehmann, nature and civilization were not opposed. Both were repositories of archetypes. He could begin a poem with an image of a lady riding a unicorn—taken from a Gobelin tapestry—and connect it with an asphalt road. Neither, to Lehmann, was more real than the other, though one might be more actual. In the same way his poem 'Nach der zweiten Sintflut' (from his collection *Noch Nicht Genug* of 1950) moves within one four-line stanza from the absence of Noah's ark to paths that have turned to stone and sand—like those in Peter Huchel's lamentations for the churned-up German roads of 1945—now that 'all human time has run out'. Only the yellowhammer sings on in this dehumanized world, and the song is understood as the voice of silence, a silence that has no more use for human voices. Shot-down bombers and rusting iron are linked to the dragons of legend that guarded treasures, but there is no treasure to guard. The poem ends with another flood, from Greek mythology, and another absence, that of Pyrrha and Deucalion. All these images and associations are packed into four rhymed iambic stanzas with short, four-stress lines. Lehmann's refusal in all his poems to moralize or explain could be more effective, artistically, than most of the heart-searching and self-justifying that German writers were to feel incumbent on them for decades to come.

In later poems, the magpie Lehmann observes is also the one seen by Wolfram von Eschenbach, the mediaeval poet; and the poem in which he makes this connection ends with the line: 'Hörst du Schritte, sind es die der Brüder Grimm' (If you hear footsteps, they're those of the brothers Grimm). Pagan and Christian figures intermingle in Lehmann's poems, sometimes harmoniously, sometimes dissonantly, as in 'Venus und Taufe' ('Venus and Baptism'). Marlene Dietrich and Claire Bloom appear in the company of Venus and Diana in the poem 'Venus und Diva', though this particular juxtaposition takes the risk of self-parody by suggesting that Lehmann's magic of synchronization could be no more than a conjuring trick, that his art could leap too easily across the ages and civilizations, leaving out too many differences in his search for analogies and fusions.

Lehmann's last book of poems, *Sichtbare Zeit*, appeared in 1967, and contains poems written up to the age of eighty-four. Its epigraph was in English, and the choice of those words by Louis MacNeice was evidence not only of his concern with English poetry, but of the isolation he had been driven into by what I have called the foreshortening of history in post-war Germany: 'Some idiot recently stated that rhyme in English poetry was now a thing of the past'. In fact it was in West Germany that rhyme was a thing of the past, at that particular moment, and according to the prescriptions of those who ruled the media and publishing industry, when the 'demon of progress in the arts' (Wyndham Lewis) went hand-in-hand not only with Marxist dogma but with capitalist marketing techniques. Lehmann's poems, though, were not affected by those pressures, any more than they had been affected by the 'demons' of reaction supreme in the Third Reich. Lehmann remained a classicist and a quiet innovator to the end. Rhyme remained essential to his poetry, as it was essential to much of Rilke's or Gottfried Benn's—as a means of discovering connections, correspondence, analogies, but also of creating order by the exercise of a process that made for impersonality, because those rhymes were found, rather than invented. To the last Lehmann remained delicately responsive to the *minutiae* of both human and non-human life. On his late visit to England in 1964—his first since the First World War, when he was a prisoner-of-war!—he not only met Robert Graves at Oxford, but visited London Zoo. His poem 'London (1964)' shows a characteristically magical progression from a street musician with his old pram and jazz records to a South East Asian owl in the Zoo and hence to *La Belle Dame sans Merci*, the realm of timeless myths and archetypes that were Lehmann's constant and unifying domain.

3

Lehmann's poem 'Nach der zweiten Sintflut' avoided the rhetoric of apocalypse by its coolness, a coolness due to the detachment that came of a long habit of looking at human life *sub specie naturae*, if not *eternitatis*. Its diction is neither archaic nor contemporary, neither high nor low, because to Lehmann things of the mind, of culture and civilization, were as continuous as the things of nature.

It was a poem by Günter Eich—a younger 'nature poet', though one closer to Peter Huchel than to Lehmann, who disowned the literary offspring attributed to him by historians and critics—that, independently of Brecht, hit on a mode of deliberate understatement and dead-pan plainness in poetry, as a prophylactic against pathos, self-pity and moral exhortation. The undated poem, 'Inventur', appeared in Eich's collection *Abgeeigene Gehöfte* of 1948. From other poems in the book one gathers that the soldier of this poem was a prisoner-of-war, but any army camp could have been the setting:

Dies ist meine Mütze,
dies ist mein Mantel,
hier ist mein Rasierzeug
im Beutel aus Leinen.

Konservenbüchse:
Mein Teller, mein Becher,
ich hab in das Weissblech
den Namen geritzt.

Geritzt hier mit diesem
kostbaren Nagel,
den vor begehrlichen
Augen ich berge.

Im Brotbeutel sind
ein Paar wollene Socken
und einiges, was ich
niemand verrate,

so dient es als Kissen
nachts meinem Kopf.
Die Pappe hier liegt
zwischen mir und der Erde.

Die Bleistiftmine
lieb ich am meisten:
Tags schreibt sie mir Verse,
die nachts ich erdacht.

Dies ist mein Notizbuch,
dies meine Zeltbahn,
dies ist mein Handtuch,
dies ist mein Zwirn.

Inventory

This is my cap,
this is my greatcoat,
and here's my shaving-kit
in its linen bag.

A can of meat:
my plate, my mug,
into its tin
I've scratched my name.

Scratched it with this
invaluable nail
which I keep hidden
from covetous eyes.

My bread bag holds
two woollen socks
and a couple of things
I show to no one,

like that it serves me
as a pillow at night.
Between me and the earth
I lay this cardboard.

This pencil lead
is what I love most:
by day it writes verses
I thought up in the night.

This is my notebook,
and this is my groundsheet,
this is my towel,
this is my thread.

    This poem was followed in the book by one called 'Latrine', in which 'Urin' rhymes with 'Hölderlin'—a more explicit affront to the solemn guardians of the German cultural heritage, but less remarkable as a poem for that very reason. The strength of 'Inventur' lies in what it does not say, what it refrains from saying; and it owed much of its shock

effect to the context of poems not only rhymed, but quite close even in theme and stance to what German readers still expected of 'nature poems'.

For nearly two decades after the end of the war, the radio play was a medium cultivated by most of the best imaginative writers in German. Yet those by Günter Eich stood out even in that distinguished company, and he was generally acknowledged to be the most original and versatile practitioner of the art, which, like Peter Huchel, he had pioneered in the 1930s. After the war, his radio plays were not only widely performed all over the German-speaking world, with its many radio stations, and beyond it, but collected into volumes that were widely read. The principal collections are *Träume* (1953), *Stimmen* (1958) and *In Anderen Sprachen* (1964). In several of his best radio plays, such as *Die Mädchen aus Viterbo* (1952/1958), Eich dealt with topical issues by resorting to parallel plots as a distancing device. In *Die Mädchen aus Viterbo* the situations interwoven are those of a Jewish father and daughter awaiting arrest in the Third Reich and a party of Italian schoolgirls on a visit to the Catacombs, in which one girl goes astray, in danger of being trapped there. As in Lehmann's poems, 'real toads' are placed in an 'imaginary garden'—with the symbolism of the Catacombs as an implicit third parallel in the case of the play—not in order to evade the moral implications of a specific horror, but to heighten it by analogy and contrast.

Unlike the stage play, the radio play is an intimate, almost introspective medium, relying for its effect on language alone, unaided by gesture, action or scenery. Its freedom, like that of poetry, is the freedom of suggestiveness. Like Eich's 'Inventur' and the increasingly laconic and sardonic poems of his later years, which left all stereotypes of 'nature poetry' far behind them, it can mean more than it says. In Günter Eich's case, it always meant more than it said, and that was the crux of his mastery. The language of his radio plays is as plain and commonplace as the language of 'Inventur', which suggested new possibilities to poets brought up to believe that verse must be edifying, above all. In the radio plays, too, the complexities and the mystery are left between the lines, between the passages of ordinary dialogue, in the vibrations set up between one thing, one order, and another.

After 1965, by which time television had largely robbed radio of its once attentive audiences, and until his death in 1972, Eich concentrated on poems more and more cryptic and condensed, and on very short prose pieces which he called *Maulwürfe* (Moles), perhaps because their meaning, too, is not so much on the surface as underground. Like Lehmann, Huchel, Ernst Meister and Paul Celan, Eich was one of the victims of the politicization of so-called imaginative, but in fact increasingly unimaginative and anti-imaginative, literature that reached its height in the late 1960s. The four-volume edition of his Collected

Works published in 1973 looked like a monument, rather than the event it deserved to be.

4

Both in prose and verse, the 'de-demonization' of German writing had made considerable progress even before Hannah Arendt reported on 'the banality of evil', on the monstrous disproportion between the destruction wrought by Nazism and the drab ordinariness of the destroyers. Independently of Hannah Arendt and her researches, many novelists and poets in the German-speaking world had been bringing home the same recognition to their readers. The strong resistance met by Hannah Arendt's book *Eichmann in Jerusalem* (1963) and by some of the imaginative writers in question proved once more that most of 'human kind cannot bear very much reality' (T. S. Eliot). The demonization of Nazism, like the related notion of corporate guilt, was more acceptable to many than an understanding of what human nature is capable of perpetrating in cold blood, possessed by no demon other than one never identified in any theology, the demon of conformism. Hitler, perhaps, was possessed by demons less drab, and his demagogy most certainly evoked them; but the system could never have been sustained for twelve years without the support of respectable citizens doing their duty.

Critics of Hannah Arendt's book were as outraged by the suggestion that Eichmann was not a 'brute', thug and sadist as by the revelation that Jews, too, could be terrorized, duped or flattered into passive connivance or active collaboration. What they could not see, because their own nationalism or racialism blinkered them, was that Arendt's de-demonizing of Nazi evil was not only true in essence, but salutary, liberating and instructive. To condemn and hate the German as the Nazi leaders condemned and hated the Jews is an emotional subterfuge that merely inverts Hitler's coarse and fanatical delusions. To demonstrate the 'banality of evil', and indeed the stupidity of that particular evil, is emotionally shocking and unacceptable only because it exposes the utter senselessness of so much suffering and destruction: to be the victims of demons or monsters is more meaningful and more dignified than to be the victims of ordinary, respectable little men. But demons and monsters are beyond our comprehension, the 'terrible and terrifying' normality of a man like Eichmann is not. By understanding Eichmann, as Hannah Arendt helped us to do, we can learn not to fall into evil as banal and stupid, and as ordinary and respectable, as his.

Perhaps the most shocking of all Hannah Arendt's revelations is that Eichmann did not even hate the Jews whom he sent to mass destruction, that he had Jewish friends and relations, that he was sympathetic to

Zionism, that he would have applied himself just as conscientiously to saving or resettling Jews if such had been his orders, as for a time they were. If there are contradictions, or seeming contradictions, in Arendt's account of Eichmann—his 'idealism' on the one hand, his upstart careerism on the other, for instance—these make her portrait all the more lifelike, and Eichmann all the more representative of countless other servants of the régime. As for many Nazis, for Eichmann idealism was a kind of insurance policy, something to 'keep his metaphysics warm'—to quote Eliot once more—when he had cause for anxiety, scruples, or disgust. It is precisely this that shows how cultural values and 'possessions' had become totally separate from real experience, to the point of becoming a 'second reality' in Doderer's sense. A century earlier, Georg Büchner had shown incomparable prescience in his revolt against a philosophical idealism that had this very function of providing an alibi for inhumanity; and it was on receiving the Büchner Prize for literature that Günter Eich delivered his challenging address on the need for German writers never again to collaborate with the apparatus of power.

Eichmann's 'idealism' was as sincere as anything else about him, as sincere as anything can be in a man totally unrelated to reality. It was his insulation from reality that enabled him to carry out his special and specialized task without more than passing scruples as to its ends; the end was not his business, but that of authority, and authority was bound to be right, because it had power. Hannah Arendt did not evade the peculiarly German aspects of this complex, analysing them with insight and acumen: but she knew that the complex arises not from an ethnic disposition, but from political, social and educational conditioning that can be changed. Eichmann's ambition, on the other hand, his snobbery and even 'his horrible gift for consoling himself with clichés' are universal enough to be even more disturbing. Most shattering of all was the extent of Eichmann's conformism, and thus of his ordinariness. Arendt was almost certainly right in arguing 'that it was not his fanaticism but his conscience that prompted Eichmann to adopt his uncompromising attitude during the last year of the war, as it had prompted him to move in the opposite direction for a short time three years before.' Even Eichmann's readiness to stand trial in Jerusalem was due not to anything as independent or spontaneous as a sense of guilt, but to his awareness that authority and power had shifted since the end of the war. As a conscientious conformist to the end, Eichmann felt the need to confront this new wave, whatever it might do to him. To the end, too, he remained closed to reality, immured not only in his glass box at the trial, but in his abstract and meaningless verbiage. As Arendt put it,

officialese became his language because he was genuinely incapable of uttering a single sentence that was not a cliché . . . The longer one listened to him, the more obvious it became that his inability to speak was closely connected with his inability to *think*, namely, to think from the standpoint of somebody else. No communication was possible with him, not because he lied but because he was surrounded by the most reliable of safeguards against the words and the presence of others, and hence against reality as such.

Eichmann went to his death unperturbed, and immured in a final cliché: 'After a short while, gentlemen, we shall meet again. Such is the fate of all men. Long live Germany, long live Argentina, long live Austria. I shall not forget them'—words as meaningless as all Eichmann's words and actions, when he had previously affirmed that he was not a Christian and did not believe in an after-life. He was despatched out of this world without so much as understanding what he had done, in terms of the sufferings inflicted on individuals more alive to reality than he was. The facts of which Eichmann undoubtedly had full knowledge were pure abstractions, because he lacked the imagination that would have made them more; and even the reality of his own death was beyond his comprehension. 'Under the gallows', Hannah Arendt wrote, 'his memory played him the last trick: he was 'elated' and he forgot that this was his own funeral.'

Eichmann was a specialist in the transportation of certain 'categories'. What happened to the categories transported was the concern of a different department. In order to ensure the non-existence of certain condemned 'categories', officials like Eichmann must become unfeeling and unthinking—except in so far as thinking is demanded by their function—just as they must switch off imagination and compassion. The slightest glimmer of awareness of another person's inner reality would make them bad servants, bad instruments. (Eichmann experienced such glimmers at times, and was conscience-stricken when he remembered that he had used his influence on behalf of a few individual Jews; but on the whole he was immune from such corruption, as from the avarice of many of his fellow bureaucrats and superiors.)

Traditional notions of good and evil, right and wrong, lost their validity in face of such a split and breakdown of reality. The madness of Eichmann was a case not of possession, but of cold vacuity. In imaginative literature, too, all attempts to come to terms with the immediate past were thwarted as long as evil was demonized and guilt established without the recognition that good and evil, right and wrong, had been utterly confounded. Yet this very process is one in which every one of us is implicated to a greater or lesser extent, if only by pursuing one or another specialization and excluding this or that order of reality from our awareness. Imaginative literature itself had become more and more specialized in this sense in the course of the last century and a half. To be resisted, this process had to be accepted and understood. Very

gradually it became clear to German writers that the 'demonic' personality of Hitler was less relevant to this urgent concern than the banality
of millions of ordinary men who differed from Eichmann only in being
differently employed.

5

To retrace all the stages of that development in West and East German,
Austrian and Swiss writing over four decades would call for an historian
and critic not only omniscient, but more convinced than I am that any
kind of linear progression can take place in a whole literature—still
produced, as it is, by individuals, with their tensions, conflicts and
regressions. Wherever the recent past was dealt with truthfully, if only
in unambitious war novels of a naturalistic type, a contribution was
made to the process of de-demonization. In more ambitious work, the
main obstacle was an alienation from every kind of society, peculiar to
German writers ever since the eighteenth century and still advocated by
Gottfried Benn after the war as 'isolationism', 'nihilism' and his version
of solipsism. Even before and after Nietzsche, this trend was so deeply
rooted in Germany—and not only in the arts—that it has become
fashionable to speak of the 'socialization' of writers, as though to be part
of society, let alone a community, were some remote consummation
devoutly to be wished.

The very first post-war German work of fiction to be translated into
English and other languages, Ernst Kreuder's short novel *Die Gesellschaft vom Dachboden* (1946; *The Attic Pretenders*), which remained
Kreuder's most widely read work, sets up a society within a society,
that of the attic of the title. It is a society of drop-outs and eccentrics
dedicated to values that are not those of either post-war Germany, any
more than those of the Third Reich. Kreuder's later, and far less
conventional, works of fiction reverted again and again to a
romanticism of isolated, remote or disused places, preferably rural; and
he was never to feel at home in the West Germany of the *Wirtschaftswunder*, one of whose policies was to industrialize agricultural regions
and villages. The consequences of that policy were not to become a
matter of general concern until after Kreuder's death in 1972, by which
time his novels, too, had been relegated to the attics of public attention.

The three short novels published by Wolfgang Koeppen in the early
1950s were more explicitly critical of the incipient *Wirtschaftswunder*.
Koeppen's virtual silence as a writer of fiction in the ensuing decades
has not detracted from the reputation he owes to those three novels, or
from their relevance to later developments. Much as Kreuder, like
Jahnn, anticipated the ecological and anti-nuclear concerns of a
younger generation; Koeppen was one of the first to voice apprehen-

sions about the Cold War and Germany's involvement in it as the most likely battlefield of a hot one. Trained as a journalist before the Third Reich, as a writer of fiction Koeppen was close to satirists of an earlier bourgeoisie like Carl Sternheim and Kurt Tucholsky. His narrative style was more idiosyncratic and vehement, in the manner of Expressionism, than that of younger post-war realists like Alfred Andersch, Siegfried Lenz or Heinrich Böll. *Tauben in Gras* (1951) has an episodic, almost cinematic structure that succeeds in conveying the hectic, chaotic character of American-German relations just after the stabilization of the West German currency—with the implication throughout that little else has been stabilized. As in most satirical writing, Koeppen's characters are less portrayed than caricatured, illuminated in flashes of sharp perception; and Koeppen may always have lacked the patience with accumulated detail indispensable for the practice of a sustained realism (and most pronounced, in post-war German writing, in the work of Uwe Johnson). It is sporadic acts, like Kay's returning of the old-fashioned jewellery given to her by Emilia, the bankrupt German heiress, that stand out in the narrative as symbolic features. Nor does Koeppen bother to keep up the realistic stance of impartiality. In all the three novels there is a central character who can be identified with the author's, as one who will take no part in the rat race, any rat race, American or German, economic or artistic. In *Tauben im Gras* it is Philipp, a writer who prefers not to write; and Koeppen's theme is shamelessly, provocatively sounded in the last sentences of his book:

> The air raid bunkers were blown up; the air raid bunkers are being put up again. Death plays his war games. *Threats, crises, conflicts, tensions.* Come-now-O-gentle-slumber. But no one can escape his world. Our dream is uneasy and oppressive. Germany lives in the field of tension, eastern world, western world, broken world, two half-worlds, strange and hostile to each other, Germany lives at their seam, at the breaking-point, time is precious, it is only a respite, a brief respite, lost, a second for taking breath, breathing space on a condemned battlefield.

The clipped, asyntactic prose is reminiscent of Gottfried Benn's, as of Sternheim's; but the message is far from nihilistic, since it posits an alternative to the danger of which it warns.

Philipp's counterpart in *Das Treibhaus* (1953) is Keetenheuve, a member of parliament in the new Bundestag, who had emigrated in the Third Reich and had hoped to be able to apply himself to such an alternative. He had married Elke, a refugee from the East, daughter of a Gauleiter; but Elke died, after becoming an alcoholic and a lesbian. This novel, too, is an overt indictment of post-war West Germany. Like the earlier and later novels, it leaves itself open both to the stricture that

Koeppen's realism is deficient in impartiality, and to the objection that his protagonist is deficient in the realism of a true politician. Significantly, Keetenheuve translates Baudelaire in his office! Like Koeppen, he is a sceptical utopian—bound to come to a sticky end, cynics will say, as did Gustav Landauer, another sceptical utopian reckless enough to involve himself briefly in politics, and killed for that in 1919. *Das Treibhaus* ends apocalyptically, rather like some of the Expressionist works of that period, with Keetenheuve's suicide after his weird involvement with a Salvation Army girl of sixteen, also a refugee from East Germany and dominated by another lesbian woman, Gerda. Once again, Koeppen declares his message. Parliamentary democracy, majority rule, in West Germany becomes no more than the lesser evil, seen as the dictatorship of self-interest, of careers and deals.

The two evils are brought together in the third novel, *Der Tod in Rom* (1954), whose protagonists are a former SS general, Judejahn, and his nephew Siegfried, a composer, who has the recurrent function of being the detached, non-conformist observer of vicious obsessions—that of the de-demonizer. Judejahn is in Rome with money provided by a Middle Eastern government in whose service he can be active in the old cause, which he thinks he can bring back to power in Germany, too, from his new base. Siegfried is in Rome for the performance of a symphony that is to be conducted by Kürenberg, an anti-Nazi with a Jewish wife. Under the Third Reich, Kürenberg had been deprived of his function and livelihood by Judejahn's brother-in-law, a fellow-travelling nationalist who is now the Burgomaster of his city. Judejahn's wife, who is loyal to the Führer and the cause, to the point of despising her husband for having escaped from Germany, has joined her sister's family, in Rome to attend the performance, but takes no part in their activities and refuses to leave her room. Judejahn's son Adolf underwent a conversion at the end of the war, when he met a Jewish boy released from a concentration camp, but on the point of dying of starvation, and tried to save his life by sharing his food with him. Adolf is in Rome to study for the priesthood. Siegfried's brother Dietrich, on the other hand, has inherited his father's opportunism, and is likely to do as well as his father in the Federal Republic. After various meetings and confrontations between these characters, Judejahn shoots Kürenberg's wife and dies in a homosexual bar after making love to its girl cashier, whom he had come close to killing also, because he was not sure whether she was an Italian or a Jewess. It is Dietrich Pfaffrath, though, who carries the message and warning in this book:

> but suddenly he had the feeling that his uncle's great time was over for good, that Judejahn was only an adventurer of insecure means and shady wealth, 'careful' a voice within Dietrich warned him, Judejahn could harm his career, and yet Dietrich would have liked to march behind Judejahn, in a position with prospects of course and close to the leadership, if Judejahn had

unfurled a banner and summoned a national assembly. But there were still places to be filled in the Federation, and Dietrich would get to them after passing his examinations. Not till Dietrich is unemployed, not till he is given no motor car to play with, not till he is kicked down into the academic proletariat, not till there is an economic crisis will Dietrich march blindly behind a specious banner, will he go off unthinking into a specious war.

6

If Koeppen's narrative pace and cataclysmic plots made him something other than a realistic novelist—perhaps one insufficiently 'socialized' for that function, as befitted a lone prophet warning of evils to come— Arno Schmidt had no use at all for the machinery of conventional fiction, long before his lexical researches and innovations led him not only to out-Joyce Joyce, but to produce scripts that defeated the ingenuity of printers, let alone the general novel-reading public. In another way though, Arno Schmidt's early prose works were hyper-realistic, just because he dispensed with the machinery of fiction, preferring a diary form that made for immediacy in his dealings with what, for all the reader knows, may have been 'real toads', not even pretending that they were to be placed in an 'imaginary garden'.

The earliest of these works, *Leviathan* (1949), is dated 20 May 1945, and begins with a letter in English written by a 'Jonny' to a Betty and reporting, amongst other things, that 'the Russians look a jolly good sort and are amiable to deal with'. It is not clear whether this Jonny is to be identified with the diarist recording events of the foregoing months. That diarist is a German NCO on his way out of Berlin with a mixed party of refugees, who have managed to board a train of sorts and find an engine for it. The diarist is certainly to be identified with Arno Schmidt in that, like the diarist of subsequent works, he expounds the philosophical, scientific, linguistic and literary preoccupations of that author, even to a clergyman in the party most averse to Schmidt's dogmatic atheism, to an old man who is more open to it, and a young woman with whom the diarist had been in love before her marriage. The horrors of that trip—the train is blown up by the Russians—are conveyed in a kind of descriptive shorthand that makes for vividness, though not for coherence. Schmidt had also begun to evolve his distinctive prose style that was to owe much to his work as a translator of English and American books by its incorporation of colloquial idiom, phonetically reproduced by Schmidt who hated the bureaucratic connotations of 'high' or standard German. To readers not wholly sympathetic to Schmidt's theorizing, carried from book to book at the risk of repetitiveness, this renewal of the German language and his ability to convey immediate observation of a wholly untheoretical kind are his most attractive features.

The diarist-narrators of his three later books, *Brands Haide* (1951), *Schwarze Spiegel* (1951) and *Aus dem Leben eines Fauns* (1953) are all outsiders—if not one and the same outsider, Schmidt himself—on the fringe of any society, whether set in the pre-war period, during the war or after the war. Yet it is in the truthful setting down of detail, both in recurrent weather reports and in snatches of reported speech rendering character, that Schmidt's books excel, even though the only sustained interaction between characters in these books is the erotic, between the narrator and Lore in *Brands Haide* and with Lisa in *Aus dem Leben eines Fauns*. Both are called 'the she-wolf', and both leave after brief co-habitation. In *Aus dem Leben eines Fauns*, with its more recognizably fictional setting in a Germany depopulated by a nuclear war and the diarist living like a latter-day Robinson Crusoe in the wilderness, Lisa almost shoots her fellow survivor before becoming his lover. (Already in *Leviathan* Schmidt had looked forward to the extermination of the human race. Lore's and Lisa's fierceness make them lovable because they share the narrator's disillusionment, at least to a certain degree.) Although the setting of this book may be implausible, because the effects of radiation and of changing climate are ignored—despite Schmidt's claims to scientific knowledge—the practical business of survival, housebuilding, foraging, making and mending, hold one's attention in the same way as the observed details in the preceding books. As for the theories and tirades, many of them, too, call for a suspension of disbelief. When Schmidt polemicizes against Goethe in *Brands Haide*, for instance, because Goethe once wrote about the 'significantly general', the tirade—'at his age he should gradually have got to know that only the significantly specific is significant!'—misses the point about Goethe, who was never a Platonist, but does tell us something about Schmidt's peculiar love of details in brief evocations of the weather, of clouds or trees. A proclivity to dubious generalization in his theories, though, is one of Schmidt's own weaknesses. One of countless instances occurs in *Schwarze Spiegel*: '*Who created cultural values?* Only Greeks, Romans, the Germanic peoples; Indians in philosophy.—The Slavs are typically cultureless: my God, chess'n a bit of music!' In its context, only the colloquialism redeems the assertion from being ponderous nonsense. Much the same applies to Schmidt's reiterated professions of atheism in all his earlier books, or his simplistic denunciations of Nietzsche, whom he held responsible for the Nazi glorification of power. It was his way with words, when reporting, describing, evoking persons and things, that made him a novelist despite himself. That, too, made him the forerunner of a new realism, though he dispensed from the start with its trappings in fiction.

7

What Schmidt had not learned from his English studies was to avoid being a bore; and being a bore—an opinionated bore, like his diarists—is a social offence, not an ethical one. In Schmidt's defence it must be said that even the opinionated ranting of his diarist-narrators can be funny; and that his experiences as a German conscript and a refugee from his home in Silesia, where he lost his early manuscripts, his library and his livelihood, were not conducive to good manners, literary or otherwise. The cheerful and benevolent misanthropy of his diarists—benevolent in their dealings with individuals, rather than the human species—also made for the necessary de-demonization. Schmidt's sense of fun and his moral toughness kept his work free from the solemnities of self-pity and self-justification, as from the prevalent compulsion to apportion blame, when that was an exercise beyond the competence of literature.

The best of Arno Schmidt's contemporaries could not succeed in the direct confrontation of twentieth-century enormities, conducted in seriousness. One instance is Hans Erich Nossack's first-person (and autobiographical) account of the intensive bombing of Hamburg, *Der Untergang*, admittedly written soon after the event, in November 1943, though not published until 1961. Nossack's attempt to make ethical sense of this mass slaughter of civilians was dignified and moving, and the more so in the light of Nossack's later novels and stories, from which it is apparent that this experience was a trauma that remained with him until his death in 1977, at the age of seventy-six. As a personal document and a sensitive rendering of the event itself, this narrative retains its validity. As an attempt to interpret the event, without seeing it as an instance of total war initiated on the German side and almost inevitably taken over by the Allies, by a process no longer subject to considerations of right and wrong other than strategic and tactical ones, it has ceased to be valid.

'After a lost war one should write comedies', Hofmannsthal had remarked in response to what was for him no less a cataclysm, the collapse and dissolution of the Austrian Empire after the First World War. After 1945, it was easier for the Swiss writers Max Frisch and Friedrich Dürrenmatt to learn that lesson, because as citizens of a neutral country they were not bedevilled, demonized, by guilt. That after 1945, comedy would tend to farce and absurdity, followed from the enormity of recent historical events. Wolfgang Hildesheimer, a refugee from Nazism who had lived in England before settling in Switzerland, was another early ironist of the monstrous, as in his stories *Lieblose Legenden* of 1952.

Since Hitler's 'final solution' had left a few survivors even of ex-termination camps, their testimony, too, was to contribute to the de-demonization of the past. In 1955 H. G. Adler published his minutely researched study of Theresienstadt, of which he had been an inmate for thirty-two months, transferred there from other camps after internment in Auschwitz, where his wife and mother-in-law had been put to death. Though a poet and novelist, Adler resisted the temptation to include any mention of his own experiences in this gruelling factual and statistical account of the organization, administration and day-to-day life of a concentration camp that differed from Auschwitz or Belsen in having been designed not primarily for the extermination of Jews, but, ostensibly, as a ghetto or asylum for distinguished, aged or otherwise privileged victims of racial policy. As such, Theresienstadt was 'self-administered'—under the direction of the SS, later of the Gestapo—intended only for persons of Jewish or partly Jewish descent, and characterized by the pretence of being designed for the welfare and protection of its inmates. Many of the inmates themselves were deceived for a time, even when a large proportion of the original ones in 1941 had already been transferred to the extermination camps proper. The most cruel mockery of all occurred between the summer of 1943 and September 1944, when Theresienstadt became a 'Jewish settlement' and showpiece for foreign visitors—complete with café, community centre and similar amenities—while those who had survived the hardships of camp life continued to be selected for 'liquidation' and removed accordingly. That an 'enforced community' of this kind could be dealt with at all in the detached and scholarly manner wisely adopted by H. G. Adler for *Theresienstadt 1941-1945: Das Antlitz einer Zwangsgemeinschaft*, and by one who had suffered in it, was to make the monstrous amenable to study, if not to comprehension, and so to de-demonize it—regardless of whether or not one accepted Adler's interpretation of the phenomenon in Part III of his book.

H. G. Adler was to draw on personal experience for his later works of fiction, such as his distinguished novel *Panorama* of 1968; and personal testimony was always woven into the philosophical essays of Jean Améry, who was liberated from Bergen-Belsen by British troops in 1945, but—like Paul Celan—could survive only physically, dying by suicide in 1978, a decade after he had begun to publish his unclassifiable books, one of which, *Lefeu oder der Abbruch* he called a 'novel-essay'. In his postscripts to that book, explaining why and how his protagonist had to choose to die, Améry also showed that only irony could respond to experiences of the kind that had left him obsessed with death:

> There was no relying on the SS doctor who palpated me in 1944 to find out whether I was ripe for slaughter. The fellow had left off, don't know why. Since 1945 I'd often wished to have his carelessness corrected. That courage which the author lacked was infused into his creature's heart.

The very first of Améry's philosophical treatises had been called *Beyond*

Guilt and Atonement (1966), followed by his book on old age, *Über das Altern: Revolte und Resignation* (1968), which included an apology for suicide.

If it was Günter Grass who produced the most thorough-going work of imaginative de-demonization of the servants of the Third Reich, with a combination of realism with fantasy and grotesquerie all his own, a counterpart from the point of view of a surviving victim, though on a smaller scale, is to be found in two early works of fiction by Jakov Lind, the book of short stories *Eine Seele aus Holz* (*Soul of Wood*) and the novel *Landschaft in Beton* (*Landscape in Concrete*), published in 1962 and 1963 respectively. Born in the same year as Grass (and at one time often seen as a kind of physical *doppelgänger* of Grass, down to the famous moustache), Lind had been schooled in absurdity before he began to write. Shipped to Holland at the age of eleven from Vienna after the Anschluss as a Jewish refugee, Lind escaped extermination in Holland by making his way to Germany as a cabin-boy, assuming an 'Aryan' identity and working in Germany as assistant to a spy, then as a minor civil servant. The precise facts of Lind's early life are not easy to establish even from his later autobiographical books, *Counting my Steps* (1970) and *Numbers* (1972), because autobiography is a form of fiction, and Lind's experiences were of a kind that blurs the borderline between fact and fantasy. After the war Lind lived in Palestine, then in England and America, with the result that he did not have even that linguistic home which many refugee writers regarded as their only secure possession, but was fluent in, and divided between, German, Dutch, Hebrew and English. Since he had also received little academic education and found it hard to place himself within any literary or cultural tradition, Lind was exempt from the start from the solemnities still expected of writers in both German republics, to the point of never being able to see himself as a man 'dedicated' to literature. His failure to establish himself as a German writer has a great deal to do with that. A writer who made grammatical mistakes, and did not care that he made them, had no hope of being taken seriously as a German writer.

In his early fiction, up to *Eine Bessere Welt* of 1966, Lind presented characters and situations whose realism rests on the premiss that, in our world, monstrosity has become the norm. Physical deformity, which recurs in those works, is merely the concomitant of psychic and mental deformities that are taken for granted. 'There is a pest called man' was Lind's epigraph for *Landschaft in Beton*. Cannibalism is only one of the seemingly fantastic varieties of behaviour that are Lind's imaginative correlatives of the realities he had experienced, much as H. G. Adler's sociological study of Theresienstadt had turned that murderous institution into a norm, by not permitting his imagination any part in the telling. Diametrically opposed as they are, the two procedures are complementary as records of undemonized monstrosity.

Since intellectual clarity and acerbity are not among Lind's strong points, the fluid mixture of observation and fantasy in his early works was more effective than his later attempts at allegory, as in the novel *Travels to the Enu* (1982), a kind of Swiftian satire that fails to be Swiftian because the focus is uncertain. Here the problem of perspective is inseparable from the problems of identity implicit—and explicit at times—in the early fiction and in the autobiographies. Where Max Frisch could make an ingenious play, his *Andorra* (1961), out of the absurdity of a man's becoming a Jew only because he is taken for a Jew, Jakov Lind had suffered such changes of identity in his own person, and had suffered the confusion that came of them. The confusion had to enter into Lind's imaginative writings, and the more spontaneously it did so, the better for his works.

Conducted too deliberately and clinically, de-demonization, too, had its dangers for writers, as the gifted novelist Gisela Elsner showed in *Die Riesenzwerge* (1964; English version, *The Giant Dwarfs*, 1965). The small boy who acts as narrator reports on actions that are meant to be typical of domestic life not in the Third Reich, but in the West Germany of the *Wirtschaftswunder*, though they are typical actions exaggerated to the point of monstrosity and absurdity. The very structure of the book, sub-titled not 'a novel' but 'a contribution'—to what?—one wonders— enacts a grotesque continuum of 'birth, copulation and death'. The work has no beginning, middle or end. Structurally it resembles that tapeworm whose composite anatomy and peculiar way of reproducing itself is described with characteristic minuteness in one of the episodes; but whereas the extent of the tapeworm's growth depends on the available food supply, the material of Gisela Elsner's book is quite literally inexhaustible. Its limits were imposed by her capacity to sustain, or her readers' capacity to endure, this account of the endlessly repetitive inanities of existence. Personages who are not individuals, as Elsner makes sure that hers are not, because she wants them to be specimens, cannot change or develop. In that regard they recall some of Samuel Beckett's characters—many of Samuel Beckett's characters— but also that Beckett's characters have an inner life, a sensibility rendered for each of them in delicately modulated prose, whereas Gisela Elsner's, in this book, is deliberately flat. Another component of the work, satirical episodes directed less at human life in general than at that of the German bourgeoisie in particular, points to the precedent of Günter Grass. Like him, Elsner uses incomplete or meaningless dialogue to convey the inarticulateness or, more often, the utterly brainless, banal, mechanical conformism of a character. Like him, too, and like other contemporaries, especially those who cultivated the *nouveau roman*, she resorts to an almost unbearably pedantic elaboration in the description of trivial scenes and events. Where humour, however black or grotesque, was also eliminated, as neither Beckett nor Grass eliminated it, de-demonization could throw out the baby with the bathwater and become de-humanization, making fiction read rather like H. G. Adler's account of an 'enforced community'. There is no doubt that Gisela Elsner's *via negativa* in her novel posited an alternative, 'a better world' that permits both humanity and individuation, but there are no pointers to it in the text, nor any indication that there is a difference in kind between her target, the domestic life of Germans in whatever era, and that in a death-camp. The dead-pan realism of her narrative, childlike only in its minutely factual and non-committal reporting of things heard and seen, can suddenly switch to surrealism or violent caricature, as in her story of the seven brothers and sisters who need an eighth sibling for their fights and force their parents, in the most brutal way possible, to provide one. Yet it is the merciless observation of such things as German eating habits, German attitudes to dogs or disabled ex-servicemen, German attitudes to authority and education, both in and out of school, that provides the only positive basis for Gisela Elsner's more than Swiftian, super-Manichean disgust in this book. By her next novel, *Der Nachwuchs* (1968), Gisela Elsner had shifted her perspective, and her subsequent development was towards a more humane, though always critical, realism; but it was her first book that won the international Formentor Prize and simultaneous publication in several languages. That circumstance made her a victim of the commercial practices which her later books expose.

8

Though a revolution took place in West German writing in the 1950s and 1960s before the would-be revolution imposed by more or less Marxian dogma from the mid-1960s to the early 1970s, the revolution should not be looked for in the kind of social realism that presupposes a large measure of agreement between imaginative writers and the society in which they were working. For all his truly imaginative response to 'ordinary people' and ordinary things, even Günter Grass was no exception. Nor was Uwe Johnson, with his almost painfully meticulous enquiries into circumstances and motives. The process of de-demonization, which was also a process of accepting human nature as it is, rather than as it might be or ought to be, was slow and arduous after the 'zero point' of 1945 and the persistence after it of the sacerdotal or prophetic stance of so many German writers after Nietzsche.

Those presumptions and solemnities were gradually abandoned. They belonged to an age of 'power-protected inwardness', as Thomas Mann called it, in which writers essentially profane served as 'guardians of the faith', or rather of so many different faiths and creeds that the centre could not hold. Yet, more than ever before, reality itself, and social reality in particular, had been called in question by the discontinuity of German political and social institutions. The banality of evil in our time was one aspect of the problem; and language itself had been on trial ever since its corruption into a vehicle not only of untruth, but of unreality, in politics, administration and advertising, the commercial equivalent of Goebbels' 'propaganda'. That is why poets like Helmut Heissenbüttel became deeply involved in semantic research and experiments, and even prose writers made a clean sweep of linguistic conventions, beginning with grammar and syntax. An acute sense of crisis coincided with a rediscovery of the essential playfulness of all art—an aspect of art familiar enough to so serious and committed a writer as Schiller in the eighteenth century, but too often ignored in the nineteenth—and it was often difficult to distinguish the verbal alchemists from the verbal tumblers. Both, perhaps, were needed for the de-demonization of the German language; but when language was being so drastically probed and re-shuffled, there was bound to be some degree of disparity between the essential element of play and a serious concern with the non-aesthetic implications of the written word.

It was Gottfried Benn who denied that an imaginative writer's word has any such implication or function. In doing so, he was speaking as a specialist; and the same specialization made him resort to a 'double life', with no contact or communication between what he called 'the isolated ego' and the social man who devoted himself to his patients. As Benn's own later poems show, in practice no such division can be consistently upheld. When Benn did emerge briefly from his isolation as a poet, it was to commit an error. As Walter Benjamin pointed out before the last war, Fascism 'aestheticizes politics', whereas Communism 'politicizes art'. Benn's error was to yield to the aesthetic appeal of Nazism, without troubling to enquire what very different specializations were covered up by that appeal. Even controversies about 'the two cultures' obscured the true issue. The arts, too, are specialized in so far as they are not 'humanities' but skills and techniques; and the sciences should not be confused with the functions to which they can be applied. As Brecht was to insist despite his politicization, every writer has to work out for himself or herself precisely how his specialized skill is to be reconciled with whatever degree of politicization the humanity of art may require.

These are some of the tensions carried over into the next decades, with violent controversies and divisions in the literatures of both German Republics—though fought out mainly in the media on one side, in committee rooms and in offices on the other. Only a few of them can be touched on in this book.

III   Towards Classicism:
Brecht and his Successors

1

Of all the German-speaking writers of his generation, Brecht alone has established himself as a 'classic', and not only in his own language—across the political divisions—but internationally. This classical status is no accident; all Brecht's work was directed towards the end of making a new classicism possible, of socializing and politicizing imaginative writing in such a way as to reverse historical trends that go back to Rousseau and the beginnings of Romanticism. In his *Lettre à d'Alembert sur les Spectacles* of 1758, Rousseau had undermined the foundations of an older classicism by trying to make a tragic hero out of Alceste in Molière's comedy *Le Misanthrope*, on the grounds that Alceste's uncompromising honesty put him in the right in his conflict with society and its corrupt consensus—at which Molière had connived by making Alceste ridiculous. What Brecht set out to do, in poetry as well as in drama, was to put the individual back in his place, society in the right again—provided, of course that it was the right society; and in the twentieth century, that was no easy matter. All the contradictions and duplicities that have been imputed to Brecht stemmed from the extreme difficulty, if not impossibility, of that endeavour.

'Terrible is the seduction to goodness'. This comment by the singer in *Der Kaukasische Kreidekreis* (*The Caucasian Chalk Circle*), one of Brecht's many substitutes for the chorus in that 'Aristotelean' drama which he thought he had superseded and replaced, sums up his moral dilemma; for it was the goodness of Alceste that Rousseau had pitted against the baseness of society and its 'common sense'. Because Brecht chose to politicize his art, and all practical politics is a choice of evils, a business that, at best, 'defends the bad against the worse' (C. Day Lewis's comment on the Allied cause in the Second World War), Brecht could not afford the goodness that comes so easily to the unpolitical.

'A Choice of Evils' was the sub-title of Martin Esslin's book of 1959, an early study in English of the man and his work. Its merit was that the author refused to be taken in by Brecht's theories—including that of the 'epic' drama—or by anything that Brecht said at various times about his outward commitment. Much of Brecht's work remained unpublished or uncollected in 1958, and his life, too, has been thoroughly combed and documented since that time; but no amount of research will resolve the central dilemmas or make Brecht less enigmatic than he wished and needed to be. The aura of 'silence, exile and cunning' which he shared not only with Joyce but with the other highly individual writers of his time was even more essential to him. So were ambiguity, contradiction and paradox. Brecht's individuality, other than as an artist, was an embarrassment to him in any case. Hence his sincere, but never wholly successful, efforts to dispose of it by merging it in corporative, impersonal undertakings. In the end it was always his individuality that prevailed, though an individuality deliberately stripped down to what he thought were general human features and functions. That Brecht had absolute commitments, constant commitments at odds with the relative commitments of politics, now makes him look much more of a utopian than he wished to be. Esslin touched on a number of these. Brecht's anti-militarism, which he often upheld in opposition to the party line, went back to his early experiences as a medical orderly in the First World War. Another constant characteristic, his preference for passive resistance by self-effacement, mock-humility or even unscrupulous prevarication (as in his brilliant and comic performance before the Committee on Un-American Activities in 1947, preserved for posterity on tape) was evident in his earliest struggles. Long before his discovery of Taoist doctrine, he had learnt the lesson of Hašek's *The Good Soldier Schweik*. (Martin Esslin traced back these Schweikian attitudes to the 'Black Forest peasantry to which his ancestors belonged'.)

It is these unchanging traits that make the *enfant terrible* of the early Berlin period, with his lorry driver's leather jacket alleged to conceal 'exquisite silk shirts', easily recognizable in the celebrated East Berlin dramatists with an Austrian passport and a bank account in Switzerland—who drove the very kind of car mentioned by Esslin in his sketch of the early years:

> He drove round Berlin at great speed and considerable risk to himself and his passengers in an open Steyr car, earned by writing an advertisement jingle for the makers, a mercenary act for which defenders of the romantic view of the poet's ethereal and spiritual mission held him in contempt.

Yet Esslin could also write of Brecht as 'an idealist of truly religious fervour behind the mask of cynicism and toughness he displayed'. This recognition gives Esslin's early study an advantage over later books on Brecht, like Ronald Hayman's biography, more concerned with what Brecht did, or is reported to have done, than with what he was. Until the late 1960s, admittedly, it was not Brecht's idealism, utopianism or absolute commitment that made him of exemplary importance to West and East German writers after the war, but his moral toughness, his avoidance of effusive pathos, and his truly dialectic treatment of human nature. Then, for a time, it was Brecht's didacticism that was widely imitated, a didacticism radically different from that of the lone prophets and visionaries who, ever since Rousseau, had been 'teaching without pupils', as Brecht called it in a poem. The man to whom no one is listening, he wrote in that poem, 'speaks too loud. He repeats himself. He says things that are wrong. No one corrects him.' In the light of German literary history, that realization alone was of revolutionary significance. Brecht's didacticism assumed that the writer is a person not only speaking, but listening, to other people; and it assumed that society—far from 'not being musical', as Thomas Mann said—participates in the act of artistic creation, as well as in the reception of a work of art. History has proved that very assumption to have been a utopian one; and Brecht's later poetry, most of which he never bothered to collect in his lifetime, shows that he knew it.

2

As early as 1917, Brecht is reported to have said to a girl friend: 'I must become famous, so as to show people what they're really like.' In his *Brecht: a Biography* (1983), Ronald Hayman quotes that extraordinarily apt and illuminating remark—made long before Brecht became a Marxist—but must have had so much material to pack into his narrative that he could not pause to consider its implications for his own undertaking—or any biography of Brecht, for that matter. At best such a biography might have shown people what Brecht was really like; and even that, by Brecht's own criteria, would have been a waste of time, because Brecht, like no contemporary of his, applied himself to a reduction of his own person to what he considered its basic ingredients.

At the very beginning of that process, when Brecht was still very self-consciously working on the image of himself most conducive to showing other people what they are really like, he admitted in his early diaries that it was only 'the bad things' about himself he had noted there. This over-emphasis on the cruder and nastier sides of human nature in general, and of himself as a specimen, became a recurrent feature of Brecht's writings. To show readers what Brecht was really like, therefore, would have called for much more than a stringing together of the miscellaneous reports and quotations from which Hayman's book was assembled. Above all, it would have called for correctives to the simplified images of himself that Brecht chose to project in all but the more delicate and differentiated of his later poems.

As it is, Hayman's book switches like some jumpy television documentary between Brecht's fornications on the one hand, his theatre business—much of which was abortive—on the other. Here I avoid the word 'love affairs' deliberately, though I do not believe that Brecht was as unloving as he made himself out to be or as Hayman's necessarily incomplete account of Brecht's relations with women suggests. As for the theatre business, the alternative to Hayman's gossip and summaries of plots, casts, sets, etc. would have been not biography, but criticism. Though Hayman quotes the odd poem—in translations by himself that leave a great deal to be desired—a reader of his book alone would never guess how much of Brecht's energy and skill went into his poetry, which he himself neglected only because he was outwardly preoccupied with the difficult business of survival and with the function of showing people 'what they're like'. The poetry, too, served that function, of course; but not as directly as Brecht's plays or tracts, and not in a way that lends itself to biographical documentation.

Because, to me, Brecht's poetry is his most durable and exemplary achievement, and Brecht's later poetry much more than the earlier, for all its brilliance and forcefulness, not only did I have great difficulty in reading this biography, but was left with serious doubts and misgivings about the usefulness of writing such literary biographies. 'Of making many books there is no end', said the Preacher; and it is to literary biographies that the reflection has come to apply more than to any other kind of book, now that full-length, or more than full-length, biographies of writers are assured of an attention increasingly denied to their works. A good many poems of Brecht remain to be translated, or published in translation, and two more volumes were added to the German corpus as late as 1982. Brecht's later diaries or *Arbeitsjournal* were a chronicle of his working life and of events relevant to it. An English version of those later diaries would have the advantage of making that chronicle, Brecht's own, available, without the accretions of a 'story' that Brecht would have regarded as utterly irrelevant and impertinent; and a story which, in my judgement, does justice neither to Brecht's person nor to his work.

'It was soon after returning to Santa Monica in March that Brecht met Charles Laughton, who fell in love with him', Hayman tells us. Since that statement is neither substantiated nor elaborated, I look up the source reference provided at the back of the book and find that the assertion is based on an interview with Joseph Losey, not on a confession by Charles Laughton. Hayman goes on to inform us that 'Laughton had deep feelings of inadequacy, which Brecht was able both to salve and to exploit.' In other words, Laughton's need for Brecht was not at all the one imputed to him by the phrase 'fell in love', based on Hollywood gossip at best. (Elsewhere Hayman implies that Brecht, like Laughton, had homosexual leanings, only because in his youth there were times when he preferred the company of his male friends; but one takes that as a bit of the spicing now obligatory for successful literary biographies.) Perhaps Hayman does not even expect his readers to believe that Laughton really 'fell in love' with Brecht, whom most of the people he met in America found positively repulsive; but in that case the phrase, without quotation marks, is irresponsible; slapdash and sub-literary. It is Hayman's readers who have to weigh up the possibility that both Laughton and Brecht were capable of a relationship more complex and delicate than a falling in love on one side, exploitation for professional advantage on the other. Yet that possibility is far more plausible and far less grotesque than Hayman's simplification.

On the one-act play *Er treibt einen Teufel aus (Driving out a Devil)* Hayman comments: 'This is the play that tells us most about the way Brecht imposed his will on both women and men . . . When Brecht was making passes, he may have felt insecure and desperate for love, but the mask had already begun to grow into the skin.' Whatever Brecht may or may not have felt when making passes, he did not write this—or any other—play to tell us what it was. Even his early self-probings and deliberate self-indulgences served him as a means of stripping down personality to its bare bones, because it was only by self-knowledge that he could arrive at the impersonality he was after. Critically, therefore, or only descriptively, the comment is an irrelevance.

Much of what is wrong with Hayman's biography has to do with the pace of the book. The compulsion to tell us whatever is known or has been surmised about the events of Brecht's life, and squeeze in the 'major' works as well, is enough to falsify the account, because too much of what matters about any writer resides in the gaps between events; and however long the written life, the lived life was much longer. The pace produces curious sentences like this one about Erich Engel: 'A short man with thick spectacles, strongly sculpted features and a driving energy which compensated for his lack of charm, he recognized the power latent in Brecht's dialogue'—thanks to his thick spectacles, one wonders, or one of his strongly sculpted features? This is only one of many non-sequiturs and nonsenses due to the biographer's need to tell us too much, too fast. Not only theatrical acquaintances or collaborators like Engel, but even personal friends of both sexes, pass in and out of the story without becoming much more than a name.

About Brecht the poet, Hayman writes: 'He was certainly the greatest twentieth century German poet, but, unlike his predecessors and unlike Gottfried Benn, he had achieved his mastery over the language by resisting disciplines, including those of scholarship.' The more closely one looks at that sentence, the more meaningless it grows, beginning with the epithet 'greatest', which Brecht, of all people, could only have laughed at, since the debunking of 'great men', including 'great poets', was one of his constant occupations. Nor did Brecht achieve his 'mastery over language' by 'resisting disciplines'. His true mastery was achieved by the most rigorous discipline imaginable, that of subordinating the expressive functions of poetry to considerations of its usefulness and relevance to others. To achieve that, Brecht resorted to models, like his unnamed 'predecessors' and like Gottfried Benn, who was less of a literary scholar than Brecht. At successive periods Brecht's models included classical poets like Horace, late medieval ones like Villon and modern ones like Rimbaud or Kipling, as well as all sorts of popular lyrics and balladry. Brecht's later poetry also profited by the example, and discipline, of Chinese and Japanese models, as made accessible to him mainly by Arthur Waley; and, as he pointed out, one model for all his writing was Luther's Bible.

Haste and carelessness may also be partly to blame for Hayman's absurd travesty of Brecht's poem 'Lob des Kommunismus', in which communism, the subject of every sentence in the poem, is gratuitously personified as 'he' in Hayman's version—only because in German 'der Kommunismus' is a masculine noun. Later (p. 326) we read of a speech made by Stefan Zweig at a peace rally in East Berlin, several years after that writer's suicide in South America. Clearly, Hayman has muddled up Stefan Zweig with an altogether different novelist who settled and died in the GDR, Arnold Zweig. Readers with no German will also be misled by the reference (p. 345) to a 'holiday resort on the Ostsee', that is, the Baltic, when earlier place names incorporating 'see' had denoted lakes, not seas, because 'der See' is a lake, 'die See' a sea.

Where Hayman does comment on specific poems of Brecht's—and Brecht's least successful or never completed plays qualify for more attention than most of his best poems—the comments can be so mis-leading as to be worse than useless. Of Brecht's poem 'Die Lösung'— his unofficial response to the Workers' Uprising of 1953—Hayman writes that the title 'means either "The Solution" or "The Dis-solution" '. It does not, since the German word for 'dissolution' is 'Auflösung', and the verb 'auflösen' occurs in the text of that poem. Of one of Brecht's last poems, 'Als ich in weissem Krankenzimmer der Charité . . .', he writes that 'it uses the blackbird's song, as he had used it before, semi-symbolically, to represent the work of the artist.' If that were so, the poem would be most un-Brechtian, both because such semi-(or pseudo-) symbolism is what Brecht got rid of in verse, and because an identification of a blackbird's song with the 'work of the artist' would have been both mawkish and trite. On the contrary, that blackbird represents nothing but itself, and its song has to do not with art but with nature. In face of his approaching death, Brecht celebrates the con-summation of a long process of unselfing, his capacity to take pleasure in a song not intended for him, not related to him any more than to those who will hear it when he is dead. That is why he wrote: 'Jetzt/ *Gelang es mir*, mich zu freuen . . .' ('Now/*I succeeded in* being glad of any blackbird's song coming after me too.') Sensitively interpreted, this poem alone could have served to correct those coarse, brash and unscrupulous images of Brecht—partly projected by himself—that dominate Hayman's book. There was much more to Brecht than any reader of this biography only could possibly guess; and the evidence for that is nowhere but in Brecht's works. Those who knew him best, like his wife Helene Weigel, were the persons least likely to reveal what they knew of him, most likely to share or respect his own contempt for the personality market.

John Willett's *Brecht in Context* (1984) is a collection of short pieces bearing on various aspects of Brecht's art and activities. As such, it complements the same author's books on the theatre of Brecht and Piscator, but opens with an account of his long-standing involvement and fascination with Brecht, to which a large English-speaking public is indebted, as to no one else, for Brecht's breakthrough into general awareness and availability. John Willett shows a rare combination of minute, specialized scholarship with concerns that extend to all the arts, as well as to social and cultural history—concerns no longer expected of scholars either within or outside the universities. It may be that this book will appeal most to readers already familiar with Brecht's plays and other writings, but any reader open to those concerns will find something in it to engage his or her interest, if only because Willett is far from sharing 'the lack of any capacity for enthusiasm' which Brecht, at one time, attributed to himself. It is the first four chapters especially— 'An Englishman looks at Brecht', 'Anglo-American forays', 'The case of Kipling' and 'The case of Auden'—that should appeal even to the majority of readers who do share that incapacity with regard to artistic trends in Germany or to the vexed question of Brecht's political commitment.

Relations between Brecht and Auden, which have elicited more comment and speculation than anything else in Willett's book, were as ambiguous and vexed as Brecht's politics, perhaps for reasons connected with the changing political stances of both men. Auden listed 'Berthold Brecht' (*sic*) among the 'elder modern poets' from whom he had learnt most. That was in his commonplace book, *A Certain World*, of 1971. Willett also quotes a letter from Charles Monteith that cites Auden as saying repeatedly that 'of the literary men he had known only three struck him as positively evil: Robert Frost, Yeats and Brecht!' According to Hayman (and presumably Elisabeth Bergner, by way of James K. Lyon's *Brecht in America*), Auden not only thought Brecht 'a most unpleasant man' but 'one of the few people who deserved the death sentence. In fact I can imagine doing it to him myself.' Stephen Spender is probably right in believing that Auden's dislike of Brecht's person was due to Brecht's not being a gentleman, though the difference between them lay less in what, socially, they were than in what either man wished to be. Significantly, though Willett has missed this point, the 'unfavourites' whom Auden refrained from listing in the common-place book are characterized as 'underbreds'. It seems quite conceivable to me that if Auden had listed both 'pets' and 'unfavourites' there, Brecht could have appeared under both headings. And since Auden's own gentlemanliness was questionable and insecure, John Willett may be right, too, in endorsing Edward Mendelson's 'private speculation' that 'Brecht and Auden were at bottom very much alike.'

Auden's misspelling of Brecht's name, as late as 1971, and of the German titles of Brecht's works elsewhere, contradicts his claim (in his letter to Willett of 1959 from Austria) that 'my German is much better now'. Very much as Brecht refused to become fluent in English when living in America, Auden would not take the trouble to acquire correct German when living in Austria; and my conversations and correspondence with Auden about German texts suggested that his approach to them was both quirky and cavalier. When I lunched with Auden at a restaurant in Kirchstetten and his guests had ordered different dishes, the waitress hesitated over a plate of pork. 'Hier das Schwein!', Auden called out, pointing at himself. The waitress almost dropped the plate, she laughed so much. That could have been a joke at his own expense, at the expense of his gentlemanliness; but it also bore on his attitude to the German language, which required the pedantic specification 'Schweinebraten'.

Another thing that Auden and Brecht had in common was their professionalism; and it may well be this professionalism, above all, that explains why Auden did not translate those poems of Brecht's which he said he admired and which Willett so wishes he had translated. To translate poems because one liked them is not compatible with Auden's professionalism. Adaptations of plays or texts for music are another matter; and both Auden and Brecht did take on such adaptations. Of the two, though, it was the ungentlemanly Brecht who was readier to break the professional code where poetry was concerned. His hundreds of posthumously published poems are the proof.

Brecht's changing political stance, like some of his unscrupulous professional dealings and his conviction that being good was a temptation to be resisted, will remain as controversial as it was complex, despite Willett's valuable clarifications in the second half of his book.

> Brecht observed political events very closely and had to do so in order to preserve his family and himself through what was indeed a dark time, but it is a mistake to regard him as a political philosopher; for interesting as his insights often are they are the product not so much of a fully worked out theory as of what is now called lateral thinking.

Just as perceptively, Willett distinguishes Brecht from doctrinaire Marxists when he writes:

> Brecht's idea, which he shared with Tretiakov [a victim of Stalin's purges] as well as with Yeats, Pound and Claudel, that the 'cultural heritage' could also embrace the works of non-European civilisations was as alien to Lukács as it would have been to Alfred Rosenberg and his 'Militant League for German culture'. Even in Stalin's multinational Union the non-Russian cultures were effectively relegated to the zone of folk art.

Though in his opening chapter Willett had confessed to 'having grown up fairly resistant to poetry in any language,' his brief appreciation of Brecht's poem 'Das Fischgerät' (The Fishing Tackle) of 1943 sums up much of what needs to be said about Brecht's later verse:

> Sixteen lines: economical, vivid, down-to-earth, moving from a precisely described object to a human tragedy of those times, then onward and outward. It is political. It is poetic. Neither aspect interferes with the other; it is perfectly fused, right down to the elements. This is what Brecht could do. Could anybody else?

The book ends with another summing-up, 'Stoppers for some commemorative gaps', which should be read by all students, biographers and academic critics of Brecht who cannot see the wood for the theoretical or anecdotal trees—of which, he points out, 'there are now more than ever'. If some of Willett's own trees—minutiae of Brecht's relations to Expressionism, to Piscator's 'epic theatre', to cinema, the visual arts and music—prove hard going for non-specialists, non-aficionados, the panoramic view of Willett's last two pages is an ample reward.

4

For two hundred years or so the progress of European and American poetry was one towards autonomy. The more 'advanced' the poet, the more his or her language differed from the language of discourse, exposition and plain talk. Not only metre, rhyme and metaphor—still regarded as 'ornament' by Dryden—served to remove poetry from those prosaic media of communication; more significantly still, the very syntax of poetry evolved in such a way that ambiguity or multiplicity of meaning came to be regarded as a distinguishing and essential feature of poetic utterance. The language of poetry, its practitioners and exegetes assumed, is unlike any other language. Far from being only a fine or memorable vehicle for thoughts, feelings or assertions that could be conveyed by other media, true poetry is at once the vehicle and substance of its utterances; not a different way of putting things, but the only way of putting things that could not be said at all in any language but the language of poetry.

Non-specialists continued to complain of the peculiar difficulty or obscurity of modern poetry. Specialists continued to relish it, accepting Archibald MacLeish's dictum that 'a poem should not mean but be', while devoting long books and articles to the analysis of difficult poems and their dubious or multiple meanings. Among sophisticated poets with a middle-class background and education, Brecht was virtually alone in writing a large and varied body of poetry that was clearly intended to convey a single meaning in a language as plain and un-figurative as the best prose. (That Brecht could also write quite dif-ferently, if he chose, is evident in early poems like his 'Psalms'.) Quite deliberately, Brecht set himself the aim of reversing the two-century-old development in question. Since believers in the aesthetic self-sufficiency of poetry—beyond the autonomy of all art he himself in-sisted on in the teeth of agit-prop and crude notions of 'socialist realism'—found it impossible to deny that Brecht was both a modern and a good poet, though his theory and practice alike contradicted their basic tenets, most of them found it prudent to ignore Brecht's poetry.

Whether we see it as a revolution or as a counter-revolution, Brecht's achievement in poetry was not only remarkable in itself but inseparable from the survival of poetry after the Second World War, at least in those parts of the world in which the very foundations of aesthetically self-sufficient poetry had been demolished by moral, social and political upheavals. If Brecht's later poetry is a kind of anti-poetry or minimal poetry by Romantic-Symbolist standards, no other kind of poetry could withstand the anti-poetic fury of those who had seen European civilization reduced to a heap of rubble. It was Brecht's anticipation of this crisis that prompted him to 'wash' the language of poetry, as he put it, long before the crisis occurred; and what he washed out of poetry was nothing less than the sediment of the whole Romantic-Symbolist era, with its aesthetic of self-sufficiency.

Needless to say, Brecht's poetic development was bound up with his political and social concerns, which led him to identify the Romantic-Symbolist aesthetic with an order dominated by the bourgeoisie and by bourgeois individualism. Yet even among Marxist poets Brecht was very nearly alone in the radicalism with which he applied historical or sociological insights to the practice of poetry. His contemporary Johannes R. Becher, who became Minister of Culture in the German Democratic Republic, reacted against Expressionist obscurity as Brecht did, but achieved no more by his language-washing than an old-fashioned banality of diction and a slackness of sentiment indis-tinguishable from that of the worst nineteenth-century versifiers. For a poet, ideology is not enough. To become effective in diction, stance and tone, the ideological commitment must enter his or her bloodstream like a food or a drug, pervading his or her entrails, his or her dreams. Having done so, it becomes something other than mere ideology. That is why Brecht's later poems, for all their didacticism, can be appreciated and assimilated by non-Marxists, as Becher's later poems cannot.

Another way of putting it is that the Romantic-Symbolist in Brecht—and throughout the 1920s and early 1930s he produced remarkable poems of a visionary, imaginatively individualistic kind—was not suppressed or silenced by an ideological decree, but remained a dialectical presence beneath the hard, dry and spare surface of the later poems. The process of reduction was gradual, organic and total, involving the whole man. It began with the projection of an image, that of the tough, hard-bitten, urban poet dramatized in the early Villonesque self-portrait 'Vom armen B.B.':

> . . . In der Asphaltstadt bin ich daheim. Von allem Anfang
> Versehen mit jedem Sterbsakrament:
> Mit Zeitungen. Und Tabak. Und Branntwein.
> Misstrauisch und faul und zufrieden am End.
>
> Ich bin zu den Leuten freundlich. Ich setze
> Einen steifen Hut auf nach ihrem Brauch.
> Ich sage: es sind ganz besonders riechende Tiere,
> Und ich sage: es macht nichts, ich bin es auch.
>
> In meine leeren Schaukelstühle vormittags
> Setze ich mitunter ein paar Frauen,
> Und ich betrachte sie sorglos und sage ihnen:
> In mir habt ihr einen, auf den könnte ihr nicht bauen . . .

> . . . In the asphalt city I'm at home. From the very start
> Provided with every unction and sacrament:
> With newspapers. And tobacco. And brandy.
> To the end mistrustful, lazy and content.
>
> I'm polite and friendly to the people. I put on
> A stiff hat because that's what they do.
> I say: they're animals with a quite peculiar smell,
> And I say: Does it matter? I am too.
>
> Sometimes in the mornings on my empty rocking-chairs
> I'll sit a woman or two, and with an untroubled eye
> Look at them steadily and say to them:
> Here you have someone on whom you can't rely . . .

The later self-portraits, of which there are many, right up to Brecht's last illness and the little poem in which he confronts his imminent death, can do without the brashness and self-conscious posturing of those lines, which were written as a provocation to the bourgeoisie and their expectation that poems ought to convey elevated sentiments. In the later poems the toughness has become more than a gesture, so that Brecht can also admit tenderness and gentleness, just as he could admit that love of nature about which he tended to feel uneasy, suspecting that it might be a residue of bourgeois self-indulgence, escapism and idyllicism. (In the self-portrait of the 1920s, pine-trees are said to 'piss' in the early morning, and the birds in them become their 'vermin'.) Above all, in the later poems he has ceased to care about his image, or about himself at all as an individual. Though he draws freely on his own experience, even on his dreams, and has no qualms about using the first person singular, he can do so just because he is not writing autobiography, but availing himself of useful material for reflections on the complexities of human motives and behaviour. Here is one such poem, written in the 1930s.

Fahrend in einem bequemen Wagen

Fahrend in einem bequemen Wagen
Auf einer regnerischen Landstrasse
Sahen wir einen zerlumpten Menschen bei Nachtanbruch
Der uns winkte, ihn mitzunehmen, sich tief verbeugend.
Wir hatten ein Dach und wir hatten Platz und wir fuhren vorüber
Und wir hörten mich sagen, mit einer grämlichen Stimme: Nein
Wir können niemand mitnehmen.
Wir waren schon weit voraus, einen Tagesmarsch vielleicht
Als ich plötzlich erschrak über diese meine Stimme
Dies mein Verhalten und diese
Ganze Welt.

Travelling in a comfortable car

Travelling in a comfortable car
Down a rainy road in the country
We saw a ragged fellow at nightfall
Signal to us for a ride, with a low bow.
We had a roof and we had room and we drove on
And we heard me say, in a morose tone of voice: No
We can't take anyone with us.
We had gone on a long way, perhaps a day's march
When suddenly I was shocked by this voice of mine
This behaviour of mine and this
Whole world.

This poem projects no image of Brecht as a poet or as a man that could distract us from his real concern, that with a general truth.

The 'I' of the poem is confined to a strict function, which is impersonal. We are not asked to condemn Brecht's callousness or to grow mawkish over his remorse. We are asked to participate in the delayed shock at an action which could be and is anyone's. The poem has political, as well as psychological, implications, but the moral is neither rubbed in nor even explained in ideological terms. It is enacted in terms of a simple occurrence simply told, yet without the simplification that would make it undialectical. The impersonality of Brecht's concern is brought out by the strange phrase 'we heard me say' and by the concluding reference to 'this whole world'. One dialectical implication of the poem, that it is not enough to be a Marxist, as the reader knows Brecht to be, would not have come across so forcefully if the first person had been squeamishly avoided.

I say 'forcefully', though the little poem dispenses with all the devices that serve to heighten the language of poetry for the sake of eloquence, euphony or evocativeness. It dispenses with rhyme and regular metre—though Brecht had been a master of both in his earlier verse—with alliteration and assonance, with metaphor and simile, with inversion and dislocation of syntax. Brecht's art has come to lie in the concealment of art, as Horace wrote that it should; in a manner as seemingly casual, throw-away, undemonstrative as possible. What distinguishes such poems from prose is a rhythmic organization inconspicuous precisely because it is right, perfectly accordant with what the poem says and does; and an economy of means, a tautness and conciseness that are rarely attained in a prose narrative. (The tautness begins with the very first word; the present participle construction unusual in German, but adopted by Brecht before English had become his second language. Latin is his more likely model here.) By renouncing emotive effects and that vagueness which Baudelaire considered an essential element in Romantic art, Brecht was able to create a didactic poetry that seems innocent of any design on the reader, but all the more persuasive and convincing for that. Brecht's language here is anyone's language, if anyone were capable of putting the right word in the right place, of saying neither more nor less than what he wants to say. Brecht's ability to do so consistently, in hundreds of poems written in this later manner, amounted to the establishment of an art at once modern and classical. To read Brecht's later verse is an experience akin to the reading of Horace—whom Brecht repeatedly read in his later years—the Catullus of the social epigrams, or any Latin poet at home not only in his art but in his world.

This does not mean that Brecht accepted his world uncritically, any more than the Latin poets accepted theirs uncritically, either before or after his residence in a Communist country. It means that in Brecht's later poems personal and public concerns are inseparable. The sequence of short poems which he called *Buckower Elegien*—though by modern criteria they are much closer to epigram than to elegy—was written after Brecht's return from Germany, yet its dominant tone is one of satirical or self-questioning unease, as in the opening poem, 'Der Radwechsel':

Ich sitze am Strassenrand
Der Fahrer wechselt das Rad.
Ich bin nicht gern, wo ich herkomme.
Ich bin nicht gern, wo ich hinfahre.
Warum sehe ich den Radwechsel
Mit Ungeduld?

Changing the Wheel

I sit on the roadside verge
The driver changes the wheel.
I do not like the place I have come from.
I do not like the place I am going to.
Why with impatience do I
Watch him changing the wheel?

I have written that Brecht's later manner dispenses with metaphor and simile, and so it does, except in so far as idiomatic usage is intrinsically figurative. Yet the very reduction of means in this short poem—more Chinese or Japanese than Latin, one would suppose—its extreme spareness and plainness of diction, invite us to read more into the poem than it says, to read it as an allegory. Since self-projection and self-expression are not what we look for in Brecht's later poems, the extension of meaning we are likely to provide in this instance is of a political or historical order; and, however we interpret them, the implications of the poem are very far from the optimism encouraged, if not positively enforced, under Communist régimes. Several other poems in the sequence quite unambiguously disparage or censure this official optimism. The impatience in 'Changing the Wheel' has little to do with it, though it could be related to Ernst Bloch's 'principle of hope' that can and must assert itself in facing up to the worst. (Bloch, an early dissident, chose to spend his last years in the other Germany.)

It could well be that this poem has no direct bearing on anything political at all. This possibility occurred to me when I came across this anonymous poem, probably medieval in origin, but transmitted in various dialect versions over the centuries. I quote the version closest to Brecht's poem, though others substitute living and dying for the travelling imagery:

Ich komme, ich weiss nicht woher,
Ich fahre, ich weiss nicht wohin,
Weiss nicht, warum ich so fröhlich bin.

62

I've come, I don't know from where,
I'm going, I don't know where,
Don't know how it is that I feel such cheer.

This is the (modernised) version of the poem quoted and praised by Gustav Landauer in a letter to his daughter Gudula in 1918. Brecht is more likely to have known it from his youth, and I have found no evidence of his ever having read Landauer, an anti-Marxist, anti-materialist socialist familiar enough to Brecht's friend Walter Benjamin. A four-line version of the poem was painted on to a house as late as 1791 at Illerbeuren, quite close to Brecht's home town, Augsburg. In any case the traditional verses must have served Brecht as a source for 'Changing the Wheel', either consciously or unconsciously; and any attempt to relate Brecht's poem to his immediate situation in the GDR must take account of the traditional, Christian, source.

If the dialect of 'Der Radwechsel' hides some of its implications between the lines, leaving room for speculation and extensions of meaning, other poems in the sequence could not be more explicit in their insistence on truthfulness: truthfulness in the dealings between government and subjects in 'Die Lösung' (The Solution), truthfulness about moral complexities, including the poet's own, in 'Böser Morgen' (A Bad Morning). Brecht's utopianism in clinging to the principle of hope through such truthfulness is the theme of another elegy, 'Die Wahrheit einigt' (Truth unites us).

The accusing fingers of working men, in 'Böser Morgen', and the poet's guilty conscience deflected into a counter-accusation of ignorance, their ignorance, point forward to Brecht's successors in the German Democratic Republic no less than does his insistence on truthfulness, on intellectual and moral rigour, and on a manner austere to the point of self-denial—though Brecht's later manner was as distinctive and unmistakable as that of any poet writing in his time. Compared to poets who grew up under the régime which granted Brecht a privileged position, he had little reason to doubt that the freedom of literature was compatible with corporative needs on the one hand, government directives on the other. Towards the end of his life he could write another poem that illuminates his Horatian classicism:

Ich benötige keinen Grabstein

Ich benötige keinen Grabstein, aber
Wenn ihr einen für mich benötigt
Wünschte ich, es stünde darauf:
Er hat Vorschläge gemacht. Wir
Haben sie angenommen.
Durch eine solche Inschrift wären
Wir alle geehrt.

63

I need no Gravestone

I need no gravestone, but
If you need one for me
I wish the inscription would read:
He made suggestions. We
Have acted on them.
Such an epitaph would
Honour us all.

Writing from later experience of the relations between intellectuals
and government in the GDR, the eminent critic Hans Mayer remarked
on the arrogance of Brecht's assumptions in that poem. (Hans Mayer
had been a Professor of Literature at Leipzig, where Uwe Johnson was
among his students, and, like Johnson, had been forced to leave for
West Germany. Mayer's volumes of autobiography document that
history.) Whether or not they are arrogant, Brecht's assumptions here
are certainly different from those of his younger successors, who would
not dare to suppose for one moment that the rulers of their country
might feel honoured to take their advice. To Brecht, though, the
question of his personal arrogance or humility was an irrelevance. What
mattered to him was not the statement about himself in this poem, but
what the poem implied about a proper relationship in a Communist
State between independent, critical thinking and government policies.
Brecht's confidence in that regard—a confidence essential to what I
have called his classicism, though both the classicism and the confidence may now look utopian—goes back to an earlier phase of revolutionary enterprise, when it did seem that independent thought and
vision would be allowed to make a real contribution to the shaping of a
new, socialist order. After Brecht's death that confidence, or that
arrogance, became the prerogative of those who were not his successors,
of the unthinking, unintelligent and uncritical purveyors of authorized
party pap to the people. It is the language that marks the difference,
palpably and immediately: the language of Brecht's successors is hard,
spare, precise like his own, cryptic only by omission and reduction.
The language of the conformists is vague, abstract, inflated, turgid with
all the poeticisms that Brecht had washed and scrubbed out of the
texture of verse.

5

Brecht's awareness that his stance had become utopian—when realism
and truthfulness were what determined that stance—can be seen in
these lines, written shortly before his death in 1956:

Und ich dachte immer

Und ich dachte immer: die allereinfachsten Worte
Müssen genügen. Wenn ich sage, was ist
Muss jedem das Herz zerfleischt sein.
Dass du untergehst, wenn du dich nicht wehrst
Das wirst du doch einsehn.

And I always thought

And I always thought: the very simplest words
Must be enough. When I say what things are like
Everyone's heart must be torn to shreds.
That you'll go down if you don't stand up for yourself—
Surely you see that.

Even these laconic and sad lines require an effort of imagination and intelligence on the reader's part. They, too, are plain bread, not the cream puffs offered by the propagandists and—so the poem suggests—preferred by the consumers. It is the reader who has to fill the gaps in their dialectic, beginning with the gap bridged by the casual, abrupt 'and' with which the poem begins. One thing the gaps tell us, but the words do not, is that Brecht must have had cause to question the effectiveness of his simple words—most probably because too many of his readers in the GDR had been too thoroughly brainwashed to respond to his language-washing. Most of his later poems became available in West Germany before they were published in his own country, and some of the more uncomfortable ones were deliberately withheld in the GDR. The person to whom these lines are addressed is not identified; that makes the person anyone or everyone who has failed to stand up for himself or herself in the Republic Brecht had once hoped he could help to shape.

In Brecht's last poems dryness, matter-of-factness and seeming casualness become cryptic again—at times more cryptic than many poems by other authors who cultivated word magic, unreason or ecstasy. Here is another instance:

Schwierige Zeiten

Stehend an meinem Schreibpult
Sehe ich durchs Fenster im Garten den Holderstrauch
Und erkenne darin etwas Rotes und etwas Schwarzes
Und erinnere mich plötzlich des Holders
Meiner Kindheit in Augsburg.
Mehrere Minuten erwäge ich
Ganz ernsthaft, ob ich zum Tisch gehen soll
Meine Brille holen, um wieder
Die schwarzen Beeren an den roten Zweiglein zu sehen.

Difficult Times

Standing at my desk
Through the window I see the elder tree in the garden
And recognize something red in it, something black
And all at once recall the elder
Of my childhood in Augsburg.
For several minutes I debate
Quite seriously whether to go to the table
And pick up my spectacles, in order to see
Those black berries again on their tiny red stalks.

How is one to read this poem? As confessional, a poem of personal experience? Or still as a didactic poem, of the kind expected of Brecht? Or perhaps as a 'nature poem', with special reference to other tree, plant and garden questions posed in earlier poems by Brecht, and in view of his famous assertion that 'conversations about trees' could be a crime at times that were always difficult? And of what kind were the difficulties named in the title? Were they personal difficulties of Brecht's? Or general, political and social ones?

Such distinctions—whose validity I question in any case—give us no access to Brecht's last poems, because in the course of the decades Brecht had politicized his thinking and feeling to such a degree that he was now free again to write poems in the first person that could not be merely confessional, merely personal, when for him anything personal had come to include its opposite, society, and every individual's part in society. For the same reason, all such poems must remain didactic poems—precisely by virtue of an implicit understanding that this was how his poems were to be read. Brecht had learned to use the observation of his own inclinations and hesitations for his didactic ends. Since to him, who had made it his business to determine the bounds of individuality, self-knowledge was something other than self-reflection, he could now assume that confessions in poems must be something other than self-confessions. His very choice of the first person singular for so many of his later poems had a political significance, for it served to correct the abuse of the 'collective', the 'people', as a stick for beating those individuals of whom the people is made up. (His poem 'The Solution' had pointedly satirized this abuse by inviting the Government to 'dissolve' the people and elect another.) The 'I' of Brecht's later and last poems is a subject that has been objectivized to a certain degree; but not to the degree of becoming an abstraction.

This does not mean—as late Marxist polemicists, especially in non-Communist countries, sometimes like to think—that everything private or subjective in poems can be dismissed as 'bourgeois', as though the 'working class' were a new variant of the human species entirely contained within its economic function and with no needs or emotions beyond it. (If that were true of anyone, it would apply to a different social class, to the administrators, functionaries and technocrats, and their fellow travellers among intellectuals.) What Brecht wanted was a balance, not a suppression or repression of individuality.

As for 'nature poetry', though we may associate it with the romanticism that Brecht opposed, Brecht was sufficiently well versed in classical literature to know that nature was celebrated in antiquity, by Greek and Latin poets for instance, as a refuge, a liberation from social ties and obligations, amongst other things. With all his scepticism towards modern nature cults and his awareness—as in his poem 'Der Bauer kümmert sich um seinen Acker' (The farmer's concern is with his field)—that workers on the land have little time for a romanticized nature, Brecht also wanted conditions in which 'conversations about trees' would not be a crime. Besides, in this poem there is no nature of which one could make a cult, in which one could lose oneself. There is an elder tree, with its black berries hanging from red stalks.

As in many late poems by Brecht, such general considerations do not enter his text, but are left between the lines, in front of them and behind them. Brecht's classical aesthetic rests on a kind of solidarity with his readers, on the expectation that every reader will be able to retrace a dialectic that is scarcely intimated—much as earlier classical writers could assume that every reader would catch even the most subtle of allusions to mythical or historical figures. What Brecht relies on, though, is not the learning, but the intelligence and sensitivity of his readers—and this to an extent astonishing in a poet who had wished to be a popular poet, like Kipling.

What makes this poem mysterious has to do with its withheld didacticism, its withheld dialectic, and its withheld conclusion; also with the deliberate, provocative triviality of the events it relates. A reader incapable of complementing the things left unsaid in this poem, or one brought up to believe, as many Germans were, that poems have to be about great resolutions, great gestures and great issues affecting 'humanity' or 'the people', could well be perplexed by this poem. He or she would ask why Brecht found it necessary to record and fix this moment of hesitation—which was not a moment, though, since it lasted several minutes—or this (sentimental?) re-emergence of a childhood memory; and Brecht, of all people, known to be so unsentimental, so hard-bitten, so cold! This very perplexity and puzzlement would induce such a reader to look for a meaning beyond the event—if he or she could be bothered at all with such work; perhaps, too, to wonder about what is great, what is small. It was to the Far East that Brecht owed many models for the smallness of his later poems, small forms and small gestures, as well as much of the mentality that prefers the small to the great (and which Robert Walser, too, called 'Chinese').

It is Brecht's scepticism, rightly, that is always emphasized; but, as every poet knows, for the fixing of such small events in poems one needs

a great confidence, a trust not only in an existing or potential readership, but in the capacity of the written text to signify more than its
occasion. (True, it can also happen out of a very naïve self-importance
or a monomania that lends every personal experience a value it does not
have for others. That Brecht was not prone to such self-effusion should
need no proving.)

Nor is 'Difficult Times' about a sentimental recollection of childhood. (What sentimental nature-worshipper, at the moment of being
moved by an image emerging from his remote childhood, would think
of putting on his spectacles?) It is about the hesitation, about being in
two minds, and also about the clear recognition of a specific phenomenon that would be a recognition, inasmuch as one never wholly forgets
a natural phenomenon that has impressed itself in childhood, but also a
new cognition, from the altered viewpoint of a man preoccupied with
other things, other experiences, and a man who might have to overcome
a certain indifference and lassitude to give in to this urge for knowledge
or confirmation, and who is standing at his writing desk, presumably in
order to work. It goes without saying that a certain tenderness for the
elder tree, a certain wonderment at the continuity of a human life and
the constancy of natural phenomena—perhaps, too, at his own sus-
ceptibility—are part of the complex; and a change in Brecht's attitude
to the things of nature, still more explicit in a poem about his own
death.

Certainly there were still other considerations and circumstances that
entered into his hesitation—personal *and* political ones to which the
title alludes, but of more interest to biographers or historians than other
readers. One supposes that the spectacles were not fetched, the black
berries and red stalks not looked at closely; but this too is neither
certain nor important. A poem has a right to its mysteries. That is why I
have not interpreted this one, only pointed to some of the background
from which this so simply and casually related small event draws its
significance.

Brecht's poem about his death, one of his very last, does not differ in
tone or manner from hundreds of earlier ones; and once again it can be
read either as a poem of experience or a didactic poem, if we are foolish
enough to distinguish between those kinds in Brecht's case:

Als ich in weissem Krankenzimmer der Charité

Als ich in weissem Zimmer der Charité
Aufwachte gegen Morgen zu
Und die Amsel hörte, wusste ich
Es besser. Schon seit geraumer Zeit
Hatte ich ja keine Todesfurcht mehr. Da ja nichts
Mir je fehlen kann, vorausgesetzt
Ich selber fehle. Jetzt

Gelang es mir, mich zu freuen
Alles Amselgesangs nach mir auch.

When in a White Ward of the Charité

When in a white ward of the Charité
I awoke around dawn
And heard the blackbird, I knew
Better. For quite some time
I had not feared death. Since there is nothing
I can lack, provided
I myself am lacking. Now
I succeeded in being glad
Of every blackbird's song after me too.

Even that in the end it was a blackbird's song that concerned Brecht, will astonish only those who had not noticed how hard it had always been for Brecht not to be a 'nature poet', that is, not to conduct 'conversations about trees' when more urgent matters claimed his attention. In the face of his own death, though, he could leave those more urgent matters to others. To have treated this death as a public, collective event, would have been truly arrogant in any case. If Brecht could be arrogant and presumptuous, it was mainly over questions of freedom and authority in public affairs, as in the poem about his gravestone. That was part of his commitment, not of his self-importance.

This poem is about pleasures, so important to Brecht in earlier poems, and the inevitable loss of pleasures; hence the very Brechtian words, 'succeeded in being glad'. It is also a poem, once more, about the relation of the individual to the species; and, since Brecht could not resort to 'another life', a life after death, for a continuity beyond death, he found it in what Ernst Bloch called 'natural time', as distinct from 'historical time'. At the end, then, Brecht confronts the loss of his pleasures and accepts it by putting himself in his place, as an individual not essentially different from others, to whom he leaves the particular pleasure of hearing the blackbird's song. Here the 'historical time' to which Brecht had devoted so much of his energy would not have served his purpose, since historical time is the arena of conflict and change.

Blackbirds, besides, are as much a part even of city life as the white ward of a hospital, and neither is more real than the other. If the poem pursues an implicit dialectic—and it does, of course—it is not a dialectic of nature as opposed to civilization, but of the selfishness of our pleasure-seeking and the bounds of individuality—one of Brecht's recurrent concerns. In a manner as matter-of-fact as ever, and as cool, Brecht strips himself of the residual selfishness that would prevent him from being glad in the face of his death; but the transcendence he celebrates goes back on nothing he had professed or practised, when to be glad of the pleasure that others will take in the blackbird's song remains a pleasure. To the last, then, Brecht remained true to himself and his unemphatically didactic art. To the last, he used himself to 'show other people what they are like'; in this case, by drawing a fine distinction between an egotism to be avoided and an individualism to be affirmed.

6

Most of Brecht's successors in the German Democratic Republic had to take over his function of truth-telling without so much as a glimmer of hope that this function would be honoured by official approval, let alone by such reciprocal usefulness as Brecht claimed for writers in 'I need no Gravestone'. Many of them were tormented by serious and recurrent doubts as to the propriety of writing poems at all under a system that denied all value to the individual conscience, the individual voice. After a 'language-washing' mainly directed at purging poetic diction of the accretions left by a long process of individuation to the point of solipsism, Brecht had been able to strike a classical balance between private and public concerns, as his liberal use of the first person singular attests. (The index to his *Collected Poems* of 1967—two supplementary volumes were to be added in 1982—lists nearly eighty poems that begin with the word 'I'. That quite a number of these poems are written in persons other than his own, confirms the importance he attributed to personal experience as the only reliable means of enacting general truths.) In the work of Brecht's immediate successors that balance was upset once more, because the relationship between private and corporative needs had become dubious, critical and precarious.

A New Year stocktaking poem by Peter Gosse (born 1938) contains these lines:

> . . . Drei Jahre, zwei Pfund Lyrik,
>   während mein Staat schuftet und schwitzt.
>   Schluss mit der Kindheit.
>   Ich werde exportreife Radars mitbaun,
>   werde Mehrprodukt machen,
>   Werde mitmischen.

> . . . Three years, two pounds of verse,
>   while my State drudges and sweats.
>   Stop being a child!
>   I shall help to make radars for export,
>   shall help to increase productivity,
>   I shall muck in.

The colloquial diction of this poem, 'Inventur Sylvester 64', is close enough to Brecht's—as distinct from the old-fashioned rhetoric of the propagandist poets—to bring us up with a shock against the loss of nerve exemplified in the literal weighing up of the poet's output over the years; and against the coarseness of a colloquialism taken over indiscriminatingly from the language of slogans and directives. This materialism has ceased to be dialectical, even if we give the poet credit for a certain irony that his diction and stance fail to enact. Yet, ironic or not, the bad conscience in the poem was real and pervasive among Brecht's immediate successors. The accusing finger that pointed at Brecht in a nightmare had become a familiar and inescapable presence in waking life.

For all its plainness and reductive simplicity, Brecht's poetic idiom was a distillation made from a great variety of components, literary and historical, as well as the current vernacular. Gosse's diction, at least in the passage quoted, is crudely mimetic. It is the contrast between his practice here and in other poems, which are verbally idiosyncratic to the point of mannerism, that leads one to suspect an ironic or satirical sub-stratum which he may not have intended.

There is no suspicion of irony in a short poem by Kurt Bartsch (born 1937) that also relates the writing of poems to the national economy, in terms less extreme and more Brechtian than Gosse's:

poesie

die männer im elektrizitätswerk
zünden sich die morgenzigarette an.
sie haben, während ich nachtsüber schrieb,
schwitzend meine arbeitslampe gefüttert.
sie schippten Kohle für ein mondgedicht.

poetry

the men at the power station
light their morning cigarettes.
while I was writing at night
sweating they fed my work lamp.
they shovelled coal for a moon poem.

Brecht's direct lineage is as evident in this poem's diction as in its structure. Its compressed dialectic is rendered in terms of factual observation, not of abstract generalities. Inferences are left open, so that the poem can be read as the discovery of a happy interdependence of poetic and manual labour, or as a condemnation of poetry for being parasitical on the exertions of working men. If the scales are weighted towards the latter reading, it is only by the single word 'moon' in the last line; and since Bartsch did not write 'moon poems', but poems of social awareness, when he worked in the GDR, the word was chosen because it heightens the dialectic and the poem's unemphatic play on contrasting sources of light. Moon poems, the undialectic materialistic would object—and the West German poet Peter Rühmkorf quite specifically placed moon poems under an interdict, at a time when it was usual for German poets to prescribe what kind of poems were, and were not, to be written at a particular historical moment—are useless to those useful men; but so are the cigarettes which they light all the same. The questions left open by those five brief lines could be debated at indefinite and boring length. One reason why Brecht's short later poems proved such a fruitful precedent for younger poets is that, even in the GDR, such poems could not be expected to debate or answer all the questions they raised; and that was a distinct advantage under an ideological censorship that was to drive Bartsch into emigration, like so many of his outstanding fellow poets.

Brecht's contractions and reductions, in fact, were carried farther by several of his successors, as by Günter Kunert (born 1929), whose early poems are like a continuation of Brecht's in their moral searchingness and their epigrammatic sharpness. It is the reader who has to fill in the background of this little poem, 'Unterschiede', and any reader with first-hand experience of totalitarian systems will know how to fill it in:

> Betrübt höre ich einen Namen aufrufen:
> Nicht den meinigen.
>
> Aufatmend
> Höre ich einen Namen aufrufen:
> Nicht den meinigen.

> *Differences*
>
> Distressed, I hear a name called out:
> Not mine.
>
> Relieved,
> I hear a name called out:
> Not mine.

Apart from making a point about vanity and fear, what this poem enacts by its sparseness of diction and gesture is that sparseness has become the precondition of survival—the survival of truthful poets and truthful poems. The 'I' of this poem is incomparably more depersonalized than Brecht's, because it has been stripped not only of idiosyncrasy but of circumstance. The 'I' of this poem is only what is left of it in the eyes of bureaucracy—if bureaucracy had eyes for anything but its function. This bureaucracy decides whether an individual is to be allowed to function or not; and it is to this alternative that the vanity and fear respond.

Where Kunert's concern was the survival not of the individual but of the species, as in his poem 'Laika', he could be a little more circumstantial, since such general concerns were not proscribed. Yet 'Laika' has the same terse structure, based on parallelism, as in the other poem, and packed into a single sentence:

> In einer Kugel aus Metall,
> Dem besten, das wir besitzen,
> Fliegt Tag für Tag ein toter Hund
> Um unsre Erde
> Als Warnung,
> Dass so einmal kreisen könnte
> Jahr für Jahr um die Sonne,
> Beladen mit einer toten Menschheit,
> Der Planet Erde,
> Der beste, den wir besitzen.

> *Laika*
> In a capsule of metal,
> The best that we have,
> Day after day around our Earth
> A dead dog rotates
> As a warning
> That so in the end
> With a cargo of human corpses
> Year after year around the sun
> This planet Earth could rotate,
> The best that we have.

Since Laika was the dog sent into space by the USSR in an early pioneering experiment, even this warning could easily have been taken amiss; but at the time Kunert enjoyed privileges not unlike those granted to Brecht and published his work in both republics. In other poems he resorted to allegory or fable for relief from the dual pressure of outer and inner censorship; for the self-effacing austerity of the kind of poems I have quoted was due to the poet's conscience as much as to the repression of independent judgement.

This can be seen most clearly in the work of Reiner Kunze (born 1933), a subtle, witty and fearless critic of bureaucracy and repression in the GDR. (Both Kunert and Kunze now live in West Germany.) The loss of Brecht's balance between personal and collective needs was the subject of this fable:

Der hochwald erzieht seine Bäume

Sie des lichtes entwöhnend, zwingt er sie,
all ihr grün in die kronen zu schicken

Die fähigkeit,
mit allen zweigen zu atmen,
das talent,
äste zu haben nur so aus freude,
verkümmern

Den regen siebt er, vorbeugend
der leidenschaft des durstes

Er lässt die bäume grösser werden
wipfel an wipfel:
Keiner sieht mehr als der andere,
dem wind sagen alle das gleiche

Holz

The timber forest educates its trees

By weaning them from light compels them
to send all their green into their tops

The ability
to breathe with every bough,
the talent
of having branches for the sheer joy of it
are stunted

The forest filters rain, as a precaution
against the passion of thirst

Lets the trees grow taller
crest to crest:
None sees more than another,
to the wind all tell the same thing

Wood

The fable here does not liberate the poet from his self-imposed austerity, since it serves only to convey something he would not be allowed to say without it; and since this something is the utter drabness of conformity, a conformity imposed and enforced, the language, too, must not depart from drabness. Kunze had no illusions about the transparency of the disguise. Another of his poems of the period was called 'Das Ende der Fabeln'. In fairy-tale guise it shows why fables—

and fairy-tales with a moral such as this one—had become too dangerous
to escape censorship:

> Es war einmal ein fuchs . . .
> beginnt der hahn
> eine fabel zu dichten
>
> Da merkt er
> so geht's nicht
> denn hört der fuchs die fabel
> wird er ihn holen
>
> Once upon a time there was a fox . . .
> the cock begins
> to make up a fable
>
> But realizes
> it can't be done like that
> for if the fox hears the fable
> he'll come and get him

So much for outer censorship, which Kunze continued to oppose and
satirize in full consciousness of the risks involved. Inner censorship
could be even more constricting, since it nagged the poet with constant
reminders that even his defiance would change nothing. Reiner Kunze
also wrote a poem that positively dissolves itself into silence and blankness, making all the crucial connections between minimal poetry,
minimal language, and the shrinking space occupied by the individual
where the 'collective' is worshipped as an omnipotent deity:

> *Entschuldigung*
>
> Ding ist ding
> sich selbst genug
>
> Überflüssig
> das zeichen
>
> überflüssig
> das wort
>
> (Überflüssig
> ich)
>
> *Apology*
>
> A thing's a thing
> sufficient to itself

superfluous
the sign

superfluous
the word

(superfluous
I)

The elliptic syntax of that poem—as compared with the regular and logical syntax of Brecht—serves to avoid the presumption of statement of assertion. This was poetry with its back to the wall, uttering the barest of dispensable words to bear witness still to the truth, even if that truth was its own dispensability.

Kunze wrote another fable called 'Das Ende der Kunst' (The End of Art), but the dialectic and paradox of poetry demand that even silence be articulated, even defeat and exasperation recorded. The danger of being silenced by force—as Wolf Biermann was within the GDR, and Kunze, who defended him, also came to be before being allowed to leave the country—did not deter him. He wrote a poem about that, too, in a poem without a fable and closely akin to Kunert's 'Differences':

Zimmerlautstärke

Dann die
zwölf jahre
durfte ich nicht publizieren sagt
der mann im radio

Ich denke an X
und beginne zu zählen

Low Volume

Then for
twelve years
I was forbidden to publish says
the man on the radio

I think of X
and start counting

The implied analogy with a writer silenced under the twelve years of National Socialist rule made this the most daring and provocative of all Kunze's poems in defence of freedom, for it was a most sensitive point in a state that claimed to have made a clean sweep of Nazism, unlike the other Germany, in which both Kunze and Biermann were ultimately compelled to settle.

Only Kunze's minimal language preserved him from the blatant and outraged defiance of the 'collective' in Biermann's poem 'Rücksichtslose Schimpferei' (All-in Tirade), with its opening assertion 'Ich ich ich'. Not only this emphatic assertion of the personal principle, but his preference elsewhere for ballads and pop-song lyrics (which were recorded in the GDR for export to the Federal Republic, while Wolf Biermann was forbidden to perform or publish them in his own country), brought Biermann closer to the position of the early, pre-Marxist Brecht than any of his East German contemporaries. Even this defiant and exasperated poem contains an admission of personal fallibility, and Biermann, too, has his place in the later Brecht's succession. With a charm and a lightness of touch peculiar to him, he employed minimal diction and epigrammatic trenchancy in this short poem:

> *Ach freund, geht es nicht auch dir so?*
>
>   ich kann nur lieben
>   was ich die Freiheit habe
>   auch zu verlassen:
>
>   dieses Land
>   diese Stadt
>   diese Frau
>   dieses Leben
>
>   Eben darum lieben ja
>   wenige ein Land
>   manche eine Stadt
>   viele eine Frau
>   aber alle das Leben

> *Oh friend, don't you find it's the same with you?*
>
>   I can only love
>   what I am also free
>   to leave:
>
>   this country
>   this city
>   this woman
>   this life
>
>   And that's the reason why
>   so few love a country
>   some love a city
>   many love a woman
>   but all love life.

A great many more poets and poems could be cited in this context; and Brecht's successors included West German poets, as well as East European poets writing in languages other than German. Brevity in itself did not necessarily arise from the needs and intentions with which I have been concerned. In America, for instance, oriental forms like the *haiku*—which also influenced Brecht—were cultivated for purposes and reasons quite different from those of Brecht or his East German successors, giving prominence to the very autonomous image that Brecht virtually banished from his later verse. Nor was Brecht's the only line of succession in the GDR. From Peter Huchel and Stephan Hermlin, Erich Arendt and Johannes Bobrowski to Volker Braun and Karl Mickel, right down to the youngest generation represented in the anthology *Berührung ist nur eine Randerscheinung* of 1985, good poetry has been written in the GDR quite independently of Brecht's lineage, and it is now as diverse as that of any pluralist society.

Historically, the whole phenomenon of minimal language in poetry, whether in East or West Germany, was never a purely literary one. Poetry has always tended towards compression, so much so that Ezra Pound wanted the German word 'dichten'—to make poetry—to be derived from the adjective 'dicht' (dense), though etymologically it is not. Brecht's language, though, was not particularly dense or condensed. Except where he was cryptic, deliberately so, for good and cunning reasons, his plain language was logical and relaxed, minimal only in its avoidance of ornament, emotive devices, and the subjective associations cultivated by Romantics and Symbolists. What Brecht wanted, and would have achieved if political developments had allowed it, was a social poetry of dialogue about matters of interest to everyone. This eminently classical relationship between writer and reader had long been made impossible by the individualism of writers and readers alike, and nowhere more so than in serious and 'advanced' poetry, with its need to escape from vulgar norms of communication in every conceivable direction. It was to put poetry and poets back where he thought they belonged, in society and in history, that Brecht undertook his drastic and rigorous revision of the functions and practice of the art.

Brecht's successors, Marxists like himself when they began, accepted his premisses and wished to work along the same lines; but the freedom granted to Brecht as a special cultural asset was not granted to most of them. Far from welcoming the advice and criticism of poets whose social and moral awareness did not turn them into conformists, the Party executives grudgingly tolerated them at best—with fluctuations not always of their choice, when the GDR itself was under pressure from the Soviet Union—publicly disgraced or silenced them at the worst, so forcing them to emigrate, if not actually expelling them. The more repressive those authorities who claimed to represent the will of the masses, the more the poets questioned the reality of such a collective will. The very medium which Brecht had evolved for plain speaking in poetry became the last remaining receptacle for frantic messages so abbreviated as to be almost more cryptic than the hermetic poetry it had replaced. To carry that development any farther would have amounted to self-imposed silence, and thus to defeat. It followed that poetry had to put on flesh again, as it did in the work of Volker Braun, Karl Mickel, and Sarah Kirsch—a poet far less austere from the start, who also left for West Germany. These, and others, also began to draw much more freely on immediate personal experience, not only of the socially exemplary kind.

Even in its extreme reduction—dispensable words set down by dispensable poets—minimal poetry should remain of interest as an instance of the extraordinary resilience of poetry, its power to survive and function when it was little more than a skeleton, stripped of all the sensuous appeal traditionally associated with it. Though by omission, ellipsis, disguise, it managed to tell the truth about itself and society, when no other medium could do so. When outer and inner pressures forbade the free play of imagination, feeling and perception, its very austerity and reticence served to uphold that freedom, if only by reminding readers of its loss. Unlike some of the protest poetry written elsewhere, in other circumstances, it cannot be dismissed as a form of self-indulgence, since it admitted no personal idiosyncrasy, no expansive gesture, no intoxicating or intoxicated eloquence; and it was written by men who had no illusions about the effectiveness of protest in poetry. Yet, by a self-effacement that was also political self-exposure, they protested none the less. If, by another dialectical twist, that desperate defiance points back to the fundamental autonomy of poetic language, Brecht himself granted that 'art is an autonomous realm', though as a Marxist he distinguished this necessary autonomy from what he called 'autarchy'. Not till after the great exodus of good poets from the GDR in the late 1970s—precipitated by the expulsion of Wolf Biermann—did there seem to be a general recognition that norms cannot be enforced in imaginative literature, simply because 'the spirit bloweth where it listeth'. Yet even the 1985 anthology I have mentioned, containing work by little-known poets who have little in common but independence, was published in the Federal Republic, though it was edited in the GDR.

IV Divided Commitments

1

During the mere seven years of his residence in East Berlin—largely
devoted to theatre work and the establishment of his own theatre
there—Brecht's favourite form of publication remained the numbered,
paper-bound series he called *Versuche*, usually containing one major
work, a play, together with shorter ones, poems or essays. As the title
suggested, these were intended to be provisional, products of his
workshop submitted for discussion, criticism and possible revision.
Most of these could appear without major textual variants in both East
and West German editions. Difficulties and delays on the East German
side became more acute over posthumous collections of his works.

This kind of almost simultaneous publication in both countries
became very rare in later decades. Many eminent West German writers
remained unknown in the GDR, except to those privileged to receive
West German publications. Yet there were curious anomalies. The first
book of poems published by Nelly Sachs, her *In den Wohnungen des
Todes* (1947), was published by the East Berlin Aufbau-Verlag that was
also to publish Brecht, long before those poems were taken over by a
West German publisher. Admittedly, the early poems of Nelly Sachs
were those that referred most specifically and directly to the persecution and mass killing of Jews in the Third Reich; and her increasingly hermetic and mystical later work was not published by any
publishing house in East Germany, with the single exception of a
selection that appeared in 1966, the year in which she was awarded the
Nobel Prize for Literature.

That only Peter Huchel's belated first book of poems, *Gedichte*,
could appear in East Germany in 1948, before its West German edition,
is understandable enough historically, since his next collection was not
ready until 1963, after his dismissal as editor of the literary periodical
Sinn und Form and his exclusion from public life in the GDR. Formally,
too, Peter Huchel's early poems accorded better with requirements in
the GDR, where there was a marked preference for traditional verse
forms; and his first book went back to his beginnings as a poet, having
been virtually completed by 1933, but withheld for the duration of the
Third Reich. Even in the brief post-war period at which Huchel came
closest to the kind of political commitment expected of him in the

GDR, writing his radio verse play *Das Gesetz* (1950; radio version 1959), his preference for rural life remained unchanged, and it was East German land reforms that engaged his sympathy and support. Much of Brecht's later work was published in *Sinn und Form* under Huchel's editorship, not only in the two book-length special issues devoted to Brecht; but it was Brecht's distinction as a writer, not his Marxist commitment, that bridged the differences between the two writers. This very insistence on artistic criteria, as against political ones, brought about Huchel's disgrace and virtual house arrest in 1962.

The case of Johannes Bobrowski—a writer much closer to Huchel in vision and sensibility than Brecht, though personal relations between them were not always happy—would be an extreme anomaly if the constitution of the GDR had not provided for the continued existence of a Christian Democratic Union. Its publishing organ, the Union-Verlag, both employed and published Bobrowski. Not only could all his books appear both in East and West Germany, but his membership of the Party and his official recognition as a Christian poet gave him an exemption from censure and censorship that even allowed him to take part in meetings of the West German *Gruppe 47*. This, in turn, led to his almost instant celebrity in West Germany after the appearance of his first book of poems in 1961. It was West German friends who tried desperately to save Bobrowski's life in 1965, with an antibiotic unobtainable in the GDR, when complications had set in after an operation for peritonitis. Since he had not returned to Germany from Soviet Russia, where he was a prisoner-of-war, until 1949, his active life as a writer of poems and prose fiction was brief, though the books he published within a mere five years included poems written some twenty-five years before his death at the age of forty-eight.

When I first saw poems by Bobrowski in the 1960 anthology *Deutsche Lyrik auf der Anderen Seite* that introduced his work, I noted only the one word 'good' and '(Hölderlin, Trakl)'. In fact Bobrowski was to claim poetic descent not from either of these poets, but from Klopstock (1724–1803), author of the Miltonic epic *Der Messias* and of classicizing odes that served as a model for Hölderlin in his youth; but one of Bobrowski's many verse tributes to the most various poets was to Trakl, though that poem appeared only posthumously. Bobrowski's poems, in any case, were as different as they could be from anything to be expected from a poet working in the GDR, whether of the Brechtian lineage or the opposing, rhetorical school. What Bobrowski's poems have in common with Hölderlin's and Trakl's was impalpable, being neither thematic nor stylistic, but rather a way of breathing, and something to do with what Hölderlin called the 'architectonics' of verse—a placing of figures in landscapes not descriptively or realistically, but according to an imaginative order also enacted in the syntax and rhythm of the verse.

This affinity was not necessarily one of derivation or imitation. Bobrowski's landscapes are always animated ones, like Trakl's, but they are not animated by an apocalyptic vision or by the 'criminal melancholy' of which Trakl accused himself. What linked Bobrowski to the Hölderlin of the late 'hymns' and fragments, across a gap of a century and a half, has to do with a 'construing' of the existing in the presentation of figures and things that could be immediately present or historical or mythical; and with 'popularity', as understood by Hölderlin, a sense of community different from the divisiveness of nationalism and free from that condescension that makes popularity vulgar; and even with the co-existence of many different orders, cultures and nationalities, as brought together in Bobrowski's 'Sarmatia' and related to what Hölderlin called 'the character of forests and the convergence of different kinds of nature'. Like Hölderlin's, too, Bobrowski's originality had a great deal to do with origins, very little with modernity in the sense of being up to date. His vocabulary of mainly very simple words included archaic ones; and his Sarmatia was a rural world already largely destroyed or superseded at the time of writing. Yet, as he put it in his poem to Klopstock, Bobrowski 'wanted the real', which, in his case, had to be evoked by a great concentration of memory and imagination.

Bobrowski's poems and prose fiction were not autobiographical or confessional, except in the religious sense of 'confessional'. Above all, they were an act of bearing witness. His imagery, therefore—though never merely descriptive or representational—was as unmetaphorical as possible. Metaphor is invention; and Bobrowski's simple naming of things like 'wood', 'river', 'lake', 'cloud', 'wind', 'sky', or 'dog', 'fence', 'wall', 'house', not particularized with epithets, avoids generality and abstraction through a placing of those things by syntax, rhythm, and line breaks that give them their peculiar function and significance within each poem. It is the poem as a whole that becomes the 'metaphor of a feeling'—Hölderlin's definition of lyrical poetry—where the feeling is also a feeling out of something outside the poet's person, an approximation to the 'real'.

The commitment out of which Bobrowski wrote is more often intimated than stated in the poems, but it became explicit in his novel *Levins Mühle* (1964) and in this statement contributed to an anthology:

I began to write near Lake Ilmen in 1941, about the Russian landscape, but as a foreigner, a German. This became a theme—something like this: the Germans and the European East—because I grew up round about the river Memel, where Poles, Lithuanians, Russians and Germans lived together and, among them all, the Jews—a long story of unhappiness and guilt, for which my people is to blame, ever since the time of the Order of Teutonic Knights. Not to be undone, perhaps, or expiated, but worthy of hope and

honest endeavour in German poems. I have been helped in this by the
example of a master, Klopstock.

Although he professed no religious commitment of this kind, Peter
Huchel also felt his post-war poetry to be a bearing witness above all;
and, though he had begun as a regional poet with a sensuous delight in
the way of life, flora and fauna of that region, his later poetry has the
same historical and mythical dimension as Bobrowski's. The Brandenburg of Huchel's youth—a landscape of rivers, marshes and woods, and
a peasantry that included the Polish labourers whose exploitation was
the theme of one of his best-known early poems—had been so utterly
changed by political upheavals and by the devastation of war that it had
to be re-construed by memory and imagination, like Bobrowski's Sarmatia. Even before the war Huchel had extended his sympathies
beyond his region by long residence abroad; and his later poems speak
through *personae* as diverse as a Lutheran pastor, an ancient Chinese
sage, an Italian heretic and a character from the Babylonian-Assyrian
epic *Gilgamesh*. It is hard to say whether the implicit commitment
behind all these personifications is a religious or a humanistic one.
Poetically the distinction would hardly arise over Bobrowski's poems
either, if Bobrowski had not found it necessary to state what his
commitment was.

2

Compared to the Brechtians in either Germany, or to the many West
German writers intent on catching up with the various avant-gardes,
both Huchel and Bobrowski were renewers of a German poetic
tradition in which Christian and secular values are not easily separable,
since they were fused even in the eighteenth-century 'enlightenment',
in the work of Lessing, Herder and Hamann (to whom Bobrowski was
especially devoted), as in the poetry of Klopstock and Hölderlin. (The
French critic Robert Minder connected even Marxism to a school of
mystical, millenarian Suabian pietism in which both Hegel and
Hölderlin were educated.) The anomaly of Bobrowski's situation in the
GDR, as opposed to Huchel's precarious one, lay in his overt affiliation
to a Church and a Party, when such an affiliation had long been the
exception, not the rule, among imaginative writers. Nor could there be
any intelligible correlation between a writer's convictions, including his
political ones, and his public status in the GDR, when that status was
subject to the most sudden and arbitrary shifts. After the Eighth Party
Congress in 1972, for instance, a selection of Reiner Kunze's poems,.
Brief mit blauem Siegel, was allowed to appear as a Reclam paperback, in
an edition of thirty thousand copies that sold out within a few days,

though Kunze had been silenced for years. In 1976 he was expelled from the Writers' Union, and in the following year he left the country.

In both Republics, though, the prestige and authority of writers remained remarkably high—for reasons that have to do with their elevation into a kind of lay, secularized clerisy in the eighteenth century. Both the sales of Reiner Kunze's book of poems and his persecution by the apparatus attest to the prestige and authority of the written word. In the Federal Republic, where public status depended not on the allocation of paper rations or directives to publishers, but on control of the media and pressures that could be ideological or commercial, there were also writers who could justly claim to have been excluded, if not as effectively silenced, as *personae non gratae* in the GDR. Apart from growing internal discord at a time when ideological commitments had begun to polarize those writers once united in the *Gruppe 47*, the charge that it had turned into a pressure group, if not a monopoly, contributed to the break-up of that association. Because, in both Republics, imaginative literature was treated as a matter of public interest and concern, all such differences tended to be debated in public. Not only the reputations of individual writers, but of whole trends, schools and movements, were constantly scrutinized and assessed, if not relegated to oblivion. Even writers critical of the West German *Wirtschaftswunder* seemed unaware that the concomitant *Kulturwunder* exacted a similar price; that its progress could be ruthless and too fast, leaving too little time for assimilation and continuity.

Much of the literature that made a stir in the immediate post-war years, and its authors, seemed to vanish without a trace; and not always because of the intrinsic anachronism on which I have touched. The poems of Hans Egon Holthusen, widely read and praised until the early 1950s, had assimilated the influence of the later Rilke and of T.S. Eliot, writers still regarded as difficult and demanding at the time; yet they had no sequel in later years, for reasons that may have more to do with politics than with literature. In 1958, in the third edition of his book *Die Zerstörung der Deutschen Literatur* (The Destruction of German Literature), the Swiss critic Walter Muschg could still maintain that the seeming recovery of German literature since 1945 was no more than 'a new façade adapted to the boom of the reconstruction era'. He asserted that 'the flood of *ersatz* products' released by a prosperous publishing industry

> serves to conceal the lack of a literary public and of significant new works. Instead of a wealth of new and considerable talents, there is an unprecedented number of literary prizes and subsidies that are showered down on young writers, so that it has almost become an art to evade this zeal on the part of the cultural powers that be.

Though he was wrong about the writers, Muschg may well have been right about the literary public, who could not possibly keep pace with the hectic demands made on their attention. In both Republics, too, a great many more writers were enabled to live by their work than in Britain or America, and in West Germany that was due to prizes and grants, such as those awarded by the cultural committee of the *Bundesverband der deutschen Industrie*, to the patronage of the Federal Republic's many radio stations, and the general availability of public and private subsidies of the arts. That even poets could live as professional writers points to another German peculiarity. The German word 'Dichter' means an imaginative writer in any medium, verse or prose. Although it became a dirty word in the 1960s and 1970s, by association with the pretensions that often attached to it at earlier periods, its inclusiveness remained active and fruitful, since imaginative writers continued to move freely between prose and verse. It was not at all unusual for a writer to be a poet, novelist and playwright, not to mention the many unclassifiable 'texts' with which they could experiment. The pressure on professional writers to produce new work of whatever kind could be as harmful to them as the pressure of publicity and fame; but the wealth and variety of German writing since the war owes a great deal to a privileged status that includes a freedom from generic constraints.

The prestige of writers in Germany, though, was bound up with the circumstance that, as servants or opponents of authority, they were associated with power. The symbolic burning of books in the early years of the Third Reich—and unofficial book burnings have occurred sporadically in the post-war period—was an inverted tribute to the might of the pen. Yet most of the post-war writers, quite especially those in the *Gruppe 47*, were determined to put an end to this tradition and disclaimed all connection with power. Whether they liked it or not, all that they did and said was invested with the nimbus of power. Even a Federal Chancellor found it necessary to attack his literary opponents in a public speech.

The *locus classicus* of the total rejection of power by West German writers was the Darmstadt address by Günter Eich at the presentation to him of the Büchner Prize—itself a public occasion, widely reported and discussed in the media—in 1959. His poem of 1951, 'Wacht auf, denn eure Traüme sind schlecht' (Wake up, for your dreams are bad) had already summed up the whole complex in its last line: 'Seid unbequem, seid Sand, nicht das Öl im Getriebe der Welt!' (Be awkward, be sand, not the oil in the works of the world!) Here is an extract from the prose elaboration of that line:

> . . . Altogether, we would rather be difficult before we are condemned to silence. It's time for mockery and satire, high time. I, for my part, suspect that 'timeless values' make power timeless, and our specious delight in

things as they are reminds me of the happily obsequious face I once had to put on. This affirmation of life in controlled language, this perpetual Strength-through-Joy motif and Be Nice to One Another! (But woe betide you if you aren't nice, and woe betide you if you don't rejoice!) Everything getting better, everything positive, our economy, our heroes and our love, why be always looking on the dark side, happiness and leisure are on the increase, don't worry about yourselves, we do the worrying for you. This pernicious optimism, so suspect because it is willed and made to measure. Eyes and ears tightly shut, and a radiant smile on every face, a song—that is how we march into the thousand and one kinds of slavery, trusting in the future.

Serious attempts are being made to create the perfectly functioning society. We have no time left to say 'yes'. If our work cannot be understood as criticism, as opposition and resistance, as an awkward question and a challenge to power, then we write in vain, then we are 'positive' and decorate the slaughterhouse with geraniums . . .

Günter Eich was an early member of the *Gruppe 47*, which was soon to be under attack not only from the neo-Nazi and neo-militarist *National- und Soldatenzeitung* but from liberal, independent critics of its growing hold over publishers and the media. The essayist Ludwig Marcuse, who had emigrated to the USA in 1939, commented as follows on the West German scene:

If I may exaggerate for the sake of brevity, I should say: The German literary machine is the last closed society in the world.

If only I still had the time, I should like to write a book on the history of literature's domination in Germany, from the classical period to that strange oligarchy of today, in which those in power inter-communicate without collusion, like communicating pipes.

Marcuse, it's true, went on to write of a 'league of trouble-makers', showing that he had a grudge against the kind of radicalism expressed by Eich, and too little understanding of it both as a reaction to the experience of Nazism and as a genuine dilemma for those who acquired power by opposing it. Günter Eich himself was to suffer both from the politicization and the commercialization of the 'literary machine' in the course of the 1970s; and his integrity was never in doubt.

3

Marcuse referred to the literary establishment in West Germany as a 'closed society'; and Walter Muschg claimed that there was no public for the work of the prize-winning writers. Yet Marcuse's essay, significantly, appeared in a paperback symposium called *I Do Not Live in the Bundesrepublik*, a complement and rejoinder to an earlier one called

I Live in the Bundesrepublik, and at least intended for a large readership. Muschg's book appeared in the same paperback series. One must assume that the proliferation of books in which writers commented on their own work, their political views and their reasons for living here or there pointed not only to their self-consciousness and self-importance, but to the representative function still accorded to them by the readers of such books. In periodicals, too, books were not only reviewed, but counter-reviewed and debated, with controversies involving editors and publishers and a general washing of dirty linen in public. One such controversy occurred as late as 1984, after the death of Uwe Johnson in England, when a literary journalist broke into his house at Sheerness and reported on private papers he had found there, among other things. The report was able to appear in book form later, despite protests at the article and the journalist's sacking in response to those protests. Uwe Johnson had chosen to live in England, in total privacy, to get away from that very West German publicity machine, only to be subjected to its most shameless prying immediately after a horrifying death. The ensuing controversies and recriminations fed that same publicity machine; and no doubt the scandal won new readers for Johnson's difficult and demanding novels.

Although the general reading public has been abused by such scandals, and overtaxed by exposure to literary business that is not theirs, the soul-searching of post-war writers, their questions about their own function and about the state of Germany, their seemingly in-bred discussions and polemics—all these must answer a real need and a real interest on the part of a considerable body of readers. If it did not, commercial considerations would have put a stop to it.

In fact, a large number of German and Austrian writers have found it preferable to live abroad, not always on grounds quite as drastic as Heinz von Cramer's, stated in the paperback symposium already mentioned:

> We have a brand-new Germany, luxury edition, in which every particle of the human body is provided for, except that they forgot that human beings have brains.
> We have a less showy (and in that, only in that, perhaps more honest) Germany, popular edition. There they are even concerned with the brains of human beings. But only to wash them.
> In neither do I wish to live.
> In neither is there a place for opposition. Because in the one the opposition strives only for power. Because in the other power permits no contradiction.
> In neither is there much worth affirming or preserving. Nor much that is convincing, without recourse to blind faith or blind obedience.
> Because in the one democracy is a lie, and freedom an idol.
> Because in the other socialism is a lie, and progress a religion.

Because in both a man who thinks independently is considered irresponsible.
The word intellectual is a dirty word again.
On both sides.
And they are hunting intellectuals again.

Such a statement is unanswerable; but it applies not only to the two German Republics, and it is too indiscriminately disgruntled to have been of any use to those on either side who were doing their best to establish the freedoms that Heinz von Cramer may have found in Italy, only because he was not implicated in Italian affairs. The statement also suggests an old German hankering after what Arno Schmidt called a 'Gelehrtenrepublik'—translated as 'egg-head republic' for the English version of his novel; and, compared to many other nations, both Germanys *are* 'egg-head republics'.

One solution to the dilemma—a necessary split between the function of the writer *qua* writer and the writer as citizen—was to be found by Günter Grass, though it must be said that he could not have assumed the political function he did assume but for the high standing of writers and intellectuals in Germany. What Grass did understand, and most of his fellow writers, in the *Gruppe 47* or outside it, did not, is that imaginative literature is not history, that it is inherently unhistorical, necessarily anachronistic and utopian, and can enter history only obliquely by impinging not on current affairs, but on the minds and awareness of human beings, in a way almost impossible to record or trace. That is why commitment is a matter for the citizen. Whether it will also impinge on the writing, depends on the exigencies of a specific work, not on its author's will or stance, because the imagination cannot be manipulated, pre-conditioned or predetermined. This is the only, and ineradicable, freedom of imaginative literature, and the reason why it has been judged subversive since Plato's time.

4

Of all the writers associated with the *Gruppe 47*, the one most generally accessible to a large reading public, and in both Republics at that, was Heinrich Böll, whose standing as a post-war *praeceptor Germaniae* was confirmed by the award to him of the Nobel Prize for Literature and many other honours. (Nelly Sachs received the prize not as a German author—she never settled in Germany after the war—but as a survivor of the 'Holocaust', sharing it with another Jewish writer S. J. Agnon. Nor was Elias Canetti ever a German author other than in language, though in his later years his work was as much part of German literature as that of Nelly Sachs or that of Paul Celan, who never lived in Germany at any period of his life. Nelly Sachs had been a German author before she became a Jewish one.) Much as Johannes Bobrowski—born in the same year as Böll, 1917—was seen as a representative of the Lutheran Church and of what had been Eastern Germany before the war, Heinrich Böll was seen as a representative of the Roman Catholic Rhineland that had become the centre of the Federal Republic after the loss of Berlin as a capital. He was also one of the first younger post-war writers to learn the lessons of the war both as an ex-soldier, and as a writer open to the example of American and British writers of fiction, especially of the short story, avoiding the German temptation to construct no less than whole sociologies or cosmologies in novel form. Together with Wolfgang Borchert, a writer much more strident than Böll, and one who did not live long enough to get over his obsession with his war-time experiences, Böll won that representative standing with his early stories about returning soldiers, followed almost at once by stories and short novels that confronted the problems of civilian life in a newly constituted West Germany still very unsure of itself. More than Alfred Andersch, who spent his later life in Switzerland, Böll never ceased to grapple with whatever issues seemed most urgent and topical in a manner straightforward enough in most of his major novels to make those issues look like anyone's concerns, yet with a seriousness and integrity that made no concessions to a specious popularity. If his work as a whole can be read as a kind of history of post-war West Germany and its tensions, this was less because he deliberately set out to be representative than because he was more identified by nature and background than most German writers with a certain way of life, in which a great many other people could recognize their own. In other words, Böll did not need to 'socialize' himself. He was social from the start—a genuine and very rare distinction where a sense of belonging could not be taken for granted among intellectuals and writers. Realistic fiction was congenial to him for that reason, though he also excelled at fantasy and satire. His radical Christian commitment, which was also a humanistic commitment, gave him the humility and compassion that made 'ordinary' people interesting enough for sustained character studies, drawn with a realism he rightly called 'sacramental'. That same realism, much less rare in other twentieth-century literatures than it is in German writing in either Republic, despite demands for 'socialist realism' in the GDR at one time, also contributed to his international accessibility.

The same commitment, however, made Böll a critic of the society of which he felt part, and a critic of the Church to which he belonged; and that function, too, went back to his beginnings, as he recorded in one of his last books, his autobiographical sketch *Was Soll aus dem Jungen bloss Werden* (1981; *What's to Become of the Boy*). This account of his last four school years, under the shadow of Nazification and remilitarization, is also a piece of history, a memoir of that period rather than an autobiography, since he was less concerned with the unique sensibility of the adolescent who was to turn into the most represen- tative of post-war West German novelists than with experiences and attitudes not peculiar to himself. For that very reason, the memoir is not only consistent with his works of fiction but a key to them. Though the story breaks off at his matriculation, before his brief apprenticeship as a bookseller, followed by labour service, university studies, military conscription and marriage, Böll's readers knew what became of the boy. What they did not know, until he told them, is that it was the adolescence that shaped the writer we know, a writer who managed to be at once representative and a highly controversial figure. He was repeatedly smeared and attacked as subversive in the West German media, especially after the publication of his long story *Die Verlorene Ehre der Katharina Blum* (1974; *The Lost Honour of Katharina Blum*), which was misread as a defence of terrorists.

From his adolescence onwards, Böll consistently avoided the intro- version and introspection which, according to Thomas Mann, had long been the moral and political alibi of other German writers in the face of unacceptable institutions and régimes. Böll's memoir begins on 30 January 1933, when Hindenburg handed over the Chancellorship to Hitler, and Böll happened to be fifteen years and six weeks old—not with any psychological pre-history or trauma that might have made his subject interesting in any but a representative way. Characteristically, too, Böll was wary of the tricks that memory plays on autobiographers more intent on fine writing than on a truthfulness that could be drab, admitting almost at once that 'I am no longer sure of how some of my personal experiences synchronize with historical events', and exposing two of his memory's tricks. I have said that autobiography is a form of fiction. Böll's little book is not an autobiography, but a memoir, because he resisted the imaginative processes that would have made it fiction. Since literal truthfulness was his purpose, he also refused to pretend that he suffered acutely under the German school system even when it came under pressure from Nazism, merely stating that he was allergic to that creed, and clarifying the allergy in these words:

> My unconquerable (and still unconquered) aversion to the Nazis was not revolt: *they* revolted *me*, repelled me on every level of my being: conscious *and* instinctive, aesthetic *and* political. To this day I have been unable to find any entertaining, let alone aesthetic, dimension to the Nazis and their era, a fact that makes me shudder when I see certain film and stage productions. I simply *could not* join the Hitler Youth, I did not join it, and that was that.

Böll's refusal to say more, or to apologise for the measure of outward compromise forced on his family for survival, makes his account much more convincing than the self-questioning and moral condemnation in which he might have indulged.

Although there are very few wholly evil or wicked characters in Böll's fiction—his realism and his compassion forbade such demonization—this early revulsion stayed with him as a distrust of officialdom and its blinkered servants, his hatred of the surveillance that was to be practised in the Federal Republic also, and his opposition to the Cold War propaganda disseminated by the powerful Springer Press. It is recognizable in the clash of principles, in *Ansichten eines Clowns* (1963), denoted by 'the sacrament of the Lamb' and 'the sacrament of the Buffalo'—where English readers must know that the German word 'Büffel' has the colloquial sense of 'lout' or 'thug'.

In the memoir, one way in which the adolescent minimized those sufferings at school which Böll calls 'mandatory for German authors' was by playing truant as often as possible, walking the streets instead; and he links that expedient to his immediate background by observing elsewhere that 'a dedicated feeling for legality does not form part of the Cologne attitude to life'. Though he tells us no more about the characters and inner lives of his parents, brothers and sisters than about his own, what the memoir conveys most vividly is the degree to which he regarded himself as the product of a particular conditioning by his family, social class, religion and region. As a self-employed cabinet maker, his father belonged to an economically imperilled and insecure class—that artisan class which would include writers also if, like Böll, they could rid themselves of the pretence that they are 'unacknowledged legislators'—whose mentality Böll described as 'that explosive mixture of lower middle class vestiges, Bohemian traits, and proletarian pride, not truly belonging to any class, yet arrogant rather than humble, in other words, almost class-conscious again.' The 'arrogance' here is independence and cussedness; and the 'class-consciousness' is only the refusal to acknowledge class superiorities, rather than spiritual and moral ones. The family's Roman Catholicism, too, was deep-rooted, yet anything but conformist. 'The elements of those three classes', Böll wrote, 'to none of which we truly belonged, had made what might be called "bourgeois" Christianity absolutely insufferable to us.' At the time of the Concordat between the Vatican and the newly established Third Reich, Böll's family considered leaving the Church, but 'Catholic was what we wanted to be and remain, in spite of all our derisive laughter and abuse.' This seemingly contradictory stance placed the family in a limbo under Nazism; and it was to lead the writer into a public controversy with an Archbishop in his opposition to what he called 'the capitulation of German Catholicism to post-war opportunism'.

As for the boy's education, though much of it was acquired in 'the school of the streets' or at home, where he read Jack London but also

Greek and Latin texts, Böll's Roman Catholic secondary or grammar school was so far from being thoroughly Nazified that it was closed down before the end of the war. It was the school of the streets that shocked Böll into the awareness essential to the story writer he became, for, relatively civilized though it remained, the other school 'prepared us not for life but for death'. The shocks that stand out in Böll's account are the Concordat, the summary decapitation, at Goering's orders, of seven young Communists, and the occupation by German troops of the previously demilitarized Rhineland. Again they are consistent with the imaginative writer's lifelong concern with the victimized and rejected—more often women than men—in his best novels, like *Gruppenbild mit Dame* (1971; *Group Portrait with Lady*), but not always. In the early novel *Und sagte kein einziges Wort* (1953; *Acquainted with the Night*) the narrative is divided impartially between the male and female protagonists. In *Ansichten eines Clowns* it is the 'clown', Schnier, who is sacrificed to the 'post-war opportunism' implicating the Church, when it is suggested that his co-habitation with Marie, who deserts him to marry a Catholic functionary, was the true sacrament—Böll's 'sacrament of the Lamb'.

That Böll came close to studying theology, rather than Classics and German, after school, and at least considered taking holy orders, will scarcely astonish careful readers of this subversive and representative writer. British readers may find it harder to understand how his economically insecure parents could afford to give all their children a university education, and without creating the kind of social and cultural estrangement the British class structure would have made inescapable at the time, and almost inescapable even now. That is why the 'class-consciousness' of which Böll wrote in the book should not be taken too literally, when in fact it was a consciousness of being classless, and liking it. Böll was never an advocate of any kind of class war, though he was a socialist; and his sympathies as a story-teller cut across the classes, as his radical Christianity demanded that it must.

Another difference between the two countries comes out when Böll refers to 'elderly and successful politicians, church dignitaries, writers, etc.'—but I have said enough about the German anomaly that placed eminent writers in that league. Not the least of Böll's distinctions was that he performed the public function expected of him in that capacity, but never succumbed to the self-importance and pomposity it so often induced in German writers similarly honoured; and that he performed it bravely and generously, paying the full price for it by provoking outrage, malice and vituperation. The memoir, too, is an utterly unpretentious work. Because he remained true to his beginnings, his family, region and convictions, the elderly and successful writer Böll became had no need to patronise, romanticise or apologise for the easy-going boy he had been. The representative standing he was able to maintain for almost four decades, as a writer who could be attacked and disparaged but never dismissed, because he stood for the values which others merely professed when that was expedient, is unlikely to be assumed by any other West German writer. The centre that held for Böll until his death in 1985—only just, in his last years—holds for few others now; and no writer can represent a society not held together by a centre of that kind.

5

Of Böll's coevals among the outstanding fiction writers—though like Böll, he also published poems in later years—Alfred Andersch was disqualified for a representative function both by his personal history and by his extreme complexity as a writer. A founder member of the *Gruppe 27*, Andersch dropped out of it before it reached the high point of its influence. Though he was an ex-soldier, his military service had been preceded by two arrests as a Communist, brief internment in Dachau and surveillance by the Gestapo after his release; and it was cut short by his desertion to the American forces in 1944, on the Italian front. The questions of conscience this desertion raised for Andersch— who carried a book by Ernst Jünger, of all people, in his kitbag on being released by the Americans from more internment—were the subject of Andersch's early book *Die Kirschen der Freiheit* (1952), and he was to take them up again as late as 1974 in his last major work of fiction, the novel *Winterspelt*. From 1945 to 1958, when he settled in Switzerland, Andersch was active in the reconstruction and reconstitution of German cultural life as assistant to Erich Kästner on the editorial staff of an American-sponsored newspaper, co-editor with Hans Werner Richter of another, so independent that its licence was withdrawn, as a radio producer, and as an editor of the most distinguished literary periodical of the period, *Texte und Zeichen* (1955–1957), comparable in its range and quality only to the East German *Sinn und Form* under Peter Huchel's editorship. When West German literature was being politicized and ideologized, Andersch was more interested in aesthetic matters and a journey to the Arctic recorded in a television film and in his book *Hohe Breitengrade* (1969). When that phase had come to an end, Andersch created a major controversy with his poem 'artikel 3 (3)', a hard-hitting protest against the 'Berufsverbote'—exclusion of politic- ally undesirable persons from employment in the educational system— brought in by the West German government in 1976, but with drastic amendments in the same year, to which the Andersch controversy may have contributed.

Alfred Andersch's excellent works were as difficult to place as his person. On the one hand, he was a realist, and a master of short stories that could be documentary in their conciseness and matter-of-factness, like 'Noch schöner wohnen' in his collection *Mein Verschwinden in Providence* (1971); not only the settings of his novels and stories, but their manner and themes, were so various and wide-ranging that his readers and critics never knew what to expect of him. His advocacy of Ernst Jünger, never retracted when Andersch's literary practice and overt commitments put him at the farthest possible remove from that writer—for a time it was Sartre's existentialism that provided Andersch with a resolution of his conflicts over the desertion in 1944—was only one of countless seeming inconsistencies that could be understood only in the light of his collected writings, not issued until 1979, and followed by a number of important posthumous publications; and even then they had to be related to constant antinomies and tensions between his aesthetic and his moral concerns. On the other hand, each of his major novels—from *Sansibar oder der Letzte Grund* (1957) and *Die Rote* (1960; new version 1972) to *Efraim* (1967) and *Winterspelt*—has intrinsic qualities of intelligence and sensibility that would have posed no such problem if each had been by a different author. Much the same is true of his collections of stories, from *Geister und Leute* (1958) to the one already mentioned, as of the posthumously published story *Der Vater eines Mörders* (1980). His many critical essays, travel sketches and autobiographical pieces have the same astonishing range and diversity. What is more—like a whole succession of post-war German writers from Martin Kessel to Günter Bruno Fuchs, Wolfgang Hildesheimer, Friedrich Dürrenmatt and Christoph Meckel—Andersch was also a visual artist, and his preference for a graphic, phenomenological realism to a socially tendentious one is connected with that. For all his seriousness, Andersch was also a defender of what Germans call 'Trivialliteratur', thrillers and the like—not the only predilection of his that was more Anglo-Saxon than German, but one as perplexing to many of his fellow writers as the unpredictability of his commitments. His last sortie into the public arena so dear to them showed both the constancy of his moral concerns and his cool disregard of all trends, conformisms and commitments worn on the sleeve, whether the left or right. It was not that his centre had shifted, but that his love of freedom, above all, induced him to keep it inscrutable, if not invisible.

Wolfgang Hildesheimer—also resident in Switzerland since 1957, and now a Swiss citizen—was even less qualified by experience and allegiance to be a spokesman for anyone or anything in West Germany. After emigrating to England, then Palestine, with his parents in 1933, he was trained as a carpenter and draftsman, furniture designer and interior decorator, studied stage design in London and lived as a painter in Cornwall just before the outbreak of war. During the war he worked as a teacher of English for the British Council in Palestine, then as an information officer for the British Government there. After the war he worked in London again, with a second visit to Cornwall, and as an interpreter at the Nuremberg trials of war criminals, becoming the general editor of the records of those trials. In 1949 he settled in Bavaria as a painter and graphic artist and—according to his own account— became a writer by accident, when weather conditions proved unfavourable for his other art. This account is characteristic of the writer he became—an ironist, satirist and fantasist, from the start, of horrors that defied any other treatment. His brilliantly witty *Lieblose Legenden* (1952; enlarged edition 1962) were followed by a succession of radio and stage plays that travestied the 'serious' realities and issues of the age to the point of farce or of pure absurdity. Hildesheimer's own seriousness, which he did his best to conceal behind frivolously evasive quips when solemn professions of commitment were demanded of him, became more apparent in his first novel, *Tynset* (1965). It is the long narrative of a sleepless night, confined to one character's memories, traumas, fantasies and futile hopes—symbolized by Tynset, the name of a remote Norwegian place picked out at random from a railway time-table—and with only one subsidiary character, a housekeeper, to confront him with present realities. Though the structure of that novel may owe something to precedents as various as Joyce's *Ulysses*, Broch's *Der Tod des Vergil* and Canetti's *Die Blendung*, its substance and manner are Hildesheimer's alone; and the novel not only gathers up many different threads from his earlier works, but gives away just what kind of despair it was out of which he had made his style. Social realism of any kind was out of the question for Hildesheimer, because he had learned too much about the nature of social realities in our time to regard them as suitable material for fiction.

His long novel *Masante* (1973) dispensed even with the foil of one subsidiary character outside the protagonist's mind. Yet, even more strikingly than in *Tynset*, that wandering, meandering mind contains a world that is also a social world, evoked in the most diverse encounters and dialogues. Despite his preference for what would seem to be a solipsistic setting and structure, Hildesheimer is the most worldly of the major German fiction writers of his generation. This paradox became even more acute in his subsequent longer works. Just as he was a novelist who could not believe in the conventions of realistic fiction, with his *Mozart* (1977) he became a biographer who could not believe in the conventions of biography, since biography turned to fiction in his hands. The outward life of Mozart, as far as the records went, could be reconstructed. His person, and quite especially the person who produced the music, was beyond a biographer's grasp. This book also showed that a third art, music, had been as important to Hildesheimer as the two with which he was associated professionally, though few had noticed the musical structures in his major literary works, including *Tynset* and *Masante*.

Having discovered that biography was fiction, Hildesheimer found it natural to write his next novel as a spoof biography, that of an early nineteenth century English aristocrat and amateur of the arts, *Marbot* (1981). Here Hildesheimer proved so adept at social and historical realism, down to long quotations from the writings of his imaginary subject, that many critics and readers were taken in by the imaginary toad placed in real gardens, in Goethe's Weimar, Leopardi's Italy or the England of the Lake Poets. In the guise of fiction, *Marbot* also served Hildesheimer as a pretext for his own reflections on the lives and characters of artists, reflections as worldly as they are sceptical and gloomy. According to his own account, this book, a pseudo-biography and pseudo-fiction, is the last of his literary travesties—though an accident can never be ruled out in Hildesheimer's case. The serious reasons behind his frivolous abandonment of this art can be gathered from yet another of Hildesheimer's versatile resorts, a poem alluding to public statements he had made in interviews about those serious reasons:

Antwort

Ganz recht, ich sagte,
es sei nicht fünf vor
zwölf, es sei vielmehr halb
drei. Das war um halb
drei. Inzwischen ist es vier. Nur
merkt ihr es nicht. Ihr lest ein Buch
über Kassandra, aber ihre Schreie
habt ihr nicht gehört. Das war
um fünf vor zwölf. Bald ist es
fünf, und wenn ihr Schreie hört,
sind es die euren.

Answer

That's right, I said
it wasn't five to
twelve, but rather half
past two. That was at half
past two. By now it's four. But you
just haven't noticed. You read a book
about Cassandra, but you didn't hear
her screams. That was
at five to twelve. Quite soon
it will be five, and if it's screams you hear
they'll be your own.

The book about Cassandra that is being read is that by the East German novelist Christa Wolf, published in 1983; and it is the kind of fiction that Hildesheimer would have to write, but will not and cannot write, to make his serious commitment more explicit than he ever chose to make it. Nor does the poem, other than by allusion and by mundane understatement, though any serious reader will know what sort of midnight the poem treats as *fait accompli*. To treat it as such could be a warning only; but Cassandra's warnings, too, were not heeded, and did not avert the catastrophe.

It is this shadow hanging over all endeavours now, not only literary ones, that has come to obscure the later work of another writer of that age-group, Peter Weiss, a refugee from the Third Reich like Hildesheimer. The commitments and choices turned into didactic plays by Weiss in his later years have come to seem almost as remote as the controversies aroused by his statements about them and so seriously fought out in the German media for a decade or so; almost as though the Vietnam war had cost Peter Weiss the imaginative verve and thrust of the Marat-Sade play for which he is mainly remembered outside Germany. That play had been preceded by prose works as personal and idiosyncratic as the later plays were inhibited by their designs on audiences and readers. The 'micro-novel' *Der Schatten des Körpers des Kutschers* (1960) owes its power to a child's eye view of the adult world that was also a painter's eye view—Peter Weiss was another of the painter-writers—and his own collages added to the effect of a hyper-realism carried to the point of surrealism. (Without resorting to collage or juxtapositions of disparate images, Günter Grass was to excel at a micro-realism of that kind both in his writing and in his graphic work; and often it was the child's eye view, with its concentration on detail unrelated to function, that invested his images with a sinister autonomy, very much as in Weiss's narrative.) It is the cool objectivity with which the adolescent narrator records his observations of every-day events in an isolated homestead that make Weiss's 'ordinary' characters and their actions cast the monstrous shadows to which the title points; but the monstrosity does not become mechanical, as in Gisela Elsner's later novel. In the adult world, and to the adolescent's innocent eye, everything ordinary becomes monstrous. One character devotes his life to a vast and indiscriminate collection of stones. Another, a doctor, is swathed in bandages that cover a mass of festering sores; and the sexual act at the end of the narrator's journal entries casts a shadow more grotesque than any. All the reported snatches of small talk bring out the monstrous banality of the things that adults do.

In his two autobiographical fictions, *Abschied von den Eltern* (1961) and *Fluchtpunkt* (1962), as in his radio play *Der Turm* (1963), Peter Weiss rendered the personal parent-child conflict whose introduction into the earlier book would have broken its unity of vision. *Abschied von den Eltern*, the shorter and more intense of the two, deals with an upper middle-class childhood in Berlin between the wars. The narrator's father is a businessman of Jewish descent, his mother a former actress who had broken off her career and a first marriage mainly, it is implied, for the sake of economic security. The circumstance that he is half-Jewish, emphasized in his family by the presence of children by his mother's first marriage who have no Jewish blood, places the protagonist at the heart of that political and social division which he records not historically, but only in terms of his own development. He is candid about his conflicting potentialities as an adherent or victim of the Nazi movement, as about the relief he feels when his half-brother tells him that his mixed descent disqualifies him from being anything but a victim. Both the pathos of an embattled bourgeoisie, desperately clinging to a hollow respectability and a hollow belief in the virtue of hard work—the same virtue without which the Third Reich could not have been maintained either in peace or war—in self-discipline and self-sacrifice to the family, and of the seething anarchy beneath it, come out much more strongly in this autobiographical story than they would have done if Weiss, in this phase, had adopted a more sociological, ideologically determined approach. His narrator does not moralize or externalize the conflict, as the later Weiss would have felt obliged to do; he renders all the tension and ambivalence of his relationship with his parents and with the world beyond his home, in so far as it impinges at all on that siege-like embattlement characteristic of German family life at the period, at least in urban, upper middle-class homes. Even his family's emigration to England, then Scandinavia, only gradually loosens the family's ethos and releases the narrator from its stranglehold on his feelings. The extent of this stranglehold is conveyed by his account of several erotic experiences, including an incestuous one, and these are treated with the same stark frankness as the political undercurrents. A connection is made between the narrator's sexual and social behaviour—as between every aspect of his private life and the history of an era—but without any deliberate attempt at social documentation. The setting is not so much described as illuminated by flashes of perception.

It is in the longer sequel, *Fluchtpunkt*, that the narrator's confined perspective and a subjectivity familiar from Hermann Hesse—who was an early mentor of Peter Weiss's, and appears as such in the book—becomes a limitation, for reasons mainly of scale and structure. Yet, taken together, both autobiographical fictions have an immediacy and authenticity that transcend their biological function; and in both works a necessary link is forged between pre-war and post-war patterns of revolt. The individualism of Peter Weiss's revolt against his parents and family background could never have been enough to sustain his later work; but, as a whole generation of younger writers was to discover more than a decade later, a single case history, imaginatively grasped, can tell us more about a whole society and era than conscientious attempts to emulate the historian's scope. Peter Weiss's personal and painterly vision—still powerfully at work in his fragment of 1963, *Das Gespräch der Drei Gehenden*—did not lend itself to the writing of neo-Brechtian parable plays or to any didactic function forced on him by his political decisions in the later 1960s. It may well have been his exposure to Nazism in his youth that, as a writer, made him a victim of the Cold War and of one of its products, the war in Vietnam.

V Versions of the Real

1

Realism of one kind or another has been the aim of generations of post-war German writers, or post-war writers in German, inasmuch as they wished to understand the continuities and discontinuities that had formed them; but because the discontinuities and divisions were so extreme, the continuities so dubious and impalpable, social realities were the last that could be taken for granted, as they have been in other societies. Even the more conventionally or recognizably 'realistic' fiction of the 1950s and 1960s had to return again and again to the Third Reich and the Second World War, or else to scrutinize a restored normality in the light of what had preceded it. At best that normality was a fragile one, when Germany had been split into two nations, with its former capital city almost as a third one, also split in two, an island at the centre of the Cold War; and when the upheavals of the earlier period had their sequel in refugees from regions no longer German, refugees from the other Germany, refugees from the Third Reich, even refugees from the Federal Republic who had chosen to emigrate after the war. All these different refugees, new and old, as well as the Austrian and German-Swiss writers, contributed their versions of reality to post-war German literature, and neither the Berlin Wall nor the militarized frontiers elsewhere could prevent the literatures of the two Germanys from interacting and interpenetrating, as they have never ceased to do over four decades.

Versions of reality, in any case, are all that any art can offer. If that were not so, realistic modes in fiction would have been rendered obsolete by statisticians and their techniques, representational modes in the visual arts by the invention of photography. For a minority of German writers—those who took up linguistic counterparts to abstraction in the visual arts, but also those who adopted documentary procedures, even in verse—any approach that could be described as realistic may, in fact, have come to seem obsolete. The majority, though, continued to offer versions of the real as reflected by a single sensibility, a single imagination, with all the distortions and transformations of generally accepted realities that artistic representation has always permitted, if not demanded. Since generally accepted realities were not easily available, least of all the social ones, these approaches were extraordinarily diverse, unstable and subject to drastic reversals. In prose fiction, for instance, character could be rendered and approached in ways as different as the ways of depth psychology are from those of behaviourist psychology—at times by the same author, in different phases or within the bounds of a single work. Because to the imagination statistical and behaviourist approaches are unreal, approximations to either in fiction tended towards satirical and grotesque effects; but reality itself had fallen into the hands of the statisticians and behaviourists of this world—to those who took no account of the individual psyche or its needs in administering societies or making 'world history'. It was not difficult, therefore, for the absurdists to claim that they were the true realists of the age.

Social realism of the kind still practised by Böll now called for a faith like his own. Several of the most gifted of his early fellow practitioners in post-war Germany and Austria—like Hans Bender and Klaus Roehler, the authors of excellent short stories that grappled with the transition to a restored normality, or Hans Lebert in Austria, another painter-writer and author of the remarkable novel *Die Wolfshaut*—did not persist as Böll did in that mode, and as Hans Werner Richter has also done over the decades. Others, like Ilse Aichinger, renounced the achievement of large-scale realistic fiction after her early novel *Die Grössere Hoffnung* (1948)—a novel that drew on her own experience of division and persecution in Austria after its annexation—in favour of prose miniatures, poems and dialogues that are a place of her own, a reality of her own rendered with an inimitable delicacy and wit. The assumption behind them must be that no generally accepted and inhabited realities can sustain her imagination, her fictions; or that her approaches to them must be as tentative and indirect as all her later ones have been. None of the successive trends and waves, from the abstract to the documentary and 'committed', had detracted from the validity of her work—any more than they could detract from the work of lyrical poets like Günter Eich (her husband), Peter Huchel, Johannes Bobrowski, Paul Celan or Ernst Meister, all of whom remained impervious to them in their concentration on very personal visions and versions of reality.

2

Even the neutrality and stability of Switzerland did not absolve its outstanding imaginative writers from shocks and questions they have shared with their German coevals. Friedrich Dürrenmatt was among the first to recognize that the whole of Europe had lost the war, and to draw the lesson that farce and black comedy were a more appropriate response to that realization, in the theatre at least, than a kind of pathos that had never been congenial to most Swiss writers in any case. He and Max Frisch had also been less out of touch with developments outside Germany—and those included the work of German emigrant writers like Brecht—than those who had grown up under Nazi censorship. Both writers were alert enough, and sensitive enough, to feel that the accident of neutrality did not absolve them from being implicated in issues that might look less urgent in Switzerland. Max Frisch's fascinating journals—his *Tagebuch 1946–1949* (1950) and its sequel covering later years—record his explorations of post-diluvian Europe; significantly, they also contain the nuclei of most of his later imaginative works, from *Stiller* (1954) to *Andorra* (1961) and *Mein Name sei Gantenbein* (1964), all of which are concerned with questions of personal identity—and therefore with questions of reality. A different kind of unreality, brought about by self-delusion rather than self-estrangement, is the subject of his 'didactic play without a moral', *Biedermann und die Brandstifter* (1958).

One of Frisch's early plays, *Nun Singen sie Wieder*, written in 1945, shows that Swiss neutrality presented difficulties, as well as advantages, to a writer who wished to engage in the moral issues posed by the Third Reich and the war. On the one hand, Frisch quarrelled with Ernst Wiechert's attempt to shift a specifically German aberration on to a plane of generality and universality that absolved individual Germans from guilt. On the other, far from de-demonizing Nazism in the play, he treated it as a kind of religious heresy quite free from 'banality of evil'. In a later note on the play, Frisch commented on the difficulty of writing about things never 'seen with one's own eyes', but also on the advantage of having no motive for resentment or revenge. In fact, Max Frisch's great advantage as a playwright and novelist was to be his remove, as a Swiss, from immediate involvement in the obsessions and compulsions of which few German writers could rid themselves, together with a sense of continuity—and so of freedom—bound up with it. In common with Dürrenmatt, he had a quality of detachment and coolness that allowed both writers to travel light across any terrain they chose, however refractory and however ravaged by historical disasters. The danger for both was a Shavian brittleness where they travelled as tourists only. Both have been at their best when the lightness was applied to their most personal, most pressing concerns. Neither of them has cultivated the loving, minute realism that comes of staying at home.

The ingenious plot and knife-edged dialogue of Frisch's play *Don Juan oder die Liebe zur Geometrie* (1953) anticipates his later distinction as a dramatist—and the dangers of a cerebral detachment he was to avoid in the best of his novels. His analytical penetration makes this comedy a de-mythologization of an archetype who, even in Mozart's opera, had a tragic dimension; but the execution is too brilliant and too neat to satisfy more than Pascal's *esprit de la géométrie*. In his novel *Stiller* (1954), Frisch showed the same psychological sharpness in exposing the weakness, vanity and self-deception of characters seemingly mature. It is the author's recurrent preoccupation with problems of personal identity that saves this novel from the danger of being the mere working out of a thesis in terms of character and situation. The greater part of the book consists of diaries—a form most congenial to Frisch— kept by Stiller, a Swiss sculptor, while he is awaiting trial for returning to his country with false papers. For reasons that become clear from accounts of his past life, Stiller persists in pretending that he is an American called White. During his imprisonment he is confronted with the wife he had deserted some six years earlier while she was seriously ill with consumption, with his younger brother, former friends, and acquaintances likely to establish his identity; but he keeps up his pretence until he is taken to his former studio. There, in the presence of his wife, his old step-father and the public prosecutor— who is also the husband of Stiller's former mistress and eventually becomes his only friend—Stiller loses his nerve, smashes his own works, and gives himself away. After his release he tries to make a new start by settling down with his wife in an isolated châlet. The complex structure of this novel, necessitated by the juxtaposition of two periods in Stiller's life, is crucial to its import, to do with time, development and identity. There are thematic links with Frisch's earlier and later works, including the Don Juan play and the suggestion, in *Andorra*, that a person's identity is what he or she thinks it is. Even the digressions—like the interpolation of the Rip van Winkle story—illuminate aspects of Stiller's character and situation.

Homo Faber (1957) has a tighter and terser structure. Its sub-title, 'a report', points to the character of its narrator, a technician, but also to the character of its author, who was trained as an architect—a *homo faber* himself, with a workmanlike efficiency most remarkable in his shorter narratives. It is in these that Frisch has merged his theses completely in a character and an action. The tragic sweep of *Homo Faber* does not even require us to reflect that its protagonist, too, is a man who has evaded his identity, brought home to him by his meeting with the illegitimate daughter he had never seen or even heard of, and the passion that destroys them both. If the Oedipus myth resonates in this work, it is not de-mythologized, but given new life by the modern setting and by the contrast between the truly prosaic, matter-of-fact telling of it and its atavistic nature. Amongst other things, this 'report' touches on matters also powerfully dealt with by Dürrenmatt in his play *Die Physiker* (1962)—concerning the blindness and madness of modern technological man; but Frisch leaves those implications to the story and its beautifully rendered setting of UNO enterprises, air travel and cosmopolitan hotels.

Mein Name sei Gantenbein (1964) can also be said to hinge on a question of identity, or on a whole complex of questions that can be crudely, vaguely, but conveniently reduced to the single term, though Frisch's concern with it is varied from work to work. What has remained constant has been his doubts as to the continuity in time and place of one's so-called identity, and hence as to the possibility of keeping one's 'true self' distinct from the various roles which it may assume in one's own eyes or in other people's. Personality, Frisch seems to suggest, is an aritifice dependent on the interplay between one's own self-conceit—in the original sense of the word—and other people's readiness to accept it. The structure of *Stiller* was complex because the dual personality of its protagonist could be enacted only by flashbacks, but the novel was held together by our knowledge that, legally and biologically, Stiller and White were one and the same man. As for the theatre, the very medium rests on the suspension of 'real' identity and has lent itself to any number of questions and answers about it, from the religious certainties of medieval allegory or the *teatro del mundo* to Pirandello's modern disquiet. Yet even in the theatre, Max Frisch's questions about the authenticity and consistency of personal identity have been so pointed and insistent that they could deprive his characters of spontaneity and turn his plots into deliberate demonstrations of a paradox. However sound the theory and however justified the doubts, what matters in every case is their imaginative fleshing, so convincing and complete in *Homo Faber*.

In *Mein Name sei Gantenbein*, the doubts are applied with a vigour—or freedom, according to how one looks at it—so uncompromising as to shatter the very foundations of the medium. It is as though Max Frisch had told himself to stop pretending that novels deal with 'real' people in 'real' circumstances, to stop fooling his readers by presenting a plausible replica of this pseudo-reality. The result was an anti-novel, if not a non-novel. It demands nothing less of the reader than a degree of honesty equal to the author's, an equal readiness to suspend not disbelief, but belief, and to renounce the conventional illusions of fiction in favour of bare truths about human behaviour. One of these is that people are capable of much more than they think they are, because their identity is as fluid as it is dubious. It follows logically—perhaps too logically—that the book has no consistent narrator, no consistent protagonist and no consistent plot, since we are perpetually reminded that any event related is no more than a conjecture or possibility, and that something quite different could have happened. (This element of conjecture or speculation may owe something to the example of Uwe Johnson's first published novel of 1959, though Johnson's perplexed realism sprang from the difficulties of establishing the facts of a case, not from doubts about identity.) Max Frisch offers several such alternatives, only to dismiss them in turn as conjectures. At several points in the book, we are left in doubt as to whether an event is being narrated by one of the two principal male characters, Gantenbein and Enderling, or by a third person. The only unquestionable unity of the book is thematic, that of relationships between men and women, with a special emphasis on jealousy

> . . . as an instance of, as a truly painful awareness of the fact, that a person on whom we depend for our own self-realization is at the same time outside ourselves. Jealousy has less to do with love between the sexes than we are led to believe; it is the gulf between the world and our delusion, and jealousy in the narrow sense of the word is only a footnote to it, the shock of discovering that the world is not identical with my partner, nor with myself, that love has united me only with my delusion.

The success of Gantenbein's marriage with the actress Lila (though in one episode Lila is deprived of her identity as an actress and tried out as an Italian countess) has always depended on his ability to act the part of a blind man and on Lila's ability to fall for this ruse, so as to be able to 'deceive' him with other men. The case, of course, is extreme once more, in the manner of Max Frisch's paradoxical theses, and the point is driven home with the help of anecdotes of the kind to be found in his published diaries, the source-book for most of his later plots. An element of contrivance—reminiscent of Gide's *Les Faux-Monnayeurs*—makes such fictional experiments less gripping than the shorter works in which Frisch has subordinated his ingenuity to the primary imagination.

Ingenious invention is very much in evidence in this book, which even seems to have been improvised to a quite uncommon degree. Yet the improvisation is guided more by the intellectual whims of an eminently clever and witty writer, than by the autonomous life that fictitious characters are apt to assume; and again and again his very theme demands the demolition of his fictions, the reminder that his characters, too, are hypothetical—an alienation effect more drastic than Brecht's. This may be why the wide range of human experience covered by this work, and rendered with humour, clarity and insight, does not convey a sense of richness. The theme itself forbids it, because the writer's awareness of the many different potentialities of his characters, and of his power to manipulate these potentialities, prevents any of the characters from being 'all there' at any one moment. Neither Gantenbein nor Enderling is vivid or memorable except in relation to the problem posed by Frisch; and even Lila, who is observed in affectionate detail, is too hypothetical, too general, to acquire an existence of her own. Her primary function, necessarily, is to demonstrate something about men, and perhaps only certain types of men at that. One of the minor characters, Burri, remarks: 'A woman is a human being before one loves her, and sometimes after one has loved

her; as soon as one loves her she is a miracle and, as such, untenable.'
This observation points to a personal obsession present in Frisch's
work at least since the Don Juan comedy, and he may have come closer
to resolving it in the later work. Towards the end he posits a durable
marriage no longer childless, and a kind of love that is not an in-
fatuation; but the ageing Gantenbein's love for his daughter is shown to
be no less 'untenable', since the relation to his daughter, too, proves to
involve the projection of his own delusions on to her.

The mask of fiction is also dropped in Frisch's long story *Montauk*
(1978), set in America, about an ageing writer's love affair with a young
woman, and acknowledged by Frisch to be autobiographical. (The
protagonist even shares his Christian name.) Here the diarist and the
imaginative writer have become one and the same, all the more so
because retrospection and self-quotation are part of the gist of this
work, a work of self-judgement. In a sense, *Montauk* is the culmination
of Frisch's investigations of love, in that both his detachment and his
rare honesty are carried farther than before, beyond the limits of
fiction; but not beyond the limits of selfhood, where only imagination
carries a writer, regardless of whether that imagination engages with an
identifiable reality or not.

At first sight *Der Mensch erscheint im Holozän* (1979)—modestly
sub-titled 'a story'—may also look like a documentary or autobiographical fiction, with its many insets in various types and shapes,
its diagrams and illustrations, its railway timetable and list of provisions
on the shelves and in the deep-freeze compartment. Yet these prove to
be not only an integral part of the story, but a means of bringing it home
with an extraordinary concreteness to the reader. All these insets are
exact reproductions of handwritten notes or clippings from books
which Herr Geiser—the principal, if not sole character in the story—
sticks to the walls of his house to make up for his failing memory; and
that failing memory, which is also the deepening isolation of old age, is
what the story is about. 'No knowledge without memory', is the
laconic, wholly unrhetorical summary in the text.

The extreme dryness and brevity of Frisch's manner in this work
does make it tend towards anti-fiction once more. Frisch has always felt
uncomfortable with the prolixity and emotiveness of conventional
fiction. The dryness is also a national characteristic, to be found in
many of the best Swiss writers; and in his case it was heightened both by
his training and practice as an architect, a primarily functional discipline, and by the impact on him—recorded in his diaries—of a
post-war Europe devastated by what had begun as emotive rhetoric and
ideology. Yet in this late work his reductive spareness is no mere
idiosyncrasy, but an enactment of the theme, a manner matched in
every particular to the matter of the story.

Herr Geiser—we are never granted the intimacy of a first name, because that would be impertinent in both senses of the word—is a retired professional man living alone in a village in Ticino. It is August, and the village has been cut off by a long period of incessant rain, causing damage to the mountain roads. The electricity supply fails. A major landslide, which could bury the whole village, is feared, though it does not occur. The possibility that it could occur is enough to induce Herr Geiser to occupy his mind not with apocalyptic fantasies—though his snippets do include a few Biblical texts, which he treats with scepticism, as he treats everything—but with factual information about geological pre-history, of the region and the whole planet, so as to arrive at a balanced view of his own situation in place and time, the Holocene of the title that is only one in a succession of geological ages. His pottering about the house and garden, a few practical chores, and an unexplained excursion across the mountains, over tracks made dangerous by flooding, erosion and thick mist, and despite a weak heart, are just about the extent of the action before Geiser suffers a fall that leaves his face partly paralysed, and his daughter arrives from Basel; but a great deal more happens between the lines.

The minimal narration leaves all sorts of gaps to be filled by the reader's imagination—and sympathy, too, though neither Geiser nor his narrator asks for it; all sorts of intriguing questions about the reason for Geiser's excursion, for instance, its connection, if any, with a mountaineering trip in his youth with his dead brother, recalled at this point, or the location and cause of Geiser's collapse. (A minor stroke seems to be implied, but no more.) This creates an extraordinary tension between the matter-of-fact precision of detail and the larger vibrations of meaning, which could be political, too, and are certainly existential and cosmological. The concentration on Geiser is intensified by a presentation that makes the character as nearly identical as possible with the narrator, even in a third-person narrative, for it has the immediacy of diary jottings, yet diary jottings without introspection or self-pity. Max Frisch lives in a similar village in Ticino, and may well have drawn on his own circumstances for many of the vividly rendered details; yet no story could read less like a confession, if only because Geiser, too, regards himself with a detached curiosity, casting a 'cold eye on life, on death'. (This has to be said only because Frisch's preceding work, *Montauk*, was read and discussed as autobiography. That is why I noted with relief that Geiser's age does not correspond with the author's at the time of writing or of publication!)

So, for once, Max Frisch achieved a work open not only to the conundrums and enigmas that have always fascinated him, but to a mysteriousness attained by the utmost clarity of outline. Whether Geiser believes them or not, even the Biblical passages add their vibrations to this mysteriousness—much as the Sophoclean under-current had to the tragic force of *Homo Faber*. Because of its density, compression and reticences, which would make it comparable to Samuel Beckett's reductions but for Frisch's avoidance of prose poetry, *Man in the Holocene* expands in the reader's mind, and seems a much longer, larger, more substantial work than a page- or word-count would indicate.

Significantly, we do not need to ask ourselves whether it is Geiser or the narrator who gives us this clue to the story's structure, manner and import:

> Novels are of no use at all on days like these, they deal with people and their relationships, with themselves and others, fathers and mothers and daughters and sons, etc, with individual souls, usually happy ones, with society, etc., as if the place for these things were assured, the earth for all time earth, the sea level fixed for all time.

The brackets I have omitted from this quotation make it read like a casual diary entry, unlike the many polished aphorisms that could be extracted from his novels, plays and diaries; but those few words tell us as much about Geiser as they do about the writing of his story, that of a man stripped down to essentials, yet concerned less with his own individuality than with the survival of life on earth. They also tell us why in this work Frisch had less use than ever for the elaborations of conventional realism.

However grim and unflinching, this virtually one-character story is neither solipsistic nor depressing. Geiser's personal relationships have simply receded from his consciousness—he has difficulty in remembering his grandchildren's names—as they must and do in old age. Yet he defies that condition, too, by braving the adverse weather and terrain on his walk, and by putting himself in his place, establishing his identity, with the help of those bits of paper.

To me, that is a more topical message than any conveyed in tendentious novels about this or that political issue—as well as a wiser one. This or that nation's revenge, even this or that nation's survival, are issues now overshadowed by the possibility that the Holocene itself could be terminated by a holocaust neither divine nor natural. The possibility is never so much as mentioned in Frisch's book, whose great distinction is that it means so much more than it says. By understatement, dryness and coolness, Frisch turned one man's consciousness, one little village, and the threat of extinction to both, into a microcosm.

3

In narrative fiction, if not in drama, Dürrenmatt has set himself less ambitious aims than Frisch, and has excelled at short works that make no bones about their indebtedness to the conventions of a humble and 'trivial' genre, the thriller, though their execution sets them apart from the common product. With a few outstanding exceptions, like the prose poem and parable *Minotaurus*—which he calls a 'ballad'—published in 1985 with Dürrenmatt's drawings, closely related to the text— Dürrenmatt has been a specialist in the deflation of myths and of history. *Minotaurus* is an exception in that it re-creates a myth, over- coming Dürrenmatt's dominant scepticism very much as Frisch could overcome his in his most imaginatively integral works. Like Frisch, too, Dürrenmatt has returned again and again to early works and themes, revising and reshaping, but also commenting on their genesis and growth. Outside the German-speaking world, but especially in Britain, his works of fiction have been sadly neglected; and even his later plays have not received the attention and performances that might have followed from the impact of his tragi-comedy *Der Besuch der Alten Dame* (1956; new version 1980; *The Visit*) or of *Die Physiker* (1962; new version 1980; *The Physicists*). Dürrenmatt's zest, intelligence and pro- ductivity have not been impaired over the decades. His farcical comedy *Achterloo* (1983) is one of a long succession of works in which Dürren- matt's debunking of history and its heroes also serves as an indirect reflector of the contemporary world; in this case Napoleon, Louis Bonaparte, Cambronne, Richelieu, Benjamin Franklin, Jan Hus, Büchner's Woyzeck and his more fictitious daughter Marion, as well as not only one Karl Marx, but five Marx Brothers are absolved from historical time to enact a farce that has an oblique bearing on con- temporary events in Poland. The black comedy remains Shavian in its irony and detachment; but not only the topical relevance, but the implicit reflections on a history that does repeat itself, as farce, in- troduce those tragic undertones never quite absent from Dürrenmatt's work, even where he does not acknowledge them, as he does in *The Visit* or in the *Minotaurus* fable.

Without repeating himself, Dürrenmatt has shown an uncommon consistency. His short novel *Grieche sucht Griechin* (1955; *Once a Greek . . .*), described as a 'prose comedy', was more closely related to his dramatic works than to his other novels. Like most of his plays, the story is a semi-realistic fable about the contemporary world; like them, too, it is drily funny, grotesque in parts, and grimly satirical through- out. Yet it is neither wholly 'absurd' nor nihilistic. The alternative endings, of which the more conventionally 'happy' one was chosen for the English version, suggests an admirable reluctance on the author's part to drive home a single moral; and this reluctance points to Dürren- matt's exceptional open-mindedness. One limitation inherent in the moral fable is that it is apt to become schematic. Another is that it tends to reduce characters to types, sacrificing the complexity and ambiguity of real persons and their motives. Dürrenmatt avoided the first danger, and the openness of his plot goes far towards compensating for the lack of characterization in depth. True, we are presented with an English couple, the archaeologists Mr and Mrs Weeman, who between them say nothing more than 'well' and 'yes'; but the farcical convention in which they have their being would have been less acceptable in so serious a work if the author had also subjected us to a preconceived moral thesis. As it is, his comic zest is beautifully integrated with his grimness as a moralist. Because it is rooted in charity, his sense of fun permits the possibility of a happy ending to do with love.

The Greek of the title, Arnolph Archilochos, is the Assistant Bookkeeper of an Assistant Bookkeeper in a large industrial concern. A celibate, teetotaller, non-smoker and vegetarian, he lives in squalid obscurity, sustained by the heroes of his 'ethical cosmos'. These include the President of the country in which he lives—a country suggesting France, but not necessarily identical with France—the almost mythical owner of the concern that employs him, and the Bishop of the Old New Presbyterians of the Penultimate Christians, the sect of which Archilochos is a fervent adherent. Together, the eight heroes of his moral cosmos represent the powers that be, though Number Eight, Arnolph's brother Bibi, with his terrible delinquent family, represent the seamy side of the social order, redeemed in Arnolph's eyes only by his own belief in his sponging brother's fundamental goodness. A complete reversal in Arnolph's status and values occurs when he advertises for a marriage partner, another Greek. It is only after the marriage ceremony that he discovers why all the heroes of his moral cosmos step down from their pedestals to accept him as their equal or superior: all of them had been lovers of his wife, the beautiful courtesan Chloe, whom he had believed to be a housemaid. For a time the meek hero-worshipper turns into a furious avenger. He is almost persuaded to assassinate the President and so lend himself to the designs of the revolutionary Fahrcks (who eventually brings off a coup, only to establish an order very much like the one he had overthrown). As in other works by Dürrenmatt, the arts are not exempted from his satirical panorama. Petit-Paysan, the tycoon, reads Hölderlin, and the great painter Passap, one of Arnolph's heroes, provides outrageous antics.

Arnolph's disillusionment makes him wise, but not cynical. Whether he returns to his former status and way of life, in a garret adjoining the lavatories in Mme Bieler's establishment, or goes off with Chloe to Greece to unearth a statue of Aphrodite, we can assume that his humility and kindness are unimpaired. The tale stops short of nihilism because Friedrich Dürrenmatt believes in the virtues of ordinariness. The values by which 'ordinary' people live may be so much cant, but in Dürrenmatt's eyes, Arnolph is the true hero.

Dürrenmatt's choice of a medium that permits only rudimentary characterization is no accident. Like other Swiss writers before and after him, he is profoundly suspicious of the pretensions that go with a highly developed individuality and its individualistic claims. One is reminded of Robert Walser's comical debunking of 'great' personalities—including writers and artists, in so far as they were public figures and celebrities—and even of Gottfried Keller's sympathetic and humorous concern with the minutiae of 'ordinary' people and their daily lives. If this nineteenth-century mode of realism is as inaccessible to Dürrenmatt as to Frisch, it is because it rested in part on a regional rootedness disrupted even in neutral Switzerland. Yet Dürrenmatt's unflagging exposure of false values, and his readiness to let satire go well beyond the limits of the plausibly real, owe less to a fashionable cult of absurdity than to the traditional didactic concerns of Swiss writers. In translation, we get the cosmopolitan awareness, the cosmopolitan range of setting, allusion and characterization. What we do not get is the vernacular quality in Dürrenmatt's standard German; and this is the vehicle of his rootedness in common sense, in a popular good sense.

4

For West German writers, the demonology—and de-demonization—of the Third Reich remained a special preoccupation throughout the 1960s and 1970s, eliciting plays, novels and biographical accounts that were widely read and discussed, like the family chronicles of Walter Kempowski (who had been sentenced to imprisonment in the GDR for a political offence, serving eight of the twenty-five years before his amnesty and departure for West Germany). Among such works, Siegfried Lenz's *Die Deutschstunde* (1968; *The German Lesson*) owed its appeal to a traditional realism of minutely observed detail, made possible by a single regional setting, to the deliberate exclusion of reference to anything outside the experience and consciousness of the characters—provincial characters at that, even though one of them is a painter with an international reputation.

Most of the action takes place during the last two years of the war, at and around Rugbüll in Schleswig-Holstein, close to the Danish border—a region familiar to Lenz from his own war experiences in the German Navy and his desertion in Denmark before the end of the war. It is narrated in retrospect by Siggi Jepsen, who has been told to write an essay on 'The Joys of Doing One's Duty' at the school for juvenile delinquents to which he was remanded after the war, for reasons bound up with the story he tells: an account of the conflict between his father—the local policeman—and the Expressionist painter Max Ludwig Nansen, whose situation and career bear a strong resemblance to those of Emil Nolde. In the policeman's relentless pursuit of the joys of doing his duty, he not only persecutes his old friend the painter, who once saved his life, but drives his own three children to rebellion and delinquency. The policeman's older son, Klaas, who is serving in the army, becomes a deserter on the run. His daughter, Hilke, poses in the nude for the painter—an offence not only against the puritanical ethos of the community but against her father's authority, since Nansen has been condemned as a 'degenerate artist', and it is Jepsen's duty to enforce the ban by making sure that no new work is done by the artist and by confiscating finished paintings. As for Siggi, a boy of eleven or twelve at the time, his defiance cannot be open or drastic. While pretending to help his father by spying on the painter, he does his best to save forbidden paintings in secret hiding-places, just as he becomes the secret ally of Klaas by hiding him.

Lenz had learned the lesson of de-demonization taught by Günter Grass, avoiding any heroic confrontations between the forces of good and evil. Jepsen does his duty; Nansen applies a related stubbornness and cunning to the business of getting on with his work. If *Die Deutschstunde* is a political novel at all—and it can be read and enjoyed as though it were not—what we gather from it is that the Nazi régime was upheld by 'decent' and conscientious executives—like any other 'law and order'. The demons of earlier fictions about the Third Reich are absent. The nearest thing to an irrational compulsion in Jepsen is his inability to leave Nansen alone after the end of the war, yet such behaviour could be attributed to his stubbornness, narrow-mindedness and inflexibility, or simply to force of habit. Similarly, Siggi cannot break his habit of concealing Nansen's paintings even when, after the war, Nansen has been rehabilitated. It is for removing paintings from a Hamburg exhibition of Nansen's work that Siggi is institutionalized as a delinquent. His father remains the policeman at Rugbüll, and we can be sure that Jepsen will serve the Federal Republic as loyally and meticulously as he had served the Third Reich.

From American writers like Hemingway, Lenz had also learned the lesson of understatement in realistic fiction. Since such realities as concentration camps, Hitler's 'final solution' or other major horrors of the war—such as the intensive bombing of German cities not very far from Rugbüll—do not impinge on the awareness of his provincials, they are not mentioned in the novel. At one point Nansen is summoned to an interrogation by the Gestapo, but Siggi—who knows or imagines all kinds of things he has not witnessed himself—is as reticent about their experience as Nansen himself. Nor are we told why Nansen's wife dies of an undiagnosed illness, although the symptoms are graphically described. That her illness is psychosomatic, is implied but never stated. Rarely does the narrator draw a moral or generalize, and when he does, within the context of a book whose ironies and satirical strands are as unobtrusive as its seriousness, the effect is almost startling.

The seriousness, in fact, comes over not as a quality of the writer's mind but of the persons in the novel, including the many subsidiary local characters. That is why *Die Deutschstunde* has a density and solidity reminiscent of nineteenth-century novels about provincial life. To the cultural dictators in Berlin, Nansen may be a degenerate artist, because the whole of the Expressionist movement, like any art that was not subservient to ideology, fell into that category; but in his local context Nansen is a man like any other, accepted by the community even when his work has been condemned. The postman and the innkeeper may not be aware that Nansen is 'their' painter, through a deep involvement with their locality, the landscape, the colours, the weather, the light, but they do know that he talks and behaves much as they do, that he belongs to the place. The same shared background accounts for the special relationship between Nansen and Jepsen, an avant-garde painter and a policeman, a relationship that would be virtually inconceivable in a more sophisticated urban environment. As somebody remarks about Nansen at the opening of his post-war exhibition in Hamburg, 'he's German to the bone, more German than six Pomeranian grenadiers put together'. Other members of the new cultural smart set smile at the painter's old-fashioned formality of dress, 'buttoned half-boots, striped stovepipe trousers, a morning coat shiny with age, silk stock and tie-pin, high stand-up collar and, on his huge, heavy head, an old-fashioned bowler'. Earnestness, stiffness and heaviness are traits that Nansen shares with all the people around Rugbüll, as with his antagonist, the policeman.

Whatever political allegory may have been worked into the realistic fabric of this novel, it is not a simple or unambiguous one. If we read the novel as an account of the Nazi era, we could object that rural Schleswig-Holstein was not Germany, that the new technology of destruction is scarcely hinted at, that the conflict between a policeman's devotion to duty and a painter's to the freedom of his art does not, and could not possibly, convey either the banality or the monstrosity of evil that distinguished National Socialism from other authoritarian systems. Nansen, we are told, had once been a supporter of the régime, as Nolde was also believed to have been; and he is among those members of the community who are called upon to form a last-minute home guard when the war is lost. Since he remains a member of that community to the end, he cannot represent the victims of Nazism, who ceased to exist not only as artists, but as human beings.

Yet, as I have suggested, political allegory need not be read into this novel at all. That is the advantage of the kind of realism of which it is a late instance—a realism of people, places, things, rather than ideas. The ironic frame of the narrative, the German lesson of the title, also shifts its relevance to post-war Germany, with its residual tradition of rigidly upheld officialdom; and beyond it, to any other society in which duty can conflict with judgement, conscience, or independence of mind, almost any society one can think of. What is more, Nansen does not merely stand for the freedom of self-expression. His function in the novel is closely related to that of Siggi as narrator and witness: it has to do with seeing—the title of one chapter—and the necessary interaction between imagination and outward reality. This makes the novel not only an example but a justification of the kind of realism its author has continued to practise.

As a painter Nansen sees and interprets the world around him. Jepsen, on the other hand, is blinkered both by his servility and by his officiousness, self-deceived even about the desire for power that motivates his obedience, so that duty can yield joys. This ambivalence comes out in Jepsen's dealings with his young son, the narrator, whom he thrashes for going out of the house without permission, yet also makes use of for his professional ends, revealing an almost abject dependence on him. As for his older son, the deserter, Jepsen no longer sees him as a son or as a human being, but is prepared to hand him over to the 'authorities' for punishment. In all such dealings Jepsen has the support of his wife, whose love for her children is not in doubt.

Lenz's deliberately narrow perspective in this novel needs no other justification than the excellence of its rendering of these family relations between people who are laconic, humourless, and contained in a patriarchal order that it never occurs to them to question. The reader is brought close to them not so much through what they say as by what they do, what they look like, what they eat; by the gestures and movements that convey what they feel and think; and it is left to him or her to draw conclusions about this patriarchal order which—at least among the peasantry and petty officialdom of provincial regions— remained almost intact behind the political and military machinery of the Third Reich. That 'the joys of doing one's duty' were still a fit subject to be assigned for a German essay in the progressive, seemingly enlightened institution in which Siggi is being reformed after the war, is one of Lenz's pervasive, but unobtrusive ironies. Another is Siggi's relationship there with his warder, Joswig, who constantly reminds Siggi that smoking is forbidden in the cells, yet supplies him with cigarettes. If we insist on looking for allegories in the book, and Joswig may be taken to be a post-war variant of the policeman father-figure, its implications for the Federal Republic, too, remain open and ambiguous.

Siegfried Lenz's absorption in his characters and their world has led him to do without one traditional ingredient of the realistic novel. Packed though it is, with the almost palpable details of the day-to-day experience, the novel scarcely touches on sexual love. Siggi's story spans his puberty; by the time he has finished telling it he is twenty-one. Yet sexual experience or sexual fantasy would have been out of place not only in his essay but in the puritanical world his narrative evokes. Instead, we get Siggi's and Nansen's emphasis on seeing, so that there is no lack of sensuous substance, but an abundance of it. Certain episodes, like that in which Siggi and his sister wade out at low tide to catch a flatfish with their hands and feet, stick in one's mind with the persistence of lived experience. So, too, does the whole natural setting, with its changing light and winds, its harshness and heaviness. If Lenz transposed certain recollections of his childhood in what was East Prussia to the vicinity of his West German home, from the Baltic to the North Sea, the imaginative graft took; and the key to that achievement, too, is the gift of seeing.

5

Rolf Hochhut established his reputation in the 1960s, when there was a widespread antagonism to closed, autonomous structures in the arts, and younger readers in West Germany came to accept many varieties of anti-fiction, semi-fiction or quasi-fiction, for the good not of their souls—souls were out of fashion—but of their social and political awareness. Even if we see Hochhut's *Eine Liebe in Deutschland* (1978; *A German Love Story*) as a belated product of this trend, which had been largely superseded, if not reversed, by 1978, it remains a strangely hybrid and anomalous piece of work.

For one thing, even in the didactic, activist and would-be dialectical 1960s, most practitioners of this kind of writing had learned from Brecht and others that enlightenment was best served if the data were presented as 'objectively' as possible, deductions left to the recipients. Although history has been his dominant interest from the start, Hochhut has never been content to let history speak for itself, but has boosted it with rhetoric as old-fashioned as that of his early blank verse play *Der Stellvertreter* (1963; *The Deputy*) or that of some of the historical passages of *Eine Liebe in Deutschland*. The intervening fifteen years, it seems, did not teach him to trust the tale, or trust his readers to trust the tale; and in one class of readers at least this lay preacher's sermonizing alone sets up an insuperable barrier of mistrust.

Although sub-titled 'a novel' *A German Love Story* was classified both as 'Fiction' and as 'History—1933–1945' in the Library of Congress Catalogue. Its German book publication, after pre-publication of part of it in a newspaper, also made it a contribution to the history of the post-war era, since it precipitated a libel action that led to the resignation of Karl Filbinger, Prime Minister of Baden-Württemberg. Its author and the editors responsible for the extract in *Die Zeit* also had the distinction of being described by Dr Franz-Josef Strauss as 'rats and bluebottles'—a distinction duly recorded in the book, though as an instance of the 'long tradition of contempt for intellectuals, for reason and the things of the mind' that Hochhut attributes to Germany. Where politicians really despise those things, they do not bother to insult mere writers of books.

In fact this is one of several dubious theses expounded by Hochhut in the formidable superstructure of historical documentation and analysis he has imposed on his rather thin fiction, the love story of the title. It is the story of an affair between a German wife and mother, separated from her husband by his war service, and a Polish prisoner-of-war working for a coal merchant in the same South-West German village. The love affair and the execution by hanging of the young Pole, Stasiek Zasada, are historical events in themselves, and Hochhut based the externals of his story on the evidence of survivors. A separate chapter explains the difficulties of writing fiction about real characters, most of them still alive, and few of them prepared to tell the whole truth, even if they remember it after a lapse of thirty-six years. If the love story itself is thin, it is because Hochhut cares more about the truth of history than about the truth of fiction; and because the political implications of Zasada's death by slow strangulation—the law demanded that he be put to death by a fellow Polish labourer, not by a practised executioner, and the killing was bungled—could not be worked into the fabric of the story itself. Committed as he is to literal truthfulness, most of the time Hochhut refrained from giving heroic dimensions to the two lovers, who are drawn to each other by sexual attraction and deprivation in the first place, not by defiance of laws that scarcely trouble them. This very discrepancy between simple human needs and a system of arbitrary prohibitions not ethical but ethnic does link the love story to the superstructure; but Pauline and Stasiek are not given the depth or individuality that would make them adequate carriers of the moral load placed on the story by Hochhut's rhetoric, as in this passage more suitable for a newspaper leader or political speech than to the most fustian of *romans à thèse*:

> We are entitled to question the purpose of human existence when human beings like Hitler, Goering or Goebbels have the power to transform a continent into a charnel-house and millions of their fellow creatures into pitiful zombies, but we must never leave it at that. Although the sun that rises above the battlefield can do nothing for the dead, it cheers the living to see how a night of tyranny can be withstood by the resolution, cunning, intelligence and tenacity of those who were so much weaker, if not well-nigh defenceless, when darkness fell. But for the knowledge that Hitler and his cronies were ultimately confronted by those who (like Churchill) had warned the world against them for a decade, and that they were lured into a position where they could be vanquished by the concerted efforts of millions upon millions, any historian would be limited to the sad and soul-destroying functions of an obituarist. All that makes war-time stories tolerable is that,

even in the twentieth century, their retelling can be a hymn to heroism, as well as a dirge.

Just because, on the personal level, Hochhut's love story is so truthful and commonplace, it could not possibly be described as a 'hymn to heroism'; and it fails to work even as a dirge, because the evil done to the protagonists—not excluding the absent husband of whom we are told that he is decent enough not to turn against his wife after her exposure—is authentic precisely by virtue of its drab banality, which grows macabre and grotesque, rather than pathetic, in the concluding account of Zasada's execution. The nearest thing to heroism on Pauline's part is the recklessness with which she visits her young lover in hospital, and her writing of the letters that will incriminate them both; but nothing in the narrative suggests that she does these things in full awareness of the likely consequences.

An early chapter is devoted to Pauline's neighbour Maria, and her desire to obtain possession of Pauline's greengrocer's shop by denouncing the relations she suspects between Pauline and Stasiek. Since Maria takes no part in Pauline's and Stasiek's incrimination, and is simply dropped from the story at that point, Maria's envious scheming, as revealed in conversation with her airman husband on leave, serves only as an exemplification of one of Hochhut's theses about the Third Reich. More blatantly still, Stasiek's last night before the execution, spent in a cell together with his reluctant executioner, Victorowicz— who, most conveniently for Hochhut, but not for his readers, happens to be a student of history—is given up to a long dialogue about the First World War and predictions of 'Poland's revenge' after the Second. Since Stasiek has not been motivated by national pride up to that point, and would have found it much harder to become Pauline's lover in the circumstances if he had been, and may possibly have been of German descent on his mother's side, this 'heroic' dialogue, too, becomes part of the superstructure, and one that creaks so loudly that it endangers the effectiveness of all that has gone before, on the level of plain, psychologically plausible story-telling.

That leaves the history—and the theses mixed up with the history, just as the history, in places, is mixed up with the story. I have already touched on one of these theses, that 'blind insensate homicidal mania, a fundamental impulse common to Hitler and a handful of his closest henchmen, came to fulfilment in Germany only because the country possesses such a long tradition of contempt for intellectuals, for reason and the things of the mind'. Even in the Third Reich—Hochhut's primary concern in this work—intellectuals were not despised, but hated and feared as a danger to the régime. Hence the burning of books. Hence the institution of a 'Ministry of Public Enlightenment and Propaganda', Goebbels' Ministry, even before the war. Hence the approaches of Goebbels to Stefan George, a poet who represented all that was most exclusive, fastidious and élitist in the German aspiration to 'Adel des Geistes'—Thomas Mann's phrase—an aristocracy of the mind. That Goebbels wanted, but could not get, the blessing of so austere a figure as George is significant because Hochhut may be right in seeing Goebbels as 'less an intellectual than a believer—one who thought what he wished to believe rather than believed what he thought': even for a German of that kind George's prestige would have been a valuable asset to the régime. The very political effectiveness of Hochhut's book contradicts his claim that this 'contempt for intellectuals' was carried over into the Federal Republic, where successful writers are granted an authority which their British and American counterparts neither claim nor receive.

On the contrary, it is just because the process of secularization I have mentioned established German intellectuals as a—largely conformist—clerisy that awkward customers among them have qualified for persecution or suppression—proof that they are not despised. Here 'things of the mind'—and the German word 'Geist' confuses the issue, because it means both intellect and spirit—must be clearly distinguished from the exercise of reason, intellectual independence and scepticism. These are not confined to intellectuals, and were often conspicuous by their absence among the German intelligentsia as a whole. In the Third Reich, and long before it, this critical function of the intellect was regarded as un-German, Jewish or French, as the case might be, and subversive. Such anti-intellectualism is far from being a German peculiarity, as any historian ought to know, though its most vehement formulations have been German ones.

Another of Hochhut's theses—also printed on the jacket of the American edition, in large type—is taken from Nietzsche: 'Insanity is a rare thing in individuals, but habitual to groups, parties, nations and ages.' This thesis is not only irrefutable, and relevant, as the other is not, but it could have justified the formal structure of Hochhut's book, his interlinking of chapters about the leaders of the Third Reich with his story about Pauline, Stasiek, their friends and persecutors—not one of whom is anything but 'sane' and 'normal' even in the act of serving the 'homicidal mania' that has been constitutionalized as law. That difficult and ambitious design, though, would have called for a more whole-heartedly imaginative and more searching fiction, as for a more rigorously selective and coherent presentation of the corporate insanity.

Hochhut's historical researches were thorough enough, and one must assume the existence of a readership that will assimilate them more readily in the form of a semi-fiction than it would as one more contribution to the already forbidding corpus of purely documentary material about the period—very much as the *Holocaust* film, another hybrid with comparable flaws, seems to have stirred the conscience of a German public with no time for the documents. If so, one must also assume that Hochhut's book accomplished what it was meant to accomplish, but with grave misgivings and regrets—not only on artistic grounds—about the continuing need for such enlightenment. Even outside Germany there has been a tendency to forget that the categories of 'Aryan' and 'non-Aryan' did not mark the limits of the coarse biologism of the Third Reich, that 'Aryan' Slavs were close to Jews and Gipsies on the extermination list, though the Slav intermixture in the German population would have proved inseparable in practice, and certain Poles could be officially 'Germanized' if their physiques accorded with a purely hypothetical 'Nordic' phenotype. Hochhut's reminders of those pernicious absurdities may have been useful; but nothing in the story or the history—least of all the 'heroic' intimations of the 'Poland's Revenge' chapter—offers any way out of the insanity (to which, alas, one must also add the stupidity) of 'groups, parties, nations and ages'. When even 'non-Aryan', black African or Arab, leaders of nations can still express admiration for Hitler, the resignation of one of his former executives in a reconstituted German State seems a small victory to be set against the truth of Nietzsche's remark.

Other small victories of that kind, won by other German writers— even poets—in the Federal Republic, after controversies in the media or libel actions, bear out what I have written about the special power of the written word in Germany; but such victories belong to history, not to imaginative literature, whose mills grind slowly and mysteriously, no matter what they are grinding—whether the stuff of history or the stuff of natural time. 'Realistic' though it may be to cross that border-line between politics and art, realism in imaginative literature is a mode that can be 'sacramental', a religious affirmation of the quiddity of people, places and things, or questioning and rebellious. What it cannot do, while remaining true to itself, is force the pace of its processes and effects for the sake of action and immediate usefulness.

6

If, to Heinrich Böll, realism was sacramental, it was so on the grounds of a religious commitment. The German post-war writer who may come to be regarded as the supreme realist, Uwe Johnson, professed no such religious commitment or faith. For him, it was the discipline of realism itself, an exploratory realism that took no accepted reality at its face value, but searched out a truth that was individual, social and political at once, with the individual consciousness as a gauge that reflected and refracted news of the world. To this exploratory realism Johnson was dedicated, religiously so, with a persistence and obstinacy that made no concessions to anyone, least of all to the lazy minds of readers—the majority of novel readers—who prefer realities that are ready-made. From the start his work was difficult, in every possible sense of the word, difficult for him and difficult for the readers whom he expected and trusted to share the difficulties with him. From the start, too, the realities that his fictions reflected and refracted were divided ones, since his later adolescence and youth, his intellectually formative years, were spent in the GDR, under a system that found him unsuitable for employment in any public institution—and literature was such a public institution. As his very first novel, *Ingrid Babendererde*, shows, even at the age of nineteen Uwe Johnson was not prepared to accept ready-made realities of an ideological kind. This extraordinary work, written between 1953 and 1956, was not published in either Republic until after Uwe Johnson's death; but it deserved to be, since it anticipates the obliqueness of Johnson's mature works, down to the syntactical and lexical oddities, as well as a consciousness divided even then between the realities of the two German nations. It was not till 1959 that Johnson crossed over to West Berlin, not as a defector to the other side—a status he always rejected—but simply because his second novel, *Mutmassungen über Jakob*, had been accepted for publication in West Germany, and there were no prospects of publication or employment for him in the GDR.

The pressures that forced anyone who dared to think for himself or herself into dissidence and, if possible, emigration—even if, like Johnson, they never ceased to be socialists, committed to the ethos of socialism but not to the bureaucratic apparatus that suppressed the ethos in practice—had dominated the first novel, about a generation of school-leavers that was Johnson's own. His second novel established him in West Germany as *the* novelist of a divided consciousness that was simplified into a consciousness of political division, if not accommodated to the terminology of the Cold War. Uwe Johnson refused to be pressed into any simple ideological position or choice. When the pressures of politicized publicity in West Germany became too much for him, he went underground—first in New York, where he worked as the anonymous editor of educational books, then to Sheerness on the Isle of Sheppey, where he lived in complete privacy as a writer, known only to a few friends beyond a group of local neighbours and pub regulars who gave him the name of 'Charlie', finding his Christian name unpronounceable in English.

Even in those last years, when those locals were his community—and to belong to a community was a prerequisite for Uwe Johnson's life and art—his loyalty had to be divided between them and a second community, that of his readers. When a family crisis and the serious illness it precipitated made it almost impossible for him to work on his last novel, only this other loyalty compelled him to complete the last of its four parts or 'instalments', as he called them; and by then the consciousness of its protagonist, Gesine Cresspahl, reflected and refracted the social and political realities of at least four different orders, those of the Third Reich, of East Germany, West Germany and of the New York of 1967–1968, its immediate setting. To those four orders one could add the pre-war England of the Richmond period in the life of Gesine's father and the ideal order, present only in the minds and needs of all Uwe Johnson's main characters, against which all his minutely registered outward realities are measured. Without this imaginative commitment, which for him was also a moral one, he could never have sustained a realism so meticulous—a realism that demanded the most minute research into an East German railway system, for *Mutmassungen über Jakob*, into the world of racing cyclists, for *Das Dritte Buch über Arnim* (1961), into countless American institutions and habits for the compendious *Jahrestage* (1970–1983)—not to mention those for the least of his minor works, like the biographical researches for his little book on Ingeborg Bachmann, *Eine Reise nach Klagenfurt* (1974), or into newspaper reports for his piece on the Second World War munitions ship still sunk and unsalvaged not far from his house in Sheerness. This was another peculiarity of Johnson's realism, as difficult for him as for his readers: that truths must be approached through facts, including facts of kinds most recalcitrant to the imagination—like the reports and leaders from the *New York Times* interwoven with the narrative of *Jahrestage*—and however dry, trivial or even boring; and not in order to 'support' foregone conclusions as evidence, as in Hochhut's book, but to be absorbed into the reader's consciousness as constituents of a highly complex reality. Uwe Johnson's powerful and idiosyncratic imagination had to submit to that discipline, his discipline of realism; and so did the imaginations of his readers, if they were prepared at all to join him in his explorations, not put off at once by the austerity and subtlety of his manner.

The intricacies of his themes, manner and plots are such that no examples or summaries can be offered here. Even the shortest and slightest of his works would cáll for more; and the 1891 pages of *Jahrestage*—only part of which, an abridged version of the first two parts, was translated for the English version, *Anniversaries*—called for a guide or skeleton book as a companion to the four volumes of the German edition. Nor is it the length of the work alone that demands repeated readings of key passages of any reader without a memory as capacious and tenacious as the author's, when the consciousness of Gesine and her daughter Marie between them extends over those four orders, and the action switches throughout from one to the other. This consciousness, in turn, is continually modified, corrected and enriched by the experience of other characters in the novel, as by the author's reflections and refractions of those multiple realities in his ordering of them and his manner—a manner whose austerity does not preclude irony and humour.

Reticent though he was about his own person and work, Johnson did provide clues to them in essays collected in the volume *Berliner Sachen* (1975)—especially in 'Versuch, eine Mentalität zu erklären', about persons brought up in the GDR, and 'Concerning an Attitude of Protesting', a piece written in English for a symposium of statements about the Vietnam War—and in his Frankfurt lectures on poetics, his own, published in 1980 as *Begleitumstände*. Two of his shorter works of fiction, *Zwei Ansichten* (1965) and *Skizze eines Verunglückten* (1982), can also help readers on the threshold of Johnson's difficult, but rewarding, explorations of reality. *Zwei Ansichten* traces the effects of the Berlin Wall on the relations between an East German nurse and a West German press photographer, in a way less tentative and speculative than that of Johnson's more demanding works. The late story, set in New York, has a tragic pathos and starkness, due not only to its brevity but to a reduction of detail in the telling, that could have initiated a new phase in Uwe Johnson's writing, had the tragedy not been his own, and his life too short.

VI   Displaced Persons

1

Nothing is more admirable about Uwe Johnson's achievement as a writer of fiction than the tenacity that enabled him to draw throughout his working life on the environment that ceased to be his in childhood. (He was born on the Mecklenburg-Pomeranian border that became part of Poland after the war.) The kind of realism he practised could not have been sustained without it. Yet his memory, imagination and sympathy could not only avail itself of that sustenance despite all his displacements—much as Joyce's could cling to his Dublin—but they could also bridge the displacements, assimilate other realities and relate themselves to other worlds—a feat so difficult and so rare that it goes far towards explaining the difficulties of Johnson's major works.

The dispersion of German literature during the Third Reich was followed by other dispersions due to the division of Germany, the loss of its Eastern territories, but also to the self-exile of many writers after the war, for the most diverse reasons, as well as to the inability of many refugees from Nazism ever to settle again in either Germany. Because a displacement of that kind was the rule, rather than the exception, social realism could not be taken for granted as a norm, as it continued to be taken for granted in other literatures after the war. Not only the extreme political discontinuity caused so many post-war German novelists to grapple with the past before they could begin to focus their attention on the present. Whole regions and whole ways of life had been lost and, with them, the roots that feed imaginative realism. Not all the displaced writers succeeded in putting down new roots, as Heinz Piontek, a Silesian by birth, did in his novels set in Munich. Another Silesian, Horst Bienek, has returned again and again to his lost homeland in his—after traumatic experiences that included a hard labour sentence of twenty-five years in the GDR, commuted after four years.

The work of Ingeborg Bachmann, whose early death in Rome was felt to be as great a loss as the suicide of Paul Celan in Paris at the age of forty-nine—the same age at which Uwe Johnson died in England—shows an extraordinary tension between her regional Austrian roots and a self-exile maintained from 1950 until her death in 1973, at the age of forty-seven. The poems to which she owed her early fame combined a modern and individual sensibility with a prosody and diction that seemed traditional, compared with the work of most of her coevals of whatever lineage, that of Benn, Brecht or the linguistically experimental that has flourished in Austria since the 1950s. The uninhibited eloquence of poems like 'An die Sonne' (To the Sun) from her second collection *Anrufung des grossen Bären* of 1956, was attributed to a peculiarly Austrian traditionalism—also striking in the work of Christine Lavant, another Carinthian even more idiosyncratic within her traditional forms, or of Christine Busta, as firmly rooted within her native Vienna. Yet already in Ingeborg Bachmann's first collection of 1953, *Die Gestundete Zeit*, there were poems much more halting and uneasy, in theme as much as in rhythm; and the lyrical flow that had reassured readers still attuned to the euphonies of an earlier era could not be carried over into her later work at all. No third collection of poems followed those early books; and her few later poems enact a loss of spontaneity that has to do with displacement.

Ingeborg Bachmann had also been a prose writer from her youth, contributing short stories to periodicals when she was in her early twenties. These were apprentice work; but two unpublished stories written before those in her book *Das dreissigste Jahr* (1961) and included in her posthumous *Werke* are remarkable. They are 'Anna Maria', a study in the conflicting views of a woman's character and conflicting rumours about her actions, that reduces realism to speculations like Uwe Johnson's about his Jakob, and 'Der Schweisser'. The welder of the story finds a book by Nietzsche in a café, reads it, and begins to live by it, losing his job, neglecting his consumptive wife and the children, and finally killing himself. The 'blinding light' in welding is linked symbolically to the 'blinding light of knowledge'. A doctor in the story tries in vain to make that connection for Reiter, the welder, but he is as fatuous as the Doctor in Büchner's *Woyzeck*, and the two orders cannot be bridged. Alienations of this kind were to preoccupy Ingeborg Bachmann as a writer of fiction. The most pervasive of these alienations has to do with an ambivalent relationship to Austria found in many Austrian writers. For Bachmann, this relationship was complicated by the clash between the values she associated with the Carinthia to which her fiction continued to return and those of Vienna, where she lived for a time. This, too, is an old antagonism for Austrian writers. The love-hate relationship to Vienna comes out most strongly in the title story of her collection *Das dreissigste Jahr*, in which Vienna becomes that 'bonfire city in which the most splendid works of music were thrown on the pyre, in which they reviled and spat on that which came from the righteous heretics, the impatient suicides, the daring explorers and inventors, and everything that was straightest in spirit'. This is part of a long rhetorical tirade more biblical, but no less damning, than some of those in the books of Thomas Bernhard, and it resembles Bernhard's, too, in suddenly veering into praise, the celebration of a Joycean 'epiphany'. Another of Ingeborg Bachmann's recurrent themes—she had studied both Heidegger and Wittgenstein, and Vienna was still haunted by the shade of Karl Kraus, the castigator of linguistic corruption as the root of all evils—is also announced in the same story: 'No new world without a new language'. Personal confession and story-telling do not quite cohere in 'Das dreissigste Jahr'. The male protagonist of the story remains a *persona*, and his antagonist, Moll, never puts on much flesh and blood, any more than the girls who appear and vanish. Reality of that kind is what eluded Ingeborg Bachmann in the city, as in later places of exile. In the collection of stories it is 'Jugend in einer österreichischen Stadt'—set in Bachmann's home town, Klagenfurt—that merges her own person in a community.

In the story 'Alles', the linguistic theme becomes part of the plot, since the experiment conducted by the parents hinges on their denying the baby they call 'Fipps' access to the old language that stands in the way of a 'new world'. Predictably, instead of finding his own language and hence his own mode of awareness, precondition of the new world, Fipps backslides into the old Adam and dies, after trying to knife another boy at school. It is the father and narrator of the story who, briefly, experiences a rebirth, before the boy's death and the father's estrangement from his wife, Hanna. Ingeborg Bachmann's quest for the new language, new awareness, and new world was also to be thwarted, whether in Vienna, Zürich, Berlin or Rome. On the political level—and, like most of her coevals, she wanted a change of heart that would transform society—one reason for that is suggested by the story 'Unter Mördern und Irren', about a reunion of war veterans in a Vienna inn and its intrusion on another gathering there of professional men, who also reminisce about the war from contrasted points of view. One thing they have in common is that they leave their wives at home, and these wives wish that their husbands would die. This feminist concern was to become more and more acute in Ingeborg Bachmann's work. In the story it is not a woman, but a stranger who appears at the inn to tell how he could not bring himself to shoot in the war, and was punished for that by imprisonment and psychiatric treatment, who speaks for the alternative order. When he moves from the gathering of professional men to the war veteran group and provokes them, he is killed by them.

The exclusion of men by an erotic transformation is weighed up in the story 'Ein Schritt nach Gomorrah'. A young girl, Mara, stays behind after a party given by Charlotte, a married woman whose husband is away on a business trip, and refuses to leave. Charlotte tries to escape Mara's demands on her by consenting to go out to a night club, though she is tired, and her husband is expected back in the morning. They return to Charlotte's flat, where Charlotte begins to consider the possibility of a liberation through a lesbian relationship. Mara becomes more and more desperate and begins to break things in the flat. The conflict in Charlotte is not resolved. The feminist concern is even more drastic in Bachmann's re-telling of the 'Undine' legend, in which every man whom Undine meets is the same 'Hans' or Jack to her, good at making and using machines, even capable at times of healing or helping, but unable to immerse in the feminine element, water.

Another aspect of the new language and the new world is at the centre of the story 'Ein Wildermuth', about a judge who has to try a namesake, a young man who killed his father and who is incapable of speaking anything but the truth. The judge, who had also loved truthfulness in his youth, suffers a breakdown in court, exasperated by factual evidence that turns on a button expert's quibbling about a button. The judge gives up his profession. His marriage, too, is unsatisfactory, because his wife, Gerda, is a woman who invents the truths by which she lives. Here Bachmann's recurrent, but many-sided, utopia founders against 'a truth of which no one dreams, which no one wants'. Evocative and provocative as they are, the stories in this book are prose complements to Ingeborg Bachmann's poems, prose correlatives never quite 'objective' enough to fuse her concerns with characters and situations that would engage us in their own right.

The later collection of stories, *Simultan* (1972), adds a more secure grasp of the externals of the alien, cosmopolitan Europe of smart sets and intellectuals that still brought Ingeborg Bachmann no closer to a 'new world'. Though the title story is set in Calabria, the man and woman who have met on their travels for a brief, unsatisfactory affair are both from Vienna. It is the character study of the man, a United Nations executive, that marks Ingeborg Bachmann's progress as a writer of the prose fictions on which she concentrated in later life. Psychological penetration, as well as a new lightness of touch, also distinguishes the story 'Probleme, Probleme', her study of a somewhat narcissistic young woman, Beatrix, who finds everything but sleeping a 'horrible imposition', not excluding her friendship with a married man, Erich, much older than herself. Apart from sleeping, only her hairdresser and her make-up are of interest to her. Sexual and personal relations have become a marginal business, with the implication that men and their world can be endured, just, as long as one does not have to take them seriously.

Fictional autonomy is also achieved in the story 'Ihr glücklichen Augen', even though the act of seeing had been celebrated in earlier poems by Ingeborg Bachmann, and diminished sight may have been a personal concern. Miranda, in the story, uses her bad sight both as a means of seeing only what she wishes to see, or can bear to see, and as a way of ensuring her husband Josef's protectiveness. When Josef becomes involved with Miranda's friend Stasi, who is about to be divorced from her husband, Miranda pretends that she, too, has a lover, so as to make the separation easier for herself and for Josef. After a meeting with Josef and Stasi she receives a blow from a revolving door, due to her near-blindness that is both organic and willed. Bachmann's new lightness of touch gives the story a fine balance between comedy and tragedy.

The two last stories in *Simultan* set up tensions between youth and old age, between the urban world of professional people and an older rural order, between new sophistication and old certainties. In 'Das Gebell', it is the attempt by the third or fourth wife of an eminent and rich psychologist to do something for his eighty-five-year-old mother living in poverty and neglect in a city that must be Vienna. The old woman is haunted by a recurrent barking associated with the dog she got rid of when it had attacked her son on one of his rare visits. Franziska, the daughter-in-law, pays with her own money for gifts to alleviate the old woman's extreme poverty, pretending that the money comes from her famous husband, whose complex relationship with his mother is rendered with subtle and mischievous wit. Franziska, though, cannot keep up her own relationship with the man. She returns to her native Carinthia and dies there. Leo Jordan, the psychologist, marries yet again. Franziska's brother receives the bill for the taxi service that had been one of Franziska's presents to the old woman. Such confrontation is even more direct in 'Drei Wege zum See', the concluding story, set in Ingeborg Bachmann's home province, Carinthia, where Elisabeth, a photographer and journalist, is on a visit to her old father. On her mountain walks and in conversation with her father she ponders her life in the cities and her love affairs. Trotta, the man she had come closest to loving wholeheartedly, had died after their separation. Once more, love between women and men is found wanting:

> There was nothing more to be made of it, and it would be best for men and women to keep a distance, have nothing to do with one another, till both have found a way out of a confusion and the distraction, the discordance of all relationships. Then one day something else could evolve, but only then, and it would be strong and mysterious and possess true grandeur, it would be something to which everyone could submit.

She is in the process of separating from her current lover, Philippe, in Paris. At an airport she has a strange encounter with Trotta's Yugoslav cousin, who has something of the aura of Mandryka in Hofmannsthal's comedy *Arabella*. The same vanished Austria of Imperial times is embodied and represented for her in her father, who clings to his old ways in rural solitude, with a dignity and self-sufficiency lost to younger generations. Elisabeth, of course, will have to resume her way of life, take up her career and entanglements. Ingeborg Bachmann was to grapple with hers in ambitious novels only partly completed before her death.

It is her later poems, though, that most poignantly enact the displacement she had chosen and could not undo. 'Exil' was published in 1957 in the international review *Botteghe Oscure*.

Ein Toter bin ich der wandelt
gemeldet nirgends mehr
unbekannt im Reich der Präfekten
überzählig in den goldenen Städten
und im grünenden Land

abgetan lange schon
und mit nichts bedacht

Nur mit Wind mit Zeit und mit Klang

der ich unter Menschen nicht leben kann

Ich mit der deutschen Sprache
dieser Wolke um mich
die ich halte als Haus
treibe durch alle Sprachen

O wie sie sich verfinstert
die dunklen die Regentöne
nur die wenigen fallen

In hellere Zonen trägt dann sie den Toten hinauf

A dead man I am who travels
not registered anywhere
unknown in the realm of the prefects
redundant in the golden cities
and in the countryside's green

written off long ago
and provided with nothing

Only with wind and with time and with sound

who cannot live among human beings

I with the German language
this cloud around me
that I keep as a house
drive through all languages

Oh, how it darkens
those muted those rain tones

only few of them fall

Up into brighter zones it will carry the dead man

That it should be language, the exile's home, that is endangered by the very displacement which has made it his only home, is clarified by the stories. There language is not only the poet's own, but the vehicle of that change in consciousness, conscience and society that Ingeborg Bachmann had left her regional home to find and help bring about. Her later poem 'Ihr Worte', dedicated to Nelly Sachs and contributed in 1961 to a volume in her honour, was followed by only six more poems written between 1964 and 1967. 'Ihr Worte' tells us why Ingeborg Bachmann had come up against a barrier which Nelly Sachs and Paul Celan could cross only by making it the starting-point and precondition of their work.

> Ihr Worte, auf, mir nach!
> und sind wir auch schon weiter,
> zu weit gegangen, geht's noch einmal
> weiter, zu keinem Ende geht's.
>
> Es hellt nicht auf.
>
> Das Wort
> wird doch nur
> andre Worte nach sich ziehn,
> Satz den Satz.
> So möchte Welt,
> endgültig,
> sich aufdrängen,
> schon gesagt sein.
> Sagt sie nicht.
>
> Worte, mir nach,
> dass nicht endgütig wird
> —nicht diese Wortbegier
> und Spruch auf Widerspruch!
>
> Lasst, eine Weile jetzt,
> keins der Gefühle sprechen,
> den Muskel Herz
> sich anders üben.
>
> Lasst, sag ich, lasst.
>
> Ins höchste Ohr nicht,
> nichts, sag ich, geflüstert,
> zum Tod fall dir nichts ein,
> lass, und mir nach, nicht mild
> noch bitterlich,

nicht trostreich,
ohne Trost
bezeichnend nicht,
so auch nicht zeichenlos—

Und nur nicht dies: das Bild
im Staubgespinst, leeres Geroll
von Silben, Sterbenswörter.

Kein Sterbenswort,
Ihr Worte!

Up, you words, follow me!
and if we have gone farther,
too far already, once more
farther let's go, to no end.

It casts no light.

The word
will only drag
other words behind it,
one sentence another.
So world
with finality
would impose itself,
be already said.
Do not say it.

Follow me, words,
so that it will not be final—
not this lust for words
and saying, gainsaying.

For a while now let
none of the feelings speak,
the muscle heart
differently exercise.

Let, I say, let
into the highest ear
nothing, I say, be whispered,
nothing occur to you about death,
let, and follow me, not gently
not bitterly,
not consolingly,
with no consolation
signifying not,
and so not signless either—

And least of all this: the image
in dust floss, empty rolling
of syllables, dying words breathed.

Don't breathe one dying word,
you words!

It would be impertinent to explain or 'interpret' that poem, which is almost untranslatable too, beginning with the German plural 'Worte', which means 'utterances' or 'statements', as distinct from the other plural form, 'Wörter' (vocables). Those two senses of the word are in conflict throughout the poem; and 'Sterbenswort' has an idiomatic sense. 'Kein Sterbenswort', idiomatically, means 'Don't breathe a word!'. Yet poetry has a habit of taking idioms literally, and the 'dying' is very much part of the sense, in a poem on the brink of silence—where even 'on' becomes ambiguous! The trilogy of novels on which Ingeborg Bachmann was working in her last years was to have the overall title *Todesarten* (Ways of Death). They are what remained of Ingeborg Bachmann's utopia, of the 'new world' and the 'new language' for which she had left her home.

2

Historically and biographically, Ingeborg Bachmann's self-imposed displacement or 'exile' could not be more different from the sudden, forcible and incomprehensible exile suffered by Horst Bienek in his youth, when he was a promising young poet and prose writer encouraged by the GDR establishment, and by Brecht. It is the imagination that blurs such distinctions, because it is has little use for motives and circumstances. I have said that Horst Bienek's arrest and punishment, which exiled him to the labour camp Vorkuta in the Northern Urals, was traumatic; and in fact his account of them, in *Traumbuch eines Gefangenen* (1957), scarcely deals with the circumstances, or the political offence imputed to him. It is a 'dreambook' that records the struggle of a mind *in extremis*, plunged—for whatever reasons—into a form of existence it cannot accept as 'real'. As a piece of writing it has more in common with Rimbaud's *Une Saison en enfer*—his account of an alienation largely self-induced, if not existentially 'chosen', in Sartre's sense—than with the countless documentary or fictionally realistic records of such imprisonment. At one point in Bienek's 'dreambook' the nightmare has turned him into an animal, which in turn regresses from an antelope to a dolphin, then to an anemone; and this process is understood as a 'way of death', a mode of dying. What Bienek attempts to render imaginatively in such passages is a loss of reality that threatened to break up his whole organism, severing the functions of his mind from those of his body, and leaving a body he can no longer feel to be his own.

Bienek came closer to fictional narrative in a later prison book, *Die Zelle* (1968), a first-person novel about a former art teacher whose anguish is due less to his physical condition than to the isolation that deprives him of all sense of time, when even his graffiti are removed from the walls of the cell; nothing happens, and it is as though nothing has ever happened, nothing will happen again, so that the convict finds himself longing even for interrogation or torture, any happening that would make him feel alive. Even in this less dream-like novel, though, Bienek was less concerned with the political system that inflicted the punishment than with the condition of extreme self-estrangement that long prison sentences induce. One reason may be that his own 'case', politically, remained incomprehensible to him, and that this incomprehensibility was part of the experience he was impelled to record. Another may be a reluctance to profit as a writer by the Cold War, as he would inevitably have done by placing more emphasis than he did on the political circumstances and implications.

A third has already been implied, and has to do with the imagination. Bienek began as a poet; and one part of his collection of poems *was war was ist* (1966), the part sub-titled 'Unsere Asche' (Our Ashes), touches on the German extermination camps, as well as on the experiences Bienek himself had suffered. Even in these poems circumstantial details matter less than the violence that political systems have inflicted on individuals in our time; and the longest poem in this section is a meditation on time and memory, on the disruption of both by violence and the possible mending of both by 'that which is/what will be'. As the poem states, 'history has no permanence'; and imagination, by its nature, engages with permanent things or tries to extract permanent meaning from things that are ephemeral. That is what Bienek set out to do both in prose and verse.

His novel *Die erste Polka* (1975) was followed closely by his book of poems *Gleiwitzer Kindheit* (1976), a selection that included work from the earlier book of poems. The setting of the novel is Bienek's home town, Gleiwitz in Upper Silesia, and the action takes place within a day or two before the outbreak of the Second World War, with distant gunfire to be heard towards the end. Flashbacks serve throughout to fill in the history not only of the main characters but also of the place and region, with its German-Polish symbiosis always threatened by political conflict. As a regional novel, *Die erste Polka* is comparable to the work of two other poet-novelists of the Eastern border regions that have proved so fertile in post-war German literature—not only because their loss has been conducive to nostalgia and so to the freedom of imagination. In this later prose work, though, Bienek's narrative approach is less idiosyncratic than either Grass's or Bobrowski's, and could seem old-fashioned but for his blunt treatment of sexual and erotic behaviour. The historical dimension is deepened by what amounts to a sub-plot, the concern of one of the characters, Montag, with the political leader Korfanty, about whom he plans to write a book. Almost melodramatic, not to say apocalyptic, as the action is, involving what may be murder, rape, and Montag's suicide at the very moment when the 'blitzkrieg' is set off, the novel manages to be neither sensational nor implausible. What is sensational is the historical moment; and plausibility is maintained by the characterization, by Bienek's refusal either to moralize or to idealize. Even the two adolescents Josel and Andreas, like the girl-friend Ulla whom they share, are humanly fallible enough to be convincing; and so is Josel's mother, Valeska, with her combination of Roman Catholic piety with shrewd business operations in real estate on the one hand, her piano teaching on the other. The character of the region, too, is bound up with the characters and conduct of the persons in the novel, and that character is cursed, as well as celebrated, in the course of the action. This rich ambivalence marked the evolution of Bienek into a true novelist. *Die erste Polka* became the first part of a sequence of novels set in Silesia during the war, ending in 1982 with the fourth volume, *Erde und Feuer*, the saturation bombing of Dresden and the Soviet occupation of Bienek's home town.

Although that evolution did not mark a break, like Ingeborg Bachmann's, with an earlier lyrical specialization, the publication of *Gleiwitzer Kindheit* did raise questions about the two media. In the sequence of poems of that name (previously published in Part III of *was war was ist*), and in the other longer poem 'Flucht, vergeblich', the same personal experiences on which Bienek drew for the Gleiwitz tetralogy of novels are evoked or drawn upon, but less persuasively, most of the time, than in the novels. Some essential structuring impetus is lacking in almost all his poems, so that they become statements or notes towards a poem rather than the real, organic thing. All of them are packed with interesting observations and thoughts, but they do not come alive poetically, because their rhythmic and syntactic articulation is not that of lyrical poetry. However close a poem may be to what we know to be Bienek's most urgent preoccupations—and many of them are very close—we rarely feel that the poem had to take this particular form, that its words had to be these words and no other words. This is so even of the later poems first published in the book of selected poems, such as the sequence about Australia, with its interesting, but somehow inappropriate, glosses on Patrick White's *Voss*. There is something marginal, too, in the sequence 'Das Haus', with the possible exception of the shortest piece in it, 'Die Katze', which does have the unity of a poem, despite its seeming casualness.

It is in prose that Bienek seems to have overcome the shock of his extreme displacements, letting imagination make up for memory and for the sensuous immediacy which displacement forbids. Both prose fiction and poetry demand a high degree of concentration, above all; but it may be that they are different kinds of concentration. To me, the prose poetry in Bienek's first book and elsewhere suggests that it is a matter of breath, because breath, in lyrical verse, is what governs movement, syntax and structure, no less than in the singing from which lyrical verse was once inseparable. Most novels can not only accommodate, but positively demand, modulations and variations of breath greater than any that a short poem can contain. Where Bienek's poems fall apart, to my ear, into thoughts, images, conceits, and feelings—all of them authentic enough in themselves—I blame the lack of a gathering breath.

3

Because physical displacement is only one of the many forms of alienation taken for granted by generations of German writers, up to those born during or even after the Second World War, countless 'cases' could be adduced here. Among the distinguished novelists, it is the exceptions, Heinrich Böll and Martin Walser, who have come closest to the modes of social realism regarded as a norm by many readers of fiction; but their regional rootedness did not absolve them from awareness of upheavals and discontinuities inescapable even for writers born and resident in Switzerland. As for Günter Grass, the West German writer younger than Böll with the widest international following, only readers outside the German-speaking nations could need to be reminded that he, too, is a displaced person, and that this displacement is of crucial relevance to the books that established his fame.

The traumatic shock suffered by Peter Härtling in his childhood was due less to his physical displacement—from Saxony to Olmütz (now Olomouc) in Moravia, hence to Austria and finally to Suabia, all before the age of eleven—than to his Nazification at school and the death of both his parents in 1946, his father's in a Russian prisoner-of-war camp, his mother's by suicide after their flight to Suabia. Härtling's early work both in verse and prose neither recorded nor hinted at the shock. Only hindsight and his later work reveal that the very playfulness of his early poems and their seeming remoteness from any social or historical concern were his way of deflecting it into art. In his prose, too, Härtling became a specialist not in impersonality but transpersonality, on the borderline of fiction and biography; and the subjects he chose were bound up with his need for the very regional roots of which he had been deprived—Slavic and possibly Hungarian on his father's side, Suabian on his mother's.

His second novel, *Niembsch oder der Stillstand* (1964), is a free set of variations—or 'suite', as he called it—based on the life of the Austro-Hungarian poet Nikolaus Lenau, who died in an asylum in 1850. Härtling takes from Lenau's life and loves only those facts and circumstances that accord with his theme; and it is the poems which Härtling had published before the novel that show us how personal a theme it was. Lenau's consuming desire to escape from time and attain a state of stillness—fulfilled in his madness, Härtling's book suggests—accords exactly with Härtling's practice as a poet at this period, with his flight from historical or directly autobiographical allusions into timeless and trans-personalized fantasy. In his poems, Härtling had created a figure, Yamin, evolved from the fantasy figure Elis in a number of poems by Georg Trakl: one of several instances of Härtling's earlier acts of trans-personification, and one that is characteristic of Härtling's difficult and gradual approach to reality by way of self-identification with figures that could be imaginary or real, as long as they were remote enough from his biological person. (Though depth psychology is something I prefer not to dabble in, it is worth pointing out that Christoph Meckel, another creator of fantasy figures in post-war German fiction—and figures sometimes close to those of Romantic fairy-tale, archetypal as Yamin—was also moved in later years to write an account of childhood relations with his father; and that, in their different ways, both Meckel's *Suchbild* (1980) and Härtling's *Nachgetragene Liebe* of the same year mark the point of intersection of fantasy with biographical reality.)

Niembsch's means of escaping time, in the novel, is to engage in a sequence of amorous adventures in the manner of Don Juan, the subject of a long poem he is trying to write at this juncture, after his return from America, where he had vainly hoped to escape from civilization in some virgin forest. His hope is that repetition, that is, the repetition of love affairs conducted for their own sake, will lead to stasis, a suspension of time. Yet he cannot quite avoid attachment to some of his mistresses as individual persons, quite especially to Karolina von Zarg (who corresponds to Sophie von Löwenthal in the historical Lenau's life). Later, he enters into a love affair with two sisters so much alike that he cannot tell them apart and makes love to both of them. He becomes engaged to a young girl of eighteen, but this relationship serves to cure him of his amorous adventures, when the girl turns out to be after his money and social rank. (Lenau was the pen-name of an aristocrat, Niembsch von Strehlenau.) He breaks off the engagement after making the girl his mistress and returns to the house of Karoline, a married woman whose husband is his friend, in time to be present at her death. At her deathbed he goes out of his mind—his last and most effectual release, other than through his art, from time and personal attachments.

In an earlier novel, Härtling had attempted to get to grips directly with historical and moral conflicts that he shared with German contemporaries, but without that prerequisite for realism which Günter Grass called 'de-demonization'. With *Niembsch* he had found the indirect way he was to make his own until he was ready to face up to realities about himself. Meanwhile he also began to find new roots, a new place in society, by a commitment both to his region, Suabia, and to the causes of disarmament and conservation.

The most daring of Härtling's operations on the border-line of fiction and biography, and within the zone of his Suabian concerns, was his *Hölderlin* (1976), a work of more than six hundred pages, sub-titled 'a novel', but open to scruples that were a biographer's. During the preceding decade, Hölderlin's status as the most poetic of German poets had been tested by the rigorous standards of 'social usefulness', in ideological controversies occasioned in part by Peter Weiss's stage play *Hölderlin* (1971) and the less tendentious radio play by the East German poet Stephan Hermlin, *Scardanelli*, published in West Berlin in 1970. Since these were the kind of controversies from which Peter Härtling had distanced himself, to his detriment, his very subject placed him on dangerous ground. In 1974, true, the literary annual *Literaturmagazin* had published an essay by Karin Struck, 'Der Dichter ist ein arbeitender Mensch' (The poet is a working man), about Hölderlin's accessibility to readers other than the academic and learned exegetes who had tended to regard him as their property; and in 1975 that scholarly establishment was challenged by the polemical prospectus for a new edition of Hölderlin's works by its non-academic editor, D. E. Sattler.

Peter Härtling could have withdrawn from this battlefield into the kind of imaginative freedom he had allowed himself in the earlier book based on Lenau's life, if his development had not been one towards realism. Had this not been so, he could have changed the names of historical personages or confined himself to a single crisis or epiphany in Hölderlin's life, as Büchner had done in his *Lenz*, Robert Walser in his *Kleist in Thun* or Thomas Mann in his *Lotte in Weimar*, re-creating his Hölderlin by self-identification, empathy and projection. Härtling did not entirely reject this *persona* procedure, and included passages of interior monologue in his book, but they serve to bridge gaps in the documentary evidence, to which Härtling was remarkably faithful. Härtling chose the hard way, that of faking as little as possible and applying the novelist's imagination to the business of re-creating not Hölderlin's inner life—this could not be re-created, only faked, and it could be left where it belongs, in Hölderlin's own writings—but his environment, circumstances, personal relationships. His Suabian adolescence helped him to render the every-day experience most vividly, despite his repeatedly explicit awareness of all that divided his own experience from Hölderlin's. Härtling's liberal use of Suabian dialect served the same end of placing Hölderlin in a recognizable regional and social setting.

The obvious objection here would be that this is a biographer's approach, not a novelist's. Härtling took on both functions at once, carefully balancing one against the other. Invention, selection and interpretation were needed, in any case, to make sense of the facts and anecdotes that had been patiently gathered by biographical research. What Härtling undertook to do was to turn them into a story, and a convincing one. Because he was so painstaking over details of Hölderlin's outer life, his fiction was even relevant to current debates about Hölderlin's political convictions. Hölderlin is presented as a radical Republican with complicated reservations about the ambiguity of all political action, as brought home to him by the progress of the French Revolution, Napoleon's imperial ambitions and, more immediately, by his involvement with German sympathizers. Hölderlin's friendship with Isaak von Sinclair, who managed to combine seemingly loyal service to the Landgrave of Homburg with a revolutionary commitment, assumes a crucial significance in Härtling's account.

Härtling did avail himself of the novelist's full licence in his treatment of Hölderlin's erotic experience—if only because the biographical records, inevitably, are reticent there. He makes much of Hölderlin's liaison with Wilhelmine Kirms, intimating that the sensual gratification that Hölderlin got from it proved irreconcilable with his need to idealize his loved ones. (Yet, characteristically, Härtling refrains from speculating as to what Hölderlin may have felt about the disappearance of this intelligent and independent woman, or about their daughter, never seen by him, who died in infancy after their separation.) Accordingly, the love affair with Susette Gontard—the only one that promised completeness—remains unconsummated in Härtling's story; and the natural sensuality, too, is shown to have given out in the end, when Hölderlin rejects the sexual advances of a Frenchwoman who put him up on his dangerous journey to Bordeaux. Hölderlin's difficult relationship with his mother, whose devotion to what she wrongly believed to be his needs is seen as a transference to the eldest son of her feelings for two husbands prematurely lost, also receives subtle and sympathetic attention, as does Hölderlin's conflict of allegiance to his 'two fathers'.

Where Härtling's book stops short, and was bound to stop short, is in relating Hölderlin's truly tragic outer life to the poetry, which both re-enacted and transcended the tragedy. A false note is struck wherever quotations of poems are introduced into the story, as in a passage of dialogue between Hölderlin and Susette. Hölderlin may well have read or quoted his poems to Susette, to whom so many of them were addressed; but Härtling had kept his narrative and dialogue on a level that does not permit the juxtaposition—for reasons of tone, not of verisimilitude. Here Härtling's new realism came up against its limits. To have brought together the poetry and the life, the vision and the experience, would have called for the very exertion that broke Hölderlin. Härtling's choice was to render the outer man, 'poor Hölderlin', the *bon enfant* loved for the purity of his aspirations, but punished for it, too, because it was presumptuous and uncompromising. Even in his poetry Hölderlin excelled in the naïve mode; but that naïvety was a triumph of his art, just as his celebrations of innocence were a triumph of his faith over his knowledge. It is the multiple knowledge, the frustration piled on frustration, the humiliation piled on humiliation, that Härtling conveyed in narrative and dialogue whose dominant mode is also naïve, but not on the level of the poetry—or even on that of the intricate theological, philosophical and aesthetic struggles that had to be fought out by Hölderlin before the language of his poetry could be naïve, spare and plain.

What Härtling did achieve is enough for one book. Hölderlin's tragedy is conveyed in it, by understatement, by a decent refusal to go beyond the limits that he set himself or satisfy the expectation of novel-readers looking for a palatable surrogate for Hölderlin's difficult poetry. The ironies of Hölderlin's life, things he did not know that could have palliated the bitter knowledge, were also within Härtling's limits; for instance the love felt for this Republican by a princess, a daughter of the same Landgrave of Homburg to whom Hölderlin dedicated a great poem, thanks to the mediation of that Landgrave's republican minister, Sinclair; or the fact that Hölderlin inherited enough money—held, or withheld, by his mother for his benefit—to have given him the independence and status he lacked throughout his life.

Because Härtling would not venture beyond those self-imposed limits, his account also stops short in time, only skimming the second half of Hölderlin's life. 'I can't get to him any more', Härtling writes in one of the interpolations that define and honestly acknowledge the limits, 'he has closed up . . . I don't know whether he remembers; what he remembers . . . He has left the world he wanted to get to grips with, the world that played cruel tricks on him; and perhaps he was only fooling that world.' The same tact that forbade Härtling more than passing references to Hölderlin's works also forbade him intrusions into the mind of the so-called madman. Nor is that 'madness' treated as a consummation, as in the earlier Lenau fiction. The brief concluding section does include a tribute to the 'simple' Suabian artisan family whose devotion to their ward showed more understanding than did most of Hölderlin's more refined and better-educated friends, not excluding his mother, who never once visited her son when he had disappointed all her hopes for him. It ends with an indirect account of Hölderlin's death in the Tübingen tower, linking his end to his student years, and suggesting once more that Hölderlin was more loved and appreciated in his lifetime, even in his death-in-life, than he knew.

Hölderlin and his friends also appear in Härtling's book of poems *Anreden* of 1977, a collection that showed a development parallel to his development as a prose writer. His later poems are as plain, spare and direct as his early ones were elaborately playful; and they are as undisguisedly personal—even where he addressed persons living or dead, like Hölderlin—as his early ones were trans-personal. This development is carried still farther in the collection *Vorwarnung* (1983), almost to the verge of prose at times, when Härtling's forewarnings of an obliteration both personal and general become so urgent as to leave no room for art; so in 'Der andere Zustand':

> Meine Sätze halten
> mich nicht mehr
> aus.
> Ich höre nichts mehr
> von mir
> Die Wörter haben
> mich verlassen
> und
> totgesagt.

> My sentences no longer
> put up with
> me.
> I hear nothing more
> of me.
> The words have
> left me
> and
> written me off.

In the context of the collection as a whole, it is the general death by war or slow destruction of the earth, rather than the personal one, that leaves no room for the personal language of art, however depersonalized by the foreknowledge. In another poem from that collection, 'Nachgeburt', Härtling's loss of language becomes that of the 'specious words' of literature which, he writes, he has already used up; and this is a poem about 'the child within the man' whom he had also confronted and accepted in his autobiographical book *Nachgetragene Liebe* of 1980. The personal and impersonal crisis grappled with throughout the book of poems has to do with Härtling's belated coming to terms with the childhood experience that culminated in the death of both his parents. As a writer of books for children, and an advocate of children's books that do not patronise children or adulterate their imaginative world,

Härtling has achieved another fusion of his personal and social concerns.

Nachgetragene Liebe retraces Härtling's relations with his father from 1938, when he was five years old, to the time of his father's death. The relationship was a bad one because of his father's silences and his failure to treat his children as anything other than 'the children', creatures treated kindly enough as long as they did not intrude on his work as a lawyer and knew their place. The father's habit of telling a single fairy tale over and over again, but incompletely, suggests that the failure is due to his inability to remember and accept 'the child within the man'. The matter is complicated by the political implications, which reverse the stock father-son conflict in post-war German writing in that it is the son who has been thoroughly Nazified, the father who resists Nazism, up to a point, cautiously and in fear. The father has an affair with a Czech woman and visits a Jewish client, when that has become dangerous, without being able to help him and prevent his deportation. Nor can the father escape his own conscription and the dissolution of his legal practice. When the boy roams the streets with his Hitler Youth friends, his father beats him while on leave. The boy takes his revenge by giving away his mother's love affair with another man. In 1944 the boy is selected for NAPOLA, special training for a Party élite. Resolution of the conflict and the breaking of those silences are prevented by the father's death as a prisoner of war, after the family's flight to Austria. The suicide of Härtling's mother soon after is not mentioned; but in *Vorwarnung* there is a poem, 'Möglicher Aufbruch', that treats suicide as a liberation and compares it to the flight of a bird. This may or may not have a bearing on the liberation from a childhood trauma in the autobiographical book—the last thing that readers of Härtling's early work would have expected of an author so adept in self-concealment. It is when one's precious 'self' becomes a person much like any other that one can dare, and afford, to expose its most painful and shameful secrets. Not every writer reaches that stage, as Härtling has done in his verse and prose, within a mere three decades of hard and various work.

4

Härtling's *Nachgetragene Liebe* has an epigraph taken from a poem by Paul Celan:

> In der Luft, da bleibt deine Wurzel, da,
> in der Luft.

> In the air, that's where your root remains, there,
> in the air.

Literalists and ideologists may question the relevance of that quotation to an account of a Nazi childhood. Other poems by Celan, including the most famous of them all, 'Todesfuge', tell us that this root in the air is that of the Jews exterminated in the death camps, a root to which Celan, the survivor, could connect himself only by lifelong remembrance, a lifelong communion with the dead. Specifically—and Celan's poetry is very specific, very precise about extremities that would have pushed most other poets into hyperbole—the root is up in the air because what remained of those exterminated Jews was smoke: 'as smoke you will rise into air', is the 'Todesfuge' version. The relevance, and propriety, of Härtling's epigraph should not be reduced to a single and simple paradox. It was the shadow of that multiple death that made it so difficult for Härtling to come to terms with his childhood. He could do so only by finding his root, which, for a long time, was as hard to reach as Celan's root in the air; and it was by a confrontation with death, his father's, and with his father's ineffectual resistance to Nazism that he succeeded in doing so. Two seemingly divergent ways of death, of dying, had to converge for him. The confrontation with death, on other levels, was carried over into his book of poems *Vorwarnung*; and into his social and political commitment to the causes of disarmament and conservation.

This is one of many instances of the complexity and circuitousness of the processes involved in the 'Vergangenheitsbewältigung'—coming to terms with the past—that has preoccupied German-language writers throughout four decades. This has long ceased to be a matter of palpable and expiable guilt—if it ever was, other than for politicians. Personal guilt, in any case, is not palpable or ponderable, other than in law courts, and that is what makes it so difficult to expiate or resolve. Corporative guilt, if truly experienced, is even less so. On rational grounds, no politician or law court could indict Peter Härtling for having been indoctrinated in his childhood—or for a betrayal of his mother's secret that was also an act of aggression against his father, and one which the child's conscience may have indicted as parricide. To Celan, a victim, it was his survival that became a source of guilt and alienation, when his root was up there, with the dead. He, too, tried to grow a new root in his displacement, and failed. It was such implications that linked Celan's lines to what, anywhere but in Germany, might have been a straightforward, unpretentious piece of autobiographical writing.

5

After the didactic austerity of the late 1960s and early 1970s, the most diverse forms of autobiographical writing came into their own. They could be strictly and laboriously factual—and so didactic by way of the personal casebook rather than social statistics—like Karin Struck's *Kindheits Ende* (1982), sub-titled 'Journal of a crisis'. This is her minute account of relations with a husband serving in the West German army, with almost daily journal entries extending over four years and including private letters and accounts of dreams: an act of almost total self-exposure bravely sustained for the sake of sociological truthfulness. They could be imaginative works, not essentially different from their authors' works of fiction, like the five autobiographies of Thomas Bernhard or Peter Handke's books about his mother and his child. They could serve to place a writer in the teeth of displacement, like the three autobiographical books of Elias Canetti, published between 1977 and 1985. In their assumption of total recall—of incidents and conversations going back sixty years and more—these works by Canetti also have their being in a border zone between autobiography and fiction, reminding one that Memory was the mother of the Muses or—less mythologically—that memory and imagination are so closely related as to be interdependent, if not inseparable. Since Canetti has published no novel later than his first of 1935—though that novel was intended to be part of a sequence on the scale of Musil's or Broch's—his imaginative search for lost time in the autobiographies assumes a Proustian character, all the more so because those works tell us less about himself than about not one, but several social and cultural worlds, all utterly vanished, beginning with the exotic, almost Arabian Nights *ambiance* of his Bulgarian-Sephardic childhood.

Quite another procedure was adopted by Wolfdietrich Schnurre for his remarkable work *Der Schattenfotograf* of 1978. A founder member of the *Gruppe 47*, Schnurre had been prolific since the end of the war as a poet, short-story writer, journalist, polemicist and writer of radio and television plays. His military service had ended in a 'Strafkompanie', a punitive unit reserved for recalcitrant soldiers; and his early poems had celebrated partisans hanged by his army, civilians victimized by it on the Eastern Front. As a writer with a special allegiance to Berlin, where he had grown up and chose to live again after 1945, he wrote strident protests against the building of the Wall that separated him from his father in East Berlin. That father also became a character in some of his best-known stories. Others dealt with the Jewish and Gipsy victims of the Third Reich; and Schnurre, in his concern for the persecuted and disadvantaged everywhere, went to the length of studying Jewish scripture. In *Der Schattenfotograf* he resorted to an autobiographical framework as a means of gathering up all the threads of his various, and seemingly heterogeneous, concerns, mixing aphoristic jottings with stories, self-reflection with polemics or day-to-day observations. Purists of the imagination could object that such a work could never amount to a synthesis of an imaginative writer's work, and they would be right, of course; but the composite structure had the advantage of presenting a writer's world, down to the professional and personal miseries, the self-doubts from which few writers are exempt, with an immediacy and frankness that no other procedure would have permitted. Schnurre's best work, in verse and prose, had always been spontaneous and brief, so much so that it was dismissed as 'slight' by some of its critics. The long book is as spontaneous in its seriousness and its humour as the earlier works, but it may well come to serve their readers as a key to the unity beneath their seeming diversity, as neither a linear narrative nor an introspective apologia would have done for this particular author; and it is a richly rewarding and engaging book in its own right.

An even more idiosyncratic autobiographical form was chosen by Martin Walser, a writer whose personal concerns had never been obtrusive in his fiction, but merged in his mastery of socially realistic modes. His early novels and plays did for the Federal Republic much what the 'angry young men' did for Britain in the 1950s, though Walser's anger proved to have more staying power than theirs, and was not disarmed by the ascendancy of the social class they represented. (The German educational system alone, together with the circumstance that regional dialects and vernaculars are not necessarily indicative of class distinctions, works against the class obsessions that have been the staple diet of so much British imaginative writing.) Yet in his first novel, *Ehen in Philippsburg* (1957), Hans Beumann's 'provincial' or regional origins make him an outsider and misfit among Philippsburg's professional classes until he beats them at their own games, integrates himself, and, at least outwardly, adopts the materialistic and snobbish values of the *Wirtschaftswunder* élite. It is the evident anger of the author, rather than of his characters, that gets in the way of Walser's social realism in this early work. His division of the novel into four more or less parallel parts, each dominated by a different character or group of characters—though Beumann links the first part to the last—does not have the effect of differentiating or enriching his social spectrum, but of hammering in the same moral four times over. Dr Benrath, the gynaecologist, Alwin, the barrister, and Klaff, the poet, may stand for very different attitudes and codes, but all of them stand for something, instead of being left to be themselves. As a satirist and social critic, Walser was outstanding from the first, both in this novel and in his book of stories, *Ein Flugzeug über dem Haus* (1953); and his verbal finesse—used to great advantage in the vernacular dialogue of his play *Eiche und Angora* (1962), an early breakthrough into the de-demonization of National Socialism—was equal to the function. It was as a realist, as distinct from caricaturist, of post-war West German society that Walser took longer to mature, despite the advantage of his regional roots. The transition from the Third Reich to the *Wirtschaftswunder*, with only opportunism and conformism as constant factors, as *Eiche und Angora* wittily and formidably brought home, did not lend itself to the impartial poise (or pose) of realism. Something like Beumann's 'socialization' was a prerequisite for his author, too, even if the inner reservations could never be overcome; and it was his seeming acceptance of the ways and standards of successful professional men and women, a growing subtlety in his rendering of them without any overt intrusion of judgement, to which Walser owes his later mastery of the realistic mode.

The vehemence and radicalism of Walser's social criticism in *Ehen in Philippsburg* and the later novel *Halbzeit* (1960) suggested at times that his real quarrel was not so much with the West Germany of the *Wirtschaftswunder*, or with any specific social and economic order, as with the depravity of anyone, anywhere, prepared to play, and win, the power game. For *Das Einhorn* (1966), Walser took over Anselm Kristlein from *Halbzeit* as his narrator and Beumann from the first novel as a character; but the main emphasis shifted from social satire to a number of themes more specific, if not more personal. Kristlein, once a copywriter, has become a novelist. A Swiss woman publisher commissions him to write a book about love. Kristlein, a married man with children, goes out to collect material, some of which is provided by an affair with the publisher herself. While staying at the villa of the industrialist Blomich, a friend of his employer, he falls in love with a girl who is camping nearby with her Dutch boyfriend. At the beginning and end of the narration Kristlein is back in his Munich flat with his wife and children, literally prostrate and utterly self-estranged.

The analysis of love, of different varieties of love, is one of the themes that holds this long novel together. The unicorn of the title is symbolic not only of the erotically questing male, but also of the outsider, Rilke's 'non-existent animal'. Kristlein's exploration of love, the story implies, is related to his social status and his ambitions as a writer. Since he is at once writing a book and turning himself into part of its material, another principal theme is the discrepancy between truth and fiction, experience and memory. It is this discrepancy that defeats Kristlein, but gives Walser ample scope for a critique both of eroticism and of fiction. His sketches of the *Wirtschaftswunder* and the concomitant *Kulturwunder*—and Walser has been implicated in both, inevitably, as a successful author—are more devastating than ever in this larger context. The two parties, in Munich and at the Lake Constance villa, are climactic points in the action, virtuoso passages complete with Joycean streams of consciousness in several languages and dialects, essayistic interpolations, flashbacks and deliberate criss-crossing of allusions. Though Walser found a distinct manner in this work, at once rich and vigorous, expressive and ironic, some of the verbalizing tends to obscure the narrative line. It is hard to tell, for instance, whether Kristlein did or did not carry through his resolution to make Orli his mistress. A single statement towards the end of the book seems to contradict everything we have learned about his painful abstinence. Yet elsewhere, too, we are warned about Kristlein's sporadic reticences; and his fantasies are as essential to the story as his actions and failures to act.

All of Walser's remarkable gifts were applied to *Das Einhorn*, which had a structure large and intricate enough to accommodate them. If even this book called for a sequel—which Walser provided in his novel *Der Sturz* of 1973—it was for reasons not strictly literary. Kristlein's wife, Birga, is only one of the female characters who remains somewhat shadowy, and not only because she is overshadowed erotically by Orli, the dream girl. It is significant that Kristlein's passion for Orli takes him back to his childhood, in a way just a little reminiscent of the novels of Günter Grass. Kristlein's final self-estrangement has to do with his failure to make the past and the present coalesce; and this failure suggests the need for a further development not only in his personal relations, but in the novel's analysis of love and, incidentally, of memory. Certain stages of love are rendered with passionate truthfulness, but Kristlein's reticences about his married life are a limitation. The fusion, in his mind, of Birga and Orli at the end of the novel looked like the beginning of another stage.

Yet it was in a shorter work, the novella *Ein fliehendes Pferd* (1978), that Walser achieved a 'seamless web' in which his most personal pre-occupations are delicately woven into their fictional correlative, a spare and linear narrative. The story is set on Walser's home ground, Lake Constance, where Helmut, a schoolmaster, is on holiday from Stuttgart with his wife Sabine. They are sitting on a café terrace, watching passers-by with sardonic curiosity, when Helmut recognizes his school and university friend Klaus Buch, though both he and his wife 'Hel' are dressed and behave as though they were not of Helmut's generation, but of the next. Hel, in fact, is Klaus's second wife, and much younger than her middle-aged husband. Reluctantly, Helmut is drawn into the wholly alien world of Klaus and Hel, who are fitness faddists, teetotallers and non-smokers, yielding to pressure from Klaus, who is intent on reviving memories of their youth which Helmut has successfully obliterated. Helmut writes a letter to Klaus as a vain defence against those pressures, but never posts it. (The unposted letter, as a vehicle of the whole, unutterable truth, is a device of which Walser made use again in his *Brief an Lord Liszt* [1982]; more crucially than in *Ein fliehendes Pferd*, but more blatantly and less convincingly.) Helmut's character and all the differences between him and Klaus, with his cult of youth and prowess, come out in the letter:

> I don't wish to speak my mind. My deepest desire is to keep things to myself. I share that desire with the majority of all the people alive at present. Our

relations with one another are like those between armoured warships. According to rules that aren't quite understandable. The sense of these rules lies in their unreasonableness. The more another person knew about me, the more power he would have over me. So . . .

Helmut wants his present to be as vague and uneventful as his past is in his memory; or, as the story puts it, 'he wanted to be past, even now'. Helmut, in fact, is the runaway horse of the title, though an actual runaway horse occurs in the story, when Klaus succeeds in bringing it to a stop. Klaus and Hel have a spaniel, and Helmut shrieks whenever the dog paws or licks him. Klaus and Hel have to leave the spaniel behind when they call on Helmut and Sabine on the day after their chance encounter. Klaus turns out to be a journalist specializing in environmental matters. The four of them set out on an excursion to the mountains and woods and are caught in a cloudburst. It is on that walk that Klaus stops the runaway horse by leaping on its back, and returns it to its owners. Over dinner Hel outrages another of Helmut's securities, when she says: 'Only people who aren't all there erotically need work.' To that Klaus adds: 'Work is a surrogate for eroticism. And the death of eroticism.' On the second of two sailing trips into which Klaus has tried to drag his friends—Sabine has excused herself from the second, and Hel, too, has dropped out—there is a squall on the lake, Helmut kicks the tiller out of Klaus's grip in his panic at Klaus's insane tacking, and Klaus is knocked into the water. Helmut manages to hang on in the yacht, which is swept ashore. After being taken back by ambulance to the holiday home, Helmut informs the police and Hel of the accident. Hel calls on them, drinks Calvados, and tells them the story of her destruction by Klaus, who forbade her to continue her work as a musician, forced her to sell her piano, and forced her into his mould. She celebrates her release by performing Schubert's 'Wanderer' Fantasy without a piano, when Klaus reappears, and takes her back to their holiday home. Helmut decides to leave at once, for Montpellier, where Hel had told them she had spent the happiest time in her life. Before that, Helmut had bought bicycles and a sports outfit for Sabine and himself, and proposed a jog in the woods. Helmut's reading of Kierkegaard on his holidays is another thread in the story, which is left open-ended, when Helmut begins to explain himself to Sabine on the train journey, but gets no farther than the opening sentence of the book. We are not told whether Klaus has been transformed, as Helmut clearly has been; or whether, erotically, Helmut's and Sabine's marriage has been improved by the loosening-up, in which Hel's attractions have had a part, though Helmut had been as loath to acknowledge them as Klaus was eager to advertise them. The circular frame of the narrative suggests that no lasting change in any of the four of them could be the outcome.

Despite vivid local colour and dialect, there is nothing specifically German about Martin Walser's concerns in his later works. His wit, irony and reticence in *Ein fliehendes Pferd* and the later novel *Das Schwanenhaus* (1980) are not qualities that foreign critics regard as typically German. In both works, true, there are symbolic overtones and undercurrents; and Walser's mundane realism can easily be translated into conflicts and problems as personal as they are social. The 'Schwanenhaus' of the later book is an *art nouveau* villa by Lake Constance, once more, and the plot revolves around the attempts of rival real estate agents to acquire it; Gottlob Zürn, the protagonist, for a client who wishes to preserve it, Kaltammer to demolish it and build luxury flats in its place. Zürn's failure—he loves the house for its own sake—becomes a liberation for him, a release from adolescent fixations into a new sense of reality. Zürn's family involvements and the operations of a third rival agent, Schatz, add complexity to the central issue of the house; and a younger generation, in the form of Zürn's four daughters and their problems, shifts the social relevance into the post-*Wirtschaftswunder* era, just as the question of the villa bears on conservationist issues that have become acute in West Germany.

Walser's autobiographical work, *Messmers Gedanken* (1985), tells no story at all, nor does it advertise itself as autobiography. It is a collection of aphorisms and observations, some of which—the most self-exposing—are attributed to an *alter ego*, Messmer, who may also be taken to be the author of the whole book by those who choose to read it as fiction. Messmer's aim is defined as 'the fourth grade of auto-biography: the weakling who takes refuge in every sort of evasion. The ideal: exposure and concealment to the same extreme degree. A language of exposure-concealment, then. The Californian climate is conducive to that, Messmer thinks.' Reticence is called for not only because that is Walser's way—and we can recognize many of the main characters of his novels in Messmer's *persona*—but because full self-confession is an impossibility. 'That which one must keep even from oneself is the truth, Messmer thinks.' Yet, in his way, Walser manages to tell us some terrible truths about himself; and those truths are worth telling because they are truths not only about himself. Messmer, therefore, becomes not only a medium but a confessor and judge.

The social criticism of Walser's fiction is not lacking in this very personal book. Walser has long been aware that the status accorded to serious writers in West Germany makes them part of the ruling classes, even economically, if they can keep up the productivity demanded of them—as of other people in the professional and business classes. Walser's sense of complicity in a system which the same writers have largely rejected, but can no longer keep at arm's length with facile generalizations about the old 'bourgeois'/artist antinomy, accounts for observations like this one: 'This patch of green. At once the shaming feeling: it belongs to you. The most pernicious effect of capitalism: that one believes, everything one can pay for belongs to one.' Simply by being writers who can keep up the productivity demanded of them, such writers are also conformists, however non-conformist their views and commitments; and this ambivalence is one that Walser has explored since his earliest works of fiction, in characters not necessarily artists or writers. Several entries in *Messmers Gedanken* expose Walser's acute unease at that pressure to produce, and the conformism in himself that yields to the pressure. There is nothing 'natural' or self-evident about the high productivity of professional writers. The natural thing could well be to write one novel in a lifetime, like that privileged amateur, the Prince of Lampedusa. Walser—or Walser's Messmer—almost seems to envy poets, who are spared the pressure because their product is a drug on the market—though in West Germany a good many poets can avoid the consequences of that. 'He longs to be able to make a poem. That he cannot express how he feels—and this, he thinks, he could do only in a poem—is an unremitting torment to him. An imposition.' Poetry, of course, is not primarily a matter of being able to express what one feels, as Walser and Messmer must know. So it must be the relative privacy of the medium they have in mind, because the privacy obviates self-evasions. In fact some of the entries come as close to poetry as Walser had ever permitted himself to come, like this one: 'So there I was full of tones, unsingable ones. My mouth was torn open, nothing came out.' That mute poet is akin to the 'musician fallen silent', who on the same page Messmer also says he would like to be.

In countries where writers of Walser's distinction are not accorded the status he enjoys and suffers, a book like *Messmers Gedanken* either could not have appeared at all or, if it had, would be sneered at as presumptuous and self-indulgent—however beautifully written and delicately dialectical. Here it must be mentioned that Walser had published an earlier book of aphorisms; that aphorisms are accepted in Germany as a literary genre, as in France, though so little of a commodity that few writers or publishers can afford to publish collections of them; and that even in this century there have been German-language writers, like the admirable Swiss writer Ludwig Hohl, who owe their deserved reputations mainly to their collections of aphorisms. Yet—Messmer or no Messmer—this one will be read as an auto-biographical work by Martin Walser, not as a collection of aphorisms; and that proves how right Walser's self-mocking and self-demolishing observations are, how truthful about the impossibility for writers to be wholly true to themselves or wholly truthful about themselves. Just like anyone else, in fact—since writers are not alone in hiding away their inmost generators, 'heart mysteries' and utopias, for which the market has no use at all.

VII   The Non-representational Alternative

1

Even if versions of the real and the 'socialization' of literature are seen as the mainstream concern of German-language writers since 1945, they were far from being the only one. Gottfried Benn and Bertolt Brecht were not the only survivors of pre-war avant-gardes whose example polarized the practices of their successors. The stylistic innovations of the later Expressionists, other than Benn, were of little help because they tended towards pathos and bombast, the very things that most younger writers wished to get out of their systems after the pathos and bombast of Nazi rhetoric. Early Expressionist innovations, especially those of August Stramm, who died in the First World War, held more potentialities for writers whose primary interest was in language as such, not as a vehicle of representation but as a material in its own right that was both medium and message. So did the work of Surrealists and Dadaists, of Carl Einstein, James Joyce, Gertrude Stein and other verbally and linguistically adventurous writers of the inter-war period. Kurt Schwitters died too soon after the Second World War to re-establish himself in Germany as one of the eminent survivors; but Hans (or Jean) Arp remained active as a poet, an exemplary one, until his death in 1966.

As early as 1962, it is true, Hans Magnus Enzensberger wrote an eloquent essay, 'Die Aporien der Avantgarde', questioning the validity of the very concept of an avant-garde in the arts, with its implication that their 'progress' and retreats could be charted like those of armies; and two years earlier he had put modernism in its place by calling his international anthology of mainly pre-1945 poems '*museum* of modern poetry'. Yet not only did he compile that anthology, but he translated and wrote about the masters of a modernism that he relegated to his museum. His polemic was directed mainly against an indiscriminate cult of novelty that had set in as a reaction to the banning of modernist art as 'degenerate' in the Third Reich; and he was perspicacious enough to see the connection between that cult of novelty in the arts and the novelties foisted on a consumer society by industry and commerce. The truth was that there is no clear dividing line between the 'representational' and the abstract uses of language, any more than between pure and applied form in the visual arts. Every good writer has to master his material, language, in its own right—or be mastered by it—quite regardless of his or her other aims and commitments, just as good representational artists have always been concerned with form, colour, texture and composition in their own right. Enzensberger had his own good reasons for disliking the purists of 'concrete' poetry—which in fact is the nearest thing to abstraction in the visual arts feasible in the medium of words—making an exception only of the linguistic experiments carried out by Max Bense and his associates with electronic instruments since the 1950s, as contributions not to art, but to science.

Not only do extremes tend to meet in the arts, but the linguistic and experimental writers in Switzerland, Austria and Germany were doing many quite different, often radically opposed, things. Extreme ways with language could serve scientific ends, but they could also be sheer play, they could become entertainment as performances and 'happenings'; they could serve expressive ends, articulating the pre-articulate, as Stramm had done; they could turn words into graphics or into musical sounds; they could apply collage techniques taken over from painters like Schwitters or Max Ernst; they could be serious and funny, or methodical to the point of boring inanity. They could make nonsense of language in the spirit of Lewis Carroll or Edward Lear, or in order to release the sub-conscious in the manner of the Surrealists, or to creat an anti-art of the fortuitous like the Dadaists, or to let language find its own meaning in grammatical permutations merely initiated by the writer. Apart from the Max Bense group based in Stuttgart, the purest 'concrete' procedures were favoured by Eugen Gomringer at Frauenfeld in Switzerland, which became the centre of an international movement. (Gomringer was born in Bolivia, and the South American wing of the international movement has remained prominent.) The Austrian 'Wiener Gruppe'—later centred more in Graz than in Vienna, and the nucleus of much excellent writing ever since the 1950s—was more eclectic, often combining all the procedures and possibilities I have listed and tending towards a spontaneity that lent itself to extemporized dramatic, or semi-dramatic, entertainments. It also favoured collaborative endeavours, as Brecht, at least in theory, did out of a commitment seemingly at the opposite extreme to theirs. In their determination to defy the machinery of professionalism, some of them, like Konrad Bayer and Hans Carl Artmann, were reluctant to publish their works at all, or to prepare definitive versions of them. Konrad Bayer's work was collected after his suicide by another member of the group, Gerhard Rühm; and several of Artmann's works owed their publication—in his lifetime—to friends and associates.

The varieties, constellations and permutations of all the primarily linguistic, non-representational kinds of writing are far too intricate to be traced here. My interest is in the meeting of extremes and in the common ground that all such writing, ultimately, has with writing of any kind. 'Bevor Dada da war, war Dada da', Hans Arp remarked, making excellent sense by adding a third 'da' to 'dada'. Arp was saying that there was nothing drastically new about the innovations of that most outrageous of movements: and he enacted that assertion by letting the German language lead him into it, producing more dada in the process of making a factual statement. The principle of fortuitousness that Arp had observed in his poetry with an almost mystical faith in that which is not willed or intended, but given or found, is a principle that had always contributed to imaginative writing. One school of medieval poets called themselves not makers but finders, 'troubadours'. Wherever rhyme has been used, that principle was at work, since rhyme does not merely serve meaning, but also directs and determines it in varying degrees, so that a poet may find the meaning by being found, struck, by a rhyme. It was mainly in rhymed poems that Arp produced the most exuberant, 'unanchored' nonsense of his Dada period proper. In later years, when his poetry tended to be anchored, weighed down by experience and by existential or metaphysical concerns, he relied more on idiom than on metre and rhyme for his findings; and such play on idioms became essential to the practice of poets like Enzensberger himself and Erich Fried, who were regarded as representational writers *par excellence*, as social realists and social critics.

So-called experiments in the arts may have results—the finished works—but they differ from experiments in the sciences in not needing to prove anything. (If they do serve to prove something, like the experiments of Max Bense and his associates, their function is more scientific than aesthetic, as Enzensberger pointed out.) By making a structural principle out of chance findings, semantic, visual or acoustic, Arp for one most certainly did not wish to prove anything. In his earlier poems at least, the sense or nonsense was left to chance. If, nevertheless, even his most nonsensical poems made sense of a sort, by being funny and by subverting logic, that bore out both the soundness of his principle and his claim that there was dada before dada was—that anti-art must always end up by being art, or nothing. That very claim was not meant to prove anything. It was a flash of insight, given to him by the fortuitousness linguistic usage; but that, again, did not prevent it from making good sense, so much so that its seven words contain the stuff of a whole treatise—on the part that chance has had in the making of poetry long before Dadaism was heard of.

A good many of Arp's later poems could dispense even with the punning on words or idioms, just as they could dispense with metre and rhyme, like this one from the sequence 'Häuser' (Houses) of 1956:

In einem Hause
hatten alle Bewohner den gleichen Traum.
Sie träumten
dass sie täglich kleiner und kleiner würden
und schliesslich stürben.
Vorsorglich zimmerten sie sich daraufhin
ihre Särge zu Särglein um
und trugen sie stets mit sich
unter dem Arm.
Sie taten recht daran.
Obwohl zuerst das Kleinerwerden
nicht der Rede wert war
und zudem unregelmässig vor sich ging
ja sogar einmal mehrere Monate stockte
übertraf es plötzlich jede Erwartung.
Eines schönen Tages
erwachten die Bewohner des Hauses
in dem alle den gleichen Traum geträumt hatten
klein wie Puppen
und passten tadellos in ihre Särglein.

In a certain house
all the occupants had the same dream.
They dreamed
that each day they grew smaller and smaller
and finally died.
Providently therefore they set to work
converting their coffins to coffinettes
and always carried them around
under their arms.
They did the right thing.
Although at first their growing smaller
was not worth talking about
and also happened sporadically
even stopping once for several months
it suddenly exceeded every expectation.
One fine day
the occupants of the house in which
all had dreamed the same dream woke up
small as dolls
and fitted perfectly into their coffinettes.

The diction of this poem is so prosaically and classically plain, so logical, that the poem could be the report of some plausible and ordinary event, in which case it would be a parable or allegory, very much like Günter Grass's existential allegory 'Im Ei' (In the Egg).

No intention of the author's forbids a reader to read it as such, as a poem about the process of ageing that is also a gradual shrinking and diminution, and about the wisdom of accepting that process, of preparing for it. Allegory had been one of Arp's resorts even in his visionary, pre-Dada poems, and his work as a whole yields something like a modern myth, by no means always or exclusively absurdist. Yet the poem is more like a fairy tale than like a deliberate parable. Perhaps we should not make the author responsible for any 'deeper significance' we can read out of or into his story, when to Arp reading was an act as much subject to chance as the act of writing. 'nature is nonsense', Arp wrote in an early manifesto; 'dada stands for nonsense, that doesn't mean idiocy. dada is senseless like nature and life, dada is for nature and against art. dada like nature wants to give each thing its appropriate and essential place.' In Arp's later poems we can forget about the antinomy of nature and art, because the anti-art of the Dadaists was directed against the misuse of art as a big 'cultural' or educational stick. When Arp's own art had become a kind of nature to him, second nature, nature could also become art. But 'senseless' or—as Arp wrote in another late poem—'mysterious' is what his art had to remain, for 'life is a mysterious breath.' The 'Houses' poem, too, hinges on the interchangeability of dream and reality, a very old and traditional theme. That the shrinking of those people in the poem begins as a dream and is carried over into waking life, strikes me as natural and 'not worth talking about'; also, that we are not told for certain whether they did not make their coffinettes and carry them around in their dream. An awakening is mentioned only at the end; and since Arp's poetry leaps over so many barriers, even that awakening could be one within a dream.

2

By not imposing meaning or sense on the things of nature—which, to him, were also the things of imagination—Arp liberated his work from the subject/object dichotomy, as perpetuated in distinctions between confessional expressive writing on the one hand, realistic writing on the other. What 'nature' was to Arp in this connection, language has been to Helmut Heissenbüttel, whose premiss was that human beings are the language that they use, and the language they are used by. Heissenbüttel's many-sided work has been an exploration and a trying-out of the behaviour of the most diverse kind of language, from that of philosophy to that of propaganda and politics, from that of idiomatic usage to that of topographical description, Romantic poetry or sentimental fiction. In his book of essays *Über Literatur* (1966), Heissenbüttel went so far as to claim that he himself had 'nothing to say'. His very substantial body of work, then, would be no more than the record of his experiments with language, and a contribution to science rather than to literature. Yet, to some readers at least, his work gives aesthetic

pleasure, whether he likes it or not; and even his personality has entered
it by a back door, as has the commitment he may have wished to keep
out of it by letting a language not his own go through its operations in
laboratory conditions.

In that regard, certainly, Heissenbüttel is a truly experimental
writer, by which I mean more than the loose sense that makes 'experimental' a synonym for 'modern' or 'avant-garde'. Not only are
these rather useless categories in any case, but Heissenbüttel agrees
with Enzensberger in relegating them to an earlier phase, and sees
himself as working within a 'tradition of the modern', if not as its
epigone. His work is truly experimental in that it is a continuous
experiment with words and sentences, conducted in a manner as nearly
scientific as his various media permit. Whether the processes and
methods he applies to language are new, matters less than the rigour
and consistency with which he applies them. Collage, montage, simul-
taneity, tautology, grammatical dislocation and permutation—all these
had been used before, by the Dadaists, by Gertrude Stein, by the
purists of 'concrete poetry' of whom Heissenbüttel is not one, by a host
of early twentieth-century innovators whose precedent Heissenbüttel
has freely acknowledged, both in his critical writings and by quotation
in his own texts. As I pointed out in *The Truth of Poetry*, one of these
precedents—the grammatical *perpetuum mobile* adopted again and again
by Heissenbüttel in his '3 × 13 mehr oder weniger Geschichten' and
elsewhere—can be traced as far back as Tristan Corbière's *Les Amours
Jaunes*, published in 1873. Again, it matters very little whether or not
this particular epigraph by Corbière, a mere *jeu d'esprit* to him, with no
sequel in his practice, served Heissenbüttel as a model for his method.
What does matter is that Heissenbüttel's method was applied to altogether different material, and produced altogether different results.
The cult of novelty for novelty's sake is bound up with an individualism
that Heissenbüttel's practice left behind.

'Anti-grammatical, anti-syntactical transformation and reproduction
of language', Heissenbüttel wrote for his Frankfurt lectures on poetics,
'are effective principles in twentieth-century literature.'

> Leaving aside that part of linguistic reproduction which can be interpreted
> in terms of social themes or cultural criticism, both principles, like their
> advocates, are described in current critical jargon as experimental (and it is
> quite conceivable that this could lead to the classification of the whole period
> as experimental, much as earlier periods are classified as 'baroque' or
> 'romantic'. Personally I regard the notion of experimental literature as a
> product of educational politics, a tactical resort, with no factual validity. Yet
> it can be used as a means of making oneself understood. Contrary to the
> usual tacit assumption, this notion of experimental literature does not stand
> in opposition to a so-called 'normal' literature. Beside it there is only one
> other literary principle, that of stylization or pseudo-stylization. In many

cases experimental and stylizing literature have formed alliances that make for complexity, but often also for perplexity, as soon as we apply those principles to specific works.

There are traces still of individual stylization in Heissenbüttel's early texts, specially those in the collection *Kombinationen* (1954). Although he has not seen fit to reprint this first collection, or to include any part of it in his later 'textbooks', it is the point of departure for the later experiments. These early texts look more or less like lyrical poems; but they are lyrical poems pervaded by the awareness that this lyricism is threatened by a drastic discontinuity. Heterogeneous prosaic reflections and perceptions intrude. Heissenbüttel's break with lyricism was gradual and inevitable. It developed from the awareness that lyrical poetry, as practised right up to his time by poets whom Heissenbüttel does not necessarily reject but found it impossible to emulate, is held together by a subjectivity that avails itself of objective or symbolic correlatives to create an order. This order, to Heissenbüttel, became an illusion or, as he calls it, a hallucination. Where, in his latest books, Heissenbüttel comes closest again to lyrical poetry of that kind, as he does in the collection *Ödipuskomplex made in Germany* (1981), he distances himself from the confessional mode by attributing it to occasions or by returning to the topographical descriptiveness of his second book, *Topographien* of 1956. His use of rhyme in those later poems, such as the landscape poems, is one of several indications that Heissenbüttel has relaxed his experimental rigour in favour of a 'stylization' that he had never condemned, only found incompatible with his procedures.

What made his early texts recognizably 'poetic' was not that they were divided into verse lines—so are many of his later texts—far less that they fell into rhyme at times, but that they had not broken with subjectivity to the point of ceasing to register experiences and perceptions that disrupted or threatened it. For that reason they remained self-expressive, even confessional, in a way that the later texts are not. By this I don't mean that autobiographical material is not used in the later texts, but that it becomes material of the same order as any other, used not for self-expression but for experiments with language. More and more, it was the verbal processes that counted. These verbal processes, in turn, served to reveal possibilities of meaning, possibilities of truth, inherent in language itself, rather than in the individual consciousness and sensibility that we expect to meet in the poems, short stories, novels and plays of writers less austerely, less rigorously, experimental. Heissenbüttel's latest works, published after the one-volume issue of his six separate *Textbücher* in 1970, make that distinction more dubious and suggest that his experiments have been largely concluded.

Almost from the start, Heissenbüttel tended as much towards narrative prose as towards poetry, writing 'quasi-stories' and 'quasi-novels' long before the publication of his novel *D'Alemberts Ende* (1970), which is also a 'quasi-novel', operating with quotations and parodies of conventional fiction. Just as his poems questioned the presuppositions of lyrical verse, his miniature quasi-novels and stories questioned the presuppositions of narrative. Miniature quasi-dramas further extended his range, though these too follow from earlier experiments and are best described by the neutral term 'texts', because—as Heissenbüttel wrote in 1963—'the development of the arts in the twentieth century shows this characteristic, among others, that it advances sporadically into areas where every genre comes up against the frontier of every other.' Not only do his texts cross the frontiers between poetry, prose fiction and drama, but they are as closely bound up with developments in philosophy, the visual arts and music as with developments in literature; and his methods are inseparable from the linguistic and sociological interests evident in everything he has written.

One does not need to refer back to the 'two cultures' debate to point out that most of the 'avant-garde' literature of an earlier period, including that of Dadaism, was anti-philosophical, anti-theoretical, anti-methodical. Though Heissenbüttel can be playful, high-spirited and funny—not only in his 'occasional poems' but even in his most methodical linguistic exercises, like the political and sociological ones in his *Textbuch 5* of 1965—it is the austerity of his aims and methods that makes many of his middle period texts difficult to read. They make little concession to the pleasure principle, unless it is the pleasure that a mathematician or logician may take in a piece of work thoroughly and efficiently carried to its conclusion. They also demand a kind of concentration that little contemporary writing demands, and less of it gets; for we expect imaginative writing to grip us, move us, carry us away—hallucinate us, in fact, to a greater or lesser degree—whereas most of Heissenbüttel's texts are meant to exercise the intellect by jolting it out of its habits and assumptions. Those habits and assumptions are not only reflected, but embodied, in the way we speak—in idioms, phrases, grammatical structures; and it is these that Heissenbüttel's texts shake up, often simply by leaving them to reduce themselves to absurdity. The end of Heissenbüttel's art is enlightenment; an enlightenment brought about without recourse to persuasion, appeal to emotional stock responses or any of the traditional devices of didactic art. Many of his texts are abstract and general to a degree we associate with science and philosophy rather than with imaginative art. Even the visual particulars of which they are full assume a function less sensuous than exemplary, just as the characters in them assume a function less individual than algebraic.

'In these developments', to quote Heissenbüttel again on twentieth-century poetics. 'method takes on a strong preponderance.'

> He who can grasp it can use it. One can imagine a state of affairs in which what is methodical about this literature could indeed become general. The arrested exemplars serve for the study of methods. The question of quality will lose its validity, as will the question of poetry (as something more elevated), of art. Success will depend not on a particular gift (the Muse's kiss) but on an attitude to language (or other media) that can be taken by anyone. The consistency of methods that decipher language, reproduce language, duplicate a language-world, is not due to its needing the subjectivity of the poet who, as it were, attracts all other subjects to himself to make literature, but to the method's ability to provide something that can be used by anyone who avails himself of it. There is a possibility (and this, though only a hypothesis, is not idle speculation) that the thing we still have to call literature will become general. That the old dream of the universal language of literature can come true, not by regression to pseudo-humanistic and pseudo-subjective clichés, as dogmatic Communist culture ideology and the restorative culture-preservers of the West would have it, but by the practice of post-subjective progressive literary methods.

This utopia or science fiction, according to how we look at it, has not come closer to fulfilment in the two decades that have passed since those words were written; and I, for one, cannot pretend that I am sorry. An element of personal choice, I note with relief, is involved even in Heissenbüttel's most rigorously methodical exercises; and even a scientist's experiments begin with hypotheses or hunches, sometimes with flashes which in poets would be called inspiration. I confess to being moved by some of Heissenbüttel's texts, such as his re-interpretation of the Job story, 'bad news', in which method is less obtrusive, less autonomous, than elsewhere. Heissenbüttel may let grammar have its head, but it is he who has harnessed it to the original proposition which it will pull from stage to stage, he who provides the fodder and the load. It is also he who must know or have a good idea in advance not perhaps where grammar's career will lead, but what kind of profit—psychological, sociological or ontological—any one trip is likely to yield. His methods have been available for a long time, but no one else has made them work quite as he makes them work. So I suspect that there will never be such a thing as a 'general literature', practicable by anyone who has grasped the methods, if only because not everyone has the desire or the equipment; and Heissenbüttel's equipment, his knowledge, intelligence and skill, not to mention the antiquated poetic sensibility his methods have never concealed, is as distinctive as his dedication to literature as 'a means of radical enlightenment'. There is no need to go into the wider implications of Heissenbüttel's one-time programme or to consider what severe limitations and losses literature would suffer if it were to become a branch of technology. Heissenbüttel's own practice has disproved his theory—and not only by his return to non-experimental kinds of writing after the six 'textbooks'. This does not detract from the value or exemplariness of his more self-obliterating texts, but it marks their limitations.

The title poem of his collection of 1981 was written in 1965, at the height not only of Heissenbüttel's programme of 'radical enlightenment' but also of the ideologization and politicization of West German literature and its media—intended as a 'radical enlightenment' on rather different premisses from Heissenbüttel's linguistic ones. Because extremes meet and Heissenbüttel's poem was one of his 'occasional' ones, unbuttoned and playful, it is very close generically to the direct social comment of non-experimental poets like Hans Magnus Enzensberger, though its scepticism is more acute than Enzensberger's was at that time, and it held a warning that was not heeded:

Ödipuskomplex made in Germany 1965

Papa hat ungefähr tausend Jahre regiert
der Ödipuskomplex des deutschen Volkes heißt
   Enesdeape danach haben wir es mit Opa versucht das war
   keine Dauerlösung nun sind wir ratlos
wer rät uns Rätselrater werden gesucht
wer hat uns die Suppe eingebrockt sagt Bild
Opa ist im Glassarg konserviert Papas Stellvertretern
   werden die Namen allmählich ausradiert aber haben
   wir Papa vergessen
es geht uns noch besser als im Dritten Reich das ist
   keine Dauerlösung
haben sie in Washington oder Moskau auch Papas unser
   Ersatzödipuskomplex heißt Pankow Opapa o Papa oder
   in Rom
Papas Regiment ist ausgestorben aber Stücke davon liegen
   noch in der Luft das ist die Berliner Luft immer noch
   der Geruch der Josef hieß
was wir fordern ist weg mit Papas und Opas Schluß
   mit Ödipuskomplexen
aufgeklärt wie wir uns haben
aufgeklärt wie wir uns haben
aufgeklärt wie wir uns haben
aufgeklärt wie wir uns haben
wer am vernünftigsten ist soll Macht haben
Mensch macht das mal

Oedipus Complex made in Germany 1965

Papa ruled for about a thousand years
the Oedipus complex of the German people is called
   Enesdeape after that we tried Grandpapa that was
   no permanent solution now we are at a loss
who can advise us solvers of puzzles are wanted

who made the bed for us asks *Bild*
Grandpapa lies embalmed in his glass coffin Grandpapa's stand-ins
  are having their names erased one by one but have we
  forgotten Papa
we're doing better even than in the Third Reich that is
  no permanent solution
do they have papas too in Washington or Moscow our
  substitute Oedipus complex is called Pankow Granddad grand papa
or in Rome
Papa's regiment has died out but pieces of it still lie
  in the air that is the air of Berlin even now
  the smell that was called Josef
what we demand is no more papas and grandpapas an end
  to Oedipus complexes
enlightened as we have grown
enlightened as we have grown
enlightened as we have grown
enlightened as we have grown
whoever's most sensible is to have power
just pull that off man

Apart from the repetition of the line about enlightenment, applied satirically here and rhetorically—with a degree of self-mockery, too, when Heissenbüttel himself was dedicated to an enlightenment less activist, but no less radical than the anti-Oedipal one—this poem dispenses with most of Heissenbüttel's strictly linguistic procedures. The repetition, four times, of the line serves to let the phrase call itself in question, and that is a procedure Heissenbüttel used again and again in his more strictly experimental texts. ('Enesdeape', by the way, is the usual abbreviation of the National Socialist Workers Party of Germany. Pankow is the administrative centre of East Berlin. *Bild* is a West German tabloid newspaper.) The poem, in fact, is as stylized and individual as the delicate landscape studies in the same collection. Before long, Heissenbüttel will be treated as a 'nature poet', amongst other things, as well as the initiator, from his early work onwards, of a new school of urban topographical writing, at once realist and subjective, like the work of Jürgen Becker; and it will be very much to Heissenbüttel's advantage not to be judged or appreciated within the bounds of his programme and theories.

3

Although he has written concrete poetry of the purest kind, Ernst Jandl began as a writer of 'representational' verse and has continued to go not his own way, but his own ways, wherever they might lead him. His first book of poems, *Andere Augen* (1956), appeared five years after the opening of the Vienna 'art club' and the formation of the Vienna Group, but neither the contents nor the design of this book, published in a series devoted to Austrian writers predominantly traditional, would have given its readers any reason to associate him with either. Yet his next publication was a preface to a book edited by H. C. Artmann, who was at the centre of the club and the Group. If that seems an in-consistency or a contradiction, it was a fruitful one, for it was out of the tension between all the possibilities open to writers in his time that Jandl drew the energy for his prolific and various work of the next three decades. His next books of poems were published in Stuttgart and at Frauenfeld, the two headquarters of experimental and concrete writing in German, his fourth, with the characteristically Anglo-German title *'mai hart lieb zapfen eibe hold'* (1965), in London. When Jandl published his substantial collection *Laut und Luise* in 1966, with an epilogue by Helmut Heissenbüttel, he was prominent mainly as a performer of his sound poems, which could communicate their energy, if not their meaning, even to the English audiences who heard them at the Albert Hall and elsewhere. His immediately popular poems were sound poems like 'schmerz durch reibung' (pain through friction) made out of the sounds in the single word 'Frau'; or 'schtzngrmm' made out of the consonants in the German word 'Schützengraben' (trench). Poems of this kind needed to be heard rather than read, since the letters on the page are a mere notation more difficult to take in through the eye than a musical score; and because no one but the poet himself can vocalize them exactly as they are meant to be vocalized, a gramophone record was issued as a complement to the text. The last line of 'schtzngrmm', for instance, 't-tt', looks like an onomatopoeic enactment of rifle or machine-gun fire on the page, whereas in the poet's reading it also conveys a dying fall and the German word 'tot'. Jandl had lived in England as a German teacher in the early 1950s, and worked as an English teacher in Vienna before becoming a full-time writer. It was to those occupations that we owe his English poems and his bilingual poems like 'calypso', which begins:

> ich was not yet
> in brasilien
> nach brasilien
> wulld ich laik du go

(where the 'du' in the last line reflects the Austrian and South German difficulty in distinguishing between 'd' and 't', but also adds a delight-ful illogicality by introducing an irrelevant 'you').

Though sound poems preponderated in that collection, these sound poems could be witty or serious, mimetic or fantastic, satirical or expressive; and there were also prose poems—like the sequence about England, 'prosa aus der flüstergalerie' (prose from the whispering gallery)—more akin to some of the experimental texts of Heissenbüttel, and other sequences whose main appeal is to the eye or to the intellect. Jandl's sound permutations draw on a great variety of idioms, particularly on Viennese dialect—in which Artmann had written a brilliant sequence of poems, 'med ana schwoazzn dintn' (1958)—and those Austrian responses to the sounds of the English language. Elsewhere his sources could be literary, like the line by Wordsworth that provided the title for his London book, or when phrases from Goethe and Hölderlin are taken up in the sequence 'zehn abend-gedichte' and in the longer variations 'klare gerührt'.

Jandl's practice has always borne out Heissenbüttel's claim that experiment and tradition are neither incompatible nor irreconcilable, and that Jandl's poems are not absolutely different from any others written in the past. Quite apart from the 'tradition of the new', many of Jandl's texts in verse and prose can be seen as developments of recognized and time-honoured forms. The sequence 'epigrams' in *Laut und Luise* is only one of many instances. Nor could Jandl ever be accused of narrowing down the resources and effects of lyrical poetry. Observation, reflection, feeling and pure invention have their place in his work, even where the material has been reduced to the components of a single word. Even the dramatic potentialities of his media, which were to be fulfilled in his stage play *Aus der Fremde* in 1980, were already latent not only in his earliest sound poems but in the little play made out of the names of three cities, London, Paris and Rome, included in *Laut und Luise*.

It is not often that a poet responds adequately when asked to talk about his own work, for reasons that are woven into the argument of Jandl's lectures *Die schöne Kunst des Schreibens* (1976; enlarged edition, 1983). Jandl's performance was not only adequate, but exemplary, because he decided that if he was going to respond at all to such an occasion he might as well make the most of it, for his audience and for himself, producing texts that not only illuminate his own practice but enter searchingly and truthfully into the whole question of what a poet can usefully say about his own craft. His conviction that, basically, a poem is one thing, whatever is said about it—by the author or anyone else—quite another, underlies all his observations; but it does not prevent him from revealing what he does know about the genesis and quiddity of his poems, and revealing it with such sustained attentiveness both to the matter itself and to the needs of his listeners that he could not fail to do more than the occasion demanded. He begins with examples of the four kinds of poems he has written: the poem that uses everyday language and normal grammar; the poem for reading aloud ('Sprechgedicht'); the pure sound poem ('Lautgedicht'), whose structure approximates to music but, in Jandl's case, does not necessarily exclude a message of sorts; and the 'silent' visual poem. (Examples of the last were projected on to a screen, and his remarks on them are not included in the first edition of the printed text, perhaps because they were extemporized.) In the process he not only analyses the examples, but explains why he found it necessary to write those different kinds of poems and why, for him, there are essential links between them. He also discusses language norms, necessary deviations from them in poetry, and the degree of serious, or not so serious, word-play that each kind of poem demands for its functioning.

> i love concrete
> i love pottery
> but i'm not
> a concrete pot

is one of his less serious explanations of why he has been able to excel in all those four kinds, including the 'straight' poem that renders an experience or insight without splitting words or syntax. Although little biographical information is relevant to Jandl's concerns in these lectures, he does comment on his formative years in England; and perceptive readers of the book will not need Jandl's acknowledgement of how much this wholly unacademic poet owes to his profession of English teacher—not least, the courtesy, patience and directness with which he communicates radical and complex discoveries.

These have to do not only with language, but with the relationship between theory and practice in literature, his distinction between three kinds of literary theory, the normative, the deductive and the prescriptively programmatic, and the reasons why it is easy for practising writers to fall into error when trying to make theoretical deductions from their own practice. Another outstanding passage deals with the relationship between a writer's person and his work. Here Jandl quietly and humorously demolishes the cult of personality—or, more precisely, of names and signatures—in the arts, showing just how little the name attached to it has to do with the essentially autonomous work, while admitting that his very opportunity to say so would not have arisen but for curiosity about his person and name. Characteristically, again, he does not sneer at this curiosity, but defines it with delicate precision and a total lack of vanity. Throughout the lectures Jandl takes nothing for granted. Just as in his poems he attains a stringent and questioning simplicity, so in his manner of elucidating them he uses plain words in sentences that may be anything but simple, because they register his awareness of countless contradictions and paradoxes.

As he mentioned in an earlier lecture of 1969, concrete poetry, to Jandl, fulfilled a desire for the 'absolute poem' that goes back to

Mallarmé, for a kind of poem that 'is an object, not a statement about an object'; but that desire or aspiration comes up against the fact that 'whoever operates with words, operates with meanings'. Art, for Jandl, is 'the perpetual implementation of a freedom', a freedom he has maintained for himself by access to the whole field of tensions between the different kinds of writing he has practised. Far from making concessions to 'the demon of progress in the arts' (Wyndham Lewis), though, Jandl did not even claim a personal 'development' for himself. Not only did he state that 'merely by writing poems' the experimental poet 'continues a tradition', although that tradition consists of many traditions, but he wrote: 'By the time I was 9 years old I had written my first poem. I still stand in the same place.'

This astonishing remark becomes clearer in the light of Jandl's later work. When—astonishingly once more—he managed to produce a second workshop report without repeating himself, his Frankfurt lectures on poetics *Das Öffnen und Schliessen des Mundes* of 1985, he had added several sub-divisions to the four kinds of poem listed in the earlier report. One of these, a variant of the 'straight' or conventional poem, was what he called 'verkindlichte Sprache', a diction made child-like; and it had been misread as a kind of 'pidgin' German akin to that spoken by some of the foreign 'guest workers' before they had mastered the new language. On the level of personal 'development', this new departure was a regression. Linguistically and poetically, it gave Jandl a whole new range of possibilities, since both childhood and in-articulateness are human realities, as valid and worthy of being enacted in poems as any other. In his books of poems *der gelbe hund* (1980) and *Selbstporträt des schachspielers als trinkende uhr* (1983), as well as in his stage play or 'opera for speaking voices', *Aus der Fremde* of 1980, Jandl was as unreservedly honest as ever about the personal crisis that had pushed him into this regressive mode. What was more important to him was to make the best of that crisis as a craftsman and artificer, persist in his struggle with language even when he had no other matter for verse than what came out of that struggle. The act of writing itself had always been of interest to Jandl. That is why his reports on it are exemplary, in their truthfulness, precision and detachment. In his very first book of poems there had been one about the act of writing, 'Stilleben' (Still Life):

Ich habe meinen Kugelschreiber, der rot-blau schreibt,
auf die Zündholzschachtel gelegt.
Das ist aufregend wie die Feuerwehr,
verglichen mit dem Schreibpapier daneben.

Das gelang mir nach dem Versuch,
einen grossartigen Gedanken zu haben.

(Ein Blatt Papier starb dabei an einem Ausschlag
von hässlichen blauen Buchstaben.)

I have laid my ball-pen which writes
red or blue on the matchbox.
That is thrilling as the fire engine,
compared with the sheet of paper beside it.

I succeeded in that after trying
to have a magnificent thought.
(In the process a sheet of paper
died of a rash of ugly blue letters.)

Even this early poem is characterized by self-detachment, humour and
frankness, but also by a childlike wonderment at things and processes
so ordinary that for most grown-up people, let alone most poets, they
would not be worth writing about, but dismissed and put away as
childish things.

der gelbe hund contains no sound or visual poem. The poems in this
book are a factual, almost day-to-day, record of a profound depression
and, at the same time, an attempt to overcome it by the act of writing, as
this one, 'der nagel' enacts in its regressive, primitive diction:

> festnageln ich will
> diesen da tag, jeden da
> jeden da tag da fest
> nageln ich will dass nicht
> mir er entkomme mir dass nicht
> mir er entkomme mehr dass nicht
> einer entkomme mir mehr nicht ein
> einziger mehr mir entkomme wie
> vorher als so viele ich nicht
> festgenagelt habe mit gedicht

> *the nail*
>
> nail down I will
> this here day, every here
> every here day here nail
> down I will so that
> it shall not slip away again
> not slip away from me so that
> not one shall slip away not one
> single day slip away from me as
> before when so many I did not
> nail down with poem one jot

This would have been a risky or impossible undertaking for any poet less skilled than Jandl in the art of letting language have its own way. As it is, these poems—carefully dated to preserve their chronological sequence—rarely fail to be engaging, instructive and witty, though they make no bones about the desperation from which they sprang. Jandl's trust in the power of words to create meaning, when everything else had grown meaningless for him, proved well-founded. An extreme honesty and an extreme indifference to the self-exposure involved in the exercise—carried even farther in *Aus der Fremde*, a play about himself, writing the play, and his long-standing association with the writer Friederike Mayröcker—were its precondition. All the data of the experiment are set down:

nichts und etwas

nichts im kopf
setze ich mich
an die maschine
spanne ein blatt ein
mit nichts darauf

mit etwas darauf
ziehe das blatt ich
aus der maschine
und lese als text
etwas aus meinem kopf

nothing and something

nothing in my head
I sit down
at the typewriter
insert a sheet
with nothing on it

with something on it
I extract the sheet
from the typewriter
and read as a text
something out of my head

This is minimal poetry with a vengeance, not even distanced here by sub-literary diction, rhyme, or by the reported speech subjunctive maintained throughout in *Aus der Fremde* and in some of the poems in this and Jandl's next collections. Yet this little poem celebrates a miracle and mystery of sorts. Something has really come out of nothing, thanks to the reductive simplicity and starkness of the act that is its own description and interpretation, with no evasion by way of metaphor, 'heightened' diction or emotive appeal. Other poems in the book are more intricate, such as the self-analysis 'a man of achievement'—the title is in English—which does resort to the distancing device of reported speech, like the dialogue in *Aus der Fremde*.

In both the play and the poems extremes meet once more, in that linguistic experiment fuses with its opposite, the most drastic realism in the rendering of psychological, biographical and social truths. For by his clinical self-detachment in dealing with his own crisis, Jandl makes it more than a personal matter, just as the verbal play in his early sound poems had not prevented them from engaging most effectively with the moral and political issues that preoccupied the 'mainstream' realists. At least one poem in *Selbstporträt des schachspielers als trinkende uhr* takes him well beyond the accurate transcription of the data and results of his desperate experiment in the defiance of blankness and silence:

das schöne bild

spar aus dem schönen bild den menschen aus
damit die tränen du, die jeder mensch verlangt
aussparen kannst; spar jede spur von menschen aus:
kein weg erinnere an festen gang, kein feld an brot
kein wald an haus und schrank, kein stein an wand
kein quell an trank, kein teich kein see kein meer
an schwimmer, boote, ruder, segel, seefahrt
kein fels an kletternde, kein wölkchen
an gegen wetter kämpfende, kein himmelstück
an aufblick, flugzeug, raumschiff—nichts
erinnere an etwas; ausser weiss an weiss
schwarz an schwarz, rot an rot, gerade an gerade
rund an rund;
so wird meine seele gesund.

the beautiful picture

withhold the human from your beautiful picture
so that you can withhold the tears for which
all human beings call; withhold the very trace:
let no path mark firm passage, no field recall bread
no forest house or wardrobe, no stone a wall
no spring their drinking, no pond no lake no sea
a swimmer, boat, oar, sail or navigation
no rock a climber, not one little cloud
those who resist the weather, no patch of sky
an upward glance or aircraft space-ship—let
nothing recall anything, but white recall white
black, black, red, red, straight recall straight
round recall round;
then shall my soul be healed, again be sound.

This poem does not shun rhetoric or pathos, and places itself most firmly in an older poetic tradition. (I, for instance, can hear an echo in it of Gonzalo's utopian speech in *The Tempest*; and this echo adds to the negative utopia of Jandl's poem, his exclusion of everything human from the picture that celebrates it by the very negation and exclusion— as though the utopia, now, can be reached only on the other side of extinction. Every negation in the poem posits its opposite; and this very appeal for an abstract picture becomes the least abstract poem in the book.) As for the personal crisis, this poem transcends it by facing up to its more than personal implications; it becomes a breakthrough, and a breakout from the language laboratory and its isolation. Jandl's experiment in that laboratory had proved that the very act of writing could wrest minimal meaning from meaninglessness. This poem is like a reward for the persistence and sheer industry the experiment had demanded. By regression in time and manner that also admits an old richness of import and allusion, it gathers up the various threads in Jandl's art and liberates all his faculties, as *homo faber, homo ludens* and *homo sapiens* combined. The antiquated thing once called inspiration, too, may well have contributed to this generally human poem about the exclusion of everything human.

4

For all its range between abstraction and realism—I have not even mentioned the radio plays, some of them written in collaboration with Friederike Mayröcker, collected in the volume *Fünf Mann Menschen* (1971)—Jandl's work is not eclectic, since the polarity and the tension were its precondition. With the exception of a number of early poems and a few later prose works, such as *Reise durch die Nacht* (1984), which has a narrative framework in time and place, Friederike Mayröcker has had as little use for the constraints of realism as for the pure verbalism of concrete poetry. Very consistently, in verse and prose, she has combined collage procedures with fantasy and free association, relying on the imaginative power, elegance and inventiveness of her language alone to make up for the loss of referential coherence, linear plots in prose or 'subjects', as distinct from themes, in poems. Whereas a commitment is implicit, if not explicit, in Jandl's most playful texts, as in Heissenbüttel's most austerely experimental ones, her combinations of the most disparate material have their being in total freedom. The quotations from books, magazines, printed matter of any kind that are as essential to her texts as to many of Heissenbüttel's serve as raw material for her imagination, not as data for an experiment that could prove anything whatever; and the same is true of the first-hand observations of persons, places and things, that are also woven into her figurations. What she has in common with most of the non-representational writers of her time is her freedom from generic conventions and specialization. Her language can function lyrically, dramatically or narratively, when she chooses to narrate or describe, or flow without transition from one mode into another.

Eclecticism and elegance have distinguished the extraordinary work of Hans Carl Artmann, a writer so adept at wearing and changing masks that he has become a legendary figure in his lifetime and a conundrum to his readers, who have been asking themselves for decades which of his many selves might be the real one, the authentic one. His early reputation and popularity were due to his Viennese dialect poems. If that suggested regional preoccupations and roots, Artmann had already confounded it by his association with Konrad Bayer and Gerhard Rühm, out-and-out innovators who were soon to feel that they were exiles and outcasts in their notoriously conservative city. Soon Artmann was to roam the *musée imaginaire* in search of quite other models and traditions, moving from ancient Celtic literature to the Persian, from Austrian baroque to the Arctic fringes, from archaizing pastiche to the sound laboratories of the international avant-garde. His styles and *personae* changed not only from book to book, but even within the confines of a single book. His collection of poems *Verbarium* (1966), for instance, begins with a series of mythical epitaphs, switches to the *verbaria* proper—concatenations of semantically unrelated words, mostly bizarre and exotic—then to a sequence of poems in seventeenth-century idiom, the 'treuherzige kirchoflieder'. Two other sections of the book, 'auf meine klinge geschrieben' and 'berliner gedichte', glorify sensuous, especially erotic, experience in imagery partly modern, partly archaic and primitve. It is almost as though the poet had set out to include all history and pre-history, and all regions from the tropics to the poles; and as though virtuosity and elegance, not a 'unifying personality', were the source and end of his performances.

Only a year later Artmann could publish his prose book *Fleiss und Industrie*, a collection of minutely descriptive miniatures devoted to artisans and craftsmen, 'all trades, their gear and tackle and trim', and dedicated to the memory of his father, a master craftsman. Although mannered, like all Artmann's work, this collection has the consistency and unity of a single concept and form; but if anyone thought that Artmann had been converted to a realism or representationalism of any sort, and could be pinned down to that, Artmann made it his business to give that person the slip. His next books were self-projections into the worlds of cannibals and of Lapland; and Artmann was to keep up these flights and tackings in every subsequent book. A characteristic one is the novel-length *Die Jagd nach Dr. U.* (1977), written during 'various stays at Rennes, Carnac, Roskoff, Exeter, Weymouth, Truro, Penzance, New Grange, in the wilderness of the Connor Pass and lastly in the rue Tholozé in Paris 18e.' In the same preface, Artmann writes that the work claims to be no more than 'reading matter', though it looks like a novel, and it has the baroque sub-title, 'Or a Lonely Looking-Glass in which Day Mirrors Itself'. The blurb interprets Artmann's 'reading matter' as meaning that the work fits into no category of fiction, but that would be taken for granted both by the author or by anyone who had read any of his books. Artmann was more likely to mean that his book had no purpose or function beyond his pleasure in writing it and other people's pleasure in reading it. The writing, as ever, is exuberant, full of verbal histrionics, high jinks, pastiche and collage—to a degree that many readers may have found intolerably frivolous. No serious concern, other than an auto-biographical one, could possibly be read into this pseudo-thriller that jumps about in place and time, with a narrator who appears under different names, usually English, in the most unlikely places, on his quest for a sinister villain no less volatile and mutable. Its many literary sources, which are also its substance, include Sweeney Todd, Dr Jekyll and Mr Hyde, Irish legends from Lady Gregory, works by Sax Rohmer, Basho, Richard Jefferies and Dafydd ap Gwylym. These and other literary reminiscences are strung on a thin thread of episodic, magic-lantern narrative, with all the breaks and knots unashamedly showing.

Autobiographically, the book does make sense, because Artmann's whole astonishing literary *oeuvre* is a succession of masks tried on by the author for the fun of it, and to find out what sort of stylistic effects could be drawn from his disguises. In this instance he has resorted to 'Trivial-literatur', spiced with more exotic and esoteric ingredients. The outcome is a late, artificial flowering of the Austrian baroque, distinctly decadent, as Artmann was well aware, and brilliantly brought off. The virtuosity and the elegance are there, as ever. The person and the purpose remain elusive behind the masks.

4

It was only in the decade or so of drastic politicization, when much German imaginative writing seemed to aspire to the condition of documentary, that linguistically experimental writing was kept quite separate from the acknowledged mainstream; and even then it was only the purists of concrete poetry, like Eugen Gomringer or Franz Mon, who could easily and fairly be relegated to a language laboratory whose experiments were 'irrelevant' to what was assumed to be the general public's needs. Not only had the most prominent of West German mainstream writers, Günter Grass, begun with poems more Dadaist or surrealist than representational, but documentary, too, was one of the materials and end products of experimental writing, not only in the work of Heissenbüttel. Konrad Bayer's austerely experimental prose work *Der Kopf des Vitus Bering*, published posthumously with a postscript by Jürgen Becker in 1966, took the form of a logbook in places, even if the entries had been processed in the language laboratory, which in this case was also a philosophical laboratory.

Jürgen Becker's own work can be placed either in the linguistic tributary of 'experimental' writing or in the mainstream that was given the name 'the new subjectivity' when the documentary spate had subsided. His three early 'prose' works, *Felder* (1964), *Ränder* (1968) and *Umgebungen* (1970), were neither novels nor stories, but compositions partly topographical, partly autobiographical, partly purely lingustic. *Ränder*, in fact, has a geometric structure of concentric circles whose centre is the two blank pages between sections 5 and 7. As of Heissenbüttel's texts, it is also impossible to say of these texts whether they are prose or poetry, prose poetry or poetic prose. Passages in which the lines are split and spaced like verse are thematically linked to passages that not only look, but read, like prose; and this prose can be realistically descriptive or anecdotal. Passages with regular syntax are mixed with passages in which usage and grammar dissolve, language becomes abstract.

Becker's books of poems of the same period, *Schnee* (1971) and *Das Ende der Landschaftsmalerei* (1974) have much more in common with 'the new subjectivity', with its indebtedness to American poetry of the Beat and New York schools, its fusion of immediate perceptions with a dynamic of immediate feelings or states of mind. It is in the larger structures of his 'prose' works that he made more use of the procedures of the linguistic experimentalists. His later prose work, *Erzählen bis Ostende* (1981) has a narrative framework, the account of a journey, but is closer nonetheless to his poems than to *Felder, Ränder* or *Umgebungen*, in that it captures moments of intense experience, recapitulated in a state of drowsiness during the train journey. Realistic and grammatically coherent though all the short prose episodes of the later work are, it owes its distinction and power to a concentration and condensation more poetic than prosaic; and it is its language, above all, that engages and holds our attention. This language has become an individual style once more, rather than a neutral material for experiment; but Becker is only one of many writers of the 1970s and 1980s who have availed themselves of experiments carried out by the primarily linguistic writers to fashion such a style.

Nor is Artmann the only Austrian prose writer of that period whose styles are so mannered as to serve as masks, even in 'straight' narratives that may or may not be autobiographical. Both the novels and the autobiographies of Thomas Bernhard owe more to a prose style at once idiosyncratic and anachronistic—in that it draws as little as possible from the current vernacular—than to the conventional resources of mimetic fiction in dialogue, description and character-drawing. Many of the 'plots' of Bernhard's novels could be reduced to a sentence or two without much loss of substance. Their true substance lies only in the telling, in the manner of the telling, which at once conveys and conceals the personality of the teller; and that is as true of the autobiographies as of the fiction, because Bernhard's style is a mask, though a single mask worn consistently, unlike Artmann's.

Peter Handke's *Kindergeschichte* (1981) is another instance. This may or may not be an autobiographical account of the author's relations with his daughter. (The sudden switches from a third-person to a first-person narrative may suggest that it is.) The daughter, however, does not even acquire a name, but remains 'the child' throughout the account. Nor does the father of the child acquire a 'character' in the round, though he tells us a good deal more about himself than about the mother, of whom we know little more than that she is an independent professional woman. Again, it is the manner of the telling that sustains our interest; and the manner, once more, is idiosyncratic and ana-chronistic, as remote as could be from any spoken idiom of our time. This anachronism is what the book is about—both in relation to child-hood, which is glorified as a state of pure timelessness and potentiality, and in relation to the father, whose consuming desire is to be free of history and who 'forswears history for his person'. This is also made explicit in the episodes that refer to political activists and dogmatists who wish to impose a 'compulsory future' on society at large or on any individual, like the father, who associates with them. The highly formal, almost archaic, style enacts and fulfils the father's desire to get out of history. The father, we learn early on, 'had in fact just completed a work in which he thought he had for once attained the self-evident, the casual and the lawful', and those highly mannered epithets also describe what is both the theme and the style of Handke's story. Only in that sense is it an essentially autobiographical work, and would remain one even if all the circumstances and actions of the characters were invented by the author. The categories of realistic or mimetic fiction are totally irrelevant, too, when the gist of the work is an almost mystical urge towards unqualified, undetermined essence.

Peter Handke had become famous as the *enfant terrible* of a literary establishment still hungry for novelty and sensations above all, as for the controversies they occasioned. Yet it was Handke who championed the work of a writer nearly thirty years older than himself, Hermann Lenz, who had been ignored by that establishment ever since the end of the war, as a quirky, freakish and backward-looking figure. What Lenz's fiction gave Handke was 'a childhood feeling—as though sud-denly all those missed were back again in the house.' All Lenz's fiction was backward-looking not only because, like Handke, he did not care for his own age, but because the utopia he opposed to it was one projected into the past, not the future. Though a Suabian, Lenz was more apt to project it into the Austria of the Habsburg dynasty than into Old Württemberg or Rome. The location did not matter greatly, since that past was a utopian one, and Lenz was delicately, ironically, aware that it was utopian. (An Austrian idea, as distinct from an Austrian reality, had been potent and pervasive in the work of earlier writers, from Grillparzer to Hofmannsthal. It was on this that they based a moral and spiritual patriotism even while the Habsburgs were still in power.) Herman Lenz's protagonists are outsiders and misfits, like most of those in German post-war fiction, not excluding Heinrich Böll's, because they have a purity and an integrity that has to do with Handke's quest for the 'self-evident, the casual and the lawful', in life as in literature. Unlike a great many West German critics, Handke could see that it made little difference whether such qualities were attributed to a lost way of life or to one still to be established. Imaginative literature, of whatever kind, does project utopias, and very properly so; but these should not be confused with political programmes. What is more, it was the realism of Herman Lenz's novel *Neue Zeit* (1975), in its treatment of the Third Reich and the Second World War, that won over a new readership, with Handke's help. Like the forward-looking majority of an earlier phase, Lenz was dedicated to nothing so much as the avoidance of a repetition of that historical era. Yet it was the climate of the 'new subjectivity' that allowed Lenz to come into his own belatedly. In 1978 he was awarded the prestigious Büchner Prize.

Compared to *Neue Zeit*, Herman Lenz's *Der Tintenfisch in der Garage* (1977) is on a small scale, with few characters and a plot so restricted in place and time as to recall the classical unities. That is why it was offered as an 'Erzählung' or 'conte', though English readers indifferent to such classifications still dear to German critics would probably call it a short novel. Despite a contemporary setting—the city of Regensburg in the early 1970s—a very young protagonist, and a narrative style informal to the point of briskness—much less formal and more up-to-date than Handke's in *Kindergeschichte—Der Tintenfisch in der Garage* still manages to be provocatively old-fashioned. Anachronism is its theme and gist. The student Ludwig is a fish out of water (or an 'octopus in the garage', as the Spanish idiom has it) because he has an almost Kaspar Hauser-like remoteness from his environment. This remoteness is ascribed not so much to 'idealism' or unworldliness— Ludwig has a robust shrewdness, humour and sensuality—as to his roots in an older order and his conviction that old institutions, old buildings, old ways of life are both better and more real than the new. The once imperial city of Ratisbon provides a palpable background of antiquities. Yet the modern age is by no means excluded, but offset against the old as the other pole and the generator of ironic tensions that sustain the work. A literary reading circle, a 'progressive' professor of literature, snatches of their intellectual talk, and telling descriptive details sketch in the world which Ludwig finds it so hard to regard as his. What makes the story old-fashioned is Lenz's ability to turn ambivalence into suspense, if not mystery—a knack that Handke may well have taken over from Lenz. Ludwig becomes involved with a young woman who, sensing his peculiar remoteness from the contemporary world, picks him up when he is riding his bicycle, she is driving her Morris car. The reader never knows any more than Ludwig does whether the elderly man she lives with is her uncle, as she makes out at first, or her husband; whether she is an impoverished aristocrat, an adventuress, or both; and whether her uncle/husband is merely permissive towards her relations with Ludwig or in collusion with her to involve Ludwig in shady business deals.

If the work has an allegorical dimension, this, too, remains ambiguous; for the story can be read as a satire on the intellectual and commercial state of West Germany or as an exposure of futile efforts to escape from it into the past. On any level it is an engaging, subtle and amusing work, even without recourse to those stylistic masks that Lenz employs in his longer and more ambitious novels and sequences of novels, with predominantly realistic structures.

It is Austrian writers, above all, from Ilse Aichinger to Jutta Schütting, Thomas Bernhard and Peter Handke, who have found it natural to maintain the primacy of style in all writing, often to the point of extreme idiosyncrasy and mannerism, regardless of the trends and ideologies to which the controlling West German book market has been subject over the decades. This proclivity does not depend on residence in Austria. It is strong in the work of Franz Tumler and Gerald Bisinger, despite their residence in Berlin, and more marked than has been widely noticed even in the work of Erich Fried, who has not lived in Austria since before the war and has been categorized as a 'political poet'.

German-Swiss writers, too, have made brilliant use of stylistic masks more crucial to their fictions than action, character-drawing, setting, and the rest. Peter Bichsel, in *Eigentlich möchte Frau Blum den Milchmann kennenlernen* (1964) and his *Kindergeschichten* (1969), has excelled at stories in which nothing happens, about people at once ordinary and fantastic. Not only in his stories for children—just as widely read by adults—his mask is one of näivety; and this näivety can accommodate the most outrageously eccentric assumptions and behaviour, simply by accepting them, as children do, as part of a given world. A related mask of simplicity characterizes the stories of Kurt Marti in *Dorfgeschichten* (1960), and some of Jörg Steiner's prose works, like his novel *Ein Messer für den ehrlichen Finder* (1971). All these writers, like Otto F. Walter in his novels *Der Stumme* (1959) and *Herr Tourel* (1962), chose regional settings for works that are not circumscribed by regional concerns. The stylistic mask is even more striking in the context of Adolf Muschg's *Liebesgeschichten* (1972), in his story 'Der Zusenn oder das Heimat', because Muschg is among the most sophisticated and cosmopolitan of contemporary German-language writers, and there is nothing specifically Swiss about most of his settings. (His 1980 novel *Baiyun oder die Freundschaftsgesellschaft* is set in China.) Unlike those other Swiss writers, too, he is eminently a psychological novelist. Bichsel's mask of näivety precludes all delving into psychological motives and complexes.

Muschg's story 'The Scythe Hand or the Homestead' can dispense with analysis of motives by leaving it to the style—an archaic, anachronistic idiom adopted by a farmer, whose normal idiom would be dialect, to explain his case to the legal authorities, in terms he considers more elevated and more appropriate. The case is the incestuous relations with his daughters into which he has been forced by isolation, poverty, and the death of his wife after a fire. But for the style, so matter-of-fact beneath its non-sequiturs and convolutions, that story would have been lurid or sensational. In the farmer's words it becomes a paradigm of the power and vagaries of love *in extremis*. All the author's skill and intelligence has gone into the making of a style as different from his own as this *tour de force* demanded. The slightest intrusion of his own judgement or his own vocabulary would have reduced the paradigm to a scandal or a dirty joke.

By the standards of 'committed' social realism, such stylistic masks in fiction are hardly less 'formalist' than the kind of experimental writing that makes language both the medium and the message. Seen differently, they are supremely realistic, too, in their artifice—an imaginative documentary in which the author becomes as invisible as Flaubert said he should be.

VIII   A Prodigious Equipoise

1

If there is one West German post-war writer who has confounded all the critical categories and classifications, it is Günter Grass; not so much because of his range of media, from lyrical poetry to drama and prose fiction, from essays and dialogues to political speeches, as because within those media he has maintained a balance peculiar to himself between otherwise divisive antinomies. That Grass has also been a boy soldier, wounded in action before the end of the war, a miner, stone-mason and sculptor, or that he remains a graphic artist of distinction and an accomplished cook might be mere biographical accidents or circumstances if Grass's diverse activities had been kept separate, if it were not his way to bring each of them to bear on the other. Günter Grass, in fact, could have been approached in the context of any of the foregoing chapters of this book, but not one of those contexts could have encompassed his significance or his scope.

In the first chapter, for instance, I wrote about the polarization of the conflicting principles and practices of Gottfried Benn on the one hand, Bertolt Brecht on the other, between Benn's 'absolute poetry'—'words assembled in a fascinating way' and not subject to moral, social or historical criteria—and Brecht's insistence on the uses and usefulness of literature. We have only to ask ourselves to which of these sides or trends Günter Grass belonged as a poet, at the time of his emergence in the early 1950s, to come up against one instance of his capacity to embrace and balance extreme opposites. Shortly after the publication of his first book, *Die Vorzüge der Windhühner* (1956), Grass wrote three short prose pieces that appeared in the periodical *Akzente* under the title 'Der Inhalt als Widerstand' (Content as Resistance), in which imagination and verisimilitude, fantasy and realism, are treated not as alternatives but as generators of a necessary tension. The middle piece, a brief dialogue between two poets, Pempelfort and Krudewil, on a walk together, presents the extreme alternatives. Pempelfort is in the habit of stuffing himself with indigestible food before going to bed, to induce nightmares and the (then fashionable) genitive metaphors he can jot down between fits of sleep; the quoted specimens of his poems place him in the line of development that includes German Expressionism and the Surrealism that was being rediscovered by young German poets at the time. Krudewil, for his part, wants to 'knit a new Muse' who is 'grey, mistrustful and totally dreamless, a meticulous housewife'. This homely and practical Muse points to the school of Brecht, who drew on dreams not for metaphors but moralities. Grass's treatment of these two characters is good-humouredly and comically impartial. Grass's own early poems, with their free associations and their synaesthesia, their polymorphic playfulness, might have biased him towards Pempelfort. In later years, when ideology reigned, his moderation—and moderation as such—was to be attacked as indifference or weakness or equivocation. In fact the dialogue was an early instance of a strength rare among German intellectuals, the strength of those who don't lose their heads in a crisis. Grass would not have bothered to write the dialogue at all if he had not been deeply involved in a conflict that was to turn German literature into a battlefield in the course of the next decade. It was by quarrelling with himself that he prepared for the battles to come.

Nearly ten years later, when Grass had become a celebrated writer and a controversial public figure, he published another prose piece in the same periodical. It was the lecture 'Vom mangelnden Selbstvertrauen der schreibenden Hofnarren unter Berücksichtigung nicht vorhandener Höfe' (On the Lack of Self-Confidence among Writing Court Fools in View of Non-existent Courts). The very title, with its baroque and ironic identification of writer with court fools, was an affront to the solemn self-righteousness of the dominant radicals, who disapproved not only of Grass's incorrigible addiction to clowning in his verse and prose fiction, but also of his commitment to a political party, the Social Democrats, more evolutionary than revolutionary, and so guilty of moderation and compromise in their view. What is more, Grass came out in favour of a position half-way between what the radicals understood by commitment—the subordination of art to political and social programmes—and the demand of art itself for the free play of imagination, the freedom that Grass, with historical wisdom, traced to the old privilege of court fools or jesters to tell the truth, however subversive that truth might be of the order that had power over them. Unlike most of his radical opponents, Grass had taken the trouble not only to think about politics and power, but to acquaint himself with their machinery by active participation—as early as 1961, through his personal association with Willy Brandt. That, of course, was only the beginning of an involvement that was to cost Grass more conflicts and bitter disappointments, all of which entered into the experience that shaped his imaginative works. If a writer is worried about the state of affairs in his own country or elsewhere, Grass argued in the lecture, the best way, in a parliamentary democracy, is to do something about it not as an imaginative writer but as a citizen. As for his writing, if it is imaginative writing, he should resist every kind of extraneous pressure that would transform it into a vehicle or a weapon. 'Poems admit of no compromises; but we live by compromises. Whoever can endure this tension every day of his life is a fool and changes the world.'

Gottfried Benn, in his exchange of letters with Alexander Lernet-Holenia of 1953, *Monologische Kunst*, had denied categorically that writers or artists can 'change the world'. Brecht had based all his practice on the assumption that they can. By insisting on the autonomy of art—as Brecht, incidentally, had also done—*and* on the need to change the world by availing oneself of the traditional freedom of court fools, Grass proved a better dialectician than his Marxist opponents. Grass had learned that in literature, as much as in practical politics or cooking, it is not a matter of this or that, but a little more of this rather than a little more of that; not of imagination or 'reality', of clowning or didacticism, of commitment or non-commitment, but of a particular blend of them all in every instance that makes for rightness and richness. Because he has borne this in mind at all times, in everything to which he has applied himself, Grass is not only an anti-specialist—the nearest thing to an all-round man the age allowed him to be, when even Goethe could be said by T. S. Eliot to have 'dabbled in' all the many activities he had tried to co-ordinate and synthesize in his mind—but an anti-ideologist. Even his theoretical pronouncements were nourished and sustained by his awareness of complexity, an awareness that he owes to first-hand experience. In his imaginative works, including his poems and his drawings, the mixture has not remained constant. Just as in his novels there has been a gradual shift away from subjective fantasy to observed realities—though never without an undercurrent of fantasy, fable or even myth—and that shift had its parallel in his plays written up to his 'German tragedy' about Brecht, *Die Plebejer Proben den Aufstand* (1966), it was his first book of poems that showed Grass at his most exuberantly and uninhibitedly clownish. This is not to say that these early poems lack moral or metaphysical seriousness, but that the element of free play in them is more pronounced and more idiosyncratic than in the later poems, in which the clown had to defend his privilege of freedom both from his own scruples and the combined attack of opponents on the Right and Left.

It has become something of a commonplace in Grass criticism to note that his imagination and invention are most prolific where he is closest to childhood experience, by which I mean both his own, as evoked in the more or less autobiographical sections of his Danzig trilogy, or in the more or less autobiographical poem 'Kleckerburg', and childish modes of feeling, seeing and behaving. Almost without exception, the poems in Grass's first book owe their vigour and peculiarity to this mode of feeling, seeing and behaving. These early poems enact primitive gestures and processes without regard for the distinctions that adult rationality imposes on the objects of perception. (This freedom, rather than an influence, may account for the striking similarities between Grass's early poems and those of Hans Arp, whose principle of fortuitousness gave him a related freedom of association. Grass, who has generously acknowledged his indebtedness as a novelist to Alfred Döblin—even endowing a literary prize in his honour and name—has acknowledged no such debt to Arp for his poetry. Affinity is what matters, in any case, not influence.) Grass's early poems have their being in a world without divisions or distinctions, full of magical substitutions and transformations. Arp's eye and ear had the same mischievous innocence, giving a grotesque twist to everyday things and banal phrases; and Arp, too, was to adapt his unanchored images and metaphors to increasingly moral and social preoccupations, not to mention the metaphysical ones which, much like Grass, he had always combined with his comic zest. Surrealist practice, too, would be relevant as a precedent if Grass's early poems were not as realistic as they are fantastic, with a realism that seems fantastic only because it is true to the polymorphous vision of childhood.

Most of the poems in *Die Vorzüge der Windhühner* deal in unanchored images, like the 'eleventh finger' that cannot be tied down to any particular plane of meaning or symbolism, but owes its genesis and function to a complex of mainly personal associations. Such unanchored and floating images were also carried over into Grass's prose, especially in *Die Blechtrommel*, and some of them had such obsessive power over Grass's imagination that they recur with variations in his poems, prose narratives, plays and drawings. (Dolls, nuns, cooks and hens, snails and fish and mushrooms are a few of those. In many cases, these, in turn, are associated with processes and movements—such as flying, in the case of nuns—that are even more important to Grass than the thing, person or animal in itself.) The substitution practised by Grass in these poems also includes drastic synaesthesia, as in the many poems connected with music, orchestras or musical instruments. Sounds are freely transposed into visual impressions and *vice versa*, as in 'Die Schule der Tenöre' (The School for Tenors):

> Nimm den Lappen, wische den Mond fort,
> schreibe die Sonne, die andere Münze
> über den Himmel, die Schultafel.
> Setze dich dann.
> Dein Zeugnis wird gut sein,
> du wirst versetzt werden,
> eine neue, hellere Mütze tragen.
> Denn die Kreide hat recht
> und der Tenor der sie singt.
> Er wird den Samt entblättern,
> Efeu, Meterware der Nacht,

Moos, ihren Unterton,
jede Amsel wird er vertreiben.

Den Bassisten, mauert ihn ein
in seinem Gewölbe
Wer glaubt noch an Fässer
in denen der Wein fällt?
Ob Vogel oder Schrapnell,
oder nur Summen bis es knackt,
weil der Äther überfüllt ist
mit Wochenend und Sommerfrische.
Scheren, die in den Schneiderstuben
das lied von Frühling und Konfektion zwitschern,—
hieran kein Beispiel.

Die Brust heraus, bis der Wind seinen Umweg macht.
Immer wieder Trompeten,
spitzgedrehte Tüten voller silberner Zwiebeln.
Dann die Geduld.
Warten bis der Dame die Augen davonlaufen,
zwei unzufriedene Dienstmädchen.
Jetzt erst den Ton den die Gläser fürchten
und der Staub
der die Gesimmse verfolgt bis sie hinken.

Fischgräten, wer singt diese Zwischenräume,
den Mittag, mit Schilf gespießt?
Wie schön sang Else Fenske, als sie,
während der Sommerferien,
in großer Höhe danebentrat,
in einen stillen Gletscherspalt stürzte,
und nur ihr Schirmchen
und das hohe C zurückließ.

Das hohe C, die vielen Nebenflüsse des Mississippi,
der herrliche Atem,
der die Kuppeln erfand und den Beifall.
Vorhang, Vorhang, Vorhang.
Schnell, bevor der Leuchter nicht mehr klirren will,
bevor die Galerien knicken
und die Seide billig wird.
Vorhang, bevor du den Beifall begreifst.

Take your duster, wipe away the moon,
write the sun, that other coin
across the sky, the blackboard.
Then take your seat.
Your report will be a good one,
you will go up one class,

wear a new, brighter cap.
For the chalk is in the right
and so is the tenor who sings it.
He will unroll the velvet,
ivy, yard-measured wares of night,
moss, its undertone,
every blackbird he'll drive away.

The bass—immure him
in his vault.
Who now believes in barrels
in which the wine-level falls?
Whether bird or shrapnel
or only a hum till it cracks
because the ether is overcrowded
with weekend and seaside resort.
Scissors which in the tailor's workshops
twitter the song of springtime and haute couture—
this is no example.

Puff out your chest, till the wind takes its devious way.
Trumpets again and again,
conical paper bags full of silver onions.
After that, patience.
Wait till the lady's eyes run away,
two dissatisfied skivvies.
Only now that tone which the glasses fear
and the dust
that pursues the ledges until they limp.

Fishbones, who will sing these gaps,
sing noon impaled with rushes?
How well did Elsie Fenner sing
when, in the summer vacation
at a great height she took a false step,
tumbled into a silent glacier crevasse
and left nothing behind but
her little parasol and the high C.

The high C, the many tributaries of the Mississippi,
the glorious breath
that invented cupolas and applause.
Curtain, curtain, curtain.
Quick, before the candelabrum refuses to jingle,
before the galleries droop
and silk becomes cheap.
Curtain, before you understand the applause.

There is no need to go into an elaborate and solemn explication that would amount to a translation of the poem into the terms of adult rationality—terms irrelevant to the poem in any case. It is enough to point out that its subject or gist is a sequence of kinetic gestures, derived in the first place from a personal response to the singing of tenors, but proceeding by a series of free substitutions and transpositions. These substitutions and transpositions observe no distinction between one order of experience and another, between aural and visual or tactile phenomena, between what is physically possible and what is not. The world of childhood becomes a *motif* at the start, with the chalk and blackboard images given a cosmographic extension, and the school caps which in Germany used to mark membership of successive classes by their colours and are associated with progress, promotion and ascent, like the tenor voice. That, however, is a simile; and in Grass's poems metaphor is autonomous, a thing is not *like* another thing but *is* the other thing for the purpose and duration of the poem, as it is in children's games. Yet, although one thing in the poem leads to another, by associations that are astonishingly fluid, the poem is held together by an organization different from automatic writing in that the initial phenomenon is never quite left behind. Ingenuity and intellectual invention, too, are part of that organization, as in metaphysical or baroque poetry and its 'conceits'. Grass's love of the seventeenth century, its picaresque fiction and metaphysical wit, can be traced in his novels from *Die Blechtrommel (The Tin Drum)* to *Das Treffen in Telgte* (1979; *The Meeting at Telgte*). Grass avails himself of the freedom of polymorphous childishness; but because he is not a child, and even his poems of innocence include his awareness of experience, wit serves him as a necessary mediator between the conscious and unconscious reservoirs that feed his art. The association of the bass voice, for instance, with a cellar, hence with wine and, most appropriately, with a wine-barrel or vat in which the fluid level falls, is so elementary as to be easily followed by anyone who has not lost all access to the sub-rational levels of his or her mind. The likening of a tenor voice to 'conical paper bags full of silver onions' is a little more far-fetched, a little more ingenious, but just as convincing; and so is all the play on light and darkness, bright and sombre sounds, leading to the dynamic analogy of cutting cloth and so to scissors, tailors and *haute couture*. Grass is at his most clownishly farcical in the passage introducing the woman singer who takes a false step, yet even her plunge into the crevasse is consistent with the whole poem's trans-sensory dynamism.

But for the wit and the more ingenious allusions in poems like 'The School for Tenors', they would belong to a realm of clown's and child's play that is amoral and asocial. Yet even in this poem satirical implications arise from references to historical phenomena like seaside resorts, shrapnel and, especially, to audiences in an opera house (which for upper class Germans had become a kind of secular, 'cultural' church). Grass makes fun of all those phenomena, as he was to make fun in his first novel even of the institutions that had shaped him in childhood and adolescence, the National Socialist Party and the Roman Catholic Church. The very short, almost epigrammatic pieces in the same first collection, though, introduce Grass the moralist looking over the shoulder of the clown and child, not least incisively in 'Familiär' (Family Matters), which compounds irony by judging the adult world from a child's point of view—a device most characteristic of the man who was to write *The Tin Drum* and later poems like 'Advent'. Incidentally, this poem is one of many reminders that Grass—a writer who has been accused of obscenity and blasphemy, has had his books burned and his house set on fire by the guardians of 'law and order'—was brought up as a Roman Catholic:

> In unserem Museum—wir besuchen es jeden Sonntag,—
> hat man eine neue Abteilung eröffnet.
> Unsere abgetriebenen Kinder, blasse, ernsthafte Embryos,
> sitzen dort in schlichten Gläsern
> und sorgen sich um die Zukunft ihrer Eltern.

> *Family Matters*

> In our museum—we always go there on Sundays—
> they have opened a new department.
> Our aborted children, pale, serious foetuses,
> sit there in plain glass jars
> and worry about their parents' future.

Here the grey, meticulous Muse of everyday life has taken over from the Muse of fantasy and dreams, as it was to do more consistently, though never completely, in Grass's second and third books of poems. Yet the didactic impact is made through fantasy—as in some of Arp's later poems—not through a consequential literalness, as practised by Brecht in short poems like the *Buckower Elegien* and by Brecht's many successors in the two German Republics. Like the opera house in 'Die Schule der Tenöre', the museum here has a specifically German connotation. It stands for the secular cult of self-improvement through art and education that tended to replace religious worship. That is why the museum is visited weekly, on Sundays. Abortion belongs to the same secularized order. His residual Catholicism—attested, not disproved, by his blasphemies—was to become another source of friction between Grass and the dogmatists of permissiveness.

Another early prose piece by Grass, his essay *Die Ballerina* first published in 1956, not long after his marriage to Anna Schwarz, a ballet student, not only compares the ballerina with tenors, whose voices may demand that they grip the back of a chair or some other physical support, but brings out the traditionalism and conservatism—with a decidedly small 'c'—as essential to Grass as the freedom to innovate.

> The ballerina, like a nun, lives exposed to every temptation, in a state of the strictest asceticism. This analogy should not surprise you, since all the art come down to us has been the product of consistent restriction, never the immoderation of genius. Even if at times breakouts into the impermissible made and make us think that all is permitted in art, always even the most mobile of minds invented rules for itself, fences, forbidden rooms. So, too, our ballerina's room is restricted, surveyable, and permits changes only within the area available to her. The demands of the age will always require the ballerina to put on a new face, will hold exotic or pseudo-exotic masks in front of it. She will join in that decorative little game, knowing that every fashion suits her. The true revolution, though, will have to take place in her own palace.
>
> How similar it is in painting. How meaningless seem all attempts to see fundamental discoveries in the invention of new materials, in exchanging oil painting for a process of lacquer sprayed on to aluminium. Never will dilettantism, easily recognizable by its mannerisms, drive out the pertinacious flow of the skill that remains conservative even within its revolutions.

Grass, too, believed in the 'palace revolutions', fought out within oneself, that have to precede all general and outward change; and, as a graphic artist, he has remained outstanding for a minute and meticulous skill like that of the old masters, however grotesque the subjects and personal the vision of his drawings and etchings. Not only in politics, moderation and asceticism have always acted as a counterweight to his exuberance and gusto. The two opposing tugs, with specific reference to the poems Grass was writing at the time, are designated once and for all in the next paragraph of the early prose piece:

> The ballerina turns her mirror into an implacable implement of asceticism. Wide awake she trains in front of its surface. Her dance is not the dance with closed eyes. The mirror to her is nothing more than a glass that throws everything back, with exaggerated clarity, a merciless moralist she is commanded to believe. What liberties a poet takes with his mirror. What mystical, illegible postcards he drops into its baroque frame. To him the mirror is an exit, entrance, he searches like a still ignorant kitten behind the pane and, at best, finds a broken little box there, filled with buttons that do not match, a bundle of old letters he never expected to find again, and a comb full of hairs. Only at moments of irreversible transformation, when our bodies seem enriched or impoverished, do we stand in front of the mirror as she does, with eyes as awake. A mirror shows girls their puberty,, no pregnancy escapes it, no missing tooth—should laughter try to provoke it. Perhaps a hairdresser, a taxi-driver, a tailor, a painter at his self-portrait, a prostitute who has furnished her little room with a number of these

clarifying shards, have something in common with the ballerina. It is the anxious gaze of the craftsman, of a person who works with his or her body, it is the searching look into the mirror of conscience before confession.

The analogy of ballerina and nun could be censured as an instance of the very secularization that Grass had satirized in 'Family Matters'; but that would be to miss the point about Grass's residual Catholicism, which, to him, was not a Sunday religion. That aspect of the faith had been discredited for him by his up-bringing 'between the Holy Ghost and photographs of Hitler', as he put it in the autobiographical poem 'Kleckerburg', a conjunction of powers—formalized in the notorious Concordat—he was to lampoon in his prose fiction.

2

Even generically, Grass's first novel *The Tin Drum* (1959) is an amalgam of disparate types, including the German *Bildungsroman*—or its sub-category, the *Künstlerroman*, which traced the evolution of an artist's character—and the picaresque, particularly Grimmelshausen's *Der Abenteuerliche Simplicissimus* (1669/1671), the novel of the Thirty Years' War on which Brecht drew for his *Mutter Courage*. Grimmels-hausen offers a number of clues to the overall structure and meaning of Grass's novel, in so far as it has an overall structure and meaning; especially to the retrospective nature of the narrative, from the stand-point of a protagonist who has retired from the world, its follies and its evils. On another level, *The Tin Drum* forms part of an autobiographical trilogy set in Danzig, continued in the novella *Katz und Maus* (1961) and *Hundejahre* (1963; *Dog Years*) and it is in the evocation of this setting that Grass fused the utmost realism with his fantastic, fairy tale and grotesque inventions. After working on the novel in Paris from 1956 to 1958, Grass found it necessary to re-visit his home town, now the Polish city of Gdansk, mainly for a topographical documentation almost as thorough as that required by Uwe Johnson for the writing of his novels. As with Grass's poems, there is little point in pulling apart the many strands joined in Grass's prose or only in the invention of Oskar Mazerath, his tin drummer, who is a monster and a clown and a messianic figure; or in pointing out that this comic masterpiece is also a deeply serious and tragic work—more so even than Heinrich Böll's apotheosis of the clown or 'holy fool' figure in a later novel.

It is Grass's blasphemies that testify to the power over him of Roman Catholic dogma, as in the excursus 'Faith Hope Charity' at the end of Book I, culminating in the Association of Christ with the 'heavenly gasman' and the institution of the Church with the institution of the Nazi gas chambers; or the scene in the church, where Oskar substitutes himself for the infant Jesus. Oskar's refusal to grow up is his refusal to be part of the fallen world, which is that of adult society. His seeming amorality is that of innocence, though one that extends to the polymorphous sexuality of childhood.

Oskar's seeming amorality makes him a vehicle for the political de-demonization achieved by Grass in his rendering of lower middle class life in and around Danzig during the Third Reich. The opening episode, with its parody of the autobiographical and *Bildungsroman* prototype, sets the tone for the whole work. Oskar's maternal grandmother provides a refuge under her four skirts for an arsonist hunted by the police, and so establishes Oskar's pedigree (of original sin). The grandfather's small stature points forward to Oskar's arrested growth at the age of three, his pyromania to Oscar's anarchic nature and his ability to shatter glass with his voice, his compensatory gift and power, which is that of art. Oskar's dubious and divided paternity, too, is significant, since it corresponds to the German-Slav division at Danzig and Oskar's divided loyalty, which turns into impartial disloyalty, since both Germans and Poles are Nazified. (Both in poems and in the novel, Grass has celebrated the Polish national character in the personification Pan Quixote or 'Pan Kiehot'; but Oskar's 'Polish father', Bronski, is no more heroic or Quixotic than his German father Mazerath, both of whom belong to the fallen world.)

Oskar's arrested growth until the end of the war, when he gives up his drumming for a time and settles down to a more or less adult way of life as a short and misshapen, but no longer diminutive, citizen of West Germany, is one instance of the allegories woven into the picaresque, fantastic and realistic texture. The end of the war in itself is no redemption; and Oskar's attempt to accommodate himself to the post-war order leads only to his final renunciation of the world and his withdrawal from it into the 'home' that is a secular counterpart of the hermit's cell. It is there that he drums out his story, on the magical drum of art that can recapitulate and recall past events, but could also control or influence present ones, as when it broke up a Nazi meeting. The more adult Oskar of Book III has lost much of his zest because he has accepted his own fallen nature. That not only confronts him with moral choices, as when he decides to work as a mason's assistant rather than in the black market, but induces him to accept responsibility for a murder he did not commit. Politically, this *metanoia* has to do with the corporate guilt felt by Germans after the war; but the theological implications are weightier, once Oskar has lost his amoral innocence and begins to think about death.

Yet few readers will have paused in their passage through Books I and II of the novel to pick up hints about the destination. They will have been wholly absorbed by its rumbustious actions on the one hand, the subliminal effects of certain episodes and descriptions on the other.

It is the physical and sensuous immediacy of Grass's writing that will have held their attention, unless they were incapable of the suspension of moral judgement that the child's eye view demands. What sticks in this reader's memory is the tenement block at Danzig and its ordinary, yet eccentric, if not monstrous, inhabitants, the cellars and shops, the topography of the city and its surroundings, the gruesome scene on the pier with the horse's head and the eels that produce a fatal trauma, the various erotic episodes and the aphrodisiac propensities of fizz, the ants that march across the floor while Oskar's German father swallows his party badge, and his Polish father's reluctant defence of the Post Office. In their own way, by the magnification and exaggeration of detail—as in Grass's drawings—these and other images build up a complex that amounts to the history of an era; and Grass's Danzig becomes a microcosm. Only the arrested innocence of an Oskar could have responded with sensuous immediacy to such a world, only his inhuman eye have registered such humanity as survived in it.

The novella *Katz und Maus*, originally written as part of a larger work, served Grass as a transition to the more adult perspective of *Dog Years*. The *novella* framework allowed him to confine it to a single level not of meaning—the theological implications of Mahlke's enlarged *Adam's* apple, which becomes a mouse to the cat his school friend Pilenz set at his throat, are less escapable than those of *The Tin Drum*—but of narrative progression. Historically, it covers the same ground as Books II of that novel, whereas *Dog Years* returns to all the three periods to which its three Books correspond, the pre-war, war and post-war periods. Although the pivotal significance of the Adam's apple, like its transformation into a mouse, links the smaller work to Grass's characteristic imaginative procedures in earlier works, poems and plays as much as the first novel, the greater realism of *Katz and Maus* leaves little scope for clowning.

But for the change of tone and manner announced in *Katz und Maus*, Grass could hardly have undertaken another large-scale novel so soon after the first; and one set in the same place, in the same periods, and drawing on the same store of recollected experience. *The Tin Drum*, though, had been dominated by a single character, and much of its rich ambivalence had been due to Grass's imaginative self-identification with that character. *Dog Years* has two protagonists, Matern and Amsel, and three narrators. The two alsatian dogs Harras and Prinz (alias Pluto) carry so much of the symbolic load as to qualify as main characters also; but Grass does not identify to any comparable extent with any character in the book, human or canine. This in itself is a major difference. Grass could not have succeeded in writing an essentially different novel if he had not subordinated some of his picaresque and fairy-tale inventions to more sober concerns. It is pointless to regret that Matern and even Amsel—for all those exploits with scarecrows that do correspond to Oskar's magical and artistic faculties—lack the tin drummer's heroic and mythical dimension, without a compensating gain in finely differentiated sensibility. Even in *Dog Years*, personal relations remain somewhat crude and infantile, and both Matern and Amsel devote a great deal of energy in their mature years to the business of coming to terms with their youth. Just as the diminutive Oskar of the earlier periods was more vivid than the adult hunchback, both Matern and Amsel seem to beome more shadowy as they grow older, their exploits less individual than representative, if not parabolic. This peculiarity is more striking in *Dog Years* because more weight falls on the later years, and because Oscar's arrested development has no parallel in the basic conception of the later novel. On the evidence of the Danzig trilogy alone, it looked very much as though Grass's imagination had remained fixed on his early years, as on the lost environment of his childhood and adolescence. Much of *Dog Years*, therefore, is sustained less by the exploration in depth and by the interaction of the principal characters than by their exploits and configuration; but though the action is not unified by a single protagonist, and even the narration is attributed to a staff of writers employed by Amsel (alias Brauxel) to chronicle the history of his scarecrow factory, all the seeming deficiencies of *Dog Years* are only the reverse side of Grass's minute recapitulation of the past and his devastating assault on the present. Among other things, the novel was the fullest and most convincing critique of Nazism yet achieved in fiction, when Oskar's monstrosity had tended to mythologize and demonize the phenomenon in the very act of de-mythologizing and de-demonizing it.

The exuberant fantasy and essential ambiguity of the first novel tended to blur its overall import. In *Dog Years* Grass managed to combine his humorous, often farcical, impartiality with a systematic deflation of Nazism. Not that the psychological ambivalences were eliminated. That would have been simplistic evasion. Matern is at once a Nazi and an anti-Nazi. Amsel, though half-Jewish and a victim of the régime, corrects the excesses of Matern's condemnation of the German national character. Yet these complexities can no longer be mistaken for an ambivalence on the author's part; they are facets of a reality which he made more palpable than any other writer before him. I shall not try to list all the means used to attain this end; but the interweaving of the dog motif with the lives of Matern, Amsel, Tulla, Harry and many minor characters is at once the most subtle and the most effective. Tulla—also prominent in *Katz und Maus*—at one time chooses to share the kennel of Harras, the sire of Prinz who becomes Hitler's favourite dog; and it is Tulla who does her best to ruin the non-Nazis Amsel and Brunies. When Matern decides to poison Harras, what he has come to see in the dog is nothing less than the embodiment of Nazism. More layers are added to this complex when Hitler, just before the end of the war, launches a vast military action to recapture his dog Prinz, and this action is both conducted and reported in a vacuously mystifying code that parodies the terminology of Heidegger's philosophical writings. Prinz runs away to the West; and ironically it is Matern who becomes his new master, though he gives him the name of Pluto.

The scarecrow motif is another that unifies the whole work, though its final elaboration in Amsel's post-war factory, a kind of modern inferno, is almost too obtrusively allegorical. Like the dog motif and the prophetic meal-worms of Matern's father, the miller, Amsel's animated scarecrows connect the early Danzig chapters to the West Germany of the *Wirtschaftswunder*, which is shown to depend on the miller's financial predictions—and, ultimately, on worms. Matern's frustrated attempts to avenge himself on his former Nazi mentors and bosses after the war, with the help of names and addresses that appear miraculously in the public lavatory of the Cologne railway station, have the scurrilous abandon of many episodes in *The Tin Drum*, but their relevance to the larger satirical scheme is never left in doubt.

An especially gruesome form of revenge is to be carried out during confession on a Roman Catholic priest, but abandoned when the priest proves to turn a literally deaf ear to those who confess to him. The same confessional, though, serves Matern for an act of adultery with the wife of another 'war criminal', and Grass's love-hatred for the Church has lost none of its vehemence. Heidegger, whom Matern also wishes to confront, completely evades him in the funniest and most metaphysical of all these 'Materniads'.

The great Nazi atrocities are only hinted at, not described, for Grass was tactful enough to keep his de-demonizing within its proper limits. The brutal beating-up and rolling into a snowball of Amsel by a gang of masked S.A. men, one of whom is his best friend and 'blood brother' Matern, only costs him all his teeth and changes him from a fat boy into a thin man—an instance of those fairy-tale transformations that Grass could still reconcile with the most astringent realism elsewhere. Grass was wise to confine himself to what he knows and understands so well, the latent cruelty, malevolence and cowardice of children that can so easily be fostered and exploited by an adult world for its ostensibly adult purposes. Mahlke in *Katz und Maus* differs from Matern in his exceptional resistance to such pressures. Amsel does not resist them, but neutralizes them by parody, much as Grass has done as an imaginative writer, before choosing resistance as a citizen.

The circumstance that Matern is at once a 'good' and a 'bad' German not only makes his early relations with Amsel all the more convincing, but is crucial to the design of the whole novel. Matern has to be saved from his self-hatred and self-disgust as a German by his half-Jewish friend; but Amsel's Jewish father had been deeply influenced by the self-hatred and self-disgust of Otto Weininger, who claimed that 'the Jew

188 After the Second Flood

has no soul. The Jew does not sing. The Jew does not play games.' The
eagerness of Amsel's father to prove that the second and third of these
assertions do not hold good for him—the first is harder to deal with—is a
valid reflection on tendencies widespread among the assimilated German
Jews. Eddi Amsel himself sings in the church choir and, with Matern's
help, learns to hold his own in a fierce German ball game.

These are a few of the threads that make *Dog Years* more than a repeat
performance. What the second novel has in common with the first is
Grass's re-creation of a whole community and way of life, his retracing
of the topography, folklore and vernacular of his native region; and, of
course, his incomparable gift of getting inside the skins of children and
adolescents, of presenting their barbarous rituals and codes as though
they had been his only yesterday. *Dog Years* goes well beyond *The Tin
Drum* in its combination of comic spontaneity with a serious and
ambitious design.

3

Grass's work on the prose trilogy, written within a mere six years and
remarkable enough to establish his international fame, had not prevented him from publishing another book of poems, the collection
Gleisdreieck, in 1960. 'Gleisdreieck' is the name of a Berlin rail junction
and station; and it is the poems that touch on divided Berlin that show
how fantasy had come to interlock with minute observation in Grass's
work. The documentation that preceded the completion of *The Tin
Drum* is one instance of a development that can also be traced in the
poems and drawings, from the high degree of abstraction in the
drawings done for *Die Vorzüge der Windhühner* to the grotesque magnification of realistic detail in the drawings done for *Gleisdreieck*, and on
to the hyper-realism of the clenched hand reproduced on the cover of
the third collection, *Ausgefragt*. Grass's growing involvement in politics
is bound up with that development. The clearance sale of the poem
'Ausverkauf' is a personal one, perhaps alluding to Grass's exploitation
of his own life and memories in the prose trilogy, but it includes this
unmistakable reference to East Berlin:

> Während ich alles verkaufte,
> enteigneten sie fünf oder sechs Strassen weiter
> die besitzanzeigenden Fürwörter
> und sägten den kleinen harmlosen Männern
> den Schatten ab, den privaten.

While I was selling it all,
five or six streets from here they expropriated
all the possessive pronouns
and sawed off the private shadows
of little innocuous men.

The underlying seriousness of Grass's clowning—as of all good clowning—is more apparent in *Gleisdreieck* than in the earlier collection. Without any loss of comic zest or invention, Grass could now write existential parables like 'Im Ei' (In the Egg) or 'Saturn', poems that take the risk of being open to interpretation in terms other than those of pure zany fantasy. One outstanding poem in *Gleisdreieck* has proved hard to translate, because its effect depends on quadruple rhymes and on corresponding permutations of meaning, for which only the vaguest equivalents can be found in another language. Grass himself has retained a special liking for this poem, the sinister nursery rhyme 'Kinderlied', perhaps because it achieved the most direct and the most drastic fusion in all his poetry of innocence and experience. This artistic fusion results from the confrontation of the freedom most precious to Grass, the freedom of child's play which is also the court fool's prerogative, with its polar opposite, the repression of individuality by totalitarian systems.

Wer lacht hier, hat gelacht?
Hier hat sich's ausgelacht.
Wer hier lacht, macht Verdacht,
dass er aus Gründen lacht.

Wer weint hier, hat geweint?
Hier wird nicht mehr geweint.
Wer hier weint, der auch meint,
dass er aus Gründen weint.

Wer spricht hier, spricht und schweigt?
Wer schweigt, wird angezeigt.
Wer hier spricht, hat verschwiegen,
wo seine Gründe liegen.

Wer spielt hier, spielt im Sand?
Wer spielt muss an die Wand,
hat sich beim Spiel die Hand
gründlich verspielt, verbrannt.

Wer stirbt hier, ist gestorben?
Wer stirbt, ist abgeworben.
Wer hier stirbt, unverdorben
ist ohne Grund verstorben.

Who laughs here, who has laughed?
Here we have ceased to laugh.
To laugh here now is treason.
The laughter has a reason.

Who weeps here, who has wept?
Here weeping is inept.
To weep here now means too
a reason so to do.

Who speaks here or keeps mum?
Here we denounce the dumb.
To speak here is to hide
deep reasons kept inside.

Who plays here, in the sand?
Against the wall we stand
players whose games are banned.
They've lost, thrown in their hand.

Who dies here, dares to die?
'Defector!' here we cry.
To die here, without stain,
is to have died in vain.

Laughing, weeping, talking, keeping silent, playing and even dying are the spontaneous and uncalculated acts to which totalitarian repression attributes subversive motives, drowning 'the ceremony of innocence'. No other poem by Grass is at once so simple and so intricate, compacts so much meaning into so few words. One difficulty about the translation is that no single English word has the familiar and horrible connotations of a German word like 'angezeigt'—reported to the police or other authority for being ideologically suspect—or 'abgeworben'— the bureaucratic equivalent of being excommunicated, blackballed, expelled, deprived of civil rights, ceasing to exist as a member of a corporative order that has become omnipotent.

By the time his third book of poems, *Ausgefragt*, appeared in 1967, the politicization of West German literature and its author's commitment to the Social Democratic Party, for which he had undertaken a strenuous electioneering campaign in 1965, made its publication a political, rather than a literary, event. The collection does contain a high proportion of poems that respond directly—perhaps too directly in some cases—to political and topical issues. Some of them, like 'In Ohnmacht gefallen' (Powerless, with a Guitar), were bound to be read as provocations by the dominant radical Left:

Wir lesen Napalm und stellen Napalm uns vor.
Da wir uns Napalm nicht vorstellen können,
lesen wir über Napalm, bis wir uns mehr
unter Napalm vorstellen können.
Jetzt protestieren wir gegen Napalm.
   Nach dem Frühstück, stumm,
   Auf Fotos sehen wir, was Napalm vermag.
   Wir ziegen uns grobe Raster
   und sagen: Siehst du, Napalm.
   Das machen sie mit Napalm.
Bald wird es preiswerte Bildbände
mit besseren Fotos geben,
auf denen deutlicher wird,
was Napalm vermag.
Wir kauen Nägel und schreiben Proteste.
   Aber es gibt, so lesen wir,
   Schlimmeres als Napalm.
   Schnell protestieren wir gegen Schlimmeres.
   Unsere berechtigten Proteste, die wir jederzeit
   verfassen falten frankieren dürfen, schlagen zu Buch.
Ohnmacht, an Gummifassaden erprobt.
Ohnmacht legt Platten auf: ohnmächtige Songs.
Ohne Macht mit Guitarre,—
Aber feinmaschig und gelassen
wirkt sich draussen die Macht aus.

We read napalm and imagine napalm.
Since we cannot imagine napalm
we read about napalm until
by napalm we can imagine more.
Now we protest against napalm.
   After breakfast, silent,
   we see in photographs what napalm can do.
   We show each other coarse screen prints
   and say: there you are, napalm.
   They do that with napalm.
Soon there'll be cheap picture books
with better photographs
which will show more clearly
what napalm can do.
We bite our nails and write protests.
   But, we read, there are
   worse things than napalm.
   Quickly we protest against worse things.
   Our well-founded protests, which at any time
   we may compose fold stamp, mount up.
Impotence, tried out on rubber façades.
Impotence puts records on: impotent songs.
Powerless, with a guitar.—
But outside, finely meshed
and composed, power has its way.

Compared with his early poems, this one gave Grass little scope for playfulness. The moralist seems to have taken over even from the court fool. Yet the poem is not a polemic against political protest. The new gravity shows that Grass is quarrelling more with himself than with others, weighing up painful dilemmas that were his own. The old exuberance does re-assert itself elsewhere in the same collection, even in thematically related poems like 'Der Dampfkessel-Effekt' (The Steam Boiler Effect) that *are* primarily polemical. As for the trilogy 'Irgendwas machen' (Do Something), its centre piece 'Die Schweine-kopfsülz' (The Jellied Pig's Head) was clearly intended to be a sustained political and satirical analogy, but somehow the cook in Grass seems to have gained the upper hand, deriving so much pleasure from his recipe in its own right that the reader, too, is carried away from the forum to the kitchen. Perhaps the happiest poem of all in *Ausgefragt*— happiest in two senses of the word—is 'Advent', since it blends social satire with the freedom and zest which, for Grass, appertain to the world of childhood. Even here, and in the autobiographical poem 'Kleckerburg', the tension has become extreme, because the amorality of childhood is at once re-enacted and judged in the light of mature social experience. 'Advent', in fact, juxtaposes the war games of children and those both of their parents and of nations. Moral judgement does not become explicit in this poem, and the implicit judgement seems to be in favour of the children who plan a family 'in which naughty is good and good, naughty' rather than of the parents 'who everywhere stand around and talk of getting children and getting rid of children.' What is certain about the poem is that Grass's new realism had not shut him off from the imaginative freedom and verbal play of his earlier work, though it is the realism that dominates even in poems about personal and domestic life like 'Ehe' (Marriage) and 'Vom Rest unterm Nagel' (Of the Residue under our Nails). The same realism underlay Grass's commitment to politics, his decision to 'defend the bad against the worse' within the framework of parliamentary democracy, rather than opt for the revolutionary utopias arrogantly demanded by fellow intellectuals who refused to dirty their hands in the business of practical politics. During the 1965 election campaign alone, Grass made 250 speeches all over West Germany.

In the midst of those activities and the controversies in which they never ceased to involve him, Günter Grass not only remained prolific as an imaginative writer, but continued to uphold the personal freedoms indispensable both to his practice and to that of his radical opponents. Unlike the ideologists, Grass did not wish to carry politics either into private life or into those artistic processes which they censured and censored as 'individualistic'. Though public concerns preponderate in the collection *Ausgefragt*, it also contains this short poem, 'Falsche Schönheit':

Diese Stille,
　　also der abseits in sich verbissne Verkehr
　　　gefällt mir,
und dieses Hammelkotelett,
　　wenn auch kalt mittlerweile und talgig,
　　　schmeckt mir,
das Leben,
　　ich meine die Spanne seit gestern bis Montag früh,
　　　macht wieder Spass:
ich lache über Teltower Rübchen
unser Meerschweinchen erinnert mich rosa,
Heiterkeit will meinen Tisch überschwemmen,
und ein Gedanke
　　immerhin ein Gedanke,
　　　geht ohne Hefe auf;
　　　　und ich freue mich,
　　　　　weil er falsch ist und schön.

Wrong Beauty

This quiet,
　　that is, the traffic some way off, its teeth stuck into itself,
　　　pleases me,
and this lamb cutlet,
　　though cold by now and greasy.
　　　tastes good,
life,
　　I mean the period from yesterday to Monday morning,
　　　is fun again:
I laugh at the dish of parsnips,
our guinea pig pinkly reminds me,
cheerfulness threatens to flood my table,
and an idea,
　　an idea of sorts,
　　　rises without yeast,
　　　　and I'm happy
　　　　　because it is wrong and beautiful.

The idea is one of those out of which Grass continued to make poems, drawings and prose books while applying himself to what would have been a full-time occupation for most men or women, his defence of the freedom to produce work that is 'wrong and beautiful'.

Grass's insistence on this freedom must be seen against the background of what was happening in West German literature, partly in response to the Vietnam War. While East German poets like Wolf Biermann and Reiner Kunze were desperately defending the individual from encroachments on his privacy on the part of an all-powerful collective, or of an all-powerful bureaucracy that claims to represent the collective, many West German writers were doing their best to deprive themselves of such liberties as they enjoyed—by self-censorship as much as by intolerance of any art they judged to be private or individualistic. In extreme cases, like that of Hans Magnus Enzensberger at one time, the conflict between social conscience and personal inclination could lead to the public renunciation of all imaginative writing, and such a renunciation, in that climate, turned into an interdict. It is true that to prescribe what could and could no longer be written had been a favourite pastime of German critics even before the politicization became extreme and dominant. Love poems were out, because love is a form of bourgeois self-indulgence; nature poems, because we live in a technological age; confessional poems, or poems of personal experience, because they are poems of personal experience; moon poems, because as Peter Rühmkorf argued well before the first moon landing—cosmonauts are better qualified to deal with the moon than poets. Needless to say, all those kinds of poems continued to be written, if in new ways, even before the tide turned and the 'new subjectivity' was proclaimed. Günter Grass openly defied those prescriptions and proscriptions, while setting definite limits to his own individualism by the very act of devoting himself to a political cause at the expense of his private life and his art.

His prodigious capacity to 'endure that tension' has been amply proved by his subsequent works. Even his book of political speeches and controversies, *Über das Selbstverständliche* (1968), is a collection so well-written, so forceful and so many-sided as to qualify as one of his literary works. Characteristically, the snail he adopted as an emblem of his political stance—evolution, as opposed to revolution—became one of those obsessive images that have nourished his imaginative work. Not only did it become his own left eye in a self-portrait of 1972—while his right eye remained open to all kinds of other things—but it entered into other drawings and etchings, and became the nucleus of another prose book, *Aus dem Tagebuch einer Schnecke* (1972), in which even practical politics intermingle with childhood innocence and fantasy. If realistic and topical concerns are uppermost in the novel *Örtlich Betäubt* (Local Anaesthetic) of 1969, fairy tale and myth came back into their own in *Der Butt* (1977; *The Flounder*) a work on the same scale and of the same quality as the Danzig trilogy, written before Grass's political achievements and frustrations.

As for Grass's poetry, it became more and more bound up with his drawing and graphic work, and its later progress is best followed in the two books *Zeichnungen und Texte 1954-1977* (1982), and *Radierungen und Texte 1972-1982* (1984), in which the intimate inter-relationship can be traced. (The snail reappears as late as 1982, in an etching called 'The Dream of a Place of One's Own', in which the home is a concrete bunker. This sums up Günter Grass's present commitment, less to a political party than to the causes of disarmament and conservation.) A self-portrait of 1982, 'With a glove, pensive', shows an older and sadder Grass, but one who has not given up fighting. That etching faces the text of his poem 'Müll unser':

> Suchte Steine und fand
> den überlebenden Handschuh
> aus synthetischer Masse.
>
> Jeder Fingerling sprach.
> Nein, nicht die dummen Segelgeschichten
> sondern was bleiben wird:
>
> Müll unser
> Strände lang.
> Während abhanden wir
> niemand Verlust sein werden.

> *Our Refuse*
>
> Looked for stones and found
> the surviving glove
> made of synthetic pulp.
>
> Every finger spoke.
> No, not those inane yachtmen's yarns
> but of that which will last:
>
> our refuse
> beaches long.
> Whereas we gone
> will be a loss to no one.

In that reflection on our age and our prospects Günter Grass is at one again with most of his former associates in the *Gruppe 47*, though few of them are now militant or hopeful enough to give active support to his untiring campaigns. The German title of the poem, by placing the possessive pronoun after the noun, parodies the Lord's Prayer—a late instance of Grass's blasphemies, 'wrong beauty', and affronts to every kind of decorum. (In 1965, at the award of the Büchner Prize for Literature, he had chosen to deliver a political speech, 'Über das Selbstverständliche' [On That which Goes Without Saying], to the assembled members of a learned academy.) In the late poem, once more, the clown's prerogative and the moralist's compulsions have come together, in the absence of those courts whose authority could set limits to the destructive power games of would-be adults and so relieve Grass of the need to blaspheme. The dispensability of our species, of course, is another blasphemy against every religious, every secular, creed, but it is one committed every day by the players of those power games, in their commercial exploits and their planning of wars. In both his capacities, and over the decades, Grass has made it his consistent business to fling back such blasphemies into the bland faces of those who live by them.

IX   The Poetry of Survival

1

It is the overriding urgency of the survival of our species and its habitat—including all the other species that are, or were, part of the habitat—that has made all the controversies about this or that kind of writing, this or that commitment, this or that writer's merits, recede into history in the course of the past decade. No new movement or school has been proclaimed since the 'new subjectivity' wave of the mid-1970s, and even that wave broke very soon, merging in a period 'loose at all ends', a state of literature in which everything is possible, everything permissible, if it can be done. The cult of novelty, too, has been largely displaced, and partly discredited, by the need for survival. Novelty and progress, now, are a currency that has lost its value for all but technicians, advertisers and salesmen—and the political administrators who have grown so nearly indistinguishable from them that the word 'statesman' has fallen into disuse. As the producers of commodities, books, writers remain subject to transactions in that currency, of course; but they have become the most sceptical of clients. 'Ein Friedenstraum in dunkler Zeit' (A Dream of Peace at a Dark Time) is the title of a lecture delivered in May 1985, by Walter Jens, eminent both as a writer associated with the *Gruppe 47* and as the Professor of Rhetoric at the University of Tübingen. The subject of that lecture is the seventeenth-century poet Andreas Gryphius, and no explicit analogy is drawn between that writer's experience of devastation and moral breakdown in the Thirty Years' Wars and the imminence of another dark age, incomparably darker still, not only for Germany. Walter Jens could rely on his audience in another learned academy to catch the relevance of that Christian poet's concerns to immediate ones, only hinted at by a passing reference to the presence of Günter Grass— who had not only drawn such an analogy in a work of fiction but was famous and notorious thoughout Germany for his repeated voicings of those immediate concerns. Only a decade earlier, Jens would have had to be more explicit both about his own commitment and about the relevance of choosing a subject like Gryphius for any public address delivered to non-specialists, because 'relevant' was a synonym for topical. Even in Munich, the theological erudition and fervour of Gryphius would have been judged 'irrelevant' by a considerable proportion of such an audience; and the eloquence that is Jens's speciality would have alienated those same persons on related grounds.

Eloquence and elegance, though, have always distinguished the work of Hans Magnus Enzensberger, a pioneer not only of the politicization of West German literature but also of those ecological preoccupations that have superseded it; not Jens's classicizing eloquence of balanced and supple periods, it is true—although lately Enzensberger has indulged in archaisms like 'Brosame' for 'crumb'—but an eloquence and elegance due to mastery of the vernacular, as of the specialized terminologies inaccessible and repulsive to most poets. In his mastery of both, as a poet and polemical essayist, Enzensberger was so fluently up-to-date as to be always ahead of his time, simply because no one else was as well-informed, as perspicacious and intelligent. When his first book of poems, *Verteidigung der Wölfe*, appeared in 1957, he was seen as the West German poet best fitted to take over the function of Brecht (who had died in the previous year) as a socially and politically committed poet; that is, as one who had taken the trouble to inform himself about the issues that his poems raised. In retrospect, it would seem that Enzensberger had less in common with Brecht than with Auden, whose positive commitments, too, are much harder to pin down than his up-to-dateness, his elegance, and his verbal skill. Both poets may have excelled at social comment and social criticism; but if constant commitments can be traced in either's work, these are more likely to be moral than strictly ideological. Enzensberger, of course, knew his Marx, as Auden knew his; but the Marx of his poem in *Blindenschrift* (1964) is a 'gigantic bourgeois' and 'gigantic traitor' to his own class, betrayed in turn by his followers and disciples, ending up as 'the iron mask of freedom'. It is a human study, above all, like some of Auden's 'potted biographies' in verse, bringing out both the irony and the pathos of Marx's life, rather than the celebration of an exemplary creed; and if a message can be extracted from the poem, it is: 'only your enemies/remained what they were'—as they undoubtedly have remained, to this day. When the simplists of the class war became dominant in West Germany, a few years after Enzensberger's poem was published, they challenged his commitment and turned against him, as they turned against T. W. Adorno or anyone else who presumed to think for himself, as Marx had done. Enzensberger's commitment could not be pinned down by simplists of the class war on either side.

Like all comparisons, though, that of Enzensberger to Auden should not be pushed very far. Being knowledgeable, *au fait*, and imperturbably poised was only Enzensberger's outward guise. Behind it there was a passion, a vehemence quite unlike anything in Auden. This came out in the hyperbole that flawed some of the poems in his first book, but also in the bitter eloquence of its 'sad poems' and its 'wicked poems', like the title poem defending the wolves against the lambs, because it is the lambs in every age that keep the wolves going; or the manifesto poem 'Ins Lesebuch für die Oberstufe' (For a Senior College Textbook), with its exhortation to read not odes but railway timetables, because they are more accurate. This anticipates Enzensberger's notorious renunciation of poetry some ten years later, his purging at one time of his own library of most of its *belles lettres* sections in favour of reference books, sociological books and scientific books of many kinds, and his editorship of the review *Kursbuch* (Railway Timetable!), devoted less to *belles lettres* than to the most rigorous contributions to those other disciplines. This, in turn, was only one extremity of a love-hate relationship to poetry. Enzensberger also worked as the editor of a whole series of books that made known the work of outstanding foreign poets of this century in bilingual selections, as well as of his important anthology relegating those same poets to a 'museum', but presenting them all the same, and another excellent one of nursery rhymes. He was also generous in his praise of fellow poets, like Nelly Sachs, whose work drew on sources quite different from railway timetables. The vehemence of his disgust with his own country was carried over into his second book, especially the longer poem 'Landessprache'— the title is a bitter travesty of a line of Hölderlin's that proclaims 'love' as the 'language of the country', Germany—and so, in places, was the hyperbole of his first book. As an essayist and editor, Enzensberger was in the forefront of those who conveyed a 'radical enlightenment' to generations of West Germans; and though his main emphasis did not fall on language or on experiment, like Heissenbüttel's, nor even on literature generally, like Walter Höllerer's, like them he was prepared to divert much of his energy from his own imaginative writing to the most various activities in the service of enlightenment and mediation. Since extremes meet, and all poets work within the same sphere of possibilities, often bumping their heads on the periphery and having to turn round, Enzensberger's anti-experimental and anti-formalist position did not prevent him from working with quotations, like Heissenbüttel, for what amounted to a *collage* or *montage* technique in his 'Sommergedicht'; and it was a poet classified as 'hermetic' and 'formalist', Paul Celan, whose later work drew on scientific knowledge, even of nuclear physics, in a way that accorded, but was not seen to accord, with Enzensberger's prescriptions and practices.

That Enzensberger's practices did not always accord with his prescriptions goes without saying, since he is a poet, and a poet does not do what he sets out to do, but what he can and must. It was Enzensberger's third collection, *Blindenschrift*, that showed the full range of his possibilities. The personal feelings reserved for love poems in the second collection and the ecological concerns anticipated there in the poem 'Das Ende der Eulen' (The End of the Owls), amongst others, had begun to fuse with his social and political themes. Self-knowledge and self-criticism had begun to both sharpen and moderate his quarrels with others, so that his eloquence was no longer marred by rhetorical excesses. Whereas in the past his longer poems had tended to be his weakest—because the sensuous data were most thinly spread—a new richness and allusiveness of texture was attained in his longer poem 'lachesis lapponica'. Here Enzensberger succeeded in co-ordinating and controlling tensions at once personal and existential, particular and general. The confrontation with solitude in bare Scandinavian landscapes served a necessary dialectical complement to the social involvement, while the social involvement itself remained intense.

How intelligent can a good poet afford to be—in, rather than behind, his poems? How variously well-informed? How tough-minded? There were times in Hans Magnus Enzensberger's writing life when these questions troubled some of his readers; and not only when Enzensberger himself posed them in his essays and statements. After his three early collections, published between 1957 and 1964, it seemed for a long time that he had no more use for the spontaneous, more personal lyricism that had balanced his public concerns; that the polemicist had taken over from the poet, deliberately and definitively. Apart from a few new poems added to his selection of 1971, *Gedichte 1955-1970*, Enzensberger had kept silent as a poet until *Mausoleum* appeared in 1975; and, however intelligent, knowing, tough-minded, well-informed and accomplished, that sequence was not distinguished by lyricism. If those thirty-seven studies 'in the history of Progress' were ballads, as he called them, they were ballads that neither sang nor danced, but nailed down their subjects with a laboratory-trained efficiency, though one that could be delicate, even tender from time to time.

This development remained relevant to *Der Untergang der Titanic* (1978; *The Sinking of the Titanic*), though in fact Enzensberger had already returned to more personal and existential preoccupations in shorter poems not collected at that time, and the long sequence, too, is less rigorously held down to a single purpose and manner. Behind the poetic development—or anti-poetic development, some would say—lay an ideological one, from what had looked like a revolutionary commitment to 'the principle of hope' at least. In fact it had been utopian and independent enough to put no strictly ideological constraint on the poet, through an arduous grappling with the hard facts of economic, political and technological power structures—as examined in Enzensberger's brilliant essays even before his first collection of them in 1962, *Einzelheiten*—to a general disillusionment with every existing social system and any likely to materialize in the near future. (This disillusionment, bravely and elegantly borne, and by no means defeatist, became most apparent in the book of essays *Politische Brosamen* of 1982.)

One crucial stage in that development was Enzensberger's visit to

Cuba in 1969. Not only was *The Sinking of the Titanic* conceived and begun there, but the Cuban experiences are worked into the broken narrative of the poem, like many other seeming interpolations, digressions, leaps in space, time, and even manner. Like most long or longer poems written in this century, it is not an epic, but a clustering of diverse, almost disparate, fragments around a thematic core. The main event of the poem, the going down of the *Titanic* in 1912, becomes a symbol and a microcosm, with extensions, parallels, repercussions on many different levels. The Titanic is also Cuba, East Berlin, West Berlin (where Enzensberger lived for many years, before returning to Bavaria, where he was born), an up-dated version of Dante's Hell, and many other places besides, including any place where any reader of the poem is likely to be. Not content with that much telescoping, Enzensberger also includes flashbacks to the fifteenth, sixteenth and nineteenth centuries, all to do with doubts, self-doubts, about art and the relation of art to reality. Other interpolations are even more explicit in their questioning of the truthfulness and usefulness of poets and poetry. These also introduce Dante by name, though he is present in the whole poem, as a paradigm of what poetry can and cannot achieve.

I shall not attempt to list all the many theses and sub-theses ironically advanced in the poem—usually to be challenged or contradicted by others—since it is the business of poems to do that as succinctly as possible. Yet one brief quotation, from Enzensberger's own English version of his text, does seem to subsume the main message: 'We are in the same boat, all of us. But he who is poor is the first to drown.' Characteristically for Enzensberger, this assertion is supported by statistics of the passengers—first class, second class, steerage and crew—drowned and saved in the *Titanic* disaster. Much other material of that kind, including a menu, has been drawn upon. The most lyrical, that is, song-like, canto of the thirty-three in the book—not counting the numbered interpolations—is the twentieth, adapted from *Deep Down in the Jungle: Negro Narrative and Folklore from the Streets of Philadelphia*. Documentary collages have been one of Enzensberger's favoured devices in verse and prose, and they are prominent as ever here, as in the Thirteenth Canto, made up of snatches of miscellaneous hymns and popular songs. Another is the permutation of simple colloquial phrases into puzzles or tautologies not simple at all, but devastating, as in the interpolated 'Notice of Loss'. Yet the most impressive and re-assuring parts of the sequence, poetically, are those in which Enzensberger lets himself go again a little, relying less on his bag of tricks—a formidable one—than on imaginative penetration of specific experience, other people's and his own. A high-spirited, often comically cynical desperation are his peculiar contribution to the range of poetry. It becomes affirmative, if not joyful, in the concluding canto, a celebration of bare survival.

As for the other side of his gifts, his sheer accomplishment and adroitness, one instance of it is his success in translating so intricate and ambitious a sequence into a language not his own, English—one of several in which he is fluent. In earlier English versions of his own poems he had allowed himself the freedom of 'imitation'. This one is a very close rendering, with no loss of vigour or exuberance, and very little diminution of the idiomatic rightness of the German original.

In 1980 Enzensberger bridged a gap of sixteen years by publishing a new book of short poems, *Die Furie des Verschwindens*. As his later volume of collected poems, *Die Gedichte* (1983), was to show, he had never quite ceased to write such poems even during his self-imposed silence; but for his readers *Die Furie des Verschwindens* linked up with his *Blindenschrift* of 1964 as a continuation of the kind of poetry that springs from moments of intense experience—experience inevitably subjective up to a point, however objective the correlatives. By this I do not mean 'confessional' poems. Even the longest poem in the new collection, 'Die Frösche von Bikini', is a semi-dramatic monologue whose speaker cannot be identified with the person of the poet—except perhaps in passages like:

> Nein, auf Selbsterfahrung lege er keinen Wert,
> und Probleme habe er nicht,
> wenigstens keine 'eigenen'.

> No, he did not care for self-knowledge
> and did not go in for problems,
> not at least of 'one's own'.

That longer poem is one of stock-taking, at once personal and impersonal, because not self-concerned enough to indulge in confessions. Most of the shorter poems, too, are character studies that achieve a new balance between social criticism and the spontaneity with which it had tended to conflict. By getting under the skin of a thirty-three-year-old woman, an uneasy male business executive, an equally uneasy employee on holiday in Spain—each a 'short history of the bourgeoisie', as another poem is called—Enzensberger presents a whole complex of delicate interactions in the fewest possible words, from the inside; and it no longer matters whether the social perceptions are subjective or objective, whether the inside is the poet's or another person's real or fictitious. The social criticism is more incisive and more searching than ever before, because Enzensberger has learned to dispense with the reformer's vantage point, as well as with the rhetorical bravura of his early verse. That, in turn, may well be because he has come to include himself among those—bourgeois or otherwise—whose prospects are summed up in the poem 'Unregierbarkeit' (Ungovernability):

Mit immer kürzer werdenden Beinen
watschelt die Macht in die Zukunft.

On legs growing shorter and shorter
power is waddling into the future.

A group of predominantly topical poems, concerned with this situation, leads to up the many-faceted longer poem, hence to a second group of short poems that have less to do with specific power structures than with more generally existential disparities. One of them, 'Besuch bei Ingres', is a brilliantly comic exposure of those disparities between life and art that had so worried Enzensberger in *The Sinking of the Titanic*; but on that score, too, Enzensberger's inhibiting self-doubts seem to be nearer to a resolution. A spark of the old utopianism still glimmers beneath the gloom and worldly wisdom of Enzensberger's later poems—though it is a utopianism inherent in the human condition rather than one imposed on it by a poet's vision; and the vigour, precision and elegance of his manner are unimpaired.

2

A decade before Enzensberger's first book of poems, Erich Fried had published two collections of 'political' poems, the booklets *Deutschland* (1944) and *Österreich* (1945). The first was published in London, where Fried lived as a refugee, the second in London and Zürich. If copies of those booklets penetrated as far as Germany after the end of the war, they were scarcely noticed; and the author was soon to regard them as juvenilia. Though conventional in diction and form, untouched by Brecht's didactic hardness, and more emotive than enlightening as 'political' poems, they not only showed the skill that was to distinguish this prolific poet in later years, but anticipated the moral passion that was to make him one of the most controversial figures in post-war German literature. His moral indictment of Nazi Germany and of Nazified Austria—where his father had been murdered by the Gestapo before Erich Fried's emigration in 1938—was mitigated, even in these early poems, by compassion with those whose complicity did not prevent their being fellow victims of the régime; as in the poem 'Trümmer' (Rubble) about the 'wounds' of Vienna at the end of the war, or the earlier poems 'Heimkehrer' (Ex-Soldier) and 'Einem Jungen Faschisten nach dem Todesurteil' (To a Young Fascist Sentenced to Death) in *Deutschland*. That magnanimity towards opponents—carried to the point of perversity in later works, many of Fried's critics would say—would have made even his first poems controversial in 1945, had they been publicly noticed. Only an explicitly religious commitment, never professed by Fried, might have defended him against that charge of perversity; and in 1960, when he published his novel *Ein Soldat und ein Mädchen*, very few theologians of any school or sect would have been prepared to offer such a defence of a novel about a sexual encounter between a young woman condemned to death for her work in a concentration camp and an American soldier of Jewish origin, her guard. This, too, was a juvenile work, drafted in 1946. A hint in the text that this sexual love-death was also a symbolic act of reconciliation and atonement seemed no less outrageous than the plot or its treatment, and hardly more plausible.

After the early poems, in fact, Fried emerged not as a 'political' poet, but as one preoccupied with language, language games that plumbed the unconscious, in the wake of Joyce's *Finnegans Wake* and of Dylan Thomas, whose translator Fried became. (From 1952 to 1968 Fried worked as a broadcaster for the BBC's German Service. His resignation followed the publication of the first of his predominantly political books of poems, *und Vietnam und*, in 1966.) His first book of short poems to be published in Germany, *Gedichte* (1958), was remarkable for not touching on any topical issues, social or political, even in the section reserved for 'traces of the war'. In his postscript to the collection, Fried specifically stated that 'sociological explanations are not enough to explain a poet, or only a single line in a single poem, adequately'. It is because I believe that caveat to be valid for all of Fried's work, early and late, as for anyone's, that I have placed the word political in inverted commas, even though Fried has come to be regarded as the political poet *par excellence*. There is no break in Fried's linguistic practices from *Gedichte* to his books published in the 1980s. Word-play of the most various kinds is as essential to his seemingly didactic verse of the later decades, as to the very personal poems in *Gedichte* or the love poems that Fried never ceased to write. Just as good a case could be made out for Fried as a linguistically experimental writer at all times, regardless of his themes, though one not aiming at abstraction, but grappling with it.

Fried indicated the reasons in the same postscript, when he denied that his work was 'English poetry written in German', defined the extent of his alleged indebtedness to English poetry, and attributed some of the peculiarities of his poems to 'a distance from everyday uses and abuses' of the language, German, in which they were written. Both the rewards and the disadvantages of writing in a language not lived in became even more apparent in Fried's *Reich der Steine* (1963), a collection of sixteen longer sequences written between 1947 and 1963. In the earlier of the sequences at least, his search for purely verbal associations and affinities, homonyms and near-homonyms, has the desperate seriousness of a man clinging to all that remains to him of his home, a language divorced from people and things. Poetically, this may be a game, played with astonishing virtuosity; but it is a game played solemnly, like children's games. Words are weighed and turned over, fondled and mishandled, arranged this way and that, in the hope that they will yield a meaning inherent in them, perhaps the material with which to reconstruct a world.

Since it is one function of poetry to explore language, to seek and find—and Fried has a prodigious sense of style, a range of forms and idioms, including traditional ones, that goes far towards making up for a loss of immediacy—his variations never fail to salvage something from his reservoir of words. Where his associations are purely aural, though, without etymological or semantic links, the element of chance becomes so pronounced that a reader is put on the defensive and refuses to follow. One instance of this occurs in the otherwise moving first sequence, 'Wanderung':

> Nun will ich Abschied nehmen
> nun will ich Abschied
> nun Abschied
> nun abnehmen
> Abschied nehmen

where the word 'abnehmen' seems to have no other *raison d'être* than its sonic relation to 'Abschied' and 'nehmen'. The passage, incidentally, suggests a closeness not to Dylan Thomas, e.e. cummings or Wilfred Owen, from whom Fried was supposed to have learned, but to the T. S. Eliot of *Ash Wednesday* on the one hand, the serial permutations of concrete poets on the other. Even in the later set of variations on a traditional rhyme, 'Erbsenlesen', the juxtaposition 'Erbsenlesen/von welcher Erbsünde lösen' would be more acceptable without the pun.

Elsewhere the fury of Fried's punning elicits no more and no less than the familiar exasperated groan, as in this passage from 'Zerklagung':

> Ein Fall der Bälle
> Ein Ball der Bälle
> Eine Baal der Bälle
> Ein Ball des Baal

ingenious and surprising though the last combination may be. The same poem, written in commemoration of a friend, exemplifies the degree of abstraction built into this sort of composition. Hardly ever, in the earlier sequences, do we get any sense of a particular person, a particular thing, a particular occasion or scene. The words are counters that may respond to an inner need and a dominant mood, but they do not mesh with any outward reality. In 'Rückschritt' the poet himself writes of 'a wall between image and world'.

It is no accident that the verbal associations are most appropriate and convincing in that sequence, an exploration of infantile fantasies that is also the most Joycean in its resort to neologisms. Something of the same felicity is to be found in the variations on fables, songs and nursery rhymes—also prominent in *Gedichte*—including the one on 'How many miles to Babylon?'; but, again, lines like 'Hummel, Leithammel vom Himmel' not merely invite parody, but achieve it, all the more so because of the serious, even metaphysical, themes. In an excellent later sequence, 'Die letzte Hand', Fried forestalls and disarms these strictures on the earlier ones. He himself writes,

> Weil aber das Wort mir zu leicht war
> muss es mir schwer werden
> Weil aber das Wort mir ein Spiel war
> muss es mir Ernst werden

> But because my word came too easily
> it must come harder
> But because my word was a game to me
> it must be in earnest

The two concluding sequences, 'Anfang des Rechtes' and 'Reich der Steine', owe their new rigour and authority to this awareness that the proliferation of mere word-play must be checked. There is no loss of invention in these later sequences; but their puns and paradoxes leave less of the meaning to chance.

Thematically, the new discipline demanded a turning outwards to observed realities. Yet in his next collection, *Warngedichte* (1964), this turning outwards was far from amounting to a politicization of Fried's work. As the title implies, the whole collection is pervaded by a sense of danger, but it would be superficial to describe this danger only as political. The danger of another war is only one disaster touched upon in the five sections of the book, each with a distinct character. Fried had now evolved the prototype of those epigrammatic *aperçus* in verse with which he was to fill book after book over the next two decades; but only some of those in *Warngedichte*—like 'Die Händler', 'Der Mitmensch', 'Totschlagen' and 'Die Überlebenden'—have a direct bearing on public affairs. As often as not, the danger is approached allegorically, psychologically, metaphysically, or in terms of personal relationships. Private life, social life and political life are not placed in separate compartments, but allowed to intersect and interpenetrate. A few poems in the book apply the same method of verbal association and variation as the earlier sequences; but near-nonsense verse like 'Die Summ-Summe' is a rare exception now, and the best poems in the book—beginning with 'Erfolg', 'Traumgespräch' and 'Völkerkunde' in the first section—show that Fried had learned to dispense with his more facile verbal games. What has remained constant in all his work is the danger of abstraction; and, since political comment in poetry that has not come out of direct experience runs this risk in any case, Fried compounded the danger by his later involvement in political causes. Not residence in a German-speaking country, but a perpetual round of protests and controversies was Erich Fried's way out of the displacement he had suffered at the age of seventeen. In his poetry, though, the linguistic and social effects of the displacement proved irreversible, as he acknowledged when he published a selection from it with the title *100 Poems without a Country* in 1974.

If that selection—and others that could be made from the later books of a poet who thinks nothing of writing more than one poem a day, in whatever circumstances and on top of whatever else he may be doing—vindicates Fried as an outstanding German-language poet of his time, it is because he has never become the 'political poet' for whom he was taken both by his supporters and by his enemies. If he has been a trouble-maker inside and outside his poems, again he has told us why he had to be—from the start, by an irresistible compulsion to stand up against bullies, liars and oppressors. His self-ironizing account of that proclivity is to be found in his book of prose pieces *Kinder und Narren* (1965), which pre-dates his emergence as a would-be 'political poet'. In the last of the twenty-nine prose pieces collected there, 'Anlauf', he tells of the exploits of a character with many names who, despite his slight build, feels compelled to charge any bully by taking a run at him—no easy or uncomplicated matter in cities, with obstructions in his way, and the need to run away from conflict before running into it, to acquire the necessary impetus. Like that character, Fried has often run into brick walls; and the history of those exploits—which is not the history of his contribution to poetry—would make a long and instructive book. The prose collection sheds light on the poems in other ways, too. Even where he tells a story, it remains hard or impossible for Fried to locate his characters in a recognizable *ambiance*. 'Die Vorahnung', for instance, has a London setting, but this setting is essential neither to the character of the protagonist, Mr Littleby, nor to the theme of the story. Erich Fried's preoccupations, in his prose as much as in his verse, are moral, psychological and linguistic. What 'Die Vorahnung' relates is an almost Freudian case history of anxiety, frustration and death-wish, though with a dialectical twist peculiar to all the pieces in the book. Mr Littleby is anyone or everyone. If this story demands at least an approximation to realistic plausibility, like the equally sinister psychological study 'Fraülein Gröschel', some of the best pieces in the book are pure fantasy or sound the hidden implications of words, proverbial sayings or well-known legends; and that is precisely what Fried's poems continued to do even when his books of poems alluded to specific topical issues, like the Vietnam War or the Zionists' treatment of the

Palestinian Arabs. Some of the prose pieces, like 'Muriel-Passage' or 'Hinter Fetzensee turnen am nassen Turm', explore the border-line between dream and reality by verbal associations that uncover infantile fantasies. In Fried's later work such probings of the unconscious are rarely unrelated to his moral and social concerns, which predominate in more sober parables like 'Vater aller Dinge'.

Fried did not need the 'new subjectivity' movement to liberate him from dogmatic or ideological constraints, for the simple reason that he had never accepted such restraints for his person or his work. All the forty-one poems in his book *und Vietnam und* may have a bearing on that war—about which he was as well-informed as a non-participant could be, appending a documentary chart of the history of Vietnam from 1859 to 1966—but in such diverse ways as to constitute not a sequence, but a collection of short lyrics and satires whose implications go beyond that war, and the Cold War in which it was an 'episode'. Characteristically, this collection of fables, epigrams and exhortations also includes a rhymed poem modelled on the work of the medieval poet Walther von der Vogelweide, when the dogmatic ideologists prided themselves on having no use for any poetry written before Brecht's. Throughout those politicized years, too, Fried continued to translate Shakespeare's plays into German—seventeen of the major plays in the twelve years before 1980.

Because of his obsessive concern with language and the morality of language, its uses and abuses, Fried will come to be seen less as a successor to Brecht than as a successor to Karl Kraus, with whom he also shares an instinctive siding with the underdog in any conflict of interests and powers. The linguistic genesis of Fried's poems—not out of an experience or a situation or anything that could be called a 'subject', but out of the behaviour of words and phrases—is their most striking and consistent feature. One example, out of hundreds of possible ones, is the poem 'Angst und Zweifel' from the collection *Gegengift* of 1974:

> Zweifle nicht
> an dem
> der dir sagt
> er hat Angst
>
> aber hab Angst
> vor dem
> der dir sagt
> er kennt keinen Zweifel

> *Fear and Doubt*
>
> do not doubt
> the man

who tells you
he's afraid

but be afraid
of the man
who tells you
he's never known doubt.

This is not one of Fried's outstanding poems—he has written many with a richer texture—but it is representative in that it is spare, epigrammatic, abstract, and a product of word play. One has only to compare such a poem of Fried's with one of Brecht's didactic poems to note at once that for Brecht, the thought or perception came first, the words to fit it, later. For Fried it is the behaviour of words that comes first; it is the words that lead him to a thought or perception which, in his later work, has to make good sense. Secondly, this poem without an 'I' is less impersonal than those didactic poems of Brecht's in which he makes use of a first person. Out of the things this minimal poem tells us, without allusion to any but verbal experience, is why Fried could never be a dogmatic ideologist.

The slightness of this poem does not detract from its rightness; and this rightness in the use of words—not only the very plain ones with which this poem makes do—is what Fried has aimed at in his later work. There have been bad misses, of course, to the delight of those whom it suited to mistake Fried's quixotic sallies for the sectarian partisanship of which he was incapable. His compulsive productivity has also worked against him. Since 1964, Fried has published some twenty books of poems, several of which were among the most widely read by a living poet in the German-speaking countries. This abnormal 'presence' alone, combined with an absence as conspicuous from the more official places reserved for poets in the Federal Republic, but also with an unending round of public appearances, made a just assessment of Fried's work an assignment that most critics preferred to shirk. The astonishing thing is that his unremitting busy-ness, which had made selection a special difficulty for him from the start, did not prevent Fried from returning again and again to the kind of poetry which, for other poets, would be quite incompatible with such a large output of verse, not to mention the translations, the polemical journalism, the dramatic and narrative works, the platform readings and discussions. That kind of poetry is one in which the words are inseparable from specific things, persons and complexes of lived experience, often 'recollected in tranquillity' (or reading as though they had been). Despite Fried's reputation as a 'political' poet, it is his collection *Liebesgedichte* (1979) that broke through the poetry enclave to what used to be called a 'general readership'; and when the necessary critical sifting has been done, that preference may well prove more sound than most of the published secondary literature. The mainsprings of Fried's writing have been personal and linguistic at all times. In different ways, language and personal relations have been the rafts to which he clung for survival, after the experience of genocide and homelessness. Because personal survival in itself is meaningless, as the planners of a Third World War would do well to remember while drafting their science fictions, it was natural for Fried to extend his personal struggle for survival to those concerns that we label 'social' or 'political'. Here his displacement was a forbidding obstacle. Even Johannes Bobrowski, who had the advantage in his displacement of being rooted in a religious community, wrote of language as being

> auf dem endlosen Weg
> zum Hause des Nachbarn.

> on its unending way
> to the neighbour's house.

Fried's language had farther to go, by the most various detours and through a pluralism of traditions and cultures. On his way, which took him back through the centuries, Bobrowski had to confront the victims who had once been neighbours. Fried's compelling need was to confront the victimizers, not to be avenged on them but to make them neighbours once more. (This had been the hidden gist of his outrageous novel about the soldier and the girl.)

In his lecture 'The End of Fiction' (1975; reprinted in *Das Ende der Fiktionen*, 1984) Wolfgang Hildesheimer wrote:

> The writer should make use of his name and his prominence to support a good cause, although we generally find him overestimating the value of his appeal. To despots and dictators he is just a tiresome grumbler. There has never been any proof whether for instance an eminent writer like Günter Grass who participated actively in the German election campaign of 1968 brought in votes for *his* party or for the opposition. All the writer *can* do is to justify the moral credit given to him by those who still believe in the ethics of his art and mission . . .

If it was never proved whether Günter Grass's strictly political commitment helped or harmed his cause, the effect of Fried's strictly non-partisan campaigns as a freelance champion of the wronged and deceived will remain even more imponderable; but ultimately it is not the effectiveness that matters, when even political victories can be invalidated by a change of direction or leadership. Hildesheimer implied as much when he went on to say of the writer: 'He has to rely on his personal hope that his message as an essential constituent of his inner microcosm, which is or should be his individual gift as well as his professional heritage, expresses itself automatically, unconsciously in his work. But he cannot choose this message. The message chooses him.'

In the light of that insight, it will also cease to matter whether or not Günter Grass had Erich Fried in mind when he wrote his poem about the ineffectuality of protest and protesters. Neither Grass's electioneering nor Fried's protests put an end to the puerilities of the Cold War, which seems likelier than ever to become hot and terminal—terminally cold, that is, after the heat. Each, in his way, delivered the message that had chosen him. Neither could be sure in his heart whether and how it would be read.

3

Hildesheimer's notion of an inherent, implicit, even unconscious commitment is much more relevant to German imaginative writing since 1945 than Sartre's *engagement*, that leap from nihilism into positive allegiance. What is also relevant to a literature that had been deliberately insulated is political and social awareness, an awareness that could inform the work of writers very far from any mode usually regarded as realistic. It was the lack of such awareness in the immediate post-war years that Peter Huchel regretted in his speech of 1947. Huchel's own post-war poetry was to show that the awareness, too, did not need to become explicit in a literary text, while being a necessary precondition for it even on grounds of form and diction.

One instance of that is the poetry of Marie Luise Kaschnitz, a writer of Peter Huchel's generation. The belated dawning of her social awareness, and its effects on the very structure and texture of her work, can be followed in her own selection *Überallnie*, published for her sixty-fifth birthday in 1966 and including work going back to 1928, or in the smaller, posthumous selection made by Peter Huchel, *Gedichte* (1975). Much of the earlier work reads as though it had been written not decades, but a century before 1965. Since she knew that, it was brave of her not to suppress any stage of her development in retrospect, despite the glaring disparity between her early neo-classicism, impervious both to images of contemporary life and the cadences of its vernacular, and her later laconic and chastened mode. The distance covered by that development corresponds to a change in consciousness—and in conscience, too, since her imperviousness had been as much a moral as an aesthetic one. In a short poem from her collection *Ein Wort Weiter* of 1965, she wrote of the 'counterfeit' currency of her early poems and the 'forged papers' with which she had travelled. That self-judgement about the grandeur and solemnity of her early manner is more to the point than Karl Krolow's remarks about its 'dignity' in his epilogue to her selection. As a religious poet, Marie Luise Kaschnitz had learned why she had no right to maintain such a dignity, literary or otherwise, only because she was privileged enough to lead a life almost shock-proof until the military defeat of her country. In her long elegiac poems of the early post-war years, isolated images and rhythmic irregularities register the shock-waves of a delayed awareness. When that awareness intensified, in the late 1950s and early 1960s, it was enacted not only in shorter lines, a less flowing rhythm, and fewer, plainer words, but also in a syntax that tended to be clipped or elliptic; as in the poems 'Nur die Augen' (Only the Eyes), 'Auferstehung' (Resurrection) and 'Demut' (Humility). The strength and the starkness of Marie Luise Kaschnitz's later and last poems owe much to what they refrain from saying, though they do not go nearly as far in the loading of interstices as the later poems of Günter Eich or of Paul Celan.

The work of Karl Krolow, a poet almost as prolific as Erich Fried, over an even longer period, has been more remarkable for consistency than for sudden intensities or intensifications of vision. The two volumes of his *Gesammelte Gedichte* (1965 and 1975) alone contain 624 pages, many of them with more than one poem to the page, and they were followed by a succession of new collections, as well as by prose books and translations. After Krolow's assimilation of mainly French and Spanish influences up to the late 1940s—he had begun to publish before the war, when his affinities were with the so-called 'nature poetry' of Loerke, Lehmann and Langgässer—his development strikes one as quite astonishingly unbroken, though it has taken him far from his early rhymed stanzas and from the near-surrealist imagery of the love poems and elegies that established his post-war reputation. Since the late 1950s, by steady progression rather than by Blakean contraries of attraction and repulsion, he evolved the manner most characteristic of him: a manner remarkable for coolness, an almost throw-away casualness of diction and stance, a deliberate avoidance of pathos and of soulfulness. Like W.H. Auden, with whom he shares a mistrust of enthusiasm and of bardic 'dottiness' (though Krolow has found quite other words to describe his preferences and aversions), he has succeeded in being a professional poet at a time when, anywhere but in Germany, that would seem to have become a contradiction in terms. Like Auden, too, he could be a little too conscious of his own performance, so that consistency of tone could lapse into self-parody. A poem of Krolow's written in 1973, 'Wir sollten endlich gehn', ends like this:

Tod ist, zum Beispiel,
eine andere Sache

Death, for instance,
is a different matter.

A predilection for the everyday in diction, experience, range of
feeling and thought, is part of Krolow's mature stance; and his professionalism rests on the assumption that the pleasures and frustrations
of daily life need not be heightened or universalized to sustain so large a
body of work in verse and prose. Poem after poem re-enacts the
happenings and impressions of a day, not excluding the season and the
weather. Even in the context of the two large volumes of collected
poems, Krolow's highly fastidious professionalism can avert the danger
of repetitiveness, though not that of monotony. The main reason is
that, by their very nature, his poems tend to be circumscribed by his
immediate perceptions and reflections, even though these may range in
space and time, into history and the arts. Where they are 'difficult' or
oblique—and they can be—more often than not it is less because
complex tensions are being worked out in the syntax, imagery or
rhythm, than because the allusions remain partly private.

For a time, in the 1960s and 1970s, social and political themes did
impinge on Krolow's awareness, as they could hardly fail to do in that
climate of general politicization, but in the poems his posture remained
as sceptical, detached and self-sufficient as ever. Of that 'real life' he has
so consistently and deftly celebrated over the decades, not without
melancholy and acerbity, but with a whole-hearted affirmation of every
sort of sensual enjoyment, he remarked in passing in his poem 'Winter.
Umwelt' (Winter.Environment) of 1973:

> In deutschen Gedichten
> kommt es zu kurz wie ein Stück Oberfläche,
> Während die Seele—denk es, Novalis!—
> unter allen Giften das stärkste bleibt.

> In German poems
> it receives less than its due like a bit of surface,
> while the soul—think upon it, Novalis!—
> remains the strongest of all the poisons.

Krolow has indeed effectively broken with what was left of German
Romantic lyricism when he began—the parenthesis addresses Novalis
but parodies Mörike—and with its twentieth-century refinement in
Rilke's 'inwardness'. What is more, he has done so on his own ground,
without yielding more than the odd inch of it to Brechtian impersonality. Within its self-imposed limits, his work is honest, inventive and poised. Yet to read it continuously and entire is to come up
against the limits of a sensibility that is never overpowered or un-

balanced by anything outside itself—or even within itself, like that poison, the soul.

It must be said that in the West Germany of the 1980s, where the Second Flood is widely felt to have been a mere prelude to the Third, Krolow's persistence in the celebration of private and domestic life is so exceptional as to look like an act of defiance. If he were primarily a novelist—as he is not, even in his autobiographical or reflective prose works—the traditional terrain of prose fiction would make it less so. The terrain of lyrical poetry, traditionally, is not bounded by the here and now. Indeed, more often than not it has needed an extension not only into the past—which Krolow does provide in his verse, by historical and literary allusion—but into the future: and the future, in Krolow's work, is little more than the certainty of personal death, a recurrent ground bass in his later poems, often thrumming against the erotic themes in which he specialized to the point of devoting separate books to them.

4

High spirits, combined with a peculiar intellectual astringency, have distinguished the work of Walter Höllerer, who has been as remarkable for the scarcity of his publications as Krolow or Fried for the great number of theirs. Since 1952, when he published *Der Andere Gast*, a collection containing some of the most delicate and flawless poems in German to come out of active war service, Walter Höllerer has been more prominent as a critic, editor, anthologist, film-maker, cross-fertilizer of the arts, mediator of successive waves of influence—including those from America—and untiring organizer of events and exhibitions than as the imaginative writer he never ceased to be. His work for the Berlin *Literarisches Colloquium* alone, which brought generations of foreign writers to Berlin and published selections from their writings, in a series of booklets also devoted to German writers both well established and little-known, attests to the gifts and energies that have gone into all those functions. Tributes to him on his sixtieth birthday in 1982 suggested that he is most famous for his laughter; and there's no getting away from it, without that memorable laughter of his the history of West German literature would not be what it is.

That he was also among the most serious of his contemporaries could have been gathered from his first book of poems, as from the subsequent collections, from his one novel *Die Elephantenuhr* (1973; shortened version 1975) or even from his no less fantastic lyrical and farcical comedy *Alle Vögel Alle* of 1978. What Höllerer's famous laughter mocked was the pretentious seriousness of the systematizers, even while, as a critic, he was often mistaken for one of them. It cannot have been an accident that the early critical study to which he owed his academic status and respectability, *Zwischen Klassik und Moderne* (1958), dealt with 'laughter and weeping' in the work of nineteenth-century writers mainly, but not exclusively, German. Laughter, to Höllerer, was always as essential to the human condition as the vulnerability of the species. If, in spite of his early poems, in which the vulnerability is more pervasive than the laughter, his seriousness tended to be overlooked, it became unmistakable with the publication of his *Gedichte 1942–1982*. There it could be seen to thread even the nonsense verse written for his children and the high-spirited occasional poems written for or about his friends. The same comprehensive collection also records the meeting and fusion of extremes in Höllerer's work over the decades—from the classical formality of his early mythologizing rhymed verse, set mainly in the Mediterranean region, to collage and permutation techniques in the longer poems of his middle years, the topographical Berlin poems, and his assimilation of American projective, 'beat' and synchronizing verse.

Höllerer was not the first German catalyst for the American influence that became very strong and widespread in the 1960s and 1970s, though his 1961 anthology, *Junge Amerikanische Lyrik*, (co-edited with Gregory Corso) preceded a breakthrough most crucial for the practice of younger writers like Nicolas Born and Rolf Dieter Brinkmann. The early death of Rainer M. Gerhardt cut off an earlier link between the two literatures in the late 1940s and early 1950s. This link is recorded in Gerhardt's 'Brief an Creeley und Olson', in his collection *Umkreisung* (1952), and in references to Gerhardt in poems and letters by those American poets. The first book of Charles Olson's *The Maximus Poems* was published in Germany in 1953. This link with the Black Mountain school—which, in any case, had owed a great deal to German antecedents—had a sequel in Höllerer's mediations, though it was the 'beat' and New York poets who dominated in the second wave of influence.

Höllerer's acute consciousness of plurality unifies and justifies what looks like an almost unacceptable diversity of forms and styles in his poetry as a whole. The same consciousness informs the anti-systematic satire in his novel and his comedy. *Systeme* was the title of his book of longer poems published in 1969. In one of them, 'lebensunwertes leben' (A Life not Worth Living) he wrote:

> . . . dieser Fleck lässt mich nicht
> einstimmen in Definitionen—
> die blutigen Narren
> hinter Tisch-
> platten die
> ihre Definitionen ausgeben

> . . . this spot does not permit me
> to join in definitions—
> those bloody fools
> behind table-
> tops who
> issue their definitions

Those 'bloody fools' are the systematizers who have subordinated life and the thousand things of life, including the animals to which Höllerer has devoted his most exuberant fantasies, to their schemes and projects.

In later years, only Höllerer, with his quick sensibility and intelligence, could have written an 'evolutionary love poem from the archeopterix to the flea', as funny as it is tender and astonishing; or the two Circe poems linking Homer to television. His 'Berichtsgedichte 1981' are complementary to the fantasies in letting the age speak for itself, in its own words: Edward Teller on the neutron bomb, for instance, that is to be used as soon as there is a major enemy movement of tanks towards the West, 'with German consent, of course'. That poem ends with the comment:

> 'Richtig, sagt sich der Fragesteller,
> irgendein Deutscher wird immer
> einverstanden sein, sitzend
> in einem sicheren
> Hauptquartier'

> 'Quite right', says the questioner,
> 'some German or other
> will always consent, sitting
> in a secure
> headquarters'

The third of the 'reporting poems' is as coolly devastating about the transplantation of hundreds of animal heads and brains by neurosurgeons in Cleveland, Ohio, and their excuses for that exercise on the grounds of 'priorities'. It is in late poems like these and 'Wind vor dem Feuer' or 'Jahrhundert-Museum für Tobias' that Höllerer has revealed the sober concerns behind his fantastic games with sounds, images and ideas. They are concerns with the sheer survival of human and non-human life on this planet; and their urgency is all the more effective in the context of a book by a writer famous for his playfulness and his laughter.

X Two Sides of a Wall

1

For obvious historical reasons, the literatures of the two German Republics have usually been treated as wholly separate and distinct literatures, though there has been more interaction between them at all times than the political division might lead one to suppose. The position and function of Brecht were anomalous ever since his return to Berlin. So, perhaps, were those of Johannes Bobrowski, whose work, if not his person, circulated without restriction between the two Republics. Yet most of the best East German writers found West German publishers for their works, and that almost regardless of their standing in their own country. Even when forbidden to publish there, Peter Huchel, Reiner Kunze and Wolf Biermann were able to publish in the Federal Republic. Traffic in the opposite direction was far more restricted; but a surprising number of West German writers, including Heinrich Böll and Christoph Meckel, did get through. Günter Eich and Erich Fried—as well as Dylan Thomas—were included in the widely distributed series of poetry leaflets, *Poesiealbum*, under the editorship of Bernd Jentzsch, and a large selection from Fried's poetry followed later. Most East German writers found ways of gaining access even to those West German publications that received no licence for East German editions; and their knowledge of such publications can often be discerned in their own work published in the GDR. The editors of some of the outstanding anthologies of poems in both Republics—from Peter Hamm's West German anthology *Aussichten* of 1966 to Bernd Jentzsch's East German one *Das Wort Mensch* of 1972—deliberately bridged the political division.

As for the movement of persons, most, but by no means all of it, was from the East to the West. Wolf Biermann had moved from West Germany to East Germany in 1953, before being forced to move again in the other direction. Adolf Endler, one of the most gifted poets still resident in the GDR, moved there from West Germany in 1955. The East-West exodus began even before the political division, towards the end of the war; but Heinz Piontek, who was part of that 'dispersion' or diaspora—mainly from the territories no longer part of either Germany—wrote poems about his lost home, Silesia, long after the event. Uwe Johnson became a West German writer as early as 1959, but could never think of himself as such. Christa Reinig moved from East Berlin to Bremen, then Munich, in 1964. Though celebrated there at first, like many later immigrants she was soon to suffer neglect. The novelist Manfred Bieler, who moved to West Germany from Czechoslovakia in 1968, was an exception once more in that he had been able to spend much of his time abroad even while he was a citizen of the GDR, going to sea on a trawler in 1960—an experience on which he drew for his novel *Bonifaz oder der Matrose in der Flasche* (1963). Something of the same freedom was accorded to Günter Kunert before his emigration, as to Stephan Hermlin. Other writers were rarely or never permitted to travel to the West, even for short professional visits. (This depended not only on the variable standing of individual writers in the eyes of officialdom, but on the general politico-cultural climate—no less changeable—and the programmes adopted at party congresses.) Reiner Kunze's poem 'Einundzwanzig Variationen über das Thema "die Post" ' (Twenty-one Variations on the Theme 'The Post') shows the imaginative appeal with which those prohibitions invested the forbidden countries, so that even their postage stamps acquired a magical significance. In 1975 Reiner Kunze was allowed to visit England for a number of readings—but not before he had been brought to the point of physical breakdown by bureaucratic harassments. He might have died in London but for an injection provided by a general practitioner there.

In 1976 the anthology *Time for Dreams* was published in East Berlin for English-speaking readers, at the very moment of an unprecedented crisis in the relations between East German poets and the officialdom that licenses or prohibits their publications. The inevitable time-lag between the selection and the printing of the contents was enough to give a bitterly ironic twist to the exercise. At least one contributor to the anthology, Reiner Kunze, could not have been included but for that time-lag, during which he was expelled from the Writers' Union and subjected to a campaign of vilification. A similar campaign at an earlier period—before the 8th Congress of the Socialist Unity Party in 1972 and the relative liberalization it granted to the arts—had silenced Wolf Biermann, whom Kunze had the courage to defend at the time. Biermann, therefore, could not be represented in the anthology. Yet it was his extradition—if that is the right word for the procedure of granting him a visa to give a concert in West Germany and refusing him re-entry—that precipitated the crisis and led to a large exodus of writers and artists from the GDR.

By February 1977 the following information could be gathered from West German newspapers. Bernd Jentzsch, an excellent poet and story writer, had decided not to return from a professional trip to Switzerland when informed that, instead of the prize awaiting him in the GDR, he was to receive a prison sentence for his open letter to Honecker protesting at the expulsion of Kunze from the Writers' Union and Biermann's 'extradition'. Action had also been taken against the twelve signatories of the letter appealing against Biermann's banishment. (The letter was submitted to an East German periodical, but published abroad when it failed to appear there.) More than a hundred signatures were added later. On 26 November 1976, the novelist Jurek Becker and Gerhard Wolf, husband of the eminent novelist Christa Wolf, were expelled from the Party, and the poet Sarah Kirsch was suspended from membership. Proceedings against Günter Kunert and Christa Wolf herself were provisionally dropped, on the grounds that these authors were in a state of mind that made them unfit to plead. (They were the signatories best-known in West Germany and internationally.) Other signatories, including the poets Volker Braun and Stephan Hermlin, received official reprimands: Hermlin a 'severe reprimand', Braun a 'simple' or 'plain' one, to adopt the official pedagogical terminology. Some three weeks later, Günter Kunert's Party membership was suspended—the official term was 'cancelled' or 'deleted'—and Christa Wolf received a 'severe' reprimand.

On 19 November the young East German writer Jürgen Fuchs was arrested in Robert Havemann's car. This arrest was followed by that of Christian Kunert and of the song-writer Gerulf Pannach, a friend of Biermann's. About forty Biermann fans were arrested in Jena, but released after a few days. Robert Havemann, the political philosopher and sociologist, was arrested, then released, and placed under house-arrest. His daughter was expelled from the Humboldt University, East Berlin. In December the young (British-born) writer Thomas Brasch, another signatory, was escorted across the Berlin border, at his request.

Early in February 1977 Reiner Kunze was allowed to receive the Austrian Trakl Prize at Salzburg, and duly returned to his home in Thuringia. By April he was part of the exodus that included Biermann, Jentzsch, Jurek Becker, Sarah Kirsch, Günter Kunert and—later, in 1980—Kurt Bartsch.

Another signatory, the novelist Stefan Heym, who had settled in East Germany as an American citizen in the McCarthy era and returned his war medals in protest against the Korean war, was expelled from the Writers' Union and forbidden to publish his works in the GDR. The interdict was still in force in 1983, though Heym continued to publish his works in West Germany, while remaining resident in East Berlin.

2

A correct assessment of these events would call for much more information, detailed analyses of each case and of the institutions of the GDR, such as the duties incumbent on members of the Socialist Unity

Party. One of these, I noted, was to 'practise criticism and self-criticism'; and, more specifically, 'not to conceal defects, or remain silent about, actions damaging to the Party and the State'. There can be no doubt that the signatories who were Party members believed that they were performing those duties by protesting.

Such circumstances ought to be irrelevant to an anthology of poems, and an anthology by no means blatantly propagandist or tendentious in character, if only because it was compiled at a time of relative thaw, and for foreign consumption at that. (A strikingly high proportion of the contents was taken over from the earlier anthology *Saison für Lyrik*, published in 1968, but put together before the Czech crisis brought about a tightening of controls that would also have made Kunze ineligible for inclusion, since he had opposed his country's intervention in Czechoslovakia.) Only the title of the later anthology raises misgivings about official views of the function of poetry. Good poets, in the GDR and elsewhere, had long ceased to be the contributors of 'dreams' of a comfortable or comforting kind.

The more repressive the measures taken against the critics and satirists among them, the more vehement their opposition became, even if, like Biermann, they were dedicated Communists who chose to live under a régime that had no use for their talents. None of the poets persecuted by the East German régime has yet been driven into an opposition as radical as Solzhenitsyn's, an opposition that would substantiate the charges of disloyalty with which they were smeared; but by the measure of expelling its critics, the East German system did its best to drive them into the enemy camp. In the process it also alienated those whose loyalty was never impugned and those who, though reprimanded, chose not to leave the country.

Unexceptionally, on literary grounds, the anthology opened with poems by Johannes Bobrowski, a poet distinguished for something quite other than the 'literary realism' which, according to the editor, Günther Deicke, the anthology was intended to exemplify. Apart from occasional howlers—the 'eternal nutcrackers', for instance, which, most unrealistically, 'make merry' in a poem by the editor are nothing more fantastic than birds, grosbeaks or hawfinches—the translation, too, is adequate on the whole and can rise to brilliance, as with wittily rhymed poems by Karl Mickel, another poet who came in for severe public rebukes. Responses to political atrocities committed on the other side—from Nazism to Vietnam—were fully and variously represented, and only readers familiar with the full range of East German verse will have noticed that there was no corresponding representation of responses to what was rotten in the poets' own State, though this, quite reasonably, was the primary concern of many of them. With very few exceptions, such as Volker Braun's 'Government Decree', a poem that calls on the workers to participate in policy-making, this concern has to be read between the lines. Braun's poem is forthright (and would be more so in Jack Mitchell's translation, if he had sensed that the definite article before 'easy chairs' and 'power' is a Germanism not only redundant but obfuscating in English; or if 'weakness' had been allowed to 'inflate itself', as in the original, instead of growing fat):

> . . . Stay silent, numbed
> By the shift norm, and weakness grows fat
> In the easy chairs. Close your lids in sweat
> And the power is lonely, lost
> To itself . . .

Since it posits an interdependence of power and labour in the State, Braun's criticism could not easily be censured by those powers who claim to represent the workers. Yet Kunze's satire and Biermann's invective were aimed at the same target, bureaucracy, from a related standpoint.

That has been one of the dilemmas of East German writers. The precise point at which 'constructive' or 'positive' criticism becomes 'revisionist' and 'subversive' is determined not by fixed rules, let alone by common sense, but by fluctuations in general policy that may have more to do with the economic state of the country, political events and Soviet directives, than with purely ideological considerations. That honest and inventive poetry has been written in such conditions points not to the advantages of 'literary realism'—a mode that has been practised much more successfully by British poets, without ideological directives—but to the extraordinary toughness of poets out to pit their versions of the truth against any prescribed 'reality' whatever, at whatever cost to themselves.

A crucial advantage enjoyed by the East German poets is that their work matters—both to a large reading public, in so far as the work is made available to it, and to the administrators. The very publication of *Time for Dreams* shows how seriously poetry was taken by the latter; and so, of course, does the suppression or persecution of the so-called dissidents among the poets. To make poets fight for every inch of freedom may do some of them good; but when a State is afraid even of its silenced poets, to the extent of having to push them out of the country, the questions that arise are not about poetry but about the power structure of the State. For more than ten years, Wolf Biermann neither published nor performed in his country, while the hard currency earned by his books and recordings in the West must have found its way into the collective till. Other undesirable citizens could be sold to West Germany for a substantial sum. Biermann's presence became intolerable because he did not wish to leave, having committed

222   After the Second Flood

himself to lambasting what to him was a perversion of Communism.

In the Federal Republic, Biermann was welcomed with hours of television time, front-page articles and the full blare of publicity. He then had the choice between sticking to his guns, knowing that this was to put them at the service of the Cold War, and making himself as awkward in the Federal Republic as he had been in the other Germany, by a complete redirection of his concerns. That has been the problem of all the emigrant writers; and the sharper their political, social and moral awareness, the more acute the problem was for them.

Reiner Kunze did dedicate a poem to Solzhenitsyn, and wrote another about the award to him of the Nobel Prize in 1970; but both poems were published in his West German collection *Zimmerlautstärke* (1972) when Kunze was still an East German poet, and was about to be rehabilitated briefly in the GDR. Kunze, too, was acclaimed in the Federal Republic immediately after his removal there, which followed the publication of his prose book *Die Wunderbaren Jahre* (1976), a collection of very short anecdotes and quotations bearing on his experiences in the GDR and in Czechoslovakia. Though no less spare and precise than his satirical verse, this book received a different kind of attention, if only because it was a prose book, accessible to a wider readership and more amenable to ideological interpretation. Needless to say, the book was withheld from those whom it concerns most and for whom it was written. Honours received in West Germany, like the award to him of the Büchner Prize in 1977, could not compensate Kunze for the loss of his true function. The frustration and resignation that loss induced are evident in Kunze's book of poems *Auf Eigene Hoffnung* (1981), as in this most minimal of Kunze's minimal poems, 'Den Literaturbetrieb fliehend' (Escape from the Literary Scene):

> Sie wollen nicht deinen flug, sie wollen
> die federn

> It is not your flight that they want, it is
> the feathers

Or the four-line poem about flying over his former home, Thuringia, 'Beim Anblick des Thüringer Waldes vom Flugzeug aus'; or, more explicitly, in 'Leben mit einem Misslungenen Werk' (Living with a Failed Life's Work):

> Zeigen hattest du wollen
> den strick, mid dem man die seelen hängt

> Gezeigt hast du
> ein würgemal

Zu gross war
das deine

Und viele gehen den henkern zur hand,
und tiefer schneidet der strick ein

What you wished to show
was the rope with which souls are hanged

what you showed was
the strangulation mark

Your own
was too large

And many are lending the hangman a hand,
and more deeply the rope incises

Such readers in the GDR as Kunze had been allowed to reach—and his Reclam paperback selection of 1973 had reached a good many—knew how to decode his minimal messages. Few readers in the West had been compelled by the same experience and circumstances to develop that special skill. Nor could the message be as urgent for them as for those to whom it was primarily addressed. That is why Kunze could feel that his life's work had failed; and why, in a sense, he has had to begin again since his emigration, slowly laying the foundations for work that will have to be different.

In 1980 an anthology of 'contemporary East German poetry' was published at Oberlin, Ohio, as a special issue of the periodical *Field*. Even after the great exodus of the late 1970s, its editor, Stuart Richard Zipser, came up against the political division and the suddenness with which poets once resident in the GDR can cease to be East German poets. My earlier anthology, *East German Poetry* (1972), had to be withdrawn when seven out of the twelve poets represented in it had left the country. Although the editor of the later anthology confined himself to work written in the foregoing decade, five of the fourteen poets it includes had moved to West Germany or Switzerland by the time it was published. One could argue, of course, that poems written in the GDR remain East German poems, regardless of where their authors have come to reside. Yet there is no getting away from the political nature of the very classification; nor, for that matter, from the political implications of every poem written by those who have stayed and those who have left. Where literature is subject to alternations of freeze and thaw, or even to a freeze-and-thaw combined, as in that period, the writing of deliberately personal, idiosyncratic and non-political verse becomes a political act.

In spite of that difficulty—which also lends a peculiar dubiousness to the word 'contemporary' in the title—Richard Zipser's choice of poets and poems can be questioned only on grounds more political than aesthetic. To the poets previously known in English translations the anthology added Erich Arendt (1903–1984), Rainer Kirsch (born 1934), Elke Erb (born 1938) and Thomas Brasch (born 1945). All the poems included are good enough to be worth reading even if they were not representative of anything but themselves. Very few of them would have been regarded as representative of anything else in their country of origin, least of all by those still not prepared to acknowledge just how alienated most of the better East German writers have become. The editor's useful Introduction traces most of the developments that have led to this alienation and to ways of writing more or less at odds with official requirements or directives.

One striking feature on which the Introduction hardly touches is the extent to which most of the work included draws on modes and models of the pre-revolutionary—and pre-modernist—past. Whereas Brecht had been a dominant influence in the 1950s and 1960s, allusions to the whole tradition of German poetry—including the Romantic one with which Brecht had most radically broken—have become crucial in the work of such poets as Volker Braun, Heinz Czechowski, Karl Mickel and Wulf Kirsten, all of whom remain East German poets, as in that of Sarah Kirsch, now one of the most widely read of West German poets. Allusiveness, to the point of mannerism, has largely replaced the elusiveness of the minimal poem, at which Günter Kunert, Reiner Kunze and Kurt Bartsch had excelled.

Where such allusions are lost or blurred in the English versions, and they are bound to be for readers not familiar with the sources, a poem may become very nearly untranslatable. An excellent poem by Kito Lorenc, a regional poet who writes both in German and in a minority language, Sorbian, is a conspicuous instance in the anthology. His 'Nachklang für Heinz Czechowski' is a virtuoso performance, hinging on the recurrence of a single end-rhyme throughout twenty-six of its twenty-seven lines, with internal rhymes thrown in for good measure, and a joking ambiguity in the omission of the rhyme in the last line. Few translators could match such virtuosity, which is as essential to that poem as its dedication to a fellow poet, and as indicative of developments in East German poetry as a whole. The 'Five Distichs' by Rainer Kirsch are another case in point. Though comparatively straightforward, they depend on an awareness of their classical antecedents. Loose rhythm and loose syntax do not convey that awareness in the English version. The most striking instance of all is Volker Braun's lament for his expatriate friends Reiner Kunze, Bernd Jentzsch and Sarah Kirsch, 'Der Müggelsee'. Besides the overt allusions to an eighteenth-century   source,   Klopstock's   classicizing   ode   'Der

Zürchersee', allusions both formal and thematic, this eloquent poem may well conceal another to the work of a more recent predecessor, Johannes Bobrowski, who looked upon Klopstock as his master and lived close to the Berlin lake of the title. Every rhythm in such a poem, every nuance of diction between the eighteenth-century formality and the twentieth-century vernacular that poignantly clashes with it, would have had to be rendered or matched. Instead, the final twist of the knife is lost by a blatant and easily avoidable mistranslation of 'Gram' (grief) as 'gram'. Sarah Kirsch's departure from East Germany becomes a 'leap over the Wall from a seventeenth floor', and all the lost friends not only go down into the 'soup of the lake' but out of gladness into the 'bitter text growled out' by Volker Braun, 'a grief not worth the sweat'.

This poem—not included in Volker Braun's East German collection of poems, *Training des Aufrechten Gangs*, first published in 1979— registers the impact of the literary purge on those who chose to remain East German writers, or at least on one of the best of them. Braun has done his utmost to uphold Brecht's function of truth-telling in matters of public concern in his poems, plays and narrative prose, at a time when those matters of public concern, of the commonweal, have been largely abandoned by East German poets in favour of personal, regional and historical themes. 'Der Müggelsee' is a personal, regional and historical poem, amongst other things. It is also 'literary' to the point of being inbred, but for reasons that have to do with a sense of solidarity between writers not easily understood where cultural life is more competitive and less embattled. This sense of solidarity has come to be extended to the dead, as to those absent in their lifetime. Braun implies as much in the poem by rendering Sarah Kirsch's departure as suicide.

Braun's desperate struggle to keep Brecht's succession alive is much more evident in the collection of 1979, and not only in his sonnet on Brecht's 'classical' and historical status, 'Zu Brecht, Die Wahrheit einigt' (On Brecht, The truth unites us). That Braun could include his honest doubts and self-doubts about no less a precursor than Marx, in a widely distributed book, shows that the East German authorities, too, learned the lessons of the purge. The poem, 'Rechtfertigung des Philosophen' (Vindication of the Philosopher) is far less unambiguous than its title.

> Aber Marx wusste was er sagte, was weiss ich?
> In diesem neunzehnten Jahrhundert, voll
> Von nackten Tatsachen, und keine Kunst
> Die sie auffrass, sah man noch durch
> Auf den Tag, an dem die Ketten reissen.
> Was immer kommen musste, schrecklicher
> So rettender wars. Das hätte schwächeres Fleisch
> Befeuert fortzudenken. Die grosse
> Gewissheit der Klassiker und die langen

226

Gesichter der Nachwelt. Wohin soll ich denken?
Nach vorn immer durch den Vorhang von Blut
Der Blick auf die Kulissen und nicht hinter.
So viele Kunst und hat nichts zu bedeuten.
In der Vorstellung verbrauchen sich die Köpfe.
Was immer kommt ist besserschlechter oder als.
Was mir die Augen, öffnet nicht die Lippen.

But Marx knew what he was saying, what do I know?
In that nineteenth century, full
Of naked facts, and no art
To devour them, one could still see all the way
Through to the day on which chains will burst.
Whatever had to come, the more terrible
The more saving it was. That would have fired
Weaker flesh to think on. The great
Certainty of the classics and the long faces
Of posterity. Where to am I to think?
Forward, always through the curtain of blood,
Eyes fixed on the wings and not behind.
So much art, and it means nothing.
Heads are used up in mere imagining.
Whatever is coming is betterworse or than.
What opens my eyes doesn't open my lips.

Braun's very mannered colloquialism and elliptic syntax may seem to have made the poem's message more cryptic and less accessible than it need have been; but they serve to enact the complexities and perplexities of an unguardedly truthful response, down to the admission—which stands out in its plainness—that the loss of ideological certainties has deprived (public) art of its meaning. That admission, in turn, is part of a still more complex dialectic that would have to be pursued through all the poems in the collection and other poems by Braun. The 'principle of hope' is very active still in other poems in the book like 'Neuer Zweck der Armee Hadrians' (New Purpose of Hadrian's Army), a rather Brechtian historical parable about the use of Hadrian's army not for conquest but for travel. The poem ends with questions:

For can we not, in the revolutions we dare
Like that army use the whole State,
If State there must be,
For his and another purpose?
Still with power over people, but at the same time
To give them power over themselves, over their communal faculties?
This unusual thing, that makes
The rules invalid, becoming the rule?
This Caesarian luxury of the masses

That makes the nations rejoice
In their living languages?

This particular hope, for the 'erect carriage' of the title of the book, personal responsibility and personal freedom without loss of community, and for peace between different communities, is another thread in Braun's dialectic.

3

Because the resolutions of the 8th Party Congress did remain operative despite the purge and led to a relaxation of official pressures on poets to conform to an ideological and aesthetic norm, every kind of facile generalization about trends in East German poetry became no less dubious than generalizations about trends on the other side. In 1966, the West German anthology *Aussichten* had drawn attention to the shared preoccupations of younger poets in the two Republics, but at a time when a minimal poetry of social and political comment was a dominant convention on both sides, and not all its practitioners in the GDR could be published and read in their own country. Less than a decade later, Adolf Endler's jocular defence of Karl Mickel—who had been censured in 1966 for his erotic poems—was able to appear in his East German collection *Das Sandkorn* (1974); and indeed the wave of the 'new subjectivity' in West Germany was not so much paralleled as anticipated by poets in East Germany.

Satire, criticism and protest had not been lacking in East German poetry before the relaxation of controls. What distinguished the new phase was the freedom to be difficult, idiosyncratic and 'subjective'. Günter Kunert has praised Adolf Endler for his 'uninhibited admission of absolute subjectivity', to which, dialectically, Kunert attributed 'the strength and realism' of Endler's work. 'Subjective', here, does not mean introspective or self-absorbed. Endler's verse is tough, sardonic, meticulously wrought, and outward-looking. His later verse is subjective only in that he relies on his own perceptions, his own way of apprehending and rendering realities. (After moving to the GDR Endler had fallen into an ideological euphoria and written verse of an altogether different kind.) In a statement printed on the blurb of *Das Sandkorn*, Endler compared his mode of singing to a crow's—an allusion to Hölderlin's apology for the difficulty of his later poems: 'On a fine day almost every mode of song makes itself heard.' Why not the crow's, Endler asked, after professing his dislike of a sort of poetry 'that could be used for tasteful travel brochures'. The epigram that opens the collection tells of the stinging nettle he keeps on his writing-table to make sure that he will never lack an opportunity to burn his fingers; and his most ingenious rhyming is reserved for a poem about writing a poem about nothing—'Das Lied vom Fleiss'—a mock-heroic and self-deflating exercise in a hundred lines. This poem concludes the third and last section of the book, 'Notes on the Science of Culture'; the preceding sections are 'Contributions to Natural History' and 'Addenda to History Lessons'. That this second section could include the autobiographical poem 'Ein Lebenslauf' is characteristic not only of Endler's ironic stance but of the new freedom. The same section could also accommodate a poem as objective, factual and topical as 'Santiago', dated 1973.

Endler's reference to Hölderlin is one of many instances of the historical and literary allusiveness which has become such a marked feature of much East German poetry; it is the directness of a topical poem like 'Santiago' which strikes one as exceptional. Heinz Czechowski, in many ways, is a regional poet, but his sensitive explorations of Saxon landscapes and townscapes are steeped in a historical awareness that makes them more than descriptive or topographical. Wulf Kirsten, Kito Lorenc and Volker Braun have made related contributions to a new poetry of places different from anything that could be classified as 'nature poetry'. Unlike Endler, a Berlin poet, Czechowski favours a delicately modulated free verse akin to that of Huchel and Bobrowski, though its antecedents in German poetry go back to the eighteenth century. His collection *Schafe und Sterne* of 1974 contains poems of tribute to Ewald von Kleist, Hölderlin, Mörike and Paul Celan—affinities that range well beyond Czechowski's regional concerns. Regional or not, his poems do what he writes they were intended to do, 'in the present moment to make visible the historical basis on which our existence rests'.

Czechowski's West German collection *An Freund und Feind* (1983) is a selection from work written over more than two decades and drawn from his East German publications. In his early poems—sparsely represented in the selection—Czechowski differed from Kunert, Kunze and Bartsch in deriving less from Brecht than from a rhetorical mode going back, by way of Johannes R. Becher, to Expressionism. Yet as early as the mid-1960s Czechowski seems to have decided that the public function of either mode, the drily understated or the grandiloquently hortatory, was not for him:

> . . . Kommunismus? Eine Vision, Durchgangsstufe
> Der Menschheit, zu welchen
> Erreichbaren Fernen? . . .

> . . . Communism? A vision, transitional stage
> Of human kind, towards what
> Attainable distances? . . .

was as far as he would commit himself in 'Wasserfahrt', from his collection of that name published in 1967; and another poem from the same book revoked 'the useless verses/ The dreams, the projections/ Into a heaven of glass' of his first phase. Thanks to those early reservations, Czechowski saved himself some of the ideological disillusionment and despondency that have become endemic in the literature of both Republics since the late 1970s.

His later poetry has a toughness that comes of a long-standing refusal to be taken in by any collective hopes, or to claim any exemplary place 'in the pantheon of literary history/That lodging without a future', as he calls it in a poem about Lessing. His own position is summed up in 'Was mich betrifft' (As for me), the title poem of a collection that appeared in the GDR in 1981: 'That I'm unable to creep/Or to change my skin/As the occasion demands/ Is a blessing, too, for which/I've no one to thank/But myself.' In 'Credo', from the same collection, Czechowski reflects on history and public affairs with a forthright scepticism and grimness unsurpassed by any of his West German—or formerly East German—contemporaries: 'No emperor and no tribune/ Will lead us out of this present/ That is our cross.'

Irony and forthrightedness interlock in Czechowski's 'K. s. gedenkend' (Thinking of K.), a letter poem that could well be addressed to Günter Kunert in West Germany. It begins: 'You also, Dear K., are one/Of those poets called German./ We often wrote to each other and talked/ In those voices of ours overlaid/ With all we had learned of the age. Are we still alive?' Both the multiple ironies that follow and this poet's predilection for awkward questions, rather than sententious answers, make it hard to be sure whether the conclusion is not a dart aimed at the recipient's gloom: 'And black is not black/ Because white is never white./ From the well of the man you do not like/ The whispering imperfect rises. But perhaps/ It's the past alone/ that we love.'

It is these later poems of Czechowski's, with their wide range of historical and literary allusion—including similarly blunted darts aimed at East German or formerly East German fellow poets—that challenge all the current preconceptions about the differences between East and West German, conformist and dissident poetry. Take away the ideological claptrap, Czechowski's poems suggest, and we are all in the same boat—a boat in very great danger of being sunk. Even his witty deflations of social and personal vanities, like 'Gesellschaft' or 'Gute Woche', strike home without any need to make allowances for differences between the two political orders. His awkward questions, at once unabashedly individual and wary of self-righteousness or self-satisfaction—his East German selection of 1982 was called *Ich, beispielweise* (I, for example)—are well worth pondering both by the friends and the enemies to whom they are addressed.

An individualism even more untrammelled distinguishes the work of Elke Erb, whose freedom extends to a defiance of generic border-lines, like that between poetry and prose. Her West German selection *Einer Schreit: Nicht!* (1976) is sub-titled 'stories and poems', but the 'stories'—whether anecdotal or parabolic—have the density and suppleness of the verse with which they are interspersed in the book. In both media, fantasy is fused with close observation. Prose poems and prose miniatures had been written by other East German poets—by Günter Kunert, Reiner Kunze and Sarah Kirsch; but in Elke Erb's East German collection *Vexierbild* (1983) the intermingling of prose and verse becomes a structural principle, a 'new form of presentation', as she calls her device of typographically broken line units in a report on her poem 'Einen Schmelz des schönen Mannes'. Such texts may look very much like the experimental, linguistic ones of Helmut Heissen-büttel—a precedent that would have been condemned as 'formalist' at an earlier period—but they remain representational, as Elke Erb ex-plains, as well as essentially poetic, in that the blank spaces correspond to pauses or rests in music, where linear presentation would make for too fast a tempo. Though she provides notes on literary allusions that range from seventeenth century German authors to the Russian poets Nikitin and Bryussov, and a poem by Hans Arp, the delicate art of her later texts demands more of her readers than most of the work of her West German coevals.

Both the moral exhortations and the didacticism, critical or other-wise, of the earlier period are conspicuous by their absence in Jürgen Rennert's *Märkische Depeschen* (1976), the first collection in book form of work by a poet younger than Endler, Czechowski or Elke Erb. Though the book was published by the Union Verlag in East Berlin, a publishing house affiliated to the Christian Democratic Union, Ren-nert's Christian faith is so far from being visible on the surface of his poems that only the closest attention would have made it apparent in the texts themselves. Yet it informs the distancing irony of Rennert's poem on Brecht, a poem so subtle in its ambiguities that it can be read both as a tribute and a dismissal, or both at once. Rennert comes closest to explicit judgement in the lines:

> . . . Und vergass nicht,
> Schuldige zu suchen. Je wahrhaftiger
> Er dabei wurde, desto weniger
> Fand er sie.

> . . . And did not forget
> To look for the guilty. The more
> Truthful he grew in that, the less
> Did he find them.

Yet what remains of Brecht, in the third section of the poem, is no more than 'A flight of clay pigeons,/Various sorts of museum weaponry,/a few seed grains of/The kind: I beseech you/(Seed grains far too heavy/ And far too light/For the crops of those earthen pigeons)/And the smell of his melancholy/ Cigar, when you/ Open the pages of his chronicles.' Whether or not a Christian judgement is implicit in those lines, they are far from celebrating Brecht in terms he would have chosen or approved. The collection as a whole moves freely in time and space, from ancient Greece to Allende's Chile, from Jean-Jacques to Henri Rousseau and Paul Klee, from the West Berlin of Rennert's childhood to the Jewish Quarter of Prague, to which he has devoted a whole sequence of commemorative poems.

Sascha Anderson's and Elke Erb's 1985 anthology *Berührung ist nur eine Randerscheinung* (Contact is only a Marginal Phenomenon), which introduces some thirty East German poets born in the 1950s and 1960s—to West German readers in the first place—also points to a drastic change in the function of imaginative writers in the GDR. No trace remains of Brecht's plain-speaking in the service of the *res publica*, his utopia of a classical integration. The poetry and prose in this anthology, Elke Erb writes in her preface,

> reflect a new social consciousness as the consciousness of a young generation no longer willing or able to be the object of an inherited civilization. Yet it responds to the chaotic, deforming, acquiescent, nihilistic tendencies that characterize the whole history of that civilization, not with chaos, deformation, acquiescence, nihilism, as before. It no longer allows itself to be infantilized by that civilization's utopian constituents and resists its compromises . . . For that reason, too, it is no longer misled into an ineffectual critical stance and has got beyond all postures of confrontation. This new self-confidence will not allow itself to be determined or restricted by the system whose inheritance it assumes. Its social maturity is the consequence of its withdrawal from the authoritarian system, its release from the guardianship of a superordinate meaning.

Since the anthology has not appeared in the GDR, it is impossible to say whether the guardians of a 'superordinate meaning', too, have become mature enough to respond to Elke Erb's very far-reaching claim with scepticism, rather than with anger and recriminations. A sceptical and benevolent response would make it possible for them to leave the testing of her claim to readers who, uncommonly receptive, might or might not be equal to texts as idiosyncratic, exploratory and difficult as most of the contents of the anthology are. If the circle of conformity and revolt has indeed been broken in East German literature—and there were indications that it has been, long before the anthology appeared in the Federal Republic—it remains to be seen whether that literature can remain a matter of general and public concern, as it was in earlier decades. The risk taken by most of the contributors to the anthology, in opting for a new freedom, is that they will not be seriously criticized and attacked, but ignored, like their fellow practitioners in the West of a kind of art unsuitable for mass consumption. After the purges, this could well seem a risk worth taking; and Elke Erb could prove to have been right in claiming that the poets and prose writers in question *reflect* a new consciousness that would respond to their work.

Whether or not the change in consciousness is as radical as Elke Erb claims, she also touches on another reason for it: 'For thirty years we have suffered no deprivation that endangers us materially. That has led to a loss of motivation which shakes up the authority of the apparatus of civilization, since it rests on material need.' The young writers in her anthology grew up in the GDR, and they have reached the stage of taking its institutions for granted. To write poems in praise of Communism at that stage, almost forty years after the founding of the State, would be as unnatural for them as for writers in the West to produce poems in praise of parliamentary democracy or private enterprise, and to do so year after year, decade after decade. What is more, on both sides the Cold War has frozen and arrested those potentialities of development that could stir the imaginations and energies of writers; it has blocked that dimension of futurity in which the 'principle of hope' used to operate. This change is as evident in the work of older writers as in that of contributors to the anthology (some of whom are also catching up with a youth culture and with an avant-gardism that have been outgrown in the West).

Erich Arendt, born in the same year as Peter Huchel in the same part of Germany, Brandenburg, was older by almost three generations than some of the contributors to the anthology. A Communist since 1926 and participant in the Spanish Civil War, Arendt settled in the GDR in 1950 after travels and tribulations that took him to Colombia, Curaçao and Trinidad, as well as into internment in French and British camps. His earlier poetry was close in spirit and sweep to that of Pablo Neruda, whose German translator he was. (It was as a translator of Spanish and Latin American poetry that Arendt was best-known beyond the GDR, until his own work was more widely published in the Federal Republic during the last decade of his life.) In the course of the 1960s and 1970s Arendt's poetry lost its rhetorical and affirmative impetus. His lines became shorter, his syntax more broken and hesitant, his imagery at once more personal and more concrete, so much so that, like Paul Celan's, his later poetry was judged to be 'hermetic'. In fact it is a poetry in which immediate social and political concerns have not been·displaced but transmuted, by an ontological and historical vision; and not a comforting one, as far as the future of the species is concerned. That vision was nourished by visits to Greece, whose civilization and mythology assumed a central importance in Arendt's later poetry and prose. Despite a tendency to neologism and mannerism, Arendt's later poetry has more in common with Peter Huchel's than with Paul Celan's. The political division of Germany has as little to do with Arendt's last poems as it has with Huchel's.

4

The series of extraditions and departures that began in 1976 had shattering repercussions on both sides, not only because it deprived the GDR of some of its best writers, but because many of them had been among those most devoted to the *res publica*, however critical they had been of its bureaucratic administration. Unlike Wolf Biermann, who was punished for it, Günter Kunert had been allowed to exercise that critical function, inherited from Brecht. Biermann's very medium, the satirical and polemical song or ballad intended for live performance above all—though his texts were widely read in West Germany, where they could be published—placed him in a line of descent that included the early Brecht, rather than the socially and politically integrated (or would-be integrated) Brecht who settled in East Berlin. With that early Brecht, Biermann shared a vehemence and stridency demanded by the medium for its immediate effects. This, rather than the radicalism of his opposition, exposed him to a censorship that could be circumvented at times by poets who wrote for the printed page, entrusting part of their messages to the spaces between the lines.

Because of his privileged standing, which also allowed him to write his many poems about America and Western Europe, his travelogues and prose fictions with settings outside the GDR, Günter Kunert had relatively little need of cryptograms. Though always a critic and a moralist—in relations to his travel impressions as much to his own country and city, Berlin—most of his later poems and prose poems are more explicit, less ambiguous and less condensed, than many of the last poems of Brecht. Long before his departure, too, they had shown a shift towards personal concerns and to themes more imaginative than representational; and his grave doubts about the utopian ends to which his work had been directed were freely recorded in poetry and prose books published in the GDR. His thirteen poems about Britain, for instance, 'Englische Gedichte', could appear both in his West German collection *Unterwegs nach Utopia* (1977) and in the East German collection *Verlangen nach Bomarzo* of the following year. That sequence of poems, the product of Kunert's residence at the University of Warwick in 1974/5, traces a breakthrough from the predominantly urban, if not anthropocentric, perspective of his earlier work to a cosmological and ecological one. It also questions the didacticism that had pervaded much of Kunert's work, despite its humour and fantasy.

Kunert's removal to West Germany did not break the continuity of his work or impair his astonishing productivity, but the shock and the deepening gloom are all the more evident in his collection *Abtötungsverfahren* of 1980. Not the least extraordinary thing about that substantial collection is that the greater part of its contents was written after the removal, which had been preceded by a state of near-breakdown. To write poems at all immediately after such a disruption, and to do so without any drastic discontinuity in theme or manner, would have proved impossible if Kunert had not already moved far away from his original didactic function as the conscience of a whole society. For a decade at least, Kunert had found it increasingly difficult to sustain the optimism required for that function in a Marxist State. Of the future one of the poems in *Abtötungsverfahren* says:

> In Europa geht ein Gespenst um
> in ihrem leidvollen
> Namen
>
> In Europe a spectre walks
> in its woebegone
> name

and in another poem, 'Gesellschaft' (Society), the future is 'a distant ruin on the horizon'. In earlier poems, Kunert had never ceased to exhort his readers not to forget the 'Second Flood' and its lessons. Now it is the Third Flood that he anticipates, as in the poem 'Vor der Sintflut', without enough hope to warn or to exhort.

There is no lack of irony in Kunert's delicate reports on his own situation as a public poet deprived of his function. Nor are they merely confessional, since Kunert had been trained and disciplined in ways highly adverse to any form of individualistic self-indulgence. Yet these later poems do lack the high-spirited virtuosity that Enzensberger, his West German coeval, has brought even to his gloomiest investigations. The poems in *Abtötungsverfahren* have to be read more than once, slowly and attentively, before they begin to yield their substance. Their tone is subdued, their rhythm halting, except where Kunert falls back, not very happily, on regular metre and rhyme. They are the work of a poet emerging from a state of traumatic shock, and their distinction is that they enact this emergence with scrupulous truthfulness.

> Du träumst
> den Traum des Jahrhunderts
> sobald du
> von amtlichen Schatten träumst

You dream
the century's dream
as soon
as you dream of official shadows

the poem 'Schlaf' begins, and it ends with a characteristic twist:

Dann willst du fliehen
wenigstens erwachen aber wenn
das gelingt
umringen sie dein Bett seit langem
weil der Traum des Jahrhunderts
keiner ist

Then you want to escape
at least wake up but when
you succeed in that
they've been surrounding your bed
because the century's dream
is no dream

Only three years later, Kunert published his collection *Stilleben*. Its title points both to the rural setting of one group of poems in the book and the tenor of all his recent work. Kunert's earlier work had been closely bound up with the city of his birth, Berlin, and he had devoted many of his best poems to its houses and streets, even as late as in *Abtötungsverfahren*. It was significant, therefore, that after his removal he chose not to settle in the other half of the city but in a rural and provincial region of West Germany. 'Wenig Hoffnung' (Little Hope) is the title of one *Stilleben* poem in which the rural stillness also becomes a more general silence falling between any event in the contemporary world and those whom it ought to concern, so that 'the cry of a new-born baby/no longer reaches the mother/The salvoes of a firing-squad/become as inaudible as/the nocturnal cries of animals/in front of your door.' It is the world of communication technology also alluded to in the little poem 'Wohnen auf dem Lande' (Living in the Country), in which the protagonist watches deer from his window every morning for a while, before 'switching off'. Nature too is a still life now, the 'nature morte' of another poem in the book. Not only hope for the future, but reality itself, seems in danger of being lost.

In so far as the diminution of hope has led to a diminution of explicit didacticism in Kunert's work, it amounts to a gain poetically, even where his very subject is the lack of immediacy affecting every kind of perception, private as well as social, once the connections have been severed. 'Yesterday that photograph/in the newspaper: the cave/of the Cumaean Sibyl/empty:/There is nothing more/to predict'—as he writes in 'Auf dem Lande'. The poetics of Kunert's later mode were indicated in 'Eine Poetik', included in *Abtötungsverfahren*, where 'The true poem' is said to 'extinguish itself'—only to flare up like a candle after its conclusion. Kunert is at his best where he resists the old habit of moralizing, generalizing or allegorizing, and trusts the observed or imagined phenomena of his poems to take care of their own meaning. Many of the country poems in the first section of *Stilleben* and the city poems in the second are of that sort. Most of them are in the ruminatively free-ranging but rhythmically taut *vers libre* which, together with the prose poem, has always been his most congenial medium. The rhymed regular stanzas in the collection are a more dubious resort, since they tend to lead Kunert less into lyricism than into a cerebration that has been more than adequately cultivated by German poets of the past. 'Das Fundament' is one instance. The theme is Kunert's own, but the metre, like the clipped syntax of the first line, is so much the property of Gottfried Benn (himself the beneficiary of late Goethe) that the poem has no chance of an independent life. If the near-parody of its first stanza is a lapse, rather than a stratagem, it is a rare one in Kunert's work. A return to set forms and a despondency about the contemporary world are wide-spread in the poetry now being written in both Germanys. What is more remarkable is Kunert's capacity to stand his ground as a poet in whatever circumstances and 'with the writing hand/hold fast the moment:/gift of a clock that takes pity', as he puts it in a poem with the Goethean title 'Verweile doch'.

To judge by her work alone, the transition from East to West was a good deal easier and less problematic for Sarah Kirsch, whose strength had always lain in her freedom from the Brechtian imperatives. From her first book of poems onwards—*Gespräch mit dem Saurier*, shared with her former husband Rainer Kirsch and published in 1965—her work had been marked by an imagination not conspicuously 'socialized', by an inventiveness often whimsical, witty or parodistic, and by an exuberant vitality. The closest she had come to 'social realism' in that book was in a poem about the guardian angels of workers on railway tracks, 'Gleisarbeiterschutzengel'. Her no less un-Brechtian affinity with Romantic writers was prefigured in her 'saurian' travesty of a poem by Heine, 'Leise zieht durch mein Gezell'. She had also written unashamedly personal love poems at a time when, in West Germany at least, that was regarded as anachronistic, if not counter-revolutionary. Neither her work nor her 'defection' to the West yielded much fuel for the Cold War; but perhaps her reception in the Federal Republic would have been colder if the 'new subjectivity' had not already lifted those ideological taboos, on both sides, and the feminist wave in the Federal Republic had not also favoured the transition. The relative neglect of another excellent woman poet, Christa Reinig, until the publication of Horst Bienek's selection from her work, the *Gesammelte Gedichte* of 1985, suggests as much. Before her feminist love epigrams or haikus, *Müssiggang ist aller liebe Anfang* (1979), Christa Reinig had written some of the most incisive political poems of the post-war period, in a manner so personal and undogmatic that their political implications were scarcely recognized, while her more fantastic and playful works in verse and prose also failed to mesh with the dominant trends.

By the time that Sarah Kirsch published her last East German collection, *Rückenwind* (1976)—a paperback selection could still follow in the same year—no such difficulties beset its West German reception. The dichotomy between 'formalism' and ideological commitment, which had never worried Sarah Kirsch, was being resolved or put aside where poetry was concerned. Another difference between the two literatures, the much more positive attitude of East German writers to history and literary tradition—most probably because they no longer felt obliged to regard them as repositories of a 'bourgeois' culture—was also in the process of being moderated, if not overcome. In *Rückenwind*, Sarah Kirsch alludes freely to Petrarch and Laura, Romeo and Juliet, and—in the sequence 'Wilpersdorf'—evokes and identifies with the Romantic writer Bettina Brentano (much as Christa Wolf was to do in her short novel *Kein Ort. Nirgends*, about a fictitious encounter between Heinrich von Kleist and Karoline von Günderode.) Such projections had been inhibited in West Germany by narrow notions of 'social relevance'. Sarah Kirsch carried them off without the slightest self-consciousness or affectation. Soon in West Germany, too, awareness of the past was to be taken for granted, as a prerequisite of an adequate response to immediate experience. So, for that matter, were the social implications of personal relationships and private acts.

The most bitter and harrowing indictments of the purge were written by a poet who had been more concerned with the furthering of other people's work than with any public posture, critical or affirmative, that would have drawn attention to his own. After 1961, when he published an early collection, his quiet, subtle and compassionate poems had to be looked for in miscellanies and anthologies. Bernd Jentzsch's *Quartiermachen*, published in West Germany in 1978, juxtaposes some of his uncollected work of an earlier period with poems and prose written since his open letter to Honecker and 'defection' to Switzerland in 1976. Perhaps because he had worked so self-effacingly in the service of East German literature, to the point of being indispensable and irreplaceable as an editor, his case was treated as nothing less than treason, and punitive measures were taken against members of his family. His wife was advised to divorce her husband. When she refused, she was dismissed from her teaching post and transferred to another, in a lower grade. His eight-year-old son was expelled from his school and not admitted to any other. Even his brother-in-law was

officially 'degraded'. Jentzsch's mother was interrogated by the
security police and repeatedly refused the exit visa for a visit to her son
to which she was entitled as a pensioner. She died by suicide in 1979.
Her effects were classified as 'antiques', so that her son could not inherit
them. The family grave was bulldozed, and Jentzsch's mother buried in
a communal grave. Although his wife and son were allowed to join him
in Switzerland, after being deprived of their GDR citizenship, the
recriminations had not ceased in 1981.

It is characteristic of Jentzsch that these facts are not stated in his
book of poems *Quartiermachen*, in so far as they pre-date the texts,
which need no sensational boosting. Of the two poems about his mother
in the book, one was written in 1967 and tells of other, earlier hardships. The second, written in 1978, enacts the desperation that was to
lead to her death:

Briefe schreiben, Briefe lesen

Und schreib, schreibt meine alte Mutter,
Sie ist alt wie Methusalems Esel, steinalt,
Schreib für die Arbeiter, wie sie
Ihr ganzes Leben lang, das kennt ihr alle nicht,
Sie kennt es und wurde krumm davon,
Und in Plauen am Westbahnhof die gefangenen Russen,
Das darf doch nicht wiederkommen,
Wenn sich das nicht rächt, wie sie die zugerichtet haben,
Aus Rache ist sie nun eingesperrt in ihr Haus,
Und bleib gesund, mein Kind, schreib mir,
Schreibt meine alte Mutter, die Geisel,
Was machen deine Nieren, mir tun die Zähne weh,
Die elende neue Prothese, bloss noch Suppen,
Ich lege ein Haar in den Brief, schreibt die Geisel,
Wenn es noch drin ist, dann weisst, du,
Ach, die unstillbare Lust, Briefe zu lesen,
Ob ich dich wiedersehen werde, wer weiss,
Ich weiss nicht, immer dieses Geraschel nachts,
Schritte die Wände hinauf, hörst du es auch?

Writing letters, reading letters

And write, writes my old mother,
She is like Methusalem's donkey, so old,
Write for the workers, and how
All their lives long they, none of you knows about that,
She knows and the knowledge bent her,
And at Plauen, the West Station, those Russian prisoners,
That must not happen again,
Won't someone pay for that, what they did to them,
In revenge now they've locked her into her house,
And look after yourself, my son, write to me,

Writes my old mother, the hostage,
How are your kidneys, my teeth ache,
That wretched new denture, nothing but soup now,
I enclose a hair, writes the hostage,
If it's still there you will know,
Ah, the insatiable pleasure of reading letters,
Will I see you again, who knows,
I don't know, always that scuttling at night,
Footsteps climbing the walls, can you hear it too?

If Jentzsch had provided circumstantial notes on that poem, he would
have disarmed objections to its roughness and deliberate incoherence.
As it was, he relied on the sensibility of his readers for an understanding
of why this particular poem had to lack the fine melopoeia of other texts
in the book. To do justice to its subject, this poem had to be socially
realistic with a vengeance—and without the ideological claptrap that
had converted social realism into 'socialist realism'. These ironies
would not have been lost on Jentzsch's readers in East Germany, where
his work and person had been obliterated from the records. They would
have understood, too, why the mother's injunction to 'write for the
workers' had to be chopped off before the end of the sentence, which
had not only become unspeakable but had always been so for a poet
whose political and social consciousness did not advertise itself; and
why the subject required an intimation of those unspeakable sentiments.

There is no self-pity even in the most personal poems in *Quartiermachen*. In 'Arioso', Jentzsch contrasts his physical immunity with the
plight of those who were not lucky enough to be in Switzerland when it
was time for them to leave:

Ich bin der Weggehetzte
Nicht der erste, nicht der letzte.

I am the man outcast.
Not the first, not the last.

Those others were blown up by mines or had bullets in their lungs or
'blood on their tongues' at least, whereas he is 'as good as new'. The site
of their escape is that of another poem, 'Ein Wiesenstück' (A Strip of
Meadow):

The shot: from a standing position, off-hand.
The bundle: collapsed.
In front of the bundle: the dog-run ditch,
In front of the dog-run ditch: the Spanish Horsemen,
In front of the Spanish Horsemen: the minefield,
In front of the minefield: the tall wire fence,

> Behind the tall wire fence: the minefield,
> Behind the minefield: the Spanish Horsemen,
> Behind the Spanish Horsemen: the dog-run ditch,
> Behind the dog-run ditch: the bundle.

('Spanish Horsemen' is the name given to x-shaped concrete and steel constructions on the borders between the two German Republics.)

As for the ideological differences, Jentzsch resorts to prose for an account of them no less spare and concentrated than his verse:

The Requirement

They required of him, forget this name, and it was the name of his country, they sowed hatred and required of him, harbour it in your heart, they required obedience, chastity and humility, exultation at daybreak, blindness in one eye, they required of him, they inquired into him, and he listened to them with his ears long-drawn, they required, only say what we say to you, and he opened his mouth, at last, and he did not speak as their hearts prompted him, but full of a keen craving, but they did not listen to him, they required of him, this we require of you, and that increased his requirement to four times the strength of their truth, insatiable, untamable, wild.

In Jentzsch's sequence of poems *Irrwisch* (Flibbertigibbet), published in 1980 in a limited edition, his political experience is integrated once more with personal experience of every other kind, into verse so subtle and polysemous that it cannot be reduced to a theme or 'subject'. Its freedom, which includes a reticence peculiar to lyrical poetry, is summed up in the line: 'Ich habe geredet wie ein Buch mit sieben Siegeln' (I have spoken like a book with seven seals).

Kurt Bartsch, a much more Brechtian poet, dramatist and novelist, did not need to respond as urgently as Jentzsch to his crossing of the border—which, in any case, was not attended with anything like the same repercussions and recriminations, only with bureaucratic miseries drily and factually rendered in Bartsch's poem published in the quarterly *Freibeuter* in 1981 'Der Pass' (The Passport). Because Bartsch crossed from East to West Berlin with no more illusions than other baggage, that poem could be as sardonic about his West German fellow passengers as about the officials who had detained him, but not them. Bartsch's account of that crossing ends like this:

> . . . Now the S-Bahn stops.
> Now I get out.
>
> Now something here is different.

Now the houses here are different.
Now the street here is different.
Now I don't know my way.

Now I ask someone.
Now he says something.

Now I cross the street.
Now I look at things I can buy.

Now I see that there's smoked eel.
Now I buy smoked eel with dill sauce.
Now I've bought a newspaper.
Now I read what threatens the Poles.
Now they've nothing left to eat, the Poles.
Now they're threatened with famine.

Now I eat my Polish eel.

Bartsch's reports, in other poems, on life in his former country had been no less forthright. A very short one, 'Stalin', shows his mastery of the minimal poem:

Immer wieder in den Nächten sein Schatten
Kommt geht an den Häuserwänden entlang
Lautlos im Rücken die Scheinwerfer

Kommt geht um die letzte Ecke
Sein Schatten fällt wie Blut auf den Platz
Die Wachposten salutieren

Again and again in the nights his shadow
Comes goes past the housefronts and the walls
In silence behind it the searchlights

Comes goes round the last corner
His shadow falls on the square like blood
The sentries salute

5

The claim, often made at one time, that the two German Republics had evolved linguistic usages so different as to set up an impassable barrier to communication was never true of imaginative literature. It was the languages of bureaucracy, above all, that did create a division. As late as 1975, the West German poet Wolfgang Weyrauch could exclude GDR poets from his anthology *Neue Expeditionen: Deutsche Lyrik 1960–1975*, but only on the grounds that he could not have given them adequate representation within the framework of that particular anthology. At that very time the intrinsic differences between the two literatures were being widely bridged—and in poetry more than in narrative fiction; and in the next few years shared apprehensions, a shared disillusionment, made for even better understanding. That is one reason why the anomaly of political division had to be maintained more drastically than before, encroaching in the most various ways on the lives and work of individual writers.

For the dramatist and poet Thomas Brasch, for instance, his crossing from East to West Berlin in 1976 created no difficulties of communication or reception. The poems in his book *Der Schöne 27. September*—his first major collection, after a booklet in Bernd Jentzsch's *Poesiealbum* series—are as much at home on either side of the Wall as they are in America; and American scenes had become familiar in West German poems well before 1980, when the book appeared. Yet this displacement had been preceded by others—from Yorkshire to East Berlin, and from East Berlin to prison in 1968, when Brasch had distributed leaflets protesting against the occupation of Czechoslovakia; and Brasch's dissidence in the GDR had been complicated by the circumstance that his father was a high-ranking Party functionary, with ministerial status at one time. The 'new subjectivity' in West German poetry had prepared the ground for the kind of poems that Brasch had written, out of immediate personal experience that, inevitably, was also social and political experience. Since the language of bureaucracy and ideology has no place in such poems—except for satirical purposes—his poems were as accessible to West German readers as they would have been to the East German readers from whom most of them were withheld. Brasch's plain and direct diction, even in historical poems like his ballad 'Van der Lubbe, Terrorist', goes to the heart of the most diverse phenomena, from leather-jacketed motorcyclists in West Berlin to a New York actress, the Bowery winos and the American murderer Gary Gilmore, who asked for the execution of his death sentence when it had been commuted to life imprisonment. Yet it is the least Brechtian poems in the book, and the most personal, that reach out beyond their occasions and their immediate effectiveness.

The novelist and short story writer Jurek Becker has also suffered more than one displacement. Born in Poland in 1937, he came to Berlin in 1945 as a survivor from a ghetto and a concentration camp. After signing the letter of protest against Biermann's expulsion, he was threatened with a prohibition to publish in the GDR. Late in 1977, he crossed to West Berlin with a visa permitting him to reside in West Germany for a limited period. Officially, therefore, he remains a citizen of the GDR, while living and publishing in the Federal Republic. One effect of that anomaly on his work is the indeterminacy of the settings of some of his later works of fiction, such as the novel *Aller Welt Freund* of 1982. This novel, about a botched and unmotivated attempt at suicide and its consequences, would meet all the requirements of tragi-comic, socially critical realism, if its setting were identifiable. As it is, the social criticism and the social relevance are suspended in a no-man's-land between the two Germanys. At least one incident—the visit of a plain-clothes official after Kilian's return from hospital to his room, to inquire into the motives for the attempted suicide and make sure that they do not make Kilian potentially dangerous to the State—points to an East German background, but most of the descriptive and narrative detail points to the other side. This indeterminacy may correspond to Jurek Becker's experience and situation, as a dweller in that no-man's-land or limbo between the systems (further alienated both by his severed roots in a non-German culture and by residence in America). Realism may be the mode that accords not only with his conditioning but with his own disposition and gifts. Imaginatively, though, the indeterminacy is incompatible with the convention within which the novel operates. His book of stories *Nach der ersten Zukunft* (1980), with settings emphatically identified, suggests that he may well be pushed in the direction either of fable, represented in this book by miniatures like 'Der Nachteil eines Vorteils', or of autobiographical reportage and reflection, like 'New Yorker Woche' in the same collection. Fable or allegory, in fact, are repeatedly intimated in the novel, if only because the very realities it narrates are called into question by the in-determinacy, and at one point the narrator wonders whether he had not dreamed his first encounter with the hospital consultant; yet neither is Kafka's freedom ever attained. Becker may have to accept that, unlike poetry, socially realistic fiction cannot draw enough sustenance from a no-man's-land even for a novel as short and succinct as this one.

It could also be argued that Becker's no-man's-land between the political systems has come to be the true habitation of a great many imaginative writers on both sides. This would not absolve Jurek Becker from his difficulties with the realistic mode; but it would make his case less anomalous than it seems, if one considers that the Cold War itself is an unprecedented anomaly. Although interrupted and confounded by the Second World War, it has been in progress since before the end of the First; and it is a war that has never been declared in all that time, while being prepared, threatened and assumed, even repeatedly re-hearsed, always as 'defence' or 'deterrence', as a means of keeping the peace. The two Germanys are at the heart of an absurdity whose only resolution remains the devastation of both sides—and more. Its con-tinuation, increasingly conducive, as it is, to the alternative, could not help displacing other forms of political and social awareness, such as those demanded for the practice of realistic fiction.

Meanwhile, in the GDR, realism and infringements of it have continued to be debated, as in the case of Christa Wolf, whose West German reception has remained much more favourable than her reception in her own country. The old spectres of 'formalism' and 'decadence' have been raised again by her later works, also inducing her to divert much of her energy to the defence and explanation of her imaginative practices. Formalism and decadence (or degeneration) were linked as early as the 1890s by Max Nordau in his widely read study *Entartung*, on the grounds not of Marxism but of a pseudo-Darwinian biologism. This biologism entered not only into the plays of the same period of Gerhart Hauptmann but into the later work of Thomas Mann, Gottfried Benn and Hans Henny Jahnn. Since it also informed the eugenics and racism of Nazi ideology, one would have thought that by now Marxist aesthetics could have learned to dispense with the big sticks of 'formalism' and 'decadence'.

The Marxist identification of social realism with health and righteousness in the arts—as upheld by Georg Lukács over the decades, with twists and turns and dialectical somersaults that enabled him to absolve Thomas Mann as a writer whose realism outweighed his decadence—troubled Christa Wolf at the time when she wrote her early fiction, *Moskauer Novelle* (1961), *Der Geteilte Himmel* (1963) and *Nachdenken über Christa T.* (1968). The opaqueness and oddity of her manner in these early works had as much to do with that trouble as with the 'subjectivity'—a related lapse from the realist norm—to which she inclined by nature. This subjectivity, too, had to be defended and justified, as though it were not self-evident that a novelist's business is to approach social realities by way of the sensibility, experience and memories of individual characters, rather than make the characters conform to preconceived notions of what those realities are; and equally self-evident that the writer's own sensibility, experience and memories—his or her 'subjectivity'—will enter into the process. That Christa Wolf has other worries now, far more pressing than those dogmatic prescriptions and interdicts, is as evident in her later fiction as in her Büchner Prize Address of 1980.

The subjectivity of her interest in Büchner is declared after the first paragraph of the address: 'To re-read Büchner is to see one's own situation more sharply.' Büchner was a revolutionary, imaginative writer and scientist who 'set out, at any risk whatever, to wrest a viable alternative from the gloomy conditions of his time'. Christa Wolf's time is even gloomier:

> Fettered by a past largely beyond our understanding, condemned to a present almost without alternatives, full of evil forebodings—how can we speak? A new cycle of historical contradictions now forming—will it be given time, under the sign of 'overkill', to develop? . . . In the age of

technical reproducibility, does not the word turn against its producers? And does not our time say what can be said about it in plastics, concrete and steel? Monstrous, sinister, self-betraying: With an impact that language cannot match. Will it, then, the language of literature, fail us? . . . The condition of the world is awry, we say tentatively, and see, that is so.

In the persons of Büchner's women characters, whom she treats subjectively as a single woman, Christa Wolf also raises the feminist issue, connecting it with those more general questions:

> Until now, wherever things grew serious, care was taken to spare her that seriousness. She was not made responsible for the construction of weapon, super-weapon and anti-weapon systems that put paid to old-fashioned individual death and, in the fantasies of nuclear planning staffs, have already radiated, reduced to ashes, pulverized every one of us seven, eight or twenty times over. Into the hidden significance of world-embracing military, economic and political strategies she—Rosetta under her many names—has not been further initiated. In the evenings she sees the upholder of the balance of terror sit in front of the television set, drained, sees the planner of economic misgrowth drift towards his heart thrombosis, the re-apportioner of hunger in the world reach out for the bottle, exhausted. They are not working only themselves to death.

Emancipation also means the involvement and complicity of women in this world of men who 'cannot love, can love only what is dead'. The survival of literature—any kind of literature, formalist, decadent, subjective or realistic, objective and socially responsible—demands a search for alternatives more daring even than Büchner's, though Büchner foresaw much of what was to come.

> With the help of a special terminology, the scientists have protected their inventions from their own feelings; would-be logical verbal constructs prop up the *idée fixe* of politicians that the salvation of human kind lies in the possibility of annihilating it many times over.
> Literature in our time must be peace research.

Out of those 'naïve' and 'unreasonable' preoccupations—as she acknowledges they will be called—Christa Wolf wrote her short novel *Kassandra* (1983), published in both German Republics. That she had already conceived that work in 1980 is apparent from her reference to Cassandra in the address as one 'who must have loved Troy more than she loved herself when she dared to forewarn her compatriots of the destruction of their city'. This reference follows from one to 'our two countries that were once called "Germany" and lost the right to that name when they befouled it with Auschwitz', the country 'on both sides of the Elbe' that would be one of the first to be erased in the case of a nuclear exchange.

To think that this address was delivered to a West German audience by an East German writer still resident in the GDR, on receiving a prestigious West German prize, makes one wonder what those painful purges were about. (Günter Kunert's Frankfurt lectures on poetics are called *Vor der Sintflut: Das Gedicht als Arche Noah* [Before the Flood: The Poem as Noah's Ark]. Cassandra occurs in them also; and one lecture is devoted to former fellow poets in the GDR.) Christa Wolf's awareness and imagination, too, have left the political division behind, in the face not only of undivided, indivisible extinction but of the shared shoddiness of the civilization that has made the extinction possible. About the place of literature in such a civilization there may still be conflicting views and policies; but those differences are too closely bound up with the political and ideological stalemate known as the Cold War to have much bearing now on the practices of writers. Christa Wolf's early work was concerned with the differences. Her later work cuts across them.

XI Afterthoughts

1

If Christa Wolf's *Kassandra* was intended to be a *roman* (or *conte*) à *thèse*, as well as the *roman* (or *conte*) à *clé* as which she has described it, not many readers would have connected it with the Cold War before reading the author's lectures on its inception, *Voraussetzungen einer Erzählung: Kassandra*, published as a separate book in West Germany and appended to the East German edition. The destruction of Troy by the Greeks provides no more substance for an imaginative counterpart to a Third World War and its preparation than any other war waged in the past or any archetypal cataclysm less universal than the Flood. T. W. Adorno implied in a controversial dictum that Auschwitz was not a fit subject for imaginative literature (though what he said was that there could be no more imaginative literature after Auschwitz, a claim that proved wrong). What a Third World War would be like can be brought home only by factually documented predictions, like those of Günther Anders and Robert Jungk, or by the projections of science fiction. Whatever parallels were intended by Christa Wolf, in the story itself her feminist concerns and her reflections on power politics as such come out more vividly than any parallel between preparations for the Trojan War and preparations, here and now, for another world war. This is inevitable, when the two orders, the two catastrophes, in question are wholly incommensurable, and she has bridged them only by making a mainly domestic tragedy, with political overtones, out of the heroic myth. Inevitably, too, the Homeric and even the Euripidean dimensions of the myth are diminished by her psychologizing and moralizing. Achilles becomes 'the brute' or 'the beast', Cassandra a sensible and sensitive woman who can see what those deluded and puerile men can not see. Her prophetic madness becomes little more than a nervous breakdown from which she has recovered. As Goethe said of his *Iphigenie*, it's all too confoundedly humane; and Goethe's blank verse alone kept him free from the pitfalls of the 'low mimetic' braved, but not avoided, by Christa Wolf's prose.

Kassandra, nonetheless, may have been an effective contribution to 'peace research', in that it warned of the folly of any war whatever, in a manner more emotive than prescient of what would make a Third World War different from any other war. As a work of fiction, the story comes up against the limits of social or historical realism, not because it is too subjective—in being narrated and felt through the persona of

Cassandra—nor even because the Trojan War does not permit a mode and treatment so alien to it; but because the very fabric of both reality and society are in the process of being atomized by a technical revolution that could not be so much as touched upon in Christa Wolf's story. The moral disintegration of Troy can no more be made representative of that process than the Trojan Horse can stand for the long-range missiles of our time or for their operators. Whether archaically heroic or anachronistically humane, those Trojans and Greeks could not begin to stand for anything that is happening in our world, because no individual characters, their inter-relations or their conflicts, can represent the de-individualization and de-socialization that threatens us. American veterans of the Vietnam War, rendered unfit for human relations and fending for themselves in forest solitudes, have more to tell us about the effect even of limited modern warfare on its surviving participants, the heroes of special units; but their cases, too, would defeat the resources of realistic fiction. It is their loss of social reality that would have to be conveyed.

2

This is not to suggest that good novels and stories can no longer be written in the realistic mode, provided that they confine themselves to pre-diluvian matters in societies that have maintained some semblance of cohesion and stability. Martin Walser, for instance, could ring new changes, tragic and witty, on what in British and American fiction has become an unpromising convention, the campus novel, in his *Brandung* (1985); ring new changes, too, on at least two varieties of love 'begotten by despair upon impossibility'. That this novel deals with German-American encounters in California helps to set it apart from the prototypes; but it is the quality of the writing, its intelligence and its penetration, peculiar to Walser, of the damage that can be done by holding back and playing safe, that redeem an almost melodramatic plot. His protagonist Halm, taken over from *Das Fliehende Pferd*, holds back and plays safe once more; and his new opposite, Mersjohann, pays the full price of wholeheartedness.

'There's nothing that stimulates people so much as reality', says Brissot, in Gert Hofmann's brilliant, post-realistic and super-realistic story 'Gespräch über Balzacs Pferd', one of four fantasies about writers of the past collected in his book with the same title (1981). The story is set in a theatre, on the night of Balzac's death and the first night of his play *Les Bourgeois*, which he has dragged himself out to attend in the company of Brissot, an Inspector of Sewers, who is to provide him with new material for a sensationally realistic work. Brissot, it turns out, has his own theatre down in the sewers, but his theatre is one of real, live brutalities, and these prove more attractive to high society in Paris than Balzac's fictions of real life. The multiple, incapsulated ironies of this invention of Hofmann's need not be unravelled here. At the very outset Balzac tells Brissot that in reality he is in his bed, dying. Yet, for the reader, too, this admission does not detract in the least from the plausibility and pathos of the story, which tells the truth about Balzac and about itself, as fiction. In all his novels and stories Hofmann has made as much use of observed, recorded or imagined verisimiltudes as the fiction needs to be meaningful and stimulating; but he does not pretend, to himself or to his readers, that it is the business of fiction to serve up slices of life or to compete with unprocessed realities. Imagination and invention are primary in his work; but his imagined and invented situations, in turn, are rooted in real experience; unlike the surrealists, Hofmann is not especially interested in plumbing or liberating the sub-conscious.

If the novellas in *Gespräch über Balzacs Pferd* have generic precedents in German literature, Georg Büchner's *Lenz* (1836) and some of Robert Walser's studies of epiphanies in the lives of writers, such as his 'Kleist in Thun', are the most remarkable. Not only does Hofmann acknowledge these precedents by making the eighteenth-century dramatist J. M. R. Lenz and Robert Walser the subjects of two other novellas in the book—the fourth is Casanova—but he defies them by risking comparison with them, most strikingly in the case of Lenz. (Casanova, too, had been fictionalized in Arthur Schnitzler's *Casanova Heimfahrt* of 1918). Hofmann's 'Lenz' can stand beside Büchner's because it is not the subject that matters, but what either writer has made of it; and the subject, too, proves to be wholly different from Büchner's, because Hofmann has concentrated on a different moment in Lenz's life and on a single relationship, that of Lenz to his father, as a prodigal son who is welcomed not with a fatted calf, but with total silence. This stone-walling, which drives Lenz to his death, is rendered with the terrible lightness of touch at which Hofmann has excelled in all his novels and stories. It was Büchner's distinction to get under the skin of a character judged to be 'mad'. It was Hofmann's to enact that madness from the outside, behaviouristically, in a single one-sided conversation that succeeds no less well in conveying the essence of Lenz's person and life. The same is true of Casanova's macabre confrontation with his mother in Hofmann's story—even if a Freudian insight underlies that invention—as of Walser's with the Swiss businessman who has generously offered a reading to that social and literary misfit. (Once again it makes no difference that Hofmann has deliberately pre-dated Walser's death by some thirty years for the purpose of his story, at least in the businessman's mind. In Hofmann's fictions truth overrides realities.)

Gert Hofmann's first medium was the radio play, a medium whose special importance in post-war German writing has already been touched upon. (Ever since the 1930s, too, it was the main source of income for many of the best German-language writers, including poets such as Peter Huchel, Günter Eich, Wolfgang Weyrauch and Ingeborg Bachmann.) Hofmann published stage plays, radio plays and essays before emerging late, at the age of forty-seven, as an author of narrative fiction; and it may be to his mastery of the radio play that his novels and stories owe one distinguishing feature, their use of what Elias Canetti called 'acoustic masks'. Radio plays render character acoustically, through language alone, and styles not so much the author's as the characters'. Hofmann does the same in his narrative fiction, beginning with the novella *Die Denunziation* (1979). Although his prose is highly stylized and highly idiosyncratic, as 'acoustic masks' need to be, it has an immediacy that can dispense with much of the tiresome machinery of conventional narrative; and a pace, a tempo—even at novel-length—which is that of thought and feeling rather than that of reported actions. The immediacy and the speed are not reduced by extreme syntactic convolutions in the speech of certain characters—or in the letters that the narrator Karl Hecht, a barrister, writes in *Die Denunziation*—because these convolutions enact tortuous thoughts and feelings, extreme tensions, ambivalences and paradoxes. They also make for the black, cruel comedy that is Hofmann's domain. Out of the most diverse idioms, ranging from the bureaucratically formal to the coarsely demotic, Hofmann has made a fine instrument for a 'high mimetic' in fiction.

Explicit topicality and recognizable settings are not what we should look for in Gerd Hofmann's works. Yet they would not be as gripping as they are if they were not a concentrate of experience no less political and social than personal. The mentality of Nazism, for instance, enters into *Die Denunziation* not as a topic or issue, but as the response of Hecht to the death of his brother in New York, to his reading of his brother's notebooks and diaries, hence to reminders of the denunciation and death of their mother just before the collapse of the Third Reich. These responses intermingle with Hecht's response to a client who feels that he has been discriminated against in the Federal Republic on ideological grounds, and whose brief Hecht decides to reject. The novel *Unsere Eroberung* (1984; *Our Conquest*) also tells of the events of 1945, but in terms of the adventures of a group of children who are sent out into a small town by their mother to look for butter said to be available at the 'piggery' or slaughterhouse. Even the number and identity of these children—only 'our Edgar' has a name—is left in doubt. Without the tendentiousness of historical realism, Hofmann re-creates the horror both of Nazism and defeat by his characteristic concentration on a single complex of responses and a single situation. The most ordinary things—a knife, a grave, a suit of clothes, or the circumstance that the children's father owns a factory that produced whips—are magnified in the children's imaginations, and so in the reader's; but the macabre humour of *Die Denunziation* and of Hofmann's first novel *Die Fistelstimme* (1980) is carried over into a work that might otherwise read like an elaborate allegory of cataclysm.

Hofmann's affinity with his Austrian coeval Thomas Bernhard— who was an established novelist when Hofmann began to publish his fiction—is apparent, though not obtrusive, in *Die Denunziation* and *Die Fistelstimme* in that both narratives are sustained monologues. Though monologue is still pronounced in the stories collected in *Gespräch über Balzacs Pferd*, especially in the title story, it is in this book that Hofmann broke through into a manner wholly his own. (His matter had always been quite different from Bernhard's.) His later novels *Auf dem Turm* (1982; *The Spectacle at the Tower*) and *Unsere Eroberung* are also first-person narratives, but they are not entirely dominated by one character's sensibility and style. The child narrator of *Unsere Eroberung* differentiates himself so little from his companions as to be a 'we' rather than an 'I'. The unpleasant narrator of *Auf dem Turm* is so much a vessel and vehicle of the civilization that made him, down to the cameras with which he burdens himself on his gruelling walk to the tower, without having any use for them, that he himself becomes a camera for the events, at once real and super-real, of the novel. His cruelty to the wife he is about to leave, also for no good reason, becomes a reflector for the more blatant, starker and bloodier cruelties with which the two of them are entertained in Sicily. Compared to the Yugoslav setting of *Die Fistelstimme*, the Sicilian setting of *Auf dem Turm* is a powerful factor in that work. It is all the more astonishing, and typical of this writer, that Hofmann worked for a long time in Yugoslavia, but had never so much as visited Sicily when he wrote the later novel. Not the mechanical verisimilitudes of literary realism, but the demands of the imagination, determine what part a setting will have in his fiction. *Auf dem Turm* is a fantasy in which everything is plausible. Social and moral criticism are imminent in every detail of its action, without the intrusion of a word of authorial comment or of any overt satirical intention.

The long story *Der Blindensturz* (1985) is another instance of Hofmann's power to transcend social realism without falling into private fantasy. Based on Bruegel's *The Parable of the Blind*, Hofmann's parable does not moralize the cruelty inflicted on those blind men both by the condition itself and by the treatment they receive. For once, though, Hofmann admits theological implications that may have been given to him by the subject or starting-point of his book, Bruegel's painting and Bruegel's world. Human cruelty, as ever, is taken for granted by Hofmann and by his characters. His blind men accept it with a moving humility and naïvety, enacted by their dialogue and narrative style. Their language is reduced to a bare and childlike simplicity by their condition as homeless outcasts, who possess nothing but their clothes and staves, and whose vocabulary, too, is progressively diminished by forgetfulness and doubt as to whether things they cannot see ever existed, ever had names. 'Is one still alive when one remembers so little?' is the question they ask. This dual poverty becomes something like a state of grace, with Franciscan connotations. Only one of the six blind men still protests and curses. Only one of them was blinded as a punishment by human agency, for stealing a saint's relics from a church. The others were blinded by crows, ravens or jackdaws in a forest, for no reason they can understand. The narrator, once more, is an unidentified spokesman for the six characters, though they become distinct in other respects. 'Even if one speaks for all, each suffers for himself', we learn at the outset.

Bruegel's world has also contributed to Hofmann's characterization of those persons in the book who can see, as well as being seen. Harshly or coarsely though they may treat the blind men, because their seeing falls short of insight and compassion, they share something of the blind men's peasant ingenuousness. The painter who chooses to make the blind men his subject is an exception, because he is more seeing and conscious to the point of obsession with cruelty and suffering. Yet the demands of his art—cruel in turn—make him no less impervious to the blind men's feelings. Though he has them fed at his expense, once he begins to paint he requires them to fall into a ditch again and again, till they are covered with gashes and bruises, simply because that falling is his subject. This is a clue to Hofmann's art also, to its relentless concentration on the essentials of his story and to his empathy, which remains implicit in what the story unfolds. His compassion is in that empathy, but must not show on the surface anywhere. That would be a distraction and a lapse into sentiment.

Empfindungen auf dem Lande (Country Sentiments) is the ambiguous and ironic title of another classically flawless story by Hofmann, published in the 1985 issue of the bi-annual *Literaturmagazin*. Just as the theme of male supremacy is subtly threaded into the texture of *Auf dem Turm*, that of sexual jealousy as a concomitant of racism is threaded into this account of the attempt of a local government official and a police officer to settle a party of black refugees in a number of Bavarian villages to which they have been allocated, in the teeth of local opposition, more economic than xenophobic or racist. Though the locals have threatened violence and burned down the building that was to house most of the refugees, it is the policeman who 'accidentally' shoots one of the refugees in the affray after their arrival in one village, wounding in the genitals a Nigerian—whose majestic appearance earns him the nickname 'The Prince'—when the waitress at the inn who has rejected the married policeman's advances has shown that she is attracted to the black man. Only because this story is set in our time and in a more or less recognizable place, it may seem more realistic and more topical than Hofmann's other fiction. Yet its power lies in Hofmann's imaginative penetration into archetypes beyond the data of his story and in the excellence of his writing, as in all his published works.

3

'. . . only the arts have been allegorical from the start and by virtue of this transferred significance remain binding at all times', Friederike Mayröcker remarks in passing in *Das Herzzerreissende der Dinge* (1985), her sequel to the autobiographical *Reise durch die Nacht*. Since her own writing in the two prose books is a *perpetuum mobile* of visual and verbal associations, with no linear narrative progression, by 'allegorical' here she cannot mean a deliberate construct of transferred or parallel significance. What her remark does suggest is that—mimetic or not, realistic or not—art cannot be a surrogate for the realities that it draws upon, but by its very nature must set up 'secondary realities'. That this applies to autobiographical writing as much as to works of fiction, in so far as they are works of art, is borne out not only by her prose books but by the work of Thomas Bernhard, Peter Handke and Botho Strauss, among others.

'Anything communicated can be nothing but fraud and forgery, so nothing but fraud and forgery has ever been communicated . . . for the truth is not communicable at all.' This is Thomas Bernhard's drastic way of putting it, in *Die Entziehung* (1976), one of his five autobiographical works that are scarcely distinguishable from his many works of fiction, if only because all his mature works speak through a single mask, and that mask is one of style. As he writes in the same autobiography, 'all my life long I have been a trouble-maker . . . Everything that I write, everything that I do, is a disturbance and an irritation.' It is also a delight to readers who can take his grimness, relish its elegance, and know how to take his stylized exaggerations. If any post-war writer in German has availed himself of the freedom of Günter Grass's 'court fool'—and consistently, in book after book—that writer is Thomas Bernhard. The court fool's function, too, was to entertain by provoking and irritating, testing and exercising the magnanimity that used to be expected of those in power. At his best, Bernhard has performed that function despite the absence of courts. In the absence of courts, in a world very different from Shakespeare's, at times his function had to be that of Jacques as well, and that of the bastard son, out to avenge the wrongs done to him from birth. His art alone made it possible for him to combine those functions.

Nearer home than Shakespeare's clowns and malcontents, Bernhard's stance has a precedent in the figure of the 'Nörgler' or Grumbler in Karl Kraus's satirical and apocalyptic documentary drama of the First World War, *Die Letzten Tage der Menschheit*—a figure not only thoroughly Austrian but representative of the peculiarly unhappy relationship of so many Austrian artists to the country they loved and could not bear. That relationship can be traced back as far as Mozart in music, Grillparzer and Stifter in literature. In the twentieth century, its history is one of violent or untimely deaths, by suicide in the cases of Georg Trakl, Stefan Zweig, Gerhard Fritsch, Paul Celan and Konrad Bayer, by other causes in those of Rilke, Hofmannsthal, Musil, Egon Schiele, Alban Berg, Anton von Webern and Ingeborg Bachmann, who was obsessed by 'ways of death', even if she did not choose her own. It was thoroughly Austrian, too, to 'learn a style from a despair' (William Empson), if not to make style the measure of all health and salvation, as Karl Kraus did.

Bernhard's personal reasons for the despair can be gathered from beneath the stylistic mask of his five autobiographies, with due allowance for the hyperbole that is part of the stylization. As a fatherless child growing up 'between the Holy Ghost and photographs of Hitler'—to quote Günter Grass's poem 'Kleckerburg'—then apprenticed to a grocer before being subjected to years of torment as a tubercular patient, when he could have become as good a singer as James Joyce, Bernhard might easily have been maimed, as well as scarred, by his formative years. The maternal grandfather engaged in a great work never quite brought to fruition was not only Bernhard's one mentor and model in his youth, but became the prototype for a succession of characters in his fiction.

Like most of his later novels, the fifth of his autobiographical books, *Ein Kind* (1982), begins with an incident that becomes the theme for variations and modulations, rather than the point of departure for a linear plot. It is the sheer dynamic of those variations—never broken by paragraphs in the later books—that sustains the writing, with a minimum of description, characterization, direct speech and even of action. Repetition is another structural principle that Bernhard has taken over from music. To an unusual degree, repetition and variation not only hold together each of his works, but are carried over from one to the next, so that it is the quality of the execution alone that distinguishes one work from another. Only where the performance flags a little, as it rarely does, can Bernhard be censured for repeating himself. Even his autobiographies do not proceed in chronological order, but almost reverse it, both in the sequence of their publication and in their structure of flashbacks and leaps. *Ein Kind* begins with a bicycle ride on a machine 'borrowed' from his guardian and step-father who is away on military service, before Bernhard had learned to ride a bicycle, at the age of seven. The bicycle breaks down, the boy walks some thirty kilometres back to his home, goes to an inn, then to his grandfather's house in the early hours of the morning and misses school next day. He narrowly escapes the usual horse-whipping to which his mother resorts in her vain attempts to keep her illegitimate son respectable. His grandfather, wholly dedicated to writing his thousand-page novel, says: 'Everything one writes is rubbish'—as Bernhard will say in book after book, but write them beautifully and prolifically all the same. The circumstances of Bernhard's birth in Holland come later, as do the humiliations suffered at home, at school, in the Nazi 'Jungvolk' and a correction camp in Thuringia. The bed-wetting that is their symptom—and cause of more humiliations, more punishment—is overcome when he is celebrated in the 'Jungvolk' as a champion runner. His fiction, too, was to be a desperate and triumphant running; and the early bicycle ride turns into a paradigm of the delinquency, frustrations and obstinate defiance that are Bernhard's recurrent themes.

Like Gert Hofmann, Bernhard is also a prolific and successful dramatist, but became known in the 1950s with lyrical poems and with the composition *Die Rosen der Einöde*—'five sentences for ballet, voices and orchestra'. After early dream-like prose more questioning and evocative than narrative—like *Ereignisse*, written in 1957, published in 1969—Bernhard began to write those novels and stories to which he owes most of his notoriety and fame, though he published a long poem as late as 1981. By 1967, when he published *Verstörung*, Bernhard had found his musical—but no longer lyrical—structures and a prose style that owes some of its speed and energy to that of Heinrich von Kleist, a (Prussian, not Austrian) predecessor who had made a style out of his despair. Kleist, too, plunged straight into the unheard-of, outrageous events of his stories, preferred reported speech to direct speech—because it could be stylized—and compressed complex situations or actions into syntactically complex sentences that could contain them, with no loss of impetus or pace. Thematically, *Verstörung* sounds the depravity and brutality of rural Austria (Steiermark), a depravity and brutality shared by the perpetrator and the victims of the gratuitous murder of an innkeeper's wife. Only the country doctor and his friend Block, a radical estate agent who has seen through the rottenness of the whole society and state, are partly exempt from Bernhard's un-disguisedly personal invectives and tirades—the Grumbler's—which became a constant feature of his work; yet at one point the country doctor is reminded of his own dead wife 'whom he loved, but never knew or understood'. It is the—often comic—sweepingness of Bernhard's intervention in his stories as the Grumbler that lends a strange impartiality to his tirades. In other works his condemnation of his city, Vienna, is quite as vehement; and every condemnation can be taken back, reversed, or turned against himself. The grumbles and tirades become stylistic devices, to be enjoyed as such rather than to be taken literally and solemnly. The last thing we should do is to mistake

Bernhard's fiction for tracts, when even the intervening author in his novels is a character no more 'real' than any other. Nor, even in his autobiographies, is Bernhard a confessional writer.

Not the inner life as such, but its failure to interlock with an outer one, is what interests him. At the worst his characters can be so isolated as to be virtually solipsistic and fall into a kind of madness—that of Prince Saurau in *Verstörung*. The part of *Verstörung* devoted to the Prince is an almost unbroken monologue of some hundred pages, because monologue is the form appropriate to a person so cut off from the world that the only communication that matters to him is the dreamed letter from his son in London who will dissolve and destroy the Prince's estate after his sucide. That dreamed letter is the only relief from monologue in the text, since the Prince's visitor, the narrator, scarcely penetrates into his awareness and serves only as a catalyst for monologue. Since the letter is a dreamed one, even that interruption is illusory. The pathos of that monologue is such that the Prince becomes an archetypal figure, not despite but because of his absurdity. He knows that his inherited estate has become an anachronism and a burden to him. He does not want it for himself, but neither does he wish to hand it over to a State that he despises or to the son whose ideology is no less inimical to his values. Like so many of Bernhard's protagonists, the Prince had once been engaged in the writing of a great work, but had given it up when it had come to seem as unreal as his situation. 'Everyone is totally on his own, although we are together in the closest possible way . . . Our whole lives are nothing but an intense endeavour to get together', the doctor says in the first part of *Verstörung*; and this is the main thematic link between the two otherwise disconnected parts. Another, related, link is the story in the first part of the industrialist— writing a great philosophical work!—living in isolation with his half-sister and shooting at a target outside his hunting-lodge, after having all the game on his estate destroyed. In the same way, the exotic birds he has collected in an aviary at his mill have been slaughtered, or are about to be slaughtered, by the miller's sons.

Such parallels, rather than the intercommunication, interaction of characters in most novels, convey the gist of Bernhard's tragi-comic variations on a dilemma that we can interpret as a psychological, existential or social one, according to how we read the symbolism. *Das Kalkwerk* (1970) has a more unified structure and the advantage of a single setting, the disused lime works of the title that becomes an 'objective' and visual correlative of the protagonist's history and situation, closely akin though it is, to the Prince's castle or the industrialist's estate in the earlier book. Conrad, the protagonist, buys the old lime works so as to be able to devote himself undisturbed to the preparation of his study of the faculty of hearing. Like the doctor in *Verstörung*, Conrad loves, and exploits, the wife on whom he depends for his work, but does not know or understand her. For his reading aloud to her in daily sessions that are part of his work, he has to alternate between the Romantic fiction she prefers, Novalis's *Heinrich von Ofterdingen*, and the political one he prefers, Kropotkin's *Memoirs of a Revolutionist*. Apart from the reading sessions, the wife knits countless mittens for her husband, who has no use for them, and then undoes them again to start on another pair. Money is running out. 'Hundreds and thousands' of unanswered letters have accumulated in the isolated building almost bare of furniture. Conrad ends by killing his invalid wife—out of pity and despair. Needless to say, the great work is never completed.

With scarcely any direct speech or action or description, after the initial event, and with a narrator less omniscient than speculative and questioning, Bernhard makes that nightmare wholly engrossing and compelling. The place is part of it, contributing minutely telling details of gloom, desolation and beauty. In some of his diatribes Bernhard claims to hate nature as much as he hates civilization; but his sites and landscapes disprove that claim. Indeed, it is the *via negativa* to which he seems to have committed himself almost as a duty. His positive commitments, his positive values, have to be inferred from the rejections and denials. Another singular feature of his work is the almost total absence in it of sexual love, the traditional subject of novelists. This, too, points to a core of reticence within his furious self-revelations, self-exposures and self-condemnations, in the autobiographies as much as in the fiction. It is never Bernhard the man whom we meet in his works, but the artist and his mask of style; and that may be because Bernhard's life did not give him the benefit of a 'personal identity', which is always a social identity also. Bernhard's fame and success as a writer have not altered his refusal to define himself as anything but the outsider his beginnings made him.

The long story *Gehen* (1971) is another charcteristically minimal *tour de force*—nothing but the walking and thinking of three friends—sustained by the intensity and resourcefulness of the writing. Karrer's fit of madness in the tailor's shop with the trousers that may be good English cloth or Czechoslovak rejects is a memorable instance of the comic side of Bernhard's outrageousness, and of his affinity with Samuel Beckett. Such hilariously sinister episodes occur in most of his subsequent novels, like *scherzi* in a symphony or quartet.

As an outsider, Bernhard makes no distinction between 'high' and 'low' life and moves freely between rural and urban settings, a prince's castle or the cheap restaurant in Vienna that is the haunt of his five characters in *Die Billigesser* (1980). One of them, Koller, is writing his great work on physiognomics. The loss of one leg after a dog's bite enables him to concentrate all his energy on this project by the time he returns to the restaurant. The other characters are a businessman whose passion is to outwit the authorities; he too has learned to eat cheaply, wear old clothes, drive an old car, and carry a gold watch that has long ceased to work, though he always knows exactly what the time is; a bookseller with a Bernhardian love-hate for the books in which he deals; a coin collector who works in the iron trade and has moved from his native Tyrol to the Leopoldstadt district of Vienna; and a professor and would-be aristocrat from Carinthia, who is homosexual. The account of their association, based on frugality, breaks off before the long-expected 'revelation' and with Koller's death. Nothing much needs to happen in a Bernhard novel or story.

The brother-sister relationship in *Beton* (1982) has an upper-middle-class setting, but hinges on the incompatibility of the brother's dedication to an intellectual project—a book on Mendelssohn—and the sister's proclivities as a businesswoman. Once again Bernhard maintains his impartiality not by suspending judgement, in the realistic mode, but by coming out forcefully on the brother's side, with the usual tirades, only to redress the balance no less vehemently. Nor can we be sure that Bernhard has intervened at all, since the brother is the narrator. In the same way, the brother's anti-socialist individualism is offset by his involvement in the case of Anna Haertl, who kills herself after the death of her young husband. That compassionate involvement prevents him once more from getting on with his great work—which, in any case, has become an 'indecency', due either to vanity or avarice. In the context of Bernhard's work as a whole, we may read that as a self-condemnation. 'I am not a good character. I am quite simply not a good man', his narrator says in *Wittgensteins Neffe* (1982), and the high point of that novel is the outrageously funny episode of the literary prize-giving that may or may not be based on Bernhard's own behaviour when he received the Grillparzer Prize or the Austrian State Prize for Literature. That matters no more than whether Wittgenstein's nephew in the book is a real or invented character. What matters is the exposure of vanity and avarice throughout Bernhard's work, an exposure from which he does not exclude himself; and that goodness which all his negations and self-accusations posit. What matters, too, is the brilliance of Bernhard's wicked clowning in that book.

These issues became acute with the publication of the novel *Holzfällen* in 1984 and its banning in Austria as a libellous work. Bernhard *was* identified with his narrator in that novel, and the other characters in the book had no difficulty in recognizing themselves behind thinly fictionalized names. Undoubtedly it was wicked of Bernhard, as well as cavalier and lazy, to pick on identifiable persons, some of whom had been close friends, for another of his farcical exposures of vanity and pretentiousness, more tirades against the depravity and decadence of Vienna, more grumbles about its music and literature. The magnanimity demanded of those travestied in that book was the recognition that their real selves could no more be identical with those characters than the narrator's persona could be identical with Bernhard's real self—or than the Glenn Gould of Bernhard's novel *Der Untergeher* (1983) had been identical with the pianist of that name—and regardless, again, of what use, if any, Bernhard had made of biographical facts for the writing of either book. Reality and personal identity are problematic, if not mysterious, in all Bernhard's work. As ever, too, there is a *volte-face* in *Holzfällen*, when all the denunciations of Vienna are taken back, the narrator exposes himself as a liar, and the funeral of the dancer Joana, who has killed herself, pricks all the bubbles the story had blown. In the last resort, it is as hard to say what a book by Bernhard is about as what a musical composition is about. In this one, the theme announced by the title enters only towards the end, when the actor, baited by silly questions, blurts out: 'Go into the wood, deep into the wood' and 'Forest, mountain forest, wood-felling'. This theme is counterpointed not only with the Vienna setting but with Bernhard's grumbles elsewhere about the brutality of country life and of nature. His impartiality is one of contradictions and ambivalence.

The tirades—against Austria, the rural province of Burgenland, against doctors and medicine, against the Catholic Church, against politicians, composers, writers and philosophers—recur with undiminished vigour and impartiality in the novel *Alte Meister* (1985), whose protagonist, Reger, a musicologist who writes for *The Times*, spends most of his time contemplating a painting by Tintoretto in a Vienna gallery, only to meet an 'Englishman from Wales' who has the same Tintoretto painting hanging over his bed at home. It is the precise nature of that contemplation by an old man of a portrait of an old man, every day of the week except Mondays, that intrigues the narrator, his friend, who has come for a meeting, but hides in the next room to contemplate the contemplator. Although Reger is isolated, and has lost his 87-year-old wife in a street accident, Bernhard has called this novel a comedy—perhaps as a warning to those German critics who are still trying to pin him down to some mode of seriousness more responsible than his own. If this novel marks a development or change, it is that the great work has become an act of contemplation. The comedy proves rather more subdued than that in earlier works.

4

Since the late 1970s, imaginative prose and poetry have come closer to being read, judged and—one hopes—enjoyed not as specimens of their distinct *genres* but as texts, as writing. The prose works of Bernhard, Hofmann, Handke and many others can be novel-length fictions with the density and idiosyncrasy of verse. Ulla Berkewicz is a younger

260 Af the Second Flood

writer who has availed herself of the new freedom in prose. Her two short fictions, *Josef Stirbt* (1982) and *Michel, Sag Ich* (1984) have the intensity of poems, with no loss of particularity or of narrative power. The most various forms of short prose—miniature stories, anecdotes, fables, fantasies, satires and prose poems—have also been cultivated by writers in both Republics, in some cases to the exclusion of other kinds of writing, more often as a complement to longer works of fiction or collections of poems. Whole books of such prose pieces have been published not only by small presses, for a minority readership, but by large and prominent publishing houses. One outstanding writer known for short prose pieces described only as 'texts' or 'prose' (but quite different from the linguistically experimental texts of earlier decades) is the former GDR author Hans Joachim Schädlich, whose *Versuchte Nähe* (1977) could be reissued as a paperback by an established firm. His later collection *Irgend etwas Irgendwie* (1984), containing pieces even farther removed by stylistic oddity and condensation from the norms of socially realistic story-telling, appeared in a series published by one of the many small presses that continue to have an important function in the Federal Republic, even though the large houses may seem to have resisted commercialization rather more successfully than their counterparts in other Western countries. It is the small presses, too, that have carried on a tradition of close collaboration between literature and the graphic arts, not only for the many authors—from Günter Bruno Fuchs, Günter Grass, Christoph Meckel and Günter Kunert to Oskar Pastior—who are also visual artists and have illustrated texts of their own.

Unlike Schädlich, a number of Berlin poets and prose writers indebted to Surrealist antecedents have scarcely emerged into general recognition, except as translators of French and English texts, and it is the small presses that have made their work available. The two-volume collection of poems and prose by one of them, Johannes Hübner, could be published only posthumously, with the help of a foundation. Lothar Klünner, Gerd Henniger and Richard Anders are among those writers. The Surrealist antecedents are more apparent in the short prose pieces of Richard Anders, his collections *Zeck* and *Ödipus und die heilige Kuh*, both published in 1979, than in his poems, *Preussische Zimmer* and *Über der Stadtautobahn* (1980, 1985); and a tension between realist and surrealist modes characterizes all these writers.

That such short prose forms are truly *sui generis*, vehicles of something that neither poems nor longer prose works can convey, will not be doubted by any reader of Elmar Schenkel's collection *Mauerrisse* (1985), pieces that the author calls 'Kürzestgeschichten' (shortest stories) or 'cosmograms'. The latter description points to this writer's affinity not to Surrealism but to the work of John Cowper Powys—a writer not associated with extreme brevity—to whom Schenkel has devoted excellent studies. With the lightest of touches and a subtle wit, such pieces substitute an esoteric and cosmic vision for the materialist logic and psychology of conventional fiction, since it is that logic and that psychology that have brought about a 'dissolution of reality' (of which a nuclear war would be the extreme and final outcome). Because it is our 'realities' and 'realisms' that have become absurd, Schenkel's stories and parables are motivated by a logic drawn from a cosmic range of historical and mythical instances, Far Eastern as well as European, animal as well as human. Each of his pieces becomes a microcosm.

5

As for lyrical poetry, it does not lend itself to historical generalization—least of all at a time when every attempt to set up new movements, schools and groupings has been thwarted and the 'demon of progress in the arts' thoroughly confounded. Good poems have continued to be written throughout the German-speaking countries, in every possible manner and mode. Even the linguistically experimental and 'concrete' poetry of earlier decades has provided one of many exemplars for younger poets to take up, assimilate, or adapt to needs and functions they had once excluded. A return to much older conventions, to regular stanzas and metres or to a more formal diction, has tempted many poets who had begun as didactic minimalists, 'new subjectivity' expansionists or even, like Heissenbüttel, had once looked like severe technicians in the language laboratory. To call these resorts 'postmodern' or 'post-modernist' is another embarrassed concession to the assumption, once so dear to German literary theorists, that poets and poems can be neatly classified, their advances and retreats charted like those of armies in wars waged long ago, and allocated to an avant-garde or rearguard accordingly. If that historicism were valid, the whole army would now seem to be in retreat, with its rearguard at the front; and the explanation would have to be that the future has been abolished, wars can no longer be won, there is no territory left to be conquered or occupied. The truth, I think, is that good poetry has never been wholly subject to such movements, except in the minds of its historians and propagandists; that it has always been more like a guerilla force, popping up here and there, taking what it could use and get in the way of provisions, equipment and accommodation.

As Yeats said long ago about his generation, there are always too many poets and poems about at any one time. No one can read them all, let alone do justice to them, sift them, place or evaluate them all. It is this impossibility that makes movements, groups and trends a convenient subterfuge for critics—and for poets, too, if they are out to attract notice and know how little chance they have of gaining it on their own. Yeats took that risk; and so did the German language post-war poets of any generation or kind whose work is most likely to remain of interest if and when the sifting can be done. These are the very poets whose work cannot decently be described, characterized or judged in a cursory fashion. The better the poet or the poem, the more oblique and complex his, her or its relation to history usually proves to be.

A historian drawing on the periodicals and media of the time would infer that in the decade or so after 1965, the poetry that mattered was one of social-political comment, criticism and protest. During that period, though, poets as different as Günter Eich, Peter Huchel, Erich Arendt, Max Hölzer, Ernst Meister, Paul Celan, Johannes Poethen, Franz Tumler, Rose Ausländer, Hilde Domin, Heinz Piontek, Wolfgang Bächler, Rainer Brambach, Margarete Hansmann, Christoph Meckel, Klaus Demus, Franz Wurm and Christine Koschel—to pick out too many and too few disparate names—were going their own ways and defying, or doing their best to ignore, programmes and prescriptions, and that regardless of whether or not they sympathized with the dominant political trends. Some of these poets lived to see the ascendancy of the 'new subjectivity' which, according to the same periodicals and media, took over for a while from the other dominance. The difference, however, was not necessarily one of commitment at all, but one of approach, emphasis and scope. As soon as we concentrate on the work of a single poet, even those two trends are seen to overlap, if not to interlock. Often it was not a poet's practice that changed, only the publicity it was likely to receive or fail to receive.

Horst Bingel, for instance, shared the political preoccupations of so many West German writers of the 1960s. His *Lied für Zement* (1975)—a selection from and re-arrangement of earlier poems, complemented by newer ones—shows an approach to political themes, as to any themes whatever, far less direct than that of the purists of didactic verse. His 'Fragegedicht (Wir Suchen Hitler)' is one of several political poems that achieve their effect neither by bluntness nor by persuasion but by puzzling and deliberately tantalizing the reader—a technique that he applies just as effectively in poems about love, music or landscapes. One of his devices is the incomplete statement, as in the Hitler poem, in which it is left to the reader to supply a missing noun, and so question his own associations and stock responses. Bingel's commitment did not prevent his work from being idiosyncratic to the point of quirkiness, especially in his sequence about a character called 'Pom'. With Hans-Jürgen Heise, too, it is hard to tell whether a poem is intended to be primarily descriptive, satirical or expressive. At a time when metaphor and simile were widely regarded as not only dispensable but as offensively 'subjective', Heise insisted on the liberating energy generated by metaphor. That preference had to do with Heise's devotion to Spanish poetry—and Spanish scenes, like his poem 'Bottled and shipped' in his collection *Vom Landurlaub zurück* of 1975. From Surrealism, too, Heise had learned that imagination can be more liberating than ideological dogma. In a manifesto speech appended to the collection, he advocated a 'paradoxizing sequence of black humour', as opposed to the solemn austerity of the minimal verse that was still in vogue. At the same period, though, Max Hölzer also drew on Surrealist practice for a poetry which, unlike Heise's, was esoteric and hermetic, because Hölzer was versed in alchemy and the kabbala.

Like Karl Krolow and Heinz Piontek, both of whom were once classified as 'nature poets', Walter Helmur Fritz wrote out of immediate personal experience throughout the politicized decade, with a quiet and stubborn independence, a peculiar spareness and bareness of utterance. Domestic life, personal relationships, travel impressions, artistic and literary discoveries are all celebrated in his many books of poems and prose poems—if 'celebrated' is the word for a kind of poetry so even and muted in tone. In Fritz's work, private and public crises are noted and recorded, rather than brought home to the reader by verbal and rhythmic urgency. There is little word play, little irony, little surface tension of any kind. His *Gesammelte Gedichte* (1979, 1981) vindicate the consistency and integrity of his delicately unassertive work.

One thing that the 'new subjectivity' movement undoubtedly achieved was to make poetry—any poetry—respectable again after the interdict placed on it in the late 1960s by Hans Magnus Enzensberger, and the tight, depersonalized verse that had managed to slip through the meshes of the interdict. Under the influence, in part, of American poetry of the projective, 'beat' and New York groups, possibly also of British 'pop' verse—though this is not mentioned in the manifestos—a poetry open to immediately personal experiences and perceptions began to replace the iron-ration minimal verse that had been dutifully produced and consumed by the 'politically conscious'. Some of the new work was as expansive as the other had been tight; and it was this expansiveness above all that showed the impact of American vitalism, the American cult of spontaneity, on minds that had been disciplined by ideological astringency.

Two books documented and promulgated this trend, which Jürgen Theobaldy, co-author of one of them and a leading practitioner, called the 'new subjectivity', 'the new sensibility' and 'the new realism'. In his and Gustav Zürcher's *Verbänderung der Lyrik* (1976)—backed up by his anthology *Und ich bewege mich doch . . .* of the following year— Theobaldy began by claiming that the death of Paul Celan in 1970 marked the end of a literary era in West Germany, one dominated by hermeticism and a 'regressive babbling' (adduced from Celan's poem 'Tübingen, Jänner', in which the babbling is that of Hölderlin in his so-called madness) that corresponded to 'the regression of society' in the war and post-war years; and that Celan was 'the last German poet, for the time being, to regard himself as a seer'. Here the word 'regressive' implies the historicism which I have mentioned; and the target of Theobaldy's polemic—leaving aside its gratuitous misunderstanding of Paul Celan's practice and position—is not so much the minimalism or the ideology of the preceding phase as a much earlier modernism, rooted in the Romantic-Symbolist aesthetic.

Gustav Zürcher, in the same book, rejects most concrete and linguistically experimental poetry, but makes an exception of those writers of the Vienna group, such as Ernst Jandl and Gerhard Rühm, who have applied the techniques of concrete poetry to moral, satirical or humorous ends. (Helmut Heissenbüttel, who did just that with remarkable ingenuity, is not treated as an exception.) Peter Handke is given credit for taking concrete poetry out of the language laboratory by a related application of its processes to concerns at once social and personal. Something of this order also happened in Paul Wühr's *Grüss Gott ihr Mütter ihr Väter ihr Töchter ihr Söhne* (1976), through a combination of concrete serial techniques with colloquial phrases, partly in dialect, for grotesquely, often scurrilously, satirical effects. The work of Oskar Pastior, a poet who came into his own when the 'new subjectivity' wave had been merged in a sea of plurality, was to show that linguistic processes had still other potentialities of development and application—in the direction of nonsense verse, with a difference, of invention by anagram, even of a new kind of translation that could dissolve the metaphors of Petrarch so as to get under the skin of his verse. Zürcher also provided a succinct account of political poetry in the 1950s and 1960s. Theobaldy's contributions—three chapters out of five in the book—are equally useful where he confines himself to facts or analysis; and the book includes a chronological table of collections and anthologies published between 1965 and 1975.

Hans Bender's and Michael Krüger's *Was Alles hat Platz in einem Gedicht?* (1977) is a less polemical miscellany of essays by various authors, many of whom touch on the same issues. It opens with Walter Höllerer's aphoristic defence of the long poem of 1965 and 1966—later more correctly construed as a defence of the 'open poem', in more than one sense of the word—and Karl Krolow's reply to it. The order in which the contributions are presented makes the collection look more documentary or historical than the undisguisedly tendentious *Veränderung der Lyrik*, but in fact the material was presented with an eye on the same trend, which was glorified in the editors' epilogue. Walter Höllerer's contribution, therefore, assumes the character of a programme or prediction, though it was written as a statement of his own predilections and preoccupations at the time, not only as a pioneer of the American connection. The long poem *was* to be written again, considerably later, by Michael Krüger, amongst others, though it may not have been the 'open poem' that Höllerer had in mind. One much later instance is Botho Strauss's *Diese Erinnerung an einen, der nur einen Tag zu Gast war* (1985), a meditative sequence whose diction and rhythms recall Rilke's *Duineser Elegien* and a whole era utterly remote from the vernacular spontaneity of the 'new subjectivity' wave. The same author's novel *Der junge Mann* of the previous year had intrigued and perplexed its readers by its leaps in time and manner, from the present to the age of Goethe and the early German Romantics.

Was alles hat Platz in einem Gedicht? cast its net very widely, and the contributions by Peter Rühmkorf, Hans Christoph Buch, Helmut Heissenbüttel, Günter Kunert and Nicolas Born were well worth reprinting in their own right, apart from their relevance to current debates. Of the other contributors, Nicolas Born was one of the outstanding poets of the 'new subjectivity' wave, as was Rolf Dieter Brinkmann, also represented in the book. Other representatives of it in the miscellany are Günter Herburger, Michael Krüger (as its co-editor, rather than as an advocate), and Jürgen Theobaldy, who contributed an early version of the first chapter of *Veränderung der Lyrik*. Like Höllerer's contribution, Peter Rühmkorf's witty and intelligent remarks on the necessary co-existence and interdependence of commitment and formalism in poetry serve as a corrective to the claims and assertions of younger writers. Written in 1967, Rühmkorf's essay draws on his own long practice as a virtuoso parodist of the poetry of past centuries for satirical and therapeutic purposes, as collected in his volume *Kunststücke* of 1962.

When the two manifesto books appeared, Peter Huchel was still writing poems at once historical and symbolic, ethically committed and what Theobaldy called 'hermetic'. In 1976, too, Max Hölzer published his three sequences *Mare Occidentis. Das verborgene Licht, Chrysopöe*, that are truly hermetic, not only visionary. In 1976 Ernst Meister published his collection *Im Zeitspalt*, poems about nothing more topical than death, time and eternity; and a selection, including still more recent work of his, in the following year. German poetry still had its 'seers', its writers of poems less empirical than metaphysical and archetypal. In East Germany, too, Erich Arendt was writing poems in that tradition. In Austria Klaus Demus, who had been a close friend of Celan's, was continuing to write sequences of cosmic celebration that are hermetic in the sense of being impervious to both the idiom and the imagery of contemporary life: *In der neuen Stille* (1974), *Das Morgenleuchten* (1979) and *Schatten vom Wald* (1983).

What is more, Paul Celan explicitly denied that he was a hermetic poet. He was a difficult poet, with difficult things to communicate; but the difficulty, more often than not, was due to the very precision with which his language responded to the complexities of real experience. It is a difficulty that distinguishes the work of any poet not content with a 'low mimetic', simplifying and stereotyping response to generally accepted realities. Nor could difficulty of another order be avoided by poets associated with the 'new subjectivity' wave. Much of Nicolas Born's poetry is difficult, because it rendered a complex of instantaneous perceptions, feelings and thoughts not obvious enough to be immediately recognizable as anyone's. Jürgen Becker's poems can be difficult for related reasons; and many of Brinkmann's poems could bewilder a reader not at home in the particular 'scenes', German, American or English, which they take for granted as a referential background.

In his note on his collection of poems *Die Piloten* (1968)—which preceded the official launching of the 'new subjectivity', like much of the best work that has been ascribed to it—Brinkmann wrote: 'I think that poems are the form most suited to a fixing of spontaneously grasped happenings and motions, an awareness that manifests itself for a moment only, concretely as a snapshot.' In poems of that kind, social and political awareness was no longer separable from personal experience. The individual returned to the centre of his or her poem, like a spider to the centre of a web that registers vibrations from every circle and thread; and what mattered was the vibration itself, not its categorization as economic or aesthetic, sexual or social, private or public. It was this spontaneity and immediacy that Brinkmann admired in American poets like Frank O'Hara, whom Brinkmann translated. At the Cambridge Poetry Festival of 1975, a few days before his fatal accident in London, Brinkmann spoke of the degree to which German poets of his age-group had been 'Americanized'; but this applies to Brinkmann's work, or one strand in his work, more than to that of most of his coevals. His collection *Westwärts 1 & 2*, published in the year of his death, included poems written in American English and poems written in American German. 'It could be', Brinkmann wrote in the preface, 'that German will soon be a dead language. It's so hard to sing in it. Usually, in that language, one has to be thinking all the time.' Brinkmann wanted the thinking to be part of the action and movement of his verse; and in many of his poems he succeeded in making it so, with a minimum of detachment or of recollection in tranquillity. At their best, Brinkmann's poems enact an instant of perception with a freshness, urgency and all-inclusiveness that makes their vitalism acceptable. At their worst, they fall into self-winding rhetoric, lose themselves in circumstantial details to whose significance and function in the context the reader is offered no clue, or become self-conscious to a degree that distracts and detracts from the experience the poem might have conveyed. Formally, too, there is a marked discrepancy between the taut lines of short poems like 'Die Orangensaftmaschine' and 'Einer jener klassischen', poems confined to the capturing and 'fixing' of a single moment in an identifiable setting, and more diffusely ambitious poems like 'Westwärts', with their division of lines into two or more columns as a means of synchronizing parallel streams of consciousness—something that only music can do. Like Frank O'Hara, Brinkmann was killed by a motor vehicle; and his poems are almost as full of motor cars, buses and parking lots as they are of bars, rock-and-roll musicians and the paraphernalia of pop culture. The transitoriness of those phenomena—and thus of the 'snapshots' taken of them by Brinkmann—makes him the victim as well as the hero of an era.

The same loosening up proved conducive to the long, longer or 'open' poem that Höllerer had advocated. Soon after Peter Handke's longer poems in *Als das Wünschen noch geholfen hat* (1974), Klaus Konjetzky published his book-length *Poem vom Grünen Eck* (1975), with an autobiographical framework. Its central location is the restaurant or inn of the title. From there its sections branch out into reminiscence—'even at twenty-eight one has a biography', Konjetzky remarks at one point—into narrative, fantasy, social comment or description of people met. At another point the poem turns into a series of aphoristic reflections. Martin Walser, in an epilogue, called the poem 'a song about people' with a scheme which 'demands that everything and anything shall happen in it'. The mainly iambic, occasionally rhymed, verse has connotations and derivations more European than Brinkmann's verse; and Konjetzky quite openly acknowledges an indebtedness to a bourgeois European culture at odds with his anti-capitalism. In its thematic scope, though not in its verbal and rhythmic texture, the poem is as rich and wide-ranging as Martin Walser claimed. It was a valiant attempt to win back for poetry some of the territory yielded long ago to prose fiction; but whether its cool, honest and intelligent verse was best described as 'song' is more questionable, even if epic, rather than lyric, song is what Walser had in mind.

Wholly different as it is from Brinkmann's or Born's longer poems, only its autobiographical framework connected Konjetzky's poem to the 'new subjectivity'. Nicolas Born published an early novel in 1965, but it was his poems of the next decade, especially those in *Das Auge des Entdeckers* (1972), on which his reputation rested before the appearance of two later novels and his early death in 1979. That reputation was confirmed by a collection of all but his last poems, *Gedichte*, in 1978. Though, like Brinkmann, Born was out to capture a totality of awareness in his poems and prose, he was a more reflective writer than Brinkmann, and a less 'subjective' one in that his concentration on one individual's perceptions and consciousness was more deliberately directed towards the whole of society, of which that individual was a gauge. This also made his subjective approach more clearly continuous with the social and political aspirations of the more 'objective' commentators in the Brechtian lineage. 'Each one is also every other', he wrote in his epilogue to *Das Auge des Entdeckers*. 'Simultaneously and in full awareness. We focus the telescopes on us. Each, round the clock, is everyone, the absolute identity.' His aim, therefore, was to speak for others through himself, with a radical and uncompromising truthfulness, in the hope of liberating potentialities which the existing society and the existing arts suppressed by the separation of inner realities from outer ones.

Born's novel *Die Erdabgewandte Seite der Geschichte* (1976) may seem even more controlled and compact than some of his poems; but the novel, too, is dominated by a single consciousness, the narrator's, and that narrator is a writer by profession. Much of the narrative has the immediacy of diary entries, producing an effect of unembellished, undisguised confession, and allowing little relief from the narrator's account of his sickness and moral disintegration. It is the sharpness and vividness of Born's prose that involves the reader in a story so relentlessly and claustrophobically gruelling. Quite deliberately, the author claims no knowledge or insight beyond his narrator's, when such knowledge or insight would not only palliate, but falsify, the situation in which he—or anyone—is trapped. The reader, too, is confined within the narrator's consciousness and situation, and the other characters are seen only as the narrator sees them. Set mainly in West Berlin, *Die Erdabgewandte Seite der Geschichte* traces the development of a 'love' affair in which sexual addiction serves only to alienate the man and the woman from each other and from themselves. On the narrator's side, the matter is complicated by a broken marriage, as by the love and guilt he feels towards the daughter to whom he can no longer be a true father. In a vain endeavour to resolve the conflict, he is compelled to bring his mistress and his daughter together. In quite other circumstances, a parallel exists in the relations between the narrator's friend, Lasski, and his girl friend, Lisa, with a similar component of hatred that can erupt into physical violence. No explanation is given for the parallel, but the implication is that the narrator's case is everyone's, in a given state of society; and a political analogy is suggested both by the narrator's ineffectual participation in the Berlin demonstration against the Shah's visit in 1967, and by what transpires about Lasski's former political commitments, which he has abandoned or set aside in favour of literary work. In the same way, Lasski's death assumes a significance never defined except in terms of the narrator's response to it, yet somehow pointing beyond that response. Born's novel, therefore, can also be read as a diagnosis of a sickness more social than individual; and that is where it links up with Born's poetry, and his assumption that personal experience, searchingly rendered, tells us more about the state of society than abstracted and generalized observations. The narrator's and Lasski's failure to communicate in erotic relationships, then, would correspond to the failure of a politically committed generation to create a new form of community. A related parallelism is traced in Born's last novel, *Die Fälschung* (1979), set in Beirut and Damur.

Jürgen Theobaldy's earlier poems, like those in his book *Zweiter Klasse* (1976), became popular because they were easily accessible to readers of his age-group and life-style. It was a poetry of those everyday events and scenes that took longer to make their way into German poetry than into the Anglo-Saxon, and he rendered them with humour, unpretentious charm, and a gift of sympathy much rarer in poetry than the so-called 'empathy' that slips so easily under other people's skins, only to turn them into masks. 'Alte Frauen' is a poem that enacts this kind of sympathy. Because it was more than a 'pop' stratagem, the persistently naïve tone of his poems did not preclude delicate and unexpected discoveries. Theobaldy wrote poems in praise of skin, cigarettes (repeatedly), old clothes, and opening tins of fish and ravioli. At his best, as in 'Spiegel', 'Die Mutter am Telefon' or the auto-biographical poem 'Mein junges Leben', he also captured the totality of a moment or phase of lived experience, in words that are plain but right. By his concentration on process, sometimes including the process of rendering it in words, he bridged the gap between personal confession and critical observation, so that his love poems—or even the poem 'Irgend etwas', which explains why he cannot love the person addressed—are as circumstantially direct as his poems about society and politics. A good deal of tact and selection have to go into such seemingly effortless work to save it from being mawkish or slapdash; and Theobaldy soon came up against the refusal of critics to identify with the group for which his poems had spoken.

Unlike other poets associated with the 'new subjectivity', Theobaldy was closer to certain English trends than to the American poets who were much more widely read in Germany. His work had been 'subjective' only in breaking the interdict on self-expression that had once been widely observed. If Theobaldy wrote about himself, it was to write about the way of life of a whole generation. That is why he could claim that the 'new subjectivity' was also a 'new realism'. The poems in his later collection, *Schwere Erde, Rauch* (1980), are more subtle, but also more personal and idiosyncratic, than those that had made him something of a cult figure. If Theobaldy was to develop as a poet, as he did, he had to forgo that too easy identification with the life-style of a generation which, in any case, was changing its ways. There are echoes still of that life-style, its music and its demonstrations, in the later poems, but those echoes have become melancholy ones. Even the title of the collection—Heavy Earth, Smoke—conveys the dominant mood. 'The utopias have been put away, have been/packed into drawers,/ narrow lines of people walk/across the fields . . .' Theobaldy writes in 'Ohne Blumen'; the poem goes on to trace a landscape of barbed wire, muddy policemen, tanks. 'And we rush after progress/or run up against it/words drop out/like teeth.' Another poem mourns the death by cancer of Nicolas Born. Throughout the collection, Theobaldy's sensitivity to particular scenes, urban and rural, has deepened. Their evocation has become more poignant, because shared experiences and environments can no longer be taken for granted; but the spontaneous zest of the 'new subjectivity' has been lost. By the time he published *Die Sommertour* in 1983, Theobaldy was writing in rhymed stanzas and Sapphic ode form, with a wealth of literary allusions more representative of what one must call the 'new academicism', though that trend may not yet have been promulgated or prescribed.

Not that there is anything intrinsically wrong about the cultivation of traditional forms, or a poetry of literary allusions. To many Austrian poets, like the religious poet Christine Busta, it was natural to remain close to the modes and diction with which she had begun. The East German poet Karl Mickel wrote in regular metre and rhyme consistently from the 1950s to the 1980s, and made that discipline so much his own that it is inseparable from his peculiar incisiveness. Literary allusions, even literary subject matter, were to be essential to the ambitious and by no means academic poetry of Gregor Laschen, whose *Die andere Geschichte der Wolken* (1983) contains a whole section of poems about writers and artists, from Hölderlin to Paul Klee and Paul Celan, that are also poems about recent history and the contemporary world. Oskar Pastior was to publish a whole book of sonnets, his *Sonetburger* (1983), in a language quite literally his own, gradually evolved out of one still recognizable as German, though drastically dislocated and alienated, in his *Vom Sichersten ins Tausende* of 1969.

The new academicism is something different, an understandable reaction to the slackness that came of too easy a reliance on the currency of shared experience, and its conveyance in whatever vernacular or jargon was readily to hand. Generous though it is in its sympathies and concerns, Günter Herburger's large collection *Ziele* (1977)—a book very much part of the 'new subjectivity' wave—included too many poems that make one ask oneself whether their matter could not have been presented just as well, or better, in prose, as a story or sketch—poems like 'Als ich Amerika sah', one of too many published at that time that brought back 'snapshots' or anecdotes from America. The same book contained more imaginative poems like 'Keine Fügung' or 'Der Gesang der Wale'; and the slackness was expunged in Herburger's later collection *Orchidee* (1979). The younger poet Johannes Schenk was also in danger of falling into prosy anecdote in his collection *Zittern* (1977), though his experience as a sailor—from the age of fourteen to the age of twenty—left him a store of scenes and impressions on which he has continued to draw, vividly and critically, in later collections up to his *Café Americain* of 1985. In his poems the vernacular has a special and proper function, even if it could lapse into bathos in his commemorative poem 'Bill Dalrymple' in the 1977 collection, or into a casualness picked up from American poets, in 'Philip Weichbergers Beschreibung des Weges zu ihm', a mere string of laconic directions too true to life to make a poem.

Although the 'new subjectivity', 'new sensibility' or 'new realism' released energies that had been checked by ideological constraints in the 1960s, and corresponded with a renewal of interest in poetry after the interdicts, it goes without saying that subjectivity as such was no more new than sensibility or realism was new; and Theobaldy was right to see the trend not as an alternative to, but an extension of, the political and social poetry of the earlier phase. What distinguished the poets of the 'new subjectivity' from Karl Krolow, say, or from Rainer Malkowski among their coevals, is that the subjectivity they practised was assumed to be that of a generation, group or class that had shaken off a bourgeois individualism and finicalness. Its continuity with the social and political concerns of the 1960s is striking in Helga M. Novak's *Balladen vom Kurzen Prozess* of 1975, and in her subsequent collections up to *Legende Transsib* of 1985. The early ballads were political poetry of the most rectilinear kind, too intent on their targets to indulge in metaphorical extravagance. Her subjects tended to be gruesome to the point of brutality, as in the story of the castrated doll that leads it owner, a small girl, to apply the same treatment to her baby brother. Both her subjects and her manner recalled popular broadsides, though their moral gist was an up-to-date radicalism directed at oppression or exploitation in Germany—both Germanys—Portugal, Sicily and Stalin's USSR.

Ursula Krechel, too, linked the 'new subjectivity' to the epigrammatic didacticism of the 1960s in *Nach Mainz!* (1977). Her diction remained sharp-edged, whether her theme was feminist, as in 'Umsturz', or socialist, as in 'Aussichten'. The political activism of the 1960s is contrasted with a later mood of apathy or despondency in 'Die Alten Freunde' and 'Busstage'. Her book-length long poem *Rohschnitt* of 1983 is an allegorical epic, using cinematic montage technique, about three women—'the beautiful one', 'the clever one' and 'the mother'— going out into the world. Her feminist and social concerns have remained constant up to her collection *Vom Feuer Lernen* (1985), though her manner has become more oblique.

Rolf Haufs, too, excelled at social satire in *Die Geschwindigkeit eines einzigen Tags*, published in 1976. His use of Berlin dialect, like Herburger's of Suabian dialect, in a few poems, was in line with a revival of regionalism in West German writing of the period. Haufs, too, had a tendency to tell stories—he had published a book of anecdotal stories, *Das Dorf S.*, in 1968—but told them by flashes conducive to lyrical effects, by leaving gaps to be filled by the reader's imagination. Domestic themes and family portraits are prominent, as in much verse and prose of that time. Herburger's 'Sturz der Götter' is a poem about his father; Schenk's *Zittern* included a poem about a great-grandfather who set up a second home and a second marriage in New York; and Ursula Krechel's *Nach Mainz!* opens with an eloquent poem about her mother. Haufs has poems about his father and a grandmother, as well as other childhood recollections. The personalization of social history was a concomitant of the 'new subjectivity'.

Gabriele Wohmann, best known as a novelist and story-writer, was also active as a poet at this period, and a poet almost exclusively of family life, with herself usually at the centre. 'In the attempt to disregard myself/I came up against myself', she commented in her poem 'So ist die Lage', from the book of that name published in 1975. The progress of her poetry can be traced in the selection *Ausgewählte Gedichte 1964-1982* (1983). Despite a tightening up of rhythm and structure in the later poems, after diffusively long poems like the one about her father's illness and her guilty conscience, 'Alte Herzen, schwere Herzen', her virtues remain those of a novelist and autobiographer. Few of her poems have the density of lyrical verse or its necessary crystallizations and 'epiphanies'. (That these, too, need not be 'hermetic' or esoteric, but can arise from the most ordinary things, can be seen in the work of an Austrian poet remote from all the trends, Andreas Okopenko, whose *Gesammelte Lyrik* was published in 1980.) The appeal of most of Gabriele Wohmann's poems is that of reports on experience, though of exceptionally honest and percipient ones.

The later work of poets who had been prominent as 'political' poets in the 1960s, like Yaak Karsunke, F. C. Delius and Guntram Vesper, also bridged the two phases. Delius, for one, had always tempered political commitment with humour, awareness of human complexities, and a lyrical response to creatures as aloof from social issues as cats. Some of the best poems in his collection *Wenn wir, bei Rot* (1969), such as 'Armes Schwein' and 'Mitläufer', brought out the contradiction between the simplifications of ideology and the realities of human behaviour. If, in the later phase, feminism, conservationism and human survival become causes more urgent than the class war, this difference cut across the political and literary factions. A poet so much a traditionalist as to have been black-listed in the Zürcher/Theobaldy manifesto, Heinz Piontek, could publish a sequence called *Vorkriegszeit*—where the pre-war is that before a Third World War—in 1980. This meditative sequence, true, ranges freely between figures and events from the Old Testament and the Apocrypha to Jakob Böhne and to the present, and suggests that wisdom will prove stronger than death.

One disturbing feature of the West German literary scene had been the speed with which it was made to shift, and one trend pushed in place of another. Some of those who promoted the process may not have been fully aware of its connection with industrial, commercial and advertising practices which they cannot have wished to emulate; but not only the manifestos, but the work of some of the poets most widely acclaimed in the late 1970s seemed to offer itself for instant consumption only, as the work of Celan, Huchel, Meister or Hölzer did not. Their work transcended individualism not by excluding private or personal experience, nor by keeping up a 'man in the street' persona, but by an exploration in depth of the human condition beyond the accidents of immediate circumstance. Ernst Meister's *Im Zeitspalt*, like Karl Krolow's *Der Einfachheit Halber* of 1977, confronted old age and death; but the language and imagery of Meister's book—'hermetic' by Theobaldy's criteria—serves to distance that preoccupation from his own person in a way that Krolow's do not. The difference is not one of generations, groups or classes, but of imaginative and intellectual concentration. If the 'seers' were indeed to be displaced by the storytellers and talkers in verse, it could be for the time being at the most, a qualification in Theobaldy's claim that does credit to him and should not have been overlooked. Theobaldy's too sudden turning-back to old verse forms and heightened diction was another instance of those accelerated actions and reactions, though a general disillusionment with novelty may have had something to do with the change.

It was the inability to believe in an assured—let alone a better—future that induced a pervasive despondency in German poetry of all kinds and schools even before the 'new subjectivity' wave had subsided. In 1977, the literary annual *Tintenfisch* was devoted to the theme 'Nature. Or why today a conversation about trees is no longer a crime'—a reference to a famous poem by Brecht. Significantly, the theme elicited contributions from poets as different in age, kind and even nationality as Rolf Haufs, Ursula Krechel, Günter Herburger, Jürgen Theobaldy, Christoph Meckel, Peter Huchel, Sarah Kirsch, Rainer Kirsch and Adolf Endler. The prose contributions included work by the Swedish poet Lars Gustafsson, statistics about pollution and the depletion of natural resources, and a challenging sequence of eleven 'theses' on 'ecological materialism' by Carl Amery, showing why 'the industrial system, ultimately, is the human option against life and for devastation', and concluding: 'Until now materialism has been content to change the world; what is needed now is to conserve it.' Since the industrial system extends across political divisions that had once been of primary importance to German writers, and beyond them to the Third World, Carl Amery's theses and their publication in a literary annual were more significant than old squabbles about conflicting pressure groups and trends. Nicolas Born contributed a speech warning that

> more and more clearly our history seems to be moving towards its annihilation . . . 80% of what we experience now, of our outer reality, consists of synthetic materials, the rest is pure wool . . . We must not only grow poorer, we must wish to grow poorer. And we now need a re-

distribution of poverty, of need, so that each one of us learns again what it means to know want.

That insight of Born's about the synthetic nature of most of our experience was crucial to his practice of a 'new subjectivity' and sets his work apart from the mere trend.

6

If only because these questions of survival have become so acute as to silence at least one eminent writer, and drive others into political action once more—such as the 1981 and 1983 international meetings of writers for peace and disarmament initiated by Stephan Hermlin and Günter Grass, and held in East Berlin and West Berlin respectively—it would be rash to infer from literary developments alone that German imaginative writing has been thoroughly normalized. The anomaly of Germany's political division, at the likely centre of a potential Third World War, persistent memories of the Second, and widespread concern at the destruction of woods and lakes, do not make for quiescence in any available normality. The book publication of the protocols of the second Berlin meeting, *Zweite Berliner Begegnung, den Frieden erklären* (1983), includes two poems by a West German poet, Guntram Vesper. Significantly, these are not protests, polemics or satires, but poems with a domestic and rural setting that bring home two different orders of destruction, by nuclear war and by hunting. Vesper introduces his poems by saying that he had come to listen rather than to speak, as an 'apprentice'. The issue of survival, too, has been complicated by a sense of every individual's complicity in group interests and assertions of power that he or she may oppose. Earlier commitments tended to be more sure of themselves, if not self-righteous. One recalls the public involvement even of poets in legal conflicts, like Erich Fried's in a libel action brought by a Chief of Police, F. C. Delius's three-year legal battle with the firm of Siemens, also about an alleged libel, in his documentary polemic *Wir Unternehmer* of 1966, or Arnfried Astel's appeal against his dismissal, on political grounds, as a radio producer. Later, too, Erich Fried engaged in a protracted campaign on behalf of a poet, Peter-Paul Zahl, jailed for his part in a political demonstration; and in the 1980s Fried applied himself to the conversion and rehabilitation of a young neo-Nazi leader. Only the anomalies of German history and the peculiar functions assumed by, and accorded to, writers in Germany accounts for such cases of activism, to which many others could be added.

The poetry of private life that may seem to have become dominant since the 'new subjectivity' demands to be read in the light of those anomalies and its continuity with what went before. A sense of the past beyond the revolutions of this century—much more marked at one time in East German than in West German poetry—contributes to the tension between everyday observations and fantasy or reflection in Friederike Roth's *Tollkirschenhochzeit* (1978), giving it an uncommon range of diction and forms. Quite a number of Karin Kiwus's poems, especially those in her earlier collection *Von beiden Seiten der Gegenwart* (1976), look like poems of immediate experience, crammed with data of a way of life that is anyone's, with commuter trains, medical prescriptions, a zip fastener that sticks, milk gone sour; but they do not merely register such things, they reflect on them and evaluate them. The more 'Americanized' poets of the 'new subjectivity' had learned to avoid metaphor and analogy, making each poem a nexus of perceptions that turned the perceiving 'I' into an active participant rather like the first-person narrator in a novel. Karin Kiwus comes close to this mode in her longer poems, with their uninhibited use of the current vernacular, but dissociates herself from it by her resort to metaphor, even to hyperbole. One difficulty of her poems is the suddenness of their transitions from recognizable sensory phenomena to their abstract or symbolic heightening. As the title of her first book implies, hers is a poetry of dualism, of tensions—between innocence and experience, inner moods and outward behaviour, acceptance and rejection of given realities. Poems like 'Ende des Illusionstheaters' and 'Es wird wieder Zeit' must be taken allegorically to be understood; others, or passages in others, are cryptically, because literally, personal. Her hyperbolic manner has the trenchancy and rhetoric of Hans Magnus Enzensberger's early work. Elsewhere she can be as laconic and sardonic as the later Günter Eich, to whose memory she dedicates a poem; and she can be tender, too, as in 'Renard' or the retrospective poem 'Im alten Land'. The diversity of her modes and moods contrasts with the assurance that she brings to them all.

In his later collections, *Das gewohnte Licht* (1976) and *Augenzeit* (1978), Harald Hartung resorts to regular metre as a distancing device and a way out of the bedevilled 'subjectivity' complex, but a metre that each poem finds and makes for itself in the first place, before it becomes a stanza scheme or pattern. Though this procedure—with its eighteenth-century precedent in Klopstock's classicizing odes—breaks with 'new subjectivity' instantaneousness, and eliminates some of its roughage, Hartung remains a poet of sensory perceptions, lovingly enacted for their own sake.

A certain formality of diction and structure has also returned in the work of Michael Krüger, a prolific and versatile poet since the late 1970s. His long meditative poems, like the title poem of his book *Aus der Ebene* (1982) and the book-length sequence *Wiederholungen* (1983), are at once autobiographical, in that they take their departure from a lived moment and a specific setting—Rome, in the case of 'Aus der

Ebene'—and impersonal in their range of concern. If Krüger speaks for more than himself in these meditations, it is not as a spokesman for a class, group or generation that can be identified by its way of life, interests or hopes. 'Not the future, that hopeless/case', he writes in 'Aus der Ebene'. This lost future is one of his recurrent themes, varied with great inventiveness, but a sustained gravity of tone. In his short poem 'Ein Baum' from the same collection, the tree has changed its nature, suffered a change that is a change in its human observer's relation to any tree, for reasons that connect with Born's remark about the synthetic components in our experience. A related awareness informs the poems 'Sommersprossen' and 'Man selbst, ich selber'—with its bitter questioning of our precious individuality—and the poem on his father's death, 'Elegie'. Characteristically, Krüger can write as eloquent an elegy on the extinction of the dodo, in his later collection *Die Dronte* (1985). This includes two more long sequences, 'Römischer Winter' and 'Ambach'. Like 'Wiederholungen', these interweave immediate and recollected experience by associations that can become somewhat self-conscious, as in the prologue to 'Ambach' about the writing of that sequence.

The manifestos, anthologies and debates have tended to ignore poets active since the early 1960s, who are more intent on discoveries than on assertions, whose work calls for the kind of attention which they themselves applied to the ordering of words and things not so much given as found. Manfred Peter Hein is such a poet, in search of visual correlatives—often discovered in remote and unlikely places—to concerns that have as much to do with history as those of the mimetic realists. The meaning of his poems is conveyed by images and cadences, not by arguments or statements. His *Gegenzeichnung* (1974) collects poems written over more than a decade.

Christine Koschel and Werner Dürrson are other poets who have avoided the language of shared domestic and social realities, not because it is common or 'unpoetic', but because it is facile and imprecise. Christine Koschel, too, entrusts her commitments to images which, in relation to other images, to rhythms and sounds, become signs, but signs that do not necessarily point to familiar places. Her selection *Zeit von der Schaukel zu Springen* (1975) includes poems from two earlier books and later work even more distinguished. Werner Dürrson's sequences in *Drei Dichtungen*, written in the 1960s, are in the same tradition of linguistic and semantic exploration that is not experiment, because language does not become a neutral and autarchic material, as in concrete poetry. The very short, elliptic poems in Dürrson's later collection *Mitgegangen Mitgehangen* (1975) have the acerbity of their moral concerns, but their diction makes no concession to a ready-made vernacular.

Even the tradition of the 'seers', then, can be maintained and renewed, as one of a plurality of traditions. Forty years after the end of the war, it is this plurality of traditions and possibilities, not a single line of development, that is most conspicuous. Many historical ghosts have been laid in the course of the last four decades; but gloom about 'the lost case' of the future is intermingling with gloom about the past, about past upheavals, divisions and displacements that cannot be wholly overcome without a 'direction towards the future', as Rilke put it in a poem. For a long time this 'direction towards the future' was a political one for the majority of writers throughout the German-speaking countries. The recession of those hopes can be seen even in the work of writers who defy it with protests and demonstrations.

In the work of Walter Neumann, a poet born in Riga, the impossibility of apportioning blame for his displacement—or deflecting sadness into the kind of resentful nationalism to which associations of displaced German-speaking minorities in the Federal Republic have been prone—led to a stance not so much non-political as anti-political, in poems about a homeland he left as a child or about violence of any colour committed in the service of a political cause. The religious grounds of this stance, complicated in turn by Neumann's awareness of living in a 'godless age', rarely become explicit in his later collections, *Jenseits der Worte* (1976) and *Mitten in Frieden* (1984). The irony of the second title—'in the midst of peace'—points to that intermingling of past and future disasters, or to their continuity, though in the poems themselves the irony is more wistful than bitter.

Survival in the teeth of displacement can also be affirmed, as it has been most remarkably in the work of Rose Ausländer, who can be said to have established herself as a German poet at the age of seventy-five, with the publication of her *Gesammelte Gedichte* in 1976. A survivor, like Paul Celan, of the German-speaking Jewish community of what was Czernowitz in Austria when she was young, then Cernauti in Romania, then Chernovtsy in the Soviet Union, she came to West Germany in 1965 from New York, where she had written poems in English. Her early German poems are lost; but all the stages of her life have left a residue in her late work, which is being issued in seven consecutive volumes. Her astonishing productivity in old age is her response to a homecoming into her first language. This return has been a second life to her, one that had to make up for the loss of all other continuity and belonging. Hilde Domin, who settled in Germany after emigration a decade earlier, in 1954, had celebrated her return to the language as a second birth, though hers was also a physical homecoming. It was the language, not the country, that held the continuity. In the four books of poems that she published between 1959 and 1970 the language itself and the act of writing in it are as much a theme as in the poems of Rose Ausländer.

The displacement of Cyrus Atabay from Iran to Berlin in childhood, during the Third Reich, was another historical and political anomaly that became a literary one. In Atabay's poems the German language has entered into a singular marriage with a culture that remains Persian, as even the title of one of his collections, *Das Auftauchen an einem anderen Ort* (1977) obliquely acknowledges—not with self-pity, but with a self-irony that makes his translations from Corbière in that book read like poems of his own. His cosmopolitanism alone—he has lived in Switzerland, Iran and England—has kept his work remote from the dominant trends since his first collection of 1956. Over the decades, Atabay's work has maintained a peculiar balance between the colloquial and the archaic, the worldly and the mystical, with constant reversions to the archetypes of his native tradition. Earlier fusions of East and West in Goethe's *Divan* poems or those of later nineteenth century German poets has not made Atabay's work more accessible. With delicacy, wit and poise, he has made his own way through the paradoxes of his identities and alienations.

One of those paradoxes was summed up by Jean Améry in his confessional essay 'Wieviel Heimat braucht der Mensch?'. His answer to the question was that 'one needs to be able to have a home to do without one', where the German word 'Heimat' means a homeland, not a roof over one's head or a room of one's own. (Rose Ausländer's homecoming was enacted in an old people's home.) Améry's question could never have been posed at all where a homeland is taken for granted, or by a person who has taken his or her homeland for granted. In fact, a regional rootedness like Heinrich Böll's or Martin Walser's has been the exception, not the rule, among German writers since the war. For Améry, the survivor of an extermination camp, there was not enough continuity in a language or literary culture alone. He could not feel at home in post-war Germany or Austria or anywhere, and ended by taking his own life.

The reverse side of Améry's paradox is the strength and certainty that come of having a homeland, physical or spiritual, as a point of departure and return. Those who have it can afford to do without it, to travel physically or spiritually, to venture out. This helps to explain the undiminished political certainty of the Swiss writer Kurt Marti, at once a regional poet who has written in the dialect of his parish in Bern, and an innovator, close at one time to Eugen Gomringer's group of concrete experimentalists. What is more, Marti is a Protestant pastor and theologian. Yet his commitment, still upheld when that once fashionable word has begun to call for inverted commas, is a revolutionary one. Marti's poems, in his collection *Abendland* (1980) and the selection from all his books *Schon Wieder Heute* (1982), celebrate the life of the spirit and the body, human and non-human nature, *agape* and *eros*, as sacraments. He has borrowed texts from feminist writers and has made a collage of the most various texts in praise of sexual love. He professes his belief in a 'goddess god'—without capital letters—and sees the Occident of his book as a conspiracy of commerce, militarism and clerical complicity against spiritual and natural life. He has a poem addressed to 'Karl Marx in his grave', in which he tells Marx:

> be glad
> that your grave is in London:
> here at least you are free
> to turn in it

and invites Marx not to rest, but go on turning in the hope that he will be resurrected:

> perhaps then
> you will
> wear no beard any more
> and bear another name

The title poem of the same collection is addressed to 'beautiful Judas', whose 'ONE betrayal', followed by repentance, 'is a small thing compared to the MANY betrayals/of the christians of churches/that curse you'. A poem called 'the kingdom of god in switzerland?' answers the question, put by a visitor from 'bobrowskiland', like this: '. . . a long time ago/god lost his ground/under our feet/ (to estate agents . . .)/worried/churches confer in whispers/at the green table/ with business concerns//meanwhile/models of democracy/we reject/ one right of codetermination/after another//at the same time/more and more fear/calls for more and more policemen/and for sharper/punitive measures/ "together with HIM/two thieves/were crucified . . ."')

Lao Tse and William Blake are among the diverse sources on which Marti has drawn for his poems, since his first collection, *Republikanische Gedichte*, of 1957. His word play in the early poems is akin to Erich Fried's, who was also to apply it to political themes. The rhymed verse of his dialect lyrics, *Undereinisch* (1973), is as uninhibited by literary or non-literary conventions as the plain-speaking free verse of *Abendland*.

In Marti's vision and forms, extremes have met once more; to generate tensions and potentialities, as they do and must in literature, not to clash, as they do in politics, or impose a truce, called peace, that paralyses energies on both sides. An earlier poet with a religious and revolutionary vision, Hölderlin, wrote that 'the poets, and those no less who/Are spiritual, must be worldly too', as Kurt Marti undoubtedly is. Because imaginative literature is not life, or politics, to be utopian is one of its functions. As long as it can function at all, one of its functions will be to provide 'directions towards the future', no matter how unlikely it is that those directions will be taken, or that there is any future to be reached.

Index